SOCIALIST REGISTER 2009

SOCIALIST REGISTER 2009

VIOLENCE TODAY

Acutally-Existing Barbarism

Edited by LEO PANITCH and COLIN LEYS

LEFTWORD BOOKS, NEW DELHI
THE MERLIN PRESS, LONDON

First published in 2008 by
The Merlin Press Ltd.

Published in India by
LeftWord Books
12 Rajendra Prasad Road
New Delhi 110001
INDIA

LeftWord Books is the publishing division of
Naya Rasta Publishers Pvt. Ltd.

www.leftword.com

ISBN 978-81-87496-79-3

British Library Cataloguing in Publication Data is available from the British Library

Library and Archives Canada Cataloguing in Publication
Socialist register 2009 : violence today : actually-existing barbarism
/ Leo Panitch and Colin Leys, editors.
1. Violence. 2. Imperialism. 3. Capitalism.
I. Panitch, Leo, 1945- II. Leys, Colin, 1931- III. Title: Violence today.
HM886.S62 2008 303.6 C2008-903393-0

ISSN. 0081-0606

Printed by
Progressive Printers
A 21 Jhilmil Industrial Area
G.T. Road
Shahadara
Delhi 110095

CONTENTS

CONTRIBUTORS

Samir Amin has been director of IDEP (the United Nations African Institute for Planning), the director of the Third World Forum in Dakar, and a co-founder of the World Forum for Alternatives.

John Berger is a British art critic, novelist, dramatist and essayist, based in France.

Henry Bernstein is professor of development studies at the School of Oriental and African Studies (SOAS), London.

Michael Brie is head of the department of policy analysis at the Rosa Luxemburg Foundation, Berlin.

Vivek Chibber is associate professor of sociology at New York University.

Ruth Wilson Gilmore is a professor at the University of Southern California and a founding member of Critical Resistance - Beyond the Prison Industrial Complex.

Philip Green is visiting professor of political science at the New School for Social Research Graduate Faculty, New York.

Barbara Harriss-White directs the new Contemporary South Asian Studies Programme at Oxford University.

Steffen Jensen works at the Rehabilitation and Research Centre for Torture Victims in Copenhagen and is affiliated to the Wits Institute for Social and Economic Research (Wiser) in Johannesburg.

Sofiri Joab-Peterside is a lecturer with the Department of Sociology, University of Port Harcourt, Nigeria and associate research fellow, Centre for Advanced Social Science (CASS).

Tania Murray Li is professor and Canada Research Chair in the department of anthropology at the University of Toronto, Canada.

Ulrich Oslender is a political geographer at the University of Glasgow.

Dennis Rodgers is senior research fellow in the Brooks World Poverty Institute, University of Manchester and visiting senior fellow in the Crisis States Research Centre, London School of Economics.

Lynne Segal is Anniversary Professor of Psychology and Gender Studies at Birkbeck College, University of London.

Joe Sim is professor of criminology in the School of Social Science, Liverpool John Moores University.

Steve Tombs is professor of sociology at Liverpool John Moores University.

Achin Vanaik is professor of international relations and global politics at the post-graduate Department of Political Science, Delhi University.

Anna Zalik is assistant professor in the Faculty of Environmental Studies at York University, Toronto.

PREFACE

This, the 45th volume of the *Socialist Register*, takes up a question that has preoccupied socialists for over a century – the likelihood that if capitalism is allowed to persist it will be characterised by increasing violence. When Rosa Luxemburg in 1916 quoted Engels' famous statement that 'Capitalist society faces a dilemma: either an advance to socialism, or a reversion to barbarism', she asked: 'What does a "reversion to barbarism" mean at the present stage of European civilisation? We have all read and repeated these words thoughtlessly, without a notion of their terrible seriousness. At this moment, one glance around us will show what a reversion to barbarism in bourgeois society means. This World War – that is a reversion to barbarism'. Given the extent and extremity of violence today, even in the absence of world war, and two decades after the end of actually-existing socialism, it is hard not to feel that we are living in another age of barbarism.

It is an unhappy coincidence that Georges Sorel's *Reflections on Violence* was published exactly 100 years ago. As the American publishers of the 1950 edition remarked, 'while all Europe fondly imagined that such things belonged to the dark past, Sorel correctly predicted a new epoch of such catastrophes'. Even after the slaughter of two world wars, the genocide of European Jewry and the creation of the United Nations, the world has often seemed no less violent than before. A chain of human catastrophes has continued without pause ever since the UN Declaration of Human Rights – from Korea and Vietnam to Palestine, Lebanon, Indonesia, Colombia, Guatemala, El Salvador, Nicaragua, Angola, Mozambique, Somalia, Eritrea, Chile, Uganda, Rwanda, Somalia, the Democratic Republic of Congo, the Central African Republic, Sudan, Bosnia, Chechnya, Northern Ireland, Bangladesh, Kashmir, Sri Lanka, Iraq, Afghanistan… Not to mention the prevalence of rape and other kinds of violence against women, drug wars, police and prison violence, etc. The total number of deaths in the twentieth century resulting from large-scale violence alone is estimated at about 140 million. And the world is now spending $1.3 *trillion* a year on weapons – surpassing the total at the peak of the Cold War. The 'peace dividend' that was supposed to flow from ending it has evaporated, along with the dream of the 'end of history' and universal peace under American hegemony. Can anyone seriously assert, in attempting to draw up a balance sheet of the opening years of the 21st century, that capitalism has outgrown its potential for barbarism?

What this volume seeks to do is to bring a clear perspective to bear on the great variety of forms and degrees of severity of violence in the world today. The contemporary forms of violence are so varied and complex, occurring at such different levels and in such widely differing contexts, that their specific links to capitalism and imperialism need a fresh understanding. It is also important to acknowledge that social and psychological factors and cultural legacies of all kinds – religious, ideological, familial, racial, legal, etc. – play a part, often a crucial one. It is equally important to avoid any inclination to minimise the violence that occurred under 'actually existing socialism', the legacy of which still needs to be taken into account when socialists address the question of violence today.

The extent of contemporary violence is far too great to be covered in any single volume. Last year's volume on *Global Flashpoints* focused on the Middle East and Latin America, from the occupation of Iraq and Israel's colonial siege of the Palestinians, to the 'war on terror' and the clash of fundamentalisms, to new forms of resistance to imperialism and neoliberalism. This volume paints on a broader canvass, with most of the essays analysing the nature and roots of paradigmatic cases and types of violence today around the world. The opening essay offers an overview of the scale and variety of contemporary violence while also taking up once again the question of socialism versus barbarism. And several of the concluding essays deal, from various standpoints, with the still important question of whether violence has any place in socialist strategy in the context of today's actually-existing barbarism. The volume ends with John Berger's 'Human Shield', a movingly intimate letter to a political prisoner, fictional but loosely based on real events, which epitomises the courage of those – so often women – who put themselves in the front line against the violence of the powerful.

We are grateful to John Berger for permission to include this story from his forthcoming book, *From A to X*, to be published by Verso. We also want to thank Rainer Rilling of the Rosa Luxemburg Foundation for making a longer German version of the essay by Michael Brie available to us, and Ingar Solty for translating it very ably and at short notice. As usual, we are heavily indebted to Alan Zuege for his editorial assistance, to Louis McKay for the cover design and to Adrian Howe and Tony Zurbrugg at the Merlin Press for their continuing support. We are more than usually grateful this year for the help our editorial collective – which we are happy to say has expanded in this last year to include Michel Lowy as our corresponding editor in Paris – gave us in planning the volume, and contributing to it. In thanking them as well as all the authors in the volume for their contributions we should note, as usual, that neither they nor we necessarily agree with everything in it.

We are sad to note the deaths in the past year of Andre Gorz, whose famous and still influential essay on 'Reform and Revolution' was published in the *Register* in 1968, and Andrew Glyn, whose 1992 essay with Bob Sutcliffe, 'Global but Leaderless?', was central to the influential debate on the nature of globalisation that the *Register* initiated that year. Their respective contributions to renewing socialism and socialist analysis are a precious legacy.

LP
CL
July 2008

REFLECTIONS ON VIOLENCE TODAY

HENRY BERNSTEIN, COLIN LEYS
AND LEO PANITCH

The scale and pervasiveness of violence today calls urgently for serious analysis – from 'the war on terror' and counter-insurgencies, involving massive expenditures of troops and weaponry, from terror and counter-terror, suicide bombings and torture, civil wars and anarchy, entailing human tragedies on a scale comparable to those of the two world wars (e.g. an estimated over 4 million deaths in the Democratic Republic of the Congo alone) – not to mention urban gang warfare, or the persistence of chronic violence against women, including in the most affluent countries of the global North. In many parts of the global South, violence has become more or less endemic – and not just in arenas of armed conflict like Iraq, Afghanistan, the Congo, Darfur, Sri Lanka and Chechnya. That the nirvana of global capitalism finds millions of people once again just 'wishing (a) not to be killed, (b) for a good warm coat' (as Stendhal is said to have put it in a different era) is, when fully contemplated, appalling.

In the so-called advanced capitalist countries of the North, while some forms of violence are much less common, *fear* of violence – from terrorists, but also from child abductors, carjackers, psychopaths, drug addicts, and the like – has become an increasingly central theme of politics. Surveillance and police powers have been steadily extended, and penal policy has shifted from prevention and rehabilitation to punishing and 'warehousing' people convicted of crimes. Media competing for circulation exaggerate the risk, scapegoating immigrants, and even social democratic political parties compete to be seen as 'tougher' than their rivals in responding to it. Civil liberties are eroded and methods of social control until recently thought barbaric, from detention without trial to isolation, shackles and torture, are restored to favour.

One of the most obvious differences between capitalism now and in earlier periods is that the major capitalist states no longer go to war against each other, or even threaten to. Instead they collaborate in subjecting all peoples of the world to universal market competition. The resulting conditions of existence of daily life, reinforced by the hubristic imposition of 'regime change' by the world's most powerful states, expose more and more people to forms of local violence – from crime to insurgencies. The so-called 'third wave' of democracy promoted by the 'international community' may have led to a large increase in the number of states holding apparently competitive elections, but no one can ignore the violence that so often precedes, accompanies and follows them, as in both Kenya and Zimbabwe in 2008. In reality, the world looks nothing like the rosy 'end of history' picture painted by the proponents of liberal democracy two decades ago. Violence pervades it everywhere.

We need, then, to disentangle the different kinds of violence currently occurring around the world, to identify their short and long-term causes, the perpetrators and victims, and the sustaining conditions (who benefits, directly and indirectly) – without preconceptions, and without confusing explanations with excuses. And without any illusions that contemporary violence is in some way exceptional, since it has always been a feature of human society. When the well-preserved body of a 5,000-year-old man was found in a glacier in Austria in 1991, it had an arrowhead in its back. When the 2000-year-old 'Tollund man' was found in a Danish peat bog in 1950, he had been strangled. The earliest recorded civilisations were founded on conquest and slaughter, and the vast war cemeteries strung along the former front lines of World War I remind us that capitalist civilisation has not been different in this respect, except for its industrialisation of the means of destruction. But whereas earlier cultures took violence and even cruelty for granted (some even celebrated it: the popularity of Homer's account of the fighting outside Troy shows that Greek humanism co-existed with a fascination with hand-to-hand fighting in all its bloodiness[1]), in our own times violence may be no less bloody (and glorified in movies and video games), but it is no longer taken for granted – or at least much less than formerly. We have to try to understand not only why violence is so extensive today, but also why, in spite of the many ways in which it is accepted and even promoted, it is also seen as wrong – in other words we must consider the ideology of violence, as well as its material reality.

The reflections that follow attempt to sketch an approach to this challenge, by addressing the violence that attends the development of capitalism; the counter-violence that resistance to capitalism and imperialism generates; the 'violence amongst the people' that is so tragically widespread under conditions of contemporary capitalism; the role of the US as 'global policeman'; and, once again, the issue of socialism or barbarism in our own time.

THE VIOLENCE OF CAPITALISM

Marx famously observed that 'capital comes (into the world) dripping from head to foot, from every pore, with blood and dirt', although he had no illusions about the 'blood and dirt' of those social formations that capitalism displaced. 'The discovery of gold and silver in America, the extirpation, enslavement and entombment in mines of the aboriginal population, the beginning of the conquest and looting of the East Indies, the turning of Africa into a warren for the commercial hunting of black-skins, signalised the rosy dawn of the era of capitalist production'.[2] He was referring to the primitive accumulation through which the transition to agrarian capitalism, and then the emergence of industrial capitalism, was accomplished, with its centre in England, between the fifteenth and eighteenth centuries. The dispossession of the peasantry, the ruin of small artisans, and the appalling working and living conditions experienced by the early factory proletariat in England, were then replicated elsewhere, with different forms and degrees of violence, throughout the world system that capitalism created.

Colonial expansion and European settlement overseas involved the widespread dispossession (and in some cases the extermination) of the indigenous peoples of the Americas, Asia, Africa and Australasia, followed by their forcible incorporation or marginalisation in a developing world capitalism. All this was facilitated by a racism that accompanied and was used to justify, in terms of a 'civilising mission', the imposition and administration of white rule. Violence was thus integral to primitive accumulation, both in what became the 'core' of the capitalist world and in the formation of its peripheries. Violence was also integral to the making of the modern capitalist state and the inter-state system, which was not completed in most of Europe until the second half of the twentieth century, and arguably continues into the twenty-first in the Balkans.

It is in Asia, Africa and Latin America that the major remaining zones of strategic natural resources continue to be enclosed and plundered – a form of primitive accumulation that persists into the era of capitalist accumulation proper.[3] This too is regularly accomplished or sustained by violent means, as Michael Klare points out:

> ...intensified production of oil, natural gas, uranium and minerals is itself a source of instability.... The nations involved are largely poor, so whoever controls the resources controls the one sure source

> of abundant wealth. This is an invitation for the monopolization of power by greedy elites who use control over military and police to suppress rivals. The result, more often than not, is wealthy strata of crony capitalists kept in power by brutal security forces and surrounded by disaffected and impoverished masses, often belonging to a different ethnic group – a recipe for unrest and insurgency. This is the situation today in the Niger Delta region of Nigeria, in Darfur and southern Sudan, in the uranium-producing areas of Niger, in Zimbabwe, in the Cabinda province of Angola (where most of that country's oil lies) and in numerous other areas suffering from what's been called the 'resource curse'.[4]

It is also in the 'South' today that interventions to achieve 'liberal peace', free markets and democracy are launched, and where the USA and its allies feel free to deploy 'exemplary' and 'pre-emptive' violence. The massacre of the Iraqi army retreating from Kuwait in 1991 was an act of massive 'exemplary' violence, as was the bombing of Serbia in 1999; the invasion and occupation of Iraq was justified in the name of 'pre-empting' aggression by the Saddam regime with 'weapons of mass destruction' that it, in fact, did not possess. Both 'exemplary' and 'pre-emptive' violence may be exercised directly, as in the instances cited, or by proxy via 'friendly' repressive regimes, for example, apartheid South Africa in the 1970s and 1980s in the name of combating 'communism'. The USA was also instrumental in the overthrow of governments it considered 'threatening' – in Guatemala and Iran in the 1950s, Indonesia in the 1960s, Chile in the 1970s, Nicaragua and Grenada in the 1980s, and more recently Kosovo, Afghanistan and Iraq – and was complicit, when not a major actor, in the violence that attended these 'regime changes'.

A CONTINUUM OF COUNTER-VIOLENCE

The processes of primitive accumulation and state-making and the various modalities of the rule of capital – from military adventurism to the enforced creation of individual and corporate property rights – have generated a range of consequential counter-violence. For the great social revolutions of the twentieth century, pre-eminently those of Russia and China, the initial conditions for their projects of socialist construction were necessarily established by violent means, in contexts of global war and imperialist offensives, and were followed by violence in the service of consolidating the party-state and of 'socialist primitive accumulation', including the great famines of the early 1930s in the USSR, and the late 1950s in China.

In the movements for independence from colonial rule in the Third World – Algeria, Vietnam, Mozambique, etc. – armed struggle was taken up in the face of the violent repression directed against any impulse for national liberation, not least on the part of the rural and urban labouring poor. It was also taken up in the face of violence, both exemplary and pre-emptive, exercised by local ruling classes and their imperialist allies against progressive political forces in Guatemala, Iran, Indonesia, Chile, Argentina, Nicaragua, South Africa, and elsewhere.

Wars for national liberation represented one manifestation of the resistance to dispossession and oppression that accompanied the process of primitive accumulation, and continue today. Such resistance also takes the form of peasant revolts, strikes, 'social banditry' and the invention and daily exercise of what James Scott termed 'weapons of the weak', all of which can involve their own dialectic of violent response to violent oppression.[5] These actions span a continuum of 'counter-violence' which ranges from national liberation struggles to responsive, often defensive, violence against the predations of landlords and land-grabbers, merchants and usurers, and against colonial and post-colonial authoritarian states and their tax-collectors, gendarmes and magistrates, priests and imams.

And then, in this grisly dialectic, the predators raise the stakes: resistance is met by the intensified violence of 'paramilitaries', private 'security' firms, 'extraordinary renditions', disappearances, torture, etc, culminating in a 'war on terror' that covers anything and anyone, and seeks to excuse all crimes and even atrocities.

VIOLENCE 'AMONG THE PEOPLE'

But the weapons of the weak are not always turned against the strong. One of the most widespread kinds of violence today is between people who are all themselves victims, in one way or another, of global capitalism, imperialism and attendant local forms of inequality and injustice. An instance is the African 'conflict zones' of Rwanda and the eastern Congo, Sudan/ Darfur, and Liberia/Sierra Leone, 'when victims become killers' as Mahmood Mamdani put it.[6] The Congo, in which 'disease and malnutrition caused by almost a decade of political violence has since 2003 been killing an average of 40,000 people a month – half of them children',[7] is possibly the most appalling example in the world at this moment.

Such conflicts often extend across porous international borders in areas with long histories of the brutal extraction of valuable resources, and/or new interests in strategic materials that reproduce and intensify extreme poverty, insecurity and social tension – and where ethnicity is refashioned and manipulated for purposes of power and economic gain by indigenous 'political entrepreneurs', typically in alliance with external forces interested in the extraction of strategic minerals and the sale of arms. Similar processes could be seen in the Balkans and Caucasus amid the ruins of former state socialism, exacerbated by Western interventions.

These conflicts also exemplify the 'informal' organisation of violence by 'warlords' of various kinds, just as the massive slums of the South are permeated by gangsterism that thrives on conditions of desperation, trading in drugs, the control of housing and jobs, 'protectionism', and services to urban political parties and 'entrepreneurs'. Life on the street in many of the world's cities can be hardly less precarious, if in a different way. In Guatemala City, for example:

> Over the past four years [2003-2007], the number of people found dead in the streets or hung from trees or pulled from ditches has climbed to mind-numbing levels. In 2002, before the violence began to escalate, roughly 2,900 people were killed. Last year, the total reached 6,033, although international observers believe that it could be as high as 8,000 (the National Civil Police doesn't count people who are injured in an attack but die later in hospital)... Every day on the streets of this city... citizens are robbed at gunpoint. It happens while they sit in their cars, and while they ride the bus... [in 2007] 76 Guatemalan bus drivers have been killed for their cash boxes. The crime wave is so bad that virtually every business in the city has armed guards, some mere teenagers, who now outnumber the police 3 to 1...[8]

According to circumstances – including the ways in which capitalism seizes on existing social and cultural differences and weaves them into its divisions of labour and class rule – responsive/defensive violence can often also develop an ethnic, religious or linguistic character that all too often permeates widespread 'violence among the people'. Thus some of the features noted above also characterise the mobilisation of communal violence by well-defined reactionary political forces like the Rashtriya Swayamsevak Sangh, the Hindu fascist organisation in India. Daily forms of individual violence within communities of the dispossessed and oppressed, such as those associated with (usually male) youth gangs, sexual and other violence against women (and children) are converted into violence against neighbours with the 'wrong' ethnic or religious identities.

Such violence does not express some kind of endemic or tribal atavism in the global South, as the media in the North are only too ready to imply. It tends to be concentrated in particular social environments at particular times: it can appear, flourish, abate or vanish. Nor is the attempt to understand its causes and patterns to seek to condone them, any more than understanding why workers might engage in communal violence, or why 'marginals', 'anti-socials' or 'lumpenproletarians' are susceptible to hire to break strikes or brutalise political opponents, is to condone those actions.[9] Behind the sometimes distinctive forms and peculiar cruelty of this kind of violence, there is so often a previous moment – or several – in which external agents intervened in internal class struggle; and this in turn precipitated the chain of events that lead to, and eventually drive the violence with its locally-derived characteristics and horrors. What is happening today in Guatemala City must be traced back to the CIA-organised coup which overthrew the elected government of the social-democratic president Arbenz in 1954, replacing it with a military dictatorship and culminating in a brutal civil war which ended without any significant redress of the extreme inequality and mass poverty which now fuels the chronic insecurity of the streets. In the same way, what is happening today in the Congo must be understood in relation to the CIA-inspired murder of Lumumba at the moment of independence from Belgian colonial rule.

Yet while the role of imperialism in stoking conflicts in Africa and elsewhere goes far to explain the extreme and cruel forms of violence, such as the widespread rape and mutilations seen today in the eastern Congo, Sierra Leone, or Darfur, for example, it does not explain everything. There are undoubtedly tendencies to violence, to cruelty, and to sadism, in all human beings, aggravated as these are by the gendered relations of power into which they are born, and the broader social conditions of human history to date. At the same time, such tendencies are shaped and allowed expression by cultural dynamics, themselves the product of historical processes and their contradictions.

In short, the desperation of the dispossessed and oppressed, and the emotional and psychological states it generates, can animate actions of quite different political significance. Mike Davis's summary of the situation in the cities of the South could just as well be extended to its countrysides:

> ...the future of human solidarity depends upon the militant refusal of the new urban poor to accept their terminal marginality within global capitalism.

> This refusal may take atavistic as well as avant-garde forms: the repeal of modernity as well as attempts to recover its repressed promises. It should not be surprising that some poor youth on the outskirts of Istanbul, Cairo, Casablanca, or Paris embrace the religious nihilism of al Salafia Jihadia and rejoice in the destruction of modernity's most overweening symbols. Or that millions of others turn to the urban subsistence economies operated by street gangs, *narcotraficantes*, militias, and sectarian political organizations. The demonizing rhetorics of the various 'wars' on terrorism, drugs, and crime are so much semantic apartheid: they constitute epistemological walls around *gecekondus*, *favelas,* and *chawls* that disable any honest debate about the daily violence of economic exclusion. And, as in Victorian times, the categorical criminalization of the urban poor is a self-fulfilling prophecy, guaranteed to shape a future of endless war in the streets.[10]

IDEOLOGIES OF VIOLENCE

The broad patterns of violence in the era of capitalism outlined above are hardly mysterious, but how they are understood and reacted to is not so straightforward. On the one hand, violence is deplored. On the other, it is threatened, condoned, and advocated. This apparent contradiction needs to be clarified.

To begin with, it is clear that in the emergent bourgeois societies of Europe and North America an 'Enlightenment' sensibility developed that gradually turned against certain types of violence – though with a notable lag in relation to colonies and slavery. One indicator is the gradual rejection of exemplary cruelty in judicial punishment: burning, boiling, flaying alive, drawing and quartering and breaking on the rack (not to mention flogging), fell out of favour. In Britain, capital punishment was abolished for over 200 crimes in 1838; the last public hanging took place in 1868. Even if it took another hundred years for 'judicial murder' carried out behind prison walls to be finally given up, its eventual abandonment in Europe and much of the rest of the world is still significant.

To explore the religious, psychosocial and cultural as well as economic and political developments responsible for this shift would take us far beyond the scope of this essay, but there is no doubting that contemporary concerns over the extent of subjective violence is genuine and strong. However, as Slavoj Žižek points out, it is also often inversely related to concern about the objective violence 'inherent in a system… the more subtle forms of coercion that sustain relations of domination and exploitation'.[11] Mark Twain made a similar point on the centenary of the French Revolution:

> There were two 'Reigns of Terror', if we would but remember it and consider it; the one wrought murder in hot passion, the other in heartless cold blood; the one lasted mere months, the other had lasted a thousand years; the one inflicted death upon ten thousand persons, the other upon a hundred millions; but our shudders are all for the 'horrors' of the minor Terror, the momentary Terror, so to speak... A city cemetery could contain the coffins filled by that brief Terror which we have all been so diligently taught to shiver at and mourn over; but all France could hardly contain the coffins filled by that older and real Terror – that unspeakably bitter and awful Terror which none of us has been taught to see in its vastness or pity as it deserves.[12]

People in the North today may wring their hands over violence in, say, Darfur, without reflecting on the global economic relationships that underlie it. Billionaire philanthropists lead the chorus of concern about humanitarian crises whose causes are closely intertwined with the economic system from which their wealth is extracted.

In other words liberal concern about violence has limits: it diminishes with distance – the farther away the victims of violence are, the less we are inclined to be concerned – and especially with perceived *difference.* It is a commonplace of modern military history that soldiers have to be trained to see the enemy as inferior beings if they are to be able to kill them enthusiastically. The American public was shocked by the photos of American soldiers abusing Iraqi prisoners at Abu Ghraib because they had not had the necessary indoctrination – the kind of indoctrination that is perhaps only possible on a mass scale under a fascist regime. In Hitler's Germany, after years of public indoctrination and the existential fear created by daily mounting brutality, a disturbingly large number of Germans were ready to write off their Jewish fellow-citizens as 'untermenschen', subhumans. Whatever the effects of the 24 hour barrage of Fox News, Americans were not prepared to accept the notion that Iraqi prisoners could be treated as subhuman.

Ideology, then, plays a crucial role in determining our view of violence, both in occluding 'objective violence', and in limiting our concern for many of the victims of 'subjective' violence by defining them as 'others' – people who for one reason or another are less entitled to our concern. Neoliberal ideology offers its own particular rationale: bourgeois civilisation and its state order are represented as intrinsically humane and peaceful. First, by contrast with what preceded them historically: thus the peaceful nature of capitalism ('industrial society') was proclaimed by such nineteenth-century social theorists as St. Simon, Comte, Spencer, and informed colonial doctrines like that of *pax Britannica*. 'Pacification' and the rule of law, along with commerce and Christianity, were the instruments of its 'civilising mission'. Second, capitalism as 'liberal peace' is contrasted with contemporary social groups, ideologies, and political formations which challenge it: the 'others' who would subvert or attack bourgeois civilisation – its enemies within and without. According to liberal ideology, the state's exercise of legitimate violence today limits itself strictly to instruments set by humane rules (rules of constraint) necessary to achieve peace and prosperity. Those institutional instruments are, 'internally', the judicial system (law-making and enforcement, hence police, courts, prisons), and, 'externally', international law-making and the military.

This ideological framework can be interrogated through analysis of the historical processes and moments that generate it and the institutions and practices that implement it. The Enlightenment sensibilities referred to above led to the replacement of brutal forms of punishment by more nuanced forms of control and regulation that nonetheless served to discipline the citizenry (and the poor, blacks and females in particular). The 'discipline' exercised by bourgeois institutions, practices and discourses that claimed to be applying reason (science) in the service of humanism, famously explored by Foucault in his studies of prisons, medicine, hospitals for the mentally ill, and sexuality, has also been charted in other key institutions involved in the regulation of labour and housing markets, and of immigration, schooling, and systems of welfare provision and social work.

In relation to the global 'South', neoliberal ideology strives both to establish itself as the unchallenged common sense of the epoch and to subsume the development of poorer countries and people in a grandiose project of social engineering that amounts to establishing bourgeois civilisation on a global scale: economic growth will be assured, poverty overcome, 'civil society' and social capital strengthened, and sound democracies established, if only the right reforms are implemented and the right policies pursued. This project of 'development', driven by the best of purposes, constructs its antagonistic others, driven by the worst. In a probably ascending register of criminality, the enemies of 'development', liberal peace and freedom comprise demagogic politicians, rent-seeking officials, and others who exemplify 'cronyism' (the corrupt), opponents of free trade and the unfettered mobility of capital (protectionists, anti-globalisation 'anarchists'), barbarous warlords ('theirs', not 'ours'), and international terrorists (of a certain religious complexion).

Against such others violence can, then, according to this ideology, be legitimately used (keeping 'collateral damage' to a minimum, naturally). Neoliberal ideology in fact creates a very wide and flexible range of 'others' who in one way or another may be pictured as threatening the liberal-democratic order, and whom the liberal-democratic state can therefore legitimately detain and punish – domestic criminals, 'gang members', 'failed asylum seekers' and the like – and in the case of people, especially foreigners, who are designated as 'terrorists' (or terrorist 'supporters' or even just 'sympathisers'), detain and interrogate, and even torture, or kill. 'Humanitarian' military interventions, or military interventions aimed at merely 'spreading democracy', have been justified on this kind of ground.[13] And then popular 'common sense', shaped by this ideology, makes the necessary exceptions to its general distaste for, and scruples about, the uses of violence.

THE GLOBAL POLICEMAN

In the era of neoliberal global capitalism, it is the instability associated with localised conflicts around the globe that has increasingly come to define what capital sees as 'the problem of order'. The collapse of the Soviet Union opened the way for the US to act with impunity as the global policeman, but at the same time fuelled the black market in modern armaments – with the buyers, moreover, now more often intending them for use rather than display or deterrence.[14] As the global policeman, however, the US state has hardly been more successful than the Los Angeles Police Department has been in south-central Los Angeles.

The deployment of its unparalleled means of violence in its interventions in the 1990s led to the transformation of NATO from a 'defensive organization into a powerful alliance prepared to intervene militarily wherever it chose to do so', in the words of Canada's former ambassador to Yugoslavia. 'And it paved the way for the unilateral US invasion of Iraq'.[15] While September 11, 2001 may have brought home to some Americans, in a horrible manner, the contradictions of policing the world, it was also the pretext for a new wave of military adventurism in the terror unleashed on Afghanistan and Iraq that in turn provoked violent insurgencies in response. The Bush Administration's sanctioning of the use of torture in investigations by the US military (and especially by the CIA), its practice of 'rendition' to torture chambers abroad, and the Patriot Act's violation of elementary legal rights of 'suspected terrorists' within the USA were accompanied by US federal government departments 'classifying documents at the rate of 125 a minute as they create new categories of semi-secrets bearing vague labels like "sensitive security information"'.[16]

It is important to register the fact that, despite claims by 'security experts' that the threat of terrorism has been increasing (and despite criticisms of the Iraq war that focus on how it has misdirected attention from alleged terrorist threats closer to home[17]), the incidence of terrorist attacks *outside* Iraq has in fact declined since 2001.[18] Of course, incidence and threat are not the same, and so the experts say that increased security measures have reduced the incidence while the threat has increased. That said, what has increased is the incidence of domestic insurgencies against foreign occupations, armed conflicts among rebels, warlords and ethnic and religious groups, and the 'one-sided violence' involved in deadly attacks against civilians (both by governments and such groups).[19]

The intensified security mentality of the US and allied states has been accompanied by surreal shifts in the language of violence and its uses. Even before 9/11 the police seized as a 'violent weapon' a toy catapult designed to throw teddy bears over a security fence at the Quebec City Free Trade Area of the Americas Summit in April 2001. Yet anti-globalisation protesters who tried to break through the police lines behind which the rich and powerful gathered, or who threw a rock at a McDonald's window along the route of a march, or who managed to get so far as to toss paint at a politician or CEO, were clearly engaged in a form of politics of a fundamentally different order in terms of intent, material employed, and effects, than the practice of armed violence by a state (such as the use of police violence in Genoa or Oaxaca). An immediate effect of 9/11 and the declaration of the war on terrorism was that rather than these important distinctions becoming clearer, they were further obscured by agencies concerned with 'state security' – including in the EU, which was quick to include 'urban violence', 'damage to government facilities' and 'seriously intimidating a population' in its post-9/11 redefinitions of terrorism, and to launch an unprecedented level of cooperation between Europol and American law enforcement agencies.[20] The distinctions were also obscured by unscrupulous politicians and journalists, one of whom wrote immediately after 9/11: 'Like terrorists, the anti-globalization movement is disdainful of democratic institutions... Terrorism, if not so heinous as what we witnessed last week, has always been part of the protesters' game plan'.[21]

Such claims are as absurd as they are mendacious. For what characterises this generation of left activists is the explicit eschewal, even among its most militant elements, of armed revolutionary struggle, let alone terrorism (along the lines of the Red Brigades or Weathermen) as a means of effecting political change. In the current era, it is not among activists on the left, but rather almost exclusively on the right that one finds violence adopted as a strategy, as among those Christian fundamentalists or American militiamen or European neo-Nazis who bomb abortion clinics, government buildings and refugee shelters, burn Roma camps and attack immigrants. And the same applies to the militants of political religion across Asia from the eastern Mediterranean to the China Sea, whether Muslim or Jewish or Hindu, whose self-identification as the scourge of secularism, and of those of other religious beliefs, is a defining element.[22]

ONCE AGAIN, SOCIALISM OR BARBARISM

That said, the barbarism 'actually existing' in so much of the world, however much it may be connected with the suppression and sometimes extermination of so many of the egalitarian, democratic and socialist projects of the 20th century, also needs to be traced back to the failures of so many parties and movements that sustained these projects. What happened in South Africa's townships in 2008 – 'a burning tire around the neck of a terrified immigrant; neighbours turning on neighbours with violent rage; hundreds huddling in police stations for fear of more bloodshed'[23] – is directly related to the ANC government's embrace of neoliberalism, the loss of influence of its partners, the SACP and COSATU, and experiences of rates of unemployment and poverty as great or greater than under apartheid. As one South African observer put it: 'We are sitting on a (time bomb). People are poor. They don't have jobs or decent housing and they are sick and tired of it. It's at a point where it is easy for anybody to incite violence... This is not just about xenophobia. The next thing you might get some lunatic in the informal settlement say, how can we be hungry when they are rich across (the highway). These conditions are ripe for that sort of uprising'.[24] Nor can the incidents of violence against the Gypsy community and Bengali shopkeepers in Italy – in the context of increased anti-Roma and anti-immigrant rhetoric coming from official authorities[25] – be properly understood without taking into account the confusion and loss of purpose that accompanied the demise of the PCI, once the most vibrant Communist party in the west.

The proliferation of barbarisms large and small needs to be understood in the context of the low point reached by the socialist project at the end of the 20th century – whether due to defeats inflicted by imperialism and domestic reaction, or to the many failures and acts of oppression of actually-existing socialism and post-colonial nationalism, or to the contradictions of social democratic reformism and its settlement with neoliberalism. This is, in fact, what Engels was getting at when he raised the possibility of a 'universal lapse into barbarism' in the Europe of his time. He saw this as likely if the nascent socialist mass movement's political transformation of *the working classes themselves* was stopped in its tracks. Marx and Engels founded their politics on the knowledge that 'for the success of the cause itself, the alteration of men on a mass scale is necessary, an alteration which can only take place in a practical movement: a *revolution*'. They called the development of the practical movement a revolution 'not only because the *ruling* class cannot be overthrown in any other way, but also because the class *overthrowing* it can only in a revolution succeed in ridding itself of all the muck of ages and become fitted to found a society anew'.[26] This was not something that could take place overnight, in an insurrectionary moment. Engels' letters in the late 1880s, while expressing his concern about the 'unparalleled devastation' of a war among the Great Powers, was most troubled by the fact that war would lead to the socialist movement being 'smashed up, disorganized, deprived of freedom of action everywhere'; and with 'the compulsory and universal suppression of our movement', would come 'a period of reaction based on "the inanition of all the peoples bled white..."'.[27]

We are in such a position now. The violence with which the world is now saturated reflects the failures of the socialist movements of the 20th century to transform the working classes so as to transcend their particularisms and develop the ambition and strength to face down and defeat ruling-class violence. The current impasse of the socialist movement is thus directly relevant to question of actually existing barbarism at the beginning of the 21st century. As Raymond Williams so well understood,

> there must be something in every socialist, from the very values involved in wanting socialism at all, wanting a revolution to bring about socialism rather than just wanting a revolution, that continually pulls towards precisely the compromises, the settlements, the getting through without too much trouble and suffering that is the great resource of longing on which the capitalist parties draw... It is only when people get to the point of seeing that the price of the contradictions is yet more intolerable than the price of ending them that they acquire the nerve to go all the way through to a consistent socialist politics.[28]

A consistent socialist politics for the 21st century remains to be developed. But it will certainly have to achieve a better balance between means and ends, values and practice, than 20th century socialist politics managed to do. The main task for the foreseeable future lies in fashioning new socialist institutions oriented to developing class identities and capacities and doing so in ways that are inclusive, democratic and potentially transformative. Only this can really put socialist revolution back on the historical agenda. The question will then remain of how far this can be brought about through peaceful means. But a consistent socialist politics, while grasping the violence of capitalism and imperialism in all its manifestations, will also have to be vigilant against the temptation to glamorise revolutionary violence, and not to mistake as revolutionary every act of violent resistance by those subjected to dispossession and oppression. For a consistent socialist politics, a very different set of values and judgements is involved, a very different existential calculus, as it were, from one which celebrates the cathartic and positive effects of 'subjective' violence against those who have inflicted violence on you, as in the position once supported by (mis)readings of Fanon. What is properly celebrated is courage and selflessness in the fight for human decency, solidarity and the emancipatory goals of socialism – not the exercise of violence.

The widespread discrediting of neoliberalism as ideology and policy today suggests that as political consent to neoliberalism declines, coercion is increasingly likely to be resorted to. In this context, while the prime task remains that of rebuilding the socialist movement, there are many other important and immediate tasks – not least those involving organisations, campaigns and movements for civil liberties and against war. It is more than ever necessary to hold liberal democracy to account for its own claims of legality and humanity, reason and peacefulness. In the current period of reaction there is political scope, and a responsibility, to test and contest the bourgeois order on its own grounds. Revealing its contradictions in this way can also help to move towards developing the consistent socialist politics needed to transcend it.

NOTES

1 'Idomeneus stabbed at the middle/ of his chest with the spear, and broke the bronze armour about him… He cried out then, a great cry, broken, the spear in him,/ and fell, thunderously, and the spear in his heart was stuck fast/ but the heart was panting still and beating to shake the butt end/ of the spear'. The Iliad, cited in David Denby, *Great Books*, New York: Simon and Schuster 1996, pp. 29-30.

2 Karl Marx, *Capital,* Volume I, Harmondsworth: Penguin, 1976, p. 926 and 914.

3 A disturbing recent form of this is the seizure of tropical forests to serve as carbon sinks as part and parcel of the carbon trading 'solution' to today's ecological crisis.

4 Michael T. Klare, 'The New Geopolitics of Energy', *The Nation*, 19 May 2008, p. 24.

5 James C. Scott, *Weapons of the Weak: Everyday Forms of Peasant Resistance*, New Haven: Yale University Press, 1985. It is striking that Scott omits violent acts of self-defence and opposition from such 'weapons'.

6 Mahmood Mamdani, *When Victims Become Killers: Colonialism, Nativism and the Genocide in Rwanda*, Princeton: Princeton University Press, 2002.

7 Human Security Report Project, *Dying to Lose: Explaining the Decline in Global Terrorism*, Burnaby: Simon Fraser University, 2007, p. 22.

8 Gary Mason, 'A Nation on the Brink', *The Globe and Mail*, 5 January 2008.

9 For a striking example of the refusal to condone, see Fidel Castro's statement at the time of the rescue of the FARC captives from the Columbian jungle in July 2008: 'Out of a basically humanist sentiment, we rejoiced at the news that Ingrid Betancourt, three American citizens and other captives had been released. The civilians should have never been kidnapped neither should the militaries have been kept prisoners in the conditions of the jungle. These were objectively cruel actions. No revolutionary purpose could justify it. The time will come when the subjective factors should be analyzed in depth'. http://www.cuba.cu/gobierno/reflexiones/2008/ing/f030708i.html.

10 *Planet of Slums*, London: Verso, 2006, p. 202.

11 *Violence*, London: Profile Books, 2008, p. 8.

12 Twain wrote this in *A Connecticut Yankee in King Arthur's Court*, published in 1889, see *Mark Twain and the Three R's: Race, Religion, Revolution – and Related Matters*, Edited by M. Geismar, New York: Bobbs-Merrill, 1973, pp. 178-9.

13 For example, the British Foreign Secretary David Miliband argues that '...mistakes made in Iraq and Afghanistan must not cloud the moral imperative to intervene – sometimes militarily – to help spread democracy throughout the world'. (*Guardian*, 13 February 2008). For a critique see Gwydion Williams, 'I'll do it my way, you'll do it my way', in *Labour and Trade Union Review*, 185(March), 2008, pp. 3-6.

14 See R.T. Naylor, 'The Rise of the Modern Arms Business and the Fall of Supply Side Control', in V. Gamba, ed., *Society Under Siege: Crime,*

Violence and Illegal Weapons, Halfway House: Institute for Security Studies, South Africa, 1998.

15 James Bissett, 'Why NATO Really Smote the Serbs', *The Globe and Mail*, 22 March 2007. Bissett was Canada's Ambassador to Yugoslavia from 1990 to 1992.

16 Scott Shane, 'Since 2001, Sharp Increase in the Number of Documents Classified by the Government', *New York Times*, 3 July 2005.

17 Thus even Noam Chomsky: 'One of the things that Bush *hasn't* been doing is improving security. So, for example, if you look at the government commission after 9-11, one of its recommendations – which is a natural one – is to improve security of the US-Canadian border. I mean, if you look at that border, it's very porous. You or I could walk across it somewhere with a suitcase holding components of a nuclear bomb. The Bush administration did not follow that recommendation. What it did instead was fortify the Mexican border, which was not regarded as a serious source of potential terrorism. They in fact slowed the rate of growth of border guards on the Canadian Border'. Noam Chomsky interviewed by Gabriel Matthew Schivone, 'United States of Insecurity', *Monthly Review*, 60(1), 2008, p. 16. See also Barack Obama's major foreign policy speech, 'The War We Need to Win' to the Woodrow Wilson Centre, August 1, 2007 at http://www.barackobama.com; and his 'Renewing American Leadership', *Foreign Affairs*, 86(4), 2007, esp. pp. 9-11.

18 See Human Security Report Project, *Dying to Lose: Explaining the Decline in Global Terrorism*, Burnaby: Simon Fraser University, 2007, pp. 1-2, 9-13, 20. http://www.humansecuritybrief.info/HSRP_Brief_2007.pdf.

19 Ibid, pp. 41-43. Counting only the 25 or more killings that must be perpetrated for a campaign of one-sided violence to be recorded by Uppsala University's Conflict Data Program (and noting civilians killed in attacks on military targets are not included), the data confirm that the number of such campaigns rose from 19 in 1989 to a high of 38 in 2004.

20 'EU Definition of "Terrorism" could still cover Protests', December, 2001, available from http://www.statewatch.org; and Nicholas Lavranos, 'Europol and the Fight Against Terrorism', *European Foreign Affairs Review*, 8(2), 2003.

21 Aaron Lukas, 'America Still the Villain', *National Post*, 18 Sept, 2001, quoted in D. Schederman and B. Cossman, 'Political Association and

the Anti-Terrorism Bill', in R.J. Daniels et al., eds., *The Security of Freedom*, Toronto: University of Toronto Press: 2001, pp. 188-9.

22 Several of the most important of these movements are analysed in the 2008 volume of the *Socialist Register, Global Flashpoints: Reactions to Imperialism and Neoliberalism.*

23 Olivia Ward, 'South Africa's Strife Exposes Deep Problems', *Toronto Star*, 26 May 2008.

24 Prince Mashele, analyst at the South African Institute for Security Studies, quoted in Phumza Macanda, 'ANALYSIS – Poverty a Recipe for Wider South Africa Unrest', *The Free Library*, 23 May 2008, available from http://www.thefreelibrary.com.

25 See Amnesty International, 'Italy: Attacks against Roma Communities in Italy', 23 May 2008, available at http://www.amnesty.org; and Richard Owen, 'Mob of Nazi Youth goes on Immigrant Rampage in "Tolerant" Rome', *The Times*, 26 May 2008.

26 K. Marx and F. Engels, 'The German Ideology', in *Collected Works*, Volume 5, London: Lawrence and Wishart, 1976, p. 53.

27 See the letters to Paul Lafargue, March 25 and October 3, 1889 in Frederick Engels and Paul and Laura Lafargue, *Correspondence*, Volume 2, Moscow: Foreign Languages Publishing House, 1960, pp. 210, 322. Engels first used the phrase 'the universal lapse into barbarism' in his Introduction to Sigismund Borkheim's 1887 Pamphlet, *In Memory of the German Blood-and-Thunder Patriots*, 1806-1807, in Marx and Engels, *Collected Works*, Volume 26, London: Lawrence and Wishart, 1987, p. 451. Engels' thinking during this period has been carefully analysed in Gilbert Achcar, 'Engels: Theorist of War; Theorist of Revolution', *International Socialism Journal*, 97, 2002.

28 Raymond Williams, *Politics and Letters*, London: Verso, 1979, p. 383.

AMERICAN MILITARISM AND THE US POLITICAL ESTABLISHMENT: THE REAL LESSONS OF THE INVASION OF IRAQ

VIVEK CHIBBER

The American invasion of Iraq has been a catastrophe of epic proportions for the Iraqi population – apart from the massive loss of Iraqi lives, the destruction of most of what was left of the country's physical infrastructure, and the creation of more than five million refugees – one-fifth of the total population. But it has also been a significant disaster for Bush and American global power more generally. Today, in the wake of this set-back, and in anticipation of a new presidency, the question that looms is: what is the likely fallout of this debacle for American strategy? Since we cannot predict the future, the most reasonable course is to examine the logic of the invasion itself – the interests involved in it, the depth of elite commitment to its goals, and the larger strategic purpose that it served. This is the best guide we have for ascertaining which elements of the whole misadventure are likely to be jettisoned, which will be adjusted and which are likely to continue uninterrupted.

In the haze of popular memory, and even in intellectual circles, the most common explanation for the invasion is a simple one: that it was the brainchild of the neo-conservative cabal grouped around Bush II, and it was motivated in large measure to open the door for American oil majors to take control of the region. It would be hard to deny the surface plausibility of this assessment. The neo-con policy experts and their allied think tanks were never shy about claiming credit for pushing through the invasion. Further, it is hard to think of any administration in recent memory that had closer links to oil interests than that of Bush II. It is hardly an inferential leap to suggest that these interests might have been the prime movers behind invading one of the largest pools of untapped oil in the world.

The impression that the invasion was pushed through by this particular grouping is further heightened by the memory of the intense public debates that preceded it. This was when stalwarts from the elder Bush's administration – Brent Scowcroft, James Baker, Lawrence Eagleburger and others – as well as prominent Democrats like Madeleine Albright, Richard Holbrooke and Bill Clinton himself, raised doubts about the wisdom of the younger Bush's strategy. It was widely held at the time that when experienced diplomats like Scowcroft or Baker issued public warnings to George W., they were in fact speaking for his father. The debate only seemed to confirm that the younger Bush was pursuing a strategy that would have been unthinkable under a different administration. Today, in the wake of the occupation's calamitous results, the memory of the outside criticism has taken on something of an iconic stature. The interventions made by Scowcroft and others are taken to have expressed the deep misgivings of, and opposition from, a policy establishment that knew better than to launch such a hazardous undertaking.

Among intellectuals and foreign policy experts this line has been taken further, to the effect that the heightened militarism embodied in the invasion reflected a watershed in foreign policy more generally, evident along several dimensions – from soft power to hard power, multilateralism to unilateralism, economic coercion to military coercion, etc. One of the most common descriptions of the Bush ascension is that it signalled the turn to a New Imperialism – in contrast to the policy orientation that preceded it, and reminiscent of the global hegemony established by England two centuries ago. To some, like Niall Ferguson, this was a development to be welcomed, a sign that America was finally accepting the responsibility that comes with power;[1] to more sober minds, of course, it was something to be deplored.

If these diagnoses were accurate, then the implication of the set-backs in Iraq would be simple – a return to the status quo ante, a turn away from unilateralism, the abandonment of aggressive militarism, and perhaps even an abatement of the imperial impulse. The task is to assess the extent to which they are in fact true. How much does the Bush interregnum represent a break from the recent past, and how much of his agenda can we expect to continue into the next administrations? We are thus obliged to turn to recent history in order to place his decisions in the longer flow of policy.

As it happens, the recent past serves us particularly well in assessing the distinctiveness of Bush's orientation – since his ascension was preceded by two consecutive terms of a Democratic presidency. Even more, the 1990s were indisputably a watershed period, as the fall of the Soviet Union in 1991 meant that the Cold War finally came to an end. The 1990s were the first decade in which the US was without a true geopolitical rival in the global order. The expectations, it might be recalled, were for a truly revolutionary shift in international affairs, away from militarism, and toward peace. If the younger Bush's turn to a new imperialism, his resort to unilateralism, etc., was as much of a break as has been claimed, it certainly should stand out against the backdrop of a Democratic presidency and the end of superpower rivalry.

FROM COLD WAR TO NEW WORLD ORDER

If the conventional account of the Cold War were accurate, then, in the 1990s, the United States ought to have embraced demilitarisation and a pacific foreign policy. The winding tentacles of American military power, embodied most of all in its hundreds of military and naval bases; the support of corrupt tyrannies; the clandestine operations around the global South – all of this had been justified in the decades of the Cold War as a necessary evil, in order to hold at bay an even greater evil. It had been presented as measures to which American presidents resorted in order to contain another power's aggression. The various elements of this strategy were subsumed under the umbrella concept of *containment*, a term that perfectly conveyed the essentially defensive posture that policy elites claimed for their actions. So after 1991, with the imperative to restrain Soviet global ambitions no longer obtaining, many observers waited for a corresponding diminution of the American imperium.

What happened, of course, was the very opposite. Far from scaling back its military spread, the US quickly moved to extend its presence into areas that had hitherto been out of reach. The elder Bush launched Operation Desert Storm in late 1991, which brought American bases back into Saudi Arabia after some decades. And Bill Clinton extended bases into Eastern Europe in two stages, each time in the wake of a military operation in the former Yugoslavia – in 1993, and then in 1999. Eastern Europe had, for obvious reasons, been inaccessible for decades as a military outpost; the Middle East had been the object of concerted expansion since the Carter Presidency, but the actual placement of bases so deep in the heartland had been out of the question till the Saudis gave their assent in 1991.

These were but two conspicuous instances of what has come to be known as 'power projection' during the first post-Cold War decade. The underlying strategy that they reflected was laid out fairly clearly by Bill Clinton's National Security Advisor, Anthony Lake, in the autumn of 1993. In a speech at Johns Hopkins University entitled 'From Containment to Enlargement', Lake announced a foreign policy vision for the new era that directly, and unmistakably, dissolved any expectations that the post-Soviet era would witness a drawing down of America's global reach. During the

Cold War, he maintained, American policy had been directed to mitigating the influence of the Soviets, and hence toward containing their influence. It had been essentially defensive in orientation. But now, Lake argued, the US had to embrace a more aggressive, more ambitious strategy. This was not the time to initiate an era of retreat for the US, but an enlargement of its sphere of influence.[2] Under the new dispensation, deterrence would give way to the open pursuit of primacy. In fairness, even though it was a Clinton appointee who enunciated this policy in the public arena, it had already been recognised by the administration that preceded his. In the waning months of the Bush presidency, Paul Wolfowitz, then the Under Secretary of Defense for Policy, had leaked a confidential planning document which had laid out virtually the same agenda.[3] To be sure, there had been some hesitation – a momentary pause – under the elder Bush, before the new imperial vision was embraced. It took the first Iraq War to jar him from his lethargy. But by the time Clinton assumed office, the foreign policy establishment had firmly settled on its course of power projection.[4]

Although Lake did convey rather accurately what the core foreign policy aim was to be during the decade, there was one respect in which his presentation was misleading – containment had never been the centrepiece of US strategy during the Cold War. It had always been guided by a vigorous expansionism, both economically and politically. In fact, American foreign policy since the Spanish-American War should be seen as a punctuated pursuit of global power, the tempo of which has increased as constraints to its operation have been removed. During the inter-war period, the main such constraint was the zonal authority of European colonial powers, which over time chiselled their empires into economic blocs. The Second World War provided an opportunity to dismantle the barriers to US capital, and to incorporate new zones into the US sphere of political influence. It is in fact remarkable how early the Roosevelt administration realised this. Within weeks of the attacks on Pearl Harbor, Roosevelt put together a massive network of post-war planning agencies which immediately took to designing a strategy for breaking up the colonial blocs and prying open Asia and the Middle East to American influence.[5] These plans formed the blueprint for American strategy in the post-war period, which Truman pursued with firm diligence. The settlement that came out of the war did, for a while, preserve the formal apparatus of the colonial spheres, but only under the protection of American power. With their fortunes now tied to American patronage, France and the UK could do little to resist. What ensued was a massive American expansion into those areas that had been outside its sphere.[6]

The noteworthy point here is that the plans for post-war expansion were drawn up before the outcome of the war was certain, and, more to the point, before Hitler's reversals on the Eastern Front had begun to accumulate. The outward thrust of American policy was thus emphatically not a response to the Soviets' own expansionist designs after the war – it had been designed independently of any actions Stalin might have undertaken, and before his fate could even have been known. To be sure, once the Soviet Union emerged from the war as a military power, American policy had to adjust to its presence. But it was just that – an adjustment of a strategy already in place.

If we recognise the actual nature of strategy in the Cold War years, it is clear that the years 1945 and 1991 each marked the eclipse of rival powers that had placed barriers to American expansion. In 1945, the US seized upon an opportunity provided by the weakened state of its rivals to dramatically increase its sphere of influence. And this is exactly what Anthony Lake was declaring to be the nucleus of policy after the fall of the Soviet Union in 1991. The strategic orientation being urged by him was not by any means an innovation.

IRAQ BEFORE BUSH II: FROM CONTAINMENT TO REGIME CHANGE

The push toward a more aggressive imperialism was thus already taking root much before the Iraq invasion. As this pursuit of primacy congealed in the early 1990s, the choice of unilateralism or multilateralism did not issue from a doctrinal commitment one way or the other, but as a practical choice – multilateralism when possible, unilateralism and militarism when necessary. This strategy called for a continual assessment of the facts on the ground and the international political environment. There was some hesitation about upsetting established diplomatic practices, long established in political culture. But by the end of the decade the hesitancy of the early half was beginning to give way. This gradual shift, in the midst of some uncertainty, was reflected very sharply in the evolving policy toward Iraq. It exploded into relief after 9/11, of course; but a decisive shift toward military aggression against Hussein had begun earlier, in Clinton's later years.

The conditions for containment

In the wake of the Gulf War of 1991, once the elder Bush had decided to leave Saddam Hussein in power, the administration settled for a policy of containment, of holding Hussein at bay under a regime of international sanctions. Bush would have preferred to push through with regime change, but, as he famously observed in his memoirs, prudential considerations induced him to settle for the fall-back option.[7] Two background conditions were critical to the containment strategy's viability. First, the US's European and Middle Eastern allies were willing to support the sanctions regime. In its initial years this was not politically burdensome to the actors involved, as there was considerable public disapproval of Hussein's attack on Kuwait, and the brutal character of his rule had become widely known. The only worrisome fallout of the sanctions was the expected decrease in oil shipments coming out of Iraq. But here, the second enabling condition became relevant, which was that world oil supplies in the early 1990s were in a very comfortable position. Furthermore, officials were optimistic that the rush of investments into the Caspian region would compensate for the shortfalls resulting from loss of Iraqi oil. It is doubtful that Bush anticipated the sanctions having to last more than a few years, for which the political and economic situation seemed manageable.

When Clinton came to power, he inherited this sanctions regime, which he then relied upon during his first administration. But the salient point here is that, while he was willing to use sanctions, this was never Clinton's preferred option. In fact, throughout his presidency, the US either organised, or indirectly encouraged, one ruse after another to depose Hussein – fomenting domestic opposition, sponsoring military uprisings, even giving support to assassination attempts.[8] The strategy came to be known, understandably enough, as 'containment plus regime change'. Of course, none of the various attempts came to anything, leading instead to a lively debate within the cabinet on the appropriate course of action. The staff charged with formulating Iraq policy congealed fairly rapidly into two broad camps, of doves and hawks, with the latter calling for a much more aggressive stance against Hussein, and hence for abandoning the containment strategy. But as long as other instruments were still available, the doves in the administration were able to hold their ground.[9]

During Clinton's second term, the balance within the administration started to shift. Iraq policy was now transferred to the hands of the more hawkish members of the cabinet, chief among whom were Sandy Berger and Madeleine Albright, but also included Martin Indyck and Leon Fuerth.[10] The consequence was a gradual but unmistakable increase in military actions against the Hussein regime. By the final two years of the Clinton Presidency, the policy orientation toward Iraq had changed dramatically from that of the early 1990s. The various schemes hatched to depose him had failed, leading to a great deal of frustration within both policy camps. One tangible consequence of this was that the more militant of the hawks, who had been the smallest of the policy currents in the administration, now began to attract more converts to their side.

It bears noting that this shift in Iraq policy was part of a more general thrust toward militarism in Clinton's second administration, stemming, it appears, from a clearer commitment to primacy in world affairs. Between 1996 and 2000, the world witnessed several displays of naked American power, in which more subtle diplomatic channels were openly flouted in favour of open, and at times illegal, aggression. The United Nations, in particular, was sidelined and even humiliated quite openly in Clinton's final years. The 1998 bombing campaign against Iraq, known as Operation Desert Fox, was never submitted to the Security Council; in fact, Clinton pointedly timed the bombing to start on the very day that the Security Council was deliberating on its legality. The bombing of Serbia was carried out under NATO auspices, precisely in order to take the initiative away from the UN, where there was resistance to permitting it. More broadly, Clinton began the process of backing out of several key international treaties, like Kyoto and the landmines agreement, a retreat which Bush later completed. While Clinton did not openly and decisively disparage the UN, in the way Bush II would a few years later, his practice was already showing a rather cavalier attitude toward international law and diplomacy.

The turn to regime change

The attractiveness of the hawkish position did not issue from frustration alone. Just as important was the fact that by 1998–99 the background conditions that had made containment viable had become unstable. European and Middle Eastern support of the sanctions regime was fraying, mainly because of public revulsion at its horrendous consequences. While Albright could get away with declaring her acceptance of the more than half-million deaths caused by the sanctions, matters were not so easy for European governments, which had to deal with less supine media and more mobilised citizenry.[11] Their willingness to offer support to Clinton on this strategy was beginning to wane. Without European support, it would be impossible for sanctions to continue, and by 1999, Clinton was meeting with considerable resistance within the Security Council against their continuation.

Compounding this problem was the changed situation in oil supply. In the early 1990s, the main fact about the oil market had been plentiful supplies and plenty of excess capacity in the key producing regions. By 2000, this situation was reversed. While prices were still low, increases in supply were no longer keeping up with the rate at which demand was increasing.[12] One factor contributing to the shortfall was that actual supply from new wells in the Caspian region had not met with expectations. But more important was that there had been very little addition to new capacity in the critical region for oil production, which was in the Gulf states. One high-level report estimated that spare capacity on a global scale was just 2 per cent below the level of demand, making for the tightest markets in recent memory.[13] This was a direct consequence of the sanctions imposed on Iran and Iraq, potentially the two most important sources of additional supplies after Saudi Arabia. So while the easy supply situation had allowed for a permissive attitude toward sanctions earlier in the decade, the situation now made a continuation of the policy seem perilous at best.

The change in these conditions cast grave doubt on the future viability of the multilateral sanctions regime. Already by the late 1990s, leading voices in policy circles had begun to question the wisdom, much less the possibility, of continuing with the strategy.[14] The natural solution to the fraying of international support for sanctions and the tight oil supply would have been to simply do away with sanctions and allow new investments to move in. The fact that this was *not* pursued, by either Clinton or Bush, is highly significant and warrants further discussion. If the ambition in official circles was simply to bring more oil on line by ushering international companies into the Gulf, all that would have been required was to lift the sanctions, which included a block on foreign investment. Saddam showed no intention of blocking the entrance of the oil majors, and in fact, he was clandestinely cutting deals with many of the non-American companies in his last years. Saddam was not the obstacle to boosting oil supplies – the sanctions were. This being the case, the simplest course of action would have been to see the writing on the wall, acknowledge that the whole framework of containment was falling apart, and to allow new investments to flow in while subduing Hussein with threats of imminent destruction. In fact, there were elements in the foreign policy establishment who pushed just this approach.[15] It was never given a serious audience.

The reason that sanctions could not simply be dismantled was that this would entail a direct, and prohibitive, *political* cost – a steady decline in power and leverage for the US in the region. It would mean that Hussein had managed to survive a decade-long campaign of strangulation, of attempts at regime change, air-strikes, bombing, vilification – all by the most powerful nation in the world, which had openly called for his overthrow. In any other region, this might have been a tolerable dénouement to the conflict, one that the US could have lived with. But in the Middle East, its ramifications were too serious to ignore.

The problem was the oil. If Iraq had been just another developing nation, and Hussein just another tin-pot dictator, his surviving the sanctions regime may very well have been tolerable, and his chest-thumping little more than an annoyance. But of course Iraq was, as Paul Wolfowitz imprudently put it, floating on a sea of oil. Given the relative decline in supply described above, Hussein was poised to take over as the swing producer in the global market[16] – i.e. as the producer with greatest spare capacity – giving him the kind of position that the Saudis had occupied for decades. But unlike the Saudis, who were an American protectorate, Hussein would almost certainly position himself as a regional rival. This would entail a direct loss of power for the US, to be sure. It would also create political challenges for its regional allies, who relied on American backing for their own political stability.

The loss in leverage would also have ramifications for American alliances more broadly, because of the critical place of the Middle East in global geopolitics. Since almost every nation in the world had to arrange some kind of access to Gulf oil, the US's hegemonic position in the region's politics gave it indirect leverage over their policy choices – not only choices directly related to Middle East policy, but more widely, since favours in one domain could be granted in exchange for concessions in others. The major oil producers relied on American patronage and protection in one way or another; this placed the US in a position to be consulted by all sides in key diplomatic negotiations. A loss of power in the region would be the first step toward losing this privileged position.

Clinton's dilemma

This, then, was Clinton's dilemma toward the end of his second term. There were two choices left for the administration – to engineer some kind of new and revamped apparatus for containment, or to push aggressively for regime change. Each had its own problems. A new sanctions regime would most likely not be supported by European or even regional allies, which would mean that the US would have to enforce it unilaterally. But its enforcement measures would have to be directed at those very allies, which would only further isolate the US. Furthermore, every month that they failed to trigger an uprising in Iraq, the relevant players would be more and more inclined to hammer out their own settlements with Hussein, thus giving them a vested interest in his survival, and further marginalising the US.

The other option was an intensified militarism. Pollack reports that within the Clinton administration, this was the path that was finally chosen. There was already a significant shift in this direction by 1998, of which the bombardment carried out under Desert Fox was the clearest indication. In

1999, the president assigned Madeline Albright the task of designing a plan for the overthrow of Saddam Hussein, a decision that most of his policy advisors supported.[17] Lurking in the background of all this was the fact that, if an ambitious military action were to be undertaken, its success in purely military terms was almost certain. Iraq was a broken state, almost incapable of defending itself. Had it been a real power, had Hussein's regime had a real mass base, and hence offered the prospect of real resistance, the lurch toward greater militarism would have been strongly resisted in American policy circles. But given that it was not, the military option loomed as an almost irresistible attraction. 'Containment plus regime change', the policy of the first Clinton term, had now been displaced by regime change pure and simple.

Now another dilemma presented itself. The most obvious instrument for effectuating regime change – a ground invasion – was fraught with too many imponderables, ranging from domestic public opinion to the risk of setting off regional political imbalances that would be hard to control. Most worrisome was the possibility of Iraq's break-up as a state, and, in such an eventuality, the boost that this would give to Iran as a regional power.[18] Clinton was caught in a bind – he had committed to an escalation of hostilities with Hussein, to use military force to overthrow him, but short of an invasion, just about every device had been tried, and had failed. But an invasion seemed not to be on the cards, given the two constraints just described.

INTO THE BREACH: THE NEO-CONS' WAR?

Bush had come into office with some kind of action against Iraq high on his agenda – that much we know. But in the first ten months of his presidency, there was little to suggest that he would actually pursue this course. Even with this desire to depose Hussein, Bush was hemmed in by the same constraints that had bound Clinton. There seemed little chance of justifying an unprovoked military invasion to depose Saddam. And then, in one stroke, Osama bin Laden removed the domestic constraint. It was the attacks on the Twin Towers on September 11, 2001, that changed the landscape. The insider accounts that have surfaced in the past two years show that within days of the attacks, Bush had ordered his advisors to find some way to connect the terrorist threat to Iraq and Saddam. It was plain that the attacks had created a window of opportunity with regard to public opinion, which was now pliant enough to allow Bush to contemplate an ambitious plan for regime change.[19]

The attacks of 9/11 in fact allowed Bush to think about advancing along *two* fronts. The first was global in scope, made possible under the rubric of the 'war on terror'. Within the political elite, the 'war on terror' was immediately perceived as an extraordinary opportunity to build upon the expansionist program of the 1990s.[20] Soon after the attacks, the United States launched a massive, unprecedented expansion of military and logistical institutions – bases, surveillance, prisons, training programs, etc. – around the world. Bush was riding the crest of a worldwide wave of sympathy, pushing through agreements in Central Asia, Latin America, Europe, and the Middle East that even in the recent past would have been inconceivable.[21] What is more, there was an unimpeachable, multilateral face to the expansion, easily packaged for public consumption. For as long as it lasted – and no-one could yet predict how long the sympathy would last – American military projection could be presented as nothing other than self-defence. Building on it was natural, almost effortless.

The second front that Bush wanted to open up, that of Iraq, would not be so easy. The American public could probably be managed, but it would be another matter to sell it globally. And this latter problem was salient because of the second constraint that had bound Clinton – the worries about containing the fallout from regime change. To many in foreign policy circles, an invasion would be foolhardy if carried out without the support of European and regional allies. But this brought with it other, related problems. If the allies were to be relied upon, then their own domestic constraints would have to be respected and this in turn would require a highly adroit management of diplomacy and propaganda. The most dovish of the American policy elite were sceptical of the viability of this project. Still, the gains to be had from this operation made it attractive to circles beyond the Bush cabinet. In the Democratic Party elite, the basic ambition to remove Hussein was already well established, and they could not have missed the significance of 9/11 as an opening for such a campaign. Despite the risks involved, the fact that there was a window of opportunity was not lost on anyone.

What separated the administration from its interlocutors was not the issue of whether or not to invade Iraq. Only a very few of the political elite rejected the idea outright. There was not even much disagreement over whether or not the US would need allies, i.e. on the choice between unilateralism and multilateralism. Bush seems to have had every intention of forging the broadest alliance he could muster. The disagreement was over two issues. The first was whether or not to prioritise the 'war on terror' – i.e. the global alliance system and its military benefits – over an invasion, at least in the immediate term. The dovish critics urged that Bush ought to concentrate on the former, because it would cement new alliances and give added strength to more venerable ones; over time, these strengthened alliances could then be put to use in a careful offensive against Saddam. The worry among these critics was that, by alienating the European and regional allies, a maladroit lurch toward war would undermine the campaign for regime change, as well as derailing the global thrust. The more hawkish critics were also worried about an invasion's potential for disrupting the wider expansionist agenda. Unlike the doves, however, they were more open to the idea of a simultaneous advance on both fronts. Nevertheless, like the doves, they insisted that the invasion be handled in a way that preserved the alliance system.

The second disagreement concerned the instruments with which to construct the coalition for the invasion. Most of the critics listed above, with the exception of Henry Kissinger, viewed the United Nations as the essential means to this. The Bush cabinet, however, seemed to regard the raw power of the United States – in all its dimensions, not just the military – as something of a gravitational force, which would enable them to attract a 'coalition of the willing' regardless of how the UN, or any other international agencies, reacted. Through much of 2002, the administration displayed a quite cavalier attitude to how the members of the Security Council were receiving their message – although by the end of the year they shifted to a more accommodating approach, in no small measure owing to the advice of their critics. It was not that they saw the members of the Council as irrelevant, they just believed that they could get the relevant members' cooperation outside the Council's bureaucratic procedures. This was also the view put forward by Kissinger, whose own views seem to be closest to the administration's. Whereas to the administration's critics, especially the doves, it seemed the height of folly. Through the summer and fall of 2002, therefore, both sets of critics launched a massive campaign to urge Bush back to the established instruments of international diplomacy.

In the public debate, prominent doves included Warren Christopher and Madeleine Albright, with Zbigniew Brzezinski occupying a position between the two groups. The hawks – who far outnumbered the doves – included James Baker, Lawrence Eagleburger, Brent Scowcroft (though Scowcroft was closer to the doves at one point) and most of the Clinton Democrats, including Clinton himself. Henry Kissinger could be included in this group too, though he was far enough on the hawkish end to be close to the Bush administration's position.

The fictional rift[22]

The bulk of the debate over invading Iraq was relatively short, lasting less than six months after the summer of 2002. Its famous first salvo was an op-ed piece by Brent Scowcroft, the elder Bush's National Security Advisor, on August 15; this was followed ten days later by an intervention by James Baker, who had been Secretary of State under the same administration. In the coming weeks, they were joined by Lawrence Eagleburger on the Republican side, and, on the Democratic side, by many members of Clinton's foreign policy team, including the ex-president himself. Adding their weight were veterans of administrations past, including Kissinger and Brzezinski.

From the cabinet members of the elder Bush, it was Scowcroft who expressed the gravest doubts about the invasion. But while the title of his piece was 'Don't Attack Saddam', its content was far less categorical. Scowcroft never made a case for abandoning the idea of an invasion; instead, he maintained that since Saddam was not an imminent threat, it would be hard to build a coalition against him at this point. On the other hand, there was already international support for the 'war on terror' – i.e. the larger project of expansion – and it was prudent to pursue this to a fuller extent, and revisit the idea of invasion later: 'the more progress we make in the war on terrorism... the greater will be the international support for going after Saddam', he concluded.[23] This was not a warning against invading – it was advice on how best to approach it.

James Baker's intervention was openly encouraging, as reflected accurately in its title, 'The Right Way to Change a Regime'.[24] He immediately pointed out that regime change was not Bush II's idea, but was a continuation of 'the policy of [his] predecessor'. Further, given that other means had failed, 'the only realistic way to effect regime change is through the application of military force, including significant ground troops to occupy the country... Anyone who thinks we can effect regime change in Iraq with anything less than this is simply not realistic'. But this commitment involved serious risks, chief among which is that 'unless we do it the right way, there will be costs to other American foreign policy interests, including our relationships with practically all other Arab countries'. The best way to minimise this risk was to avoid having 'to go it alone'. Again, like Scowcroft, the call was not to abandon the idea of regime change, but to recognise that it would have to be done with the help of allies. Virtually the same position was taken by Lawrence Eagleburger, also from the first Bush administration. In an interview just days after Baker's editorial, he expressed his agreement with the need for regime change, but warned that it would be 'very wrong for us, without allies, to go in'.[25] The invasion could not work without allied support, and for that, Bush had to carry a coalition along with him, especially Iraq's neighbours.

On the Democratic side, the reasoning was very similar, beginning with Richard Holbrooke, who endorsed the commitment to topple Saddam: 'The administration has rightly called for regime change'. But he warned that 'few other nations in the world, and especially in the region, will *openly* subscribe to such a goal'.[26] The only way to make it possible for allies to sell the agenda to their publics was to acquire a resolution from the UN Security Council, allowing the use of force if Hussein refused the entrance of weapons inspectors. In the coming weeks, Sandy Berger and former Assistant Secretary of State Jamie Rubin both went on the air, declaring their support for regime change – but with the proviso that it be handled in a fashion that carried the allies along, preferably through the UN.[27] But most significant was the support of Clinton himself in several appearances during the fall and winter of that year. He never, on any occasion, declared his opposition to an invasion. He observed instead that 'I think there is the right way and the best way to do it', which was to seek a Security Council resolution authorising the US to use force.[28]

If the need was to go to the Security Council, then, regardless of whatever back-room manoeuvring Bush and Powell relied upon, they also had to help any state supporting the US there to win over their domestic constituencies. For this, the advice was simple – Bush had to 'make his case' before the public, present enough evidence of Hussein's military threat, to pass muster in the public eye. This is what worried both groups of critics, the doves and the hawks, the most. Unless Bush handled this part of the campaign skilfully, potential allies would not be able to line up with him, because they would be too embattled at home. As Madeline Albright explained, the 'challenge… is to *frame a choice* for Europe that most of Europe can embrace with dignity'.[29] Clinton also made the same point: 'Here's what's going on', he told the NBC, '[America's allies] don't want it to look like they're being railroaded into going by [i.e. around] the UN... So we have to look like we're determined, but not eager, to go to war'.[30]

The critics were not engaging Bush on the actual facts of the matter, or to derail the plans for an invasion. Had they wanted to, they could have made their stand on the weapons issue. Because of its absolute centrality to Bush's public relations effort, the claim about Hussein's weapons programme was open to devastating attack – especially by members of the Clinton administration – if they were interested in scuttling Bush's attack plans. But, instead, Clinton backed the general authenticity of Bush's accusations, while urging him to make a credible *public* case. Thus, he declared during an interview in September that 'I think that Saddam Hussein clearly has chemical and biological weapons' and that, however many he may have had in 1998, 'he's doubtless developed more'.[31] The task for Bush was to package a propaganda campaign that would create the political space to act on this. 'I think we should try to get a – a United Nations resolution through calling for free, clear, and unfettered inspection, because that will give us a chance to build a much broader international coalition if we do actually attack Iraq' – inspections were thus called for, not to discover if biological and chemical weapons existed, but to help cobble together the needed coalition. Once it was in place, Bush not only could go in, but should: 'then we *have to attack*, to get rid of this vast store of biological and chemical weapons *that I believe he has*'.[32]

A spurious multilateralism

On the basic matter of regime change, then, there was no objection from either wing of the foreign policy establishment. The debate was over how Bush should organise the campaign to depose Hussein, and what the appropriate timing ought to be. As to the first issue, the advice coming from the critics seemed to be warning Bush away from a unilateral approach. Certainly, this is how the argument has come to be remembered in many quarters – a struggle between Bush's unilateralism and the critics' call for multilateralism. But if we examine the critics' statements, their interpretation of multilateralism drained it of any real content.

For Bush, there were two dangers involved in going to the UN. The first was that the Security Council might not play along. On this, Bush's critics were very careful not to suggest that the invasion should be *conditional* on the Council's permission. Again, there was complete agreement between the Republicans and Democrats on this. 'We should', Baker advised, '*try our best* to not have to go it alone'. Eagleburger advised that 'I would *do what I could to try* and build an international consensus'.[33] Zbigniew Brzezinski, in an op-ed in December, pointed to the dangers of rebuffing the UN – yet concluded not with a demand that the UN be respected, but only that 'if [rebuffing the UN] can be avoided, every effort should be exerted to make that happen'.[34]

No-one expressed the cynicism of this tactic more openly than Henry Kissinger.[35] In his television appearance in mid-August, Kissinger agreed that, no doubt, it was important to bring the allies along. But the really critical issue was 'whether one should give them a veto' over any decision Bush might want to make', i.e. whether he should predicate the invasion on international consensus.[36] And the answer to this was categorically negative.

Kissinger then issued a remonstration to Scowcroft. When asked whether Bush II ought not to follow the advice of Scowcroft and try to first build an international consensus around the need for war, Kissinger simply rejected the premise. 'I disagree with his analogies', he announced. The first Bush had never allowed himself to be dictated to by his allies:

> In the first Gulf campaign, President Bush solved the problem [of potential resistance from allies] by deploying a massive American force in the region *well before* he had a coalition. And so if countries wanted any influence over our action, they were almost obliged to join the coalition. And I think if one looks at the record, one will find that most of the allies joined the coalition after... 'Bush 41' had made clear that he would defend the independence of Kuwait, *if necessary, alone.*[37]

The basic principle of Kissinger's position was that a Great Power does not allow itself to be bound by the demands of lesser nations – and on this, there was agreement across a spectrum of critics. In the event that the Security Council slapped down Bush's requests, all of them, from dove to hawk, agreed: having made a 'best-faith effort', as Holbrook called it, Bush could then turn to his allies and launch an invasion – with allies, but, if need be, without the UN's backing.[38] The term 'international consensus' thus referred, not to the actual body of opinion in the world, but the opinion of those powers that agreed with the US.

Still, this did not settle the matter, for there was a second danger. It might turn out that even if a resolution was passed making new demands on Hussein, he might very well agree to them. This would then derail the plans for regime change. For this, Clinton and Holbrook had a practical suggestion: make the demands of the resolution so stringent that Iraq could not possibly accept them. The resolutions, Clinton advised, 'have to be totally intrusive. They have to be non-limited… And the resolution should also say that if he doesn't allow or if, later, he stops them [the inspectors], then the United Nations is authorized to use force'.[39] Holbrooke also called for 'air-tight, no-notice, anywhere, anytime inspections', as did Brzezinski.[40] The attractiveness of this, Holbrooke observed, was that, 'it is highly unlikely that Saddam will agree if… it's an air-tight, no-notice, any-time, anywhere inspection regime'. The likelihood of Saddam's refusal was thus being built into the resolution. Holbrooke concluded that the beauty of the plan was that 'he will sooner or later violate it if the inspectors go in, and we'll have the cause for war if we need to proceed'.[41] Here too, there was complete agreement, across the spectrum. The point of the whole exercise was not to discover if his weapons existed; it was, instead, to acquire the diplomatic cover needed to *justify* the invasion to the public.

Two points seem to emerge fairly clearly from the preceding discussion. First, there was no real dissent from the plans for regime change, or even of its taking the form of an invasion. The concern was about its timing. This was best expressed by Albright, who was perhaps the most sceptical about Bush's course of action. But while she continued in her public appearances to express doubts about Bush's strategy, in closed settings she was more forthcoming about her motives. She saw very well the need for regime change, but she was worried that Bush simply did not have either the alliances or the post-invasion logistics set up for the operation to work. In testimony before the Senate Foreign Relations Committee she observed that the basic rationale for going to the UN was to 'buy time' to set up the needed support structure for a successful action – not just logistical, but the needed political alliances and, just as importantly, post-invasion plans.[42] This meant, in practical terms, putting off the invasion for some time and using the political capital, and the breathing space, from the 'war on terror', to work toward preparing for the eventual invasion. The call to focus on the anti-terror campaign was thus not intended to displace the commitment to regime change in Iraq, but to make it more effective.[43]

The second point to emerge is that the purported urging of a multilateral approach by Bush's critics is something of a red herring. Bush never denied his need for allies; his critics, on the other hand, never intended that he should actually defer to his allies in any meaningful sense. The disagreement was over the instrument, or the strategy, with which to secure the alliance, on the United States' terms. While Bush did threaten to undertake the invasion alone, by the late summer of 2002 his administration had committed itself to seeking allies – both for material reasons, and for public relations. It was just that, to achieve this end, the Bush strategists took the UN as something of a nuisance. If the point was to put together a coalition, why not just forge ahead, in the manner recommended by Kissinger, and then wait for the flock to gather? Bush's declarations of his willingness to go it alone were designed to convince allies of the seriousness of his resolve – they were not meant to deter alliances.

To the critics, this just ignored the basic political realities. Allies could not simply line up behind him with an indifference to public opinion. Bush seemed to be operating under a false assumption that he could just follow the path his father had taken, as described by Kissinger. But there was a fundamental difference between the situation in 1991, and that which obtained in 2002. While Hussein was clearly an aggressor in the earlier instance, and a threat to neighbouring countries, there was no clear sign of impending danger from him in the latter instance. Such a case would have to be constructed – and until it was, allies would find it much harder to slide in behind him than they had ten years prior. Bush was urged to go to the UN because, in this context, making a case to invade Iraq would be impossible without its cover and its sanction. The UN endowed the alliance with a level of legitimacy essential to the whole enterprise. The critics were perfectly clear that if the ruse did not work, if the Security Council did not relent, then he was free to gather up his allies and move in – so why not try? If this was multilateralism, then it was, as Robert Kagan wryly observed, 'multilateralism American style'.[44]

Against the backdrop of all the portentous claims that have been made about the revolt of the elders, the deep rifts, the lurch to unilateralism, etc., the actual difference between the administration and its critics may appear almost trivial. But to suppose this would be a mistake. There was a real, and serious, tactical issue involved. The problem with Bush's approach was that he failed to appreciate the reality of his allies' predicament. Every time he announced that he intended to remove Hussein regardless of what the UN recommended, he inflamed public opinion in Europe and the Middle East, making it that much harder for potential allies to line up behind him. When members of the Bush administration encountered resistance, their reaction was to pour scorn on their counterparts, again arousing nationalist resentment, and further isolating themselves. There was a system in place for engineering allies' consent, which Bush was ignoring: the usual combination of bribes, threats, and inducements, all of which were usually carried out behind the scenes, while a script was to be carefully followed in public, allowing allies to come into the fold. Bush's folly was that he was pulling the rug from under his allies' feet.

There was an even bigger stake involved. Bush had decided to advance on two fronts at once, the global expansion under the 'war on terror', and regime change in Iraq. But if the latter was mishandled, the lead-up to it could create rifts and fissures where they had not existed before. And this could, in turn, undermine not only the possibility of a successful regime change in Iraq, but also the global strategy. Hence, even though it was a debate over tactics, the stakes involved were significant. Bush was gambling that he could not only advance on both fronts, but also that he could parlay success in Iraq into a large advance in his broader global agenda; his critics were worried that, through his mis-steps, he could squander the opening that 9/11 had presented, and undermine the advance on both fronts.

The dénouement

Since the critics' ire was directed primarily at Bush's tactics, it should not be surprising that, as Bush softened his stance over time, the attacks began to dissipate. Starting in September 2002, Bush did in fact launch something of a rapprochement with the United Nations. His address to the General Assembly on September 12 initiated a six-month campaign to 'play out the UN string', as Albright pithily advised.[45] In November he secured a new resolution, UN 1441, which provided for the intrusive inspections that Clinton, Brzezinski, Holbrooke, and others had called for. And then, as a crowning act, Powell delivered his largely fictional presentation to the Security Council on February 5, 2003. As this campaign progressed, the critics responded by offering kudos to Bush for finally seeing the light, prodding him to stay the course and continue to make his case with public opinion.

In early September, after it became known that Bush was about to address the UN General Assembly, Brent Scowcroft resurfaced, in his first public appearance after the August op-ed. When asked if he was still critical of the administration, he maintained the media representation of his opposition had been exaggerated. He added that he 'ha[d] no problem with regime change', but was worried that an invasion of Iraq might conflict with the 'war on terror'. He continued, 'I am not saying don't go after him. I'm saying let's put all this in perspective and remember that when we go after him, we need to have the support of the world community behind us because we need that support for the war on terrorism'. So, three weeks after his intervention, he admitted that he was feeling 'much better now, because I think that the direction the president is taking is exactly the right direction, to reach out to our friends, to get the UN involved. *That's exactly what I was trying to get across*'.[46]

Having signalled that he was willing to 'play out the UN string', Bush now went to Congress to seek a broad-ranging mandate to enforce the UN inspections on Hussein, with force if need be. Among rank-and-file liberal democrats, there was considerable resistance to the idea, especially the open-ended character of the power Bush was seeking. There was an effort among these forces, and even centrists like Joseph Biden, to block the resolution, or at least to significantly curtail the authority it would grant Bush. But as word of this got out, in September, it was the Democratic Party leadership that moved swiftly to squelch the opposition. Richard Holbrooke, Madeline Albright, Dennis Ross, Kenneth Pollock, and weapons expert David Kay organised a series of secret meetings with Democratic congressmen, in which they were told in no uncertain terms to vote for Bush's resolution. The party leadership made the case that military force was the only viable option for dealing with Hussein. When, as a last ditch effort, Joe Biden tried to water down the resolution's provisions, Richard Gephardt added his weight to the other side, derailing the effort to craft an alternative resolution.[47] Bush was granted his wish.

In the end, it is remarkable how far Bush did move towards adopting the recommendations of the political establishment. He even went beyond them in seeking a second resolution from the UN Security Council, something the Democrats and the Bush I advisors explicitly warned him against.[48] But Blair prevailed upon him, seeing it as crucial for his own political survival. The problem was, in part, that this was too little too late. When the Security Council met right before the invasion, it did not give an explicit assent. The months of chest-thumping, vilification, name-calling, etc. seemed to have been counterproductive. But the Security Council's recalcitrance was fundamentally due to the fact that the invasion of Iraq was, when stripped to its essentials, an unprovoked attack on a devastated, defenceless nation, which posed no imminent danger to anyone, and which had already suffered grievous losses over the past decade. Even if Bush had gone to the UN right at the outset, even if he had managed his public relations more effectively, it should not be assumed that he would have successfully brought the European allies into the fold. Bush's strategy of using American power as a gravitational force, independently of the UN, did not just fail because of it intrinsic flaws. It failed also because the cause that it was trying to sell, to package, was, to public opinion outside the US, blatantly false.

RETHINKING THE OIL CONNECTION

The absence of any deep division within the political class on the Iraq issue has some important implications. The first and most obvious is that it requires scaling down the attribution of responsibility to the Bush strategists for pushing through the invasion. The argument that the attack on Iraq was the work of a neo-con cabal, or that it was pushed through over the objections of the wider establishment, cannot be sustained. There was in fact a quite deep elite consensus on the desirability of military action. The neo-cons were still absolutely central to the actual push for war – it did not issue from sheer momentum or from a collective mobilisation of the entire political class. But it is important for the moment to move on to a further implication of the discovery that the push toward Iraqi regime change was strongly bipartisan. And this has to do with oil.

Here, though, the obsession that journalists and intellectuals have had with the role of Cheney's oil connections seems misplaced. It is sometimes argued that Cheney's commitment to the invasion reflected the outlook of the oil majors, who were eager to move into the region and establish their dominance. Cheney's ascension to office created an opening for the pursuit of this agenda. Dilip Hiro, for example, concludes that 'gaining privileged access to Iraqi oil for American companies was a primary objective of the Pentagon's invasion of Iraq'.[49] If the desire to open up Iraq for new investment had been a primary motivation, then simply lifting the sanctions would have sufficed. It did not require an invasion. The retort to this, as expressed by Hiro, is that that oil majors did not just want access to the fields, but wanted to dictate the terms on which access was secured – better guaranteed returns, more upstream investments, and even a chance at grabbing the region for themselves, to the exclusion of majors from other countries.

Even if that motivation had been present among the majors, and even if it had been what drove Cheney, the preceding analysis demotes it as a main interest behind the invasion. It has acquired its status as a prime cause of the invasion because of the assumption, widespread among commentators, that the broader elite was deeply sceptical about regime change. If most of the political establishment was hesitant about the war, then it elevates the motives of the war's proponents as its primary cause – if it was only the oil interests who really wanted the war, then it is their narrow interests that explain the war's occurrence. But in light of the preceding analysis, the most that can be said about oil interests is that they were but one in a much wider constellation of interests committed to regime change. Oil contracts may have been one goal for attacking Iraq, but they cannot, without further evidence, be elevated to the primary interest. To find the motives for the war, it then becomes important to uncover the source of the wider consensus, which bound the coalition together.

The wider consensus was linked to oil, but more broadly. It is highly unlikely that the policy establishment would have been so easily recruited to the project of regime change – with all its risks, all its regional and international ramifications for the global expansionist project – if its main function was to swell the oil companies' profits. The concern was a broader one. It was that with Iraq's ascension to the top of the oil market, the prospect of its independence from American domination carried intolerable political consequences. If sanctions were to be lifted, and if Hussein remained in power, it would mean a loss in power for the US and its regional allies, and an increase in power for not only Hussein, but also for other rival powers. So if the sanctions had to go, so did Hussein. Had the stakes in the invasion been less portentous, the conflict within the political elite during the run-up to the invasion would no doubt have been a great deal more intense.[50]

WHAT THE NEO-CONS' ROLE WAS – AND WAS NOT

I have tried to show that, in fact, there were doubts within the foreign policy establishment about Bush's approach to the Iraq problem. But they were about the actual capacity to carry out the invasion, not about the need for it, or to its morality. And they were not inconsiderable. But two factors intervened to keep the misgivings within limits. The first was that, in the changed situation of the post Cold War era, there had not really been a test of what actual American capabilities were. It had been thirty years since the US had been involved in a major neocolonial occupation, and it was the first time since its rise to global status that it did not face any serious rival. This made it a more open question than it had been for some decades what American geopolitical and military capabilities actually were. No doubt, there was a keen awareness of the potential dangers involved in toppling a state. But there was also room for considerable optimism about the defence and diplomatic corps' abilities to impose their will on the subject populations.

This is where the second factor made its impression. The grandiose claims being made by the neo-conservative ideologues about American prowess, in both the diplomatic and the military realm, were able to attract adherents. For almost a decade, talk of a 'revolution in military affairs', which was ideal for the new world order, and which would catapult the military to new heights, had been gathering momentum in defence circles.[51] Added to this were the predictions about the welcome that American troops would receive in Iraq, the natural alliance waiting to be forged with the Shias, their antipathy toward Iran, etc. In political as well as military matters, the neo-cons and policy wonks were predicting easy success.[52] In normal circumstances, these claims would have not acquired an audience. But in the context of post-9/11 America, they served as a palliative, to paper over the lingering doubts that elites harboured. Since the capacity of the empire in this new world was something of an unknown, since the target regime was broken and powerless, the promises coming from neo-conservative intellectuals had a surface plausibility. What to many outside elite circles seemed an outrageous and irrational plan, did not elicit the same reaction within the halls of power. It seemed, instead, like an audacious leap – risky, yes, but with enough chance of success to make it a gamble worth taking. Critics, while sceptical, were willing to give the scheme a chance.

Only in this limited sense was the war a creature of the neo-cons. They provided a concrete plan of action, and political prognosis, which made a venture that once seemed prohibitively dangerous, now appear realizable. But the background commitments – to a new imperialism, the turn away from containment, the preference for regime change, the shift to a military focus, and the cynical approach to the UN – all this was accepted by Democrats and internalised by virtually all of the wider establishment.

This does not by any means imply that the contribution of the ideologues and strategists around Bush was trivial. In a period where doubts about the practicalities of an invasion coexisted with genuine confidence in American capabilities, the contributions of neo-cons and the militarists was critical to swinging the balance toward war. It certainly cannot be predicted with any confidence that, had Gore been president, he would have invaded just as Bush did. The Democrats did not *call* for war – they gave it their assent and their support *after* Bush placed it on the agenda. They were willing to be persuaded, just as were the older policy experts. Had they been in the White House, it is not clear that, lacking the ideologues' clarity of purpose, they would have overcome their doubts and moved ahead. But given their background assumptions, and the opening provided by 9/11 to break out of the impasse on Iraq, it is certainly a distinct possibility that they would have.

CONCLUSION

The concern during the lead-up to the war had been that, if mishandled, the invasion and its fallout could not only backfire regionally, but also undermine the wider global agenda that the US was pursuing. Five years later, this is precisely where the US finds itself. The diplomatic cover that 9/11 had provided has not only dissipated, but has been turned into its opposite by the disaster in Iraq. In global perceptions, American standing is at the lowest ebb it has ever been in recent history. The military capabilities of its empire are stretched to their limits as Iraq has become a sinkhole for its forces. And politically, it has become marginalised in global and regional developments to an extent unimaginable a decade ago. In Asia, Latin America, and even the Middle East, alliances and agreements are being forged which not only ignore the US, but which explicitly contravene its dictat.

Nowhere are these predicaments more deeply felt than in the Middle East, the epicentre of Bush's debacle. The question that confronts the next administration – and the political elite more generally – is how to prevent a further erosion of power in the region, and, even more, how to restore it. The most common conclusion drawn is that the setbacks in Iraq spell the end of the neo-conservative experiment. This may be true, but the issue is to gauge what the distinctive components of this experiment were, which set it apart from the status quo, and which of those will be rejected.

It is virtually certain that the commitment to global expansion, to the consolidation of American military and economic primacy, will not be open to question, whoever leads the next administration. The adjustment will certainly be of the means, and not the ends, of foreign policy. On the question of the means, the most common projection among commentators is that Bush's departure will signal a return to multilateralism. Is that not, after all, what Bush's critics were urging in late 2002? They were certainly calling for a multilateral approach, but this was to be 'multilateralism, American style' – and it is certain to be the kind that is practised in the future. And a return to *this* status quo does not mean a turn away from militarism, or a greater appreciation for international law. Bush's critics were not motivated by either of these concerns. Their worry was a practical one, that unless the invasion was carried out carefully, with the logistical and political supports in place, the subsequent occupation could very well spin out of control. This carries two central, and worrisome, implications.

The first is that, in a return to traditional statecraft toward the Middle East, the commitment to American primacy and 'multilateralism, American style', most likely means a strategy that relies to a great extent on the use, or the threat, of force. In other words, the central problem with a return to the status quo, is that the status quo itself rested to a large measure on the use of force. But now, with American credibility having been dealt a serious blow by the debacle in Iraq, the most pressing problem will be to restore this credibility – through a demonstration of American power and resolve. Thus, a return to the status quo cannot be taken to mean a retreat from the use of violence and militarism. If the Iraq occupation's setbacks are to trigger a new, less bellicose US policy in the region, it will have to be based on a fundamental rethinking of America's role in the region, and of the region's place in its global strategy. This hardly seems likely.

This brings us to the second implication of the concern expressed by the political elite. Since it was a practical concern, a concern about the *management* of the occupation, the lessons they draw may very well relate to this narrow issue, and not to the broader problem of an occupation itself. Hence, the lesson that they draw may not be that occupations in this day and age are a political impossibility – but rather that, next time, they will get it right. Though this seems unlikely, it is hard to ignore the fact that the dominant framing of the occupation's implosion is not that it was doomed to failure from the start, but rather that the Bush administration *mishandled* it. In many of the most widely discussed books and documentaries since 2004, this has emerged as the most common criticism – a focus on what they did wrong.[53] It is only the rare exception that hazards the view that, given Iraqi political realities, there was almost no chance of a smooth transition to a new regime that would be stable and cohesive without a long occupation.[54] And so long as there was going to be an occupation of some duration, it would meet with deep and unyielding resistance.

The upshot is that while there will no doubt be a great deal of hand-wringing about what went wrong in Iraq, there is no reason to assume that it will lead to a turn away from militarism and aggression. To do so would require a deep shift in the overall US strategy in the Middle East. Certainly, the most recent developments in Iraq, and in the American political debate around the occupation, offer little grounds for optimism. Bush has been negotiating a permanent presence of US troops in Iraq, located in at least four massive military bases, and as many as 58 – a goal that McCain has endorsed.[55] While Obama has been cagey on the issue of troops,[56] his rhetoric on more general matters in the region has been extraordinarily bellicose, from the notorious threat to attack Pakistan, to the sabre-rattling against Iran, and, most recently, the astonishing promise to hand over an undivided Jerusalem to Israel – a promise that, according to Israeli commentator Uri Avnery, goes beyond anything promised by a presidential candidate in recent memory.[57] Hence, the impulse to continue with traditional patterns of coercive diplomacy is unmistakably strong.

But pulling in the other direction is the fact that the two basic constraints that have tempered American aggression – domestic public opinion and the state's practical capabilities – are now more binding than ever. With its military over-stretched, and an economic recession – or worse – well in train, the domestic resource base for militarism is thinner than at any time during the past century; while its regional allies – especially Israel – may want to support a display of force in the region, it is now infinitely harder to sell to their populations than it was five years ago. With regard to domestic public opinion in the US, the sentiment against the occupation is so strong that, even before news of a potential recession started to appear, Bush's popularity was the lowest of any president in recent history. A new military venture, or continued brinksmanship by the next administration, will only exacerbate the fatigue and further erode political legitimacy.

The political elite is thus in a bind – and it is doubtful that there is any real sense among the key protagonists as to what is the best course of action. For progressives, however, this should heighten the sense of urgency. The stakes involved for American global power are such that, to break out of the impasse, the political elite could very well settle on a high-risk, high-returns gamble. This has almost certainly been Cheney's motivation for his unceasing efforts to manage a confrontation with Iran – and during the Democratic primaries, the candidates' participation in the threats and intimidation are a sign that they are willing to keep that option on the table.

On the other hand, the impasse also provides an opening for mobilisation. There are elements within the political establishment who are calling for a thorough re-evaluation of American foreign policy – within both the Democratic and Republican parties. While it is out of reach to push for a turn away from the basic imperial agenda, there is nevertheless room, even with the current level of political organisation, to call for a more modest programme – for the United States to follow international law, respect national sovereignty, and withdraw immediately and unconditionally from Iraq. This would be the first step to changing the basis for American diplomacy in the Middle East, and potentially, beyond. It will have to come from the weight of popular pressure, for as we have seen, the commitment to traditional, coercive diplomacy runs very deep in the US political establishment.

NOTES

This paper has benefited greatly from the advice and comments of Bashir Abu-Manneh, Gilbert Achcar, Robert Brenner, Thomas Ferguson, Jeff Goodwin, Nivedita Majumdar, and Michael Schwartz.

1 Niall Ferguson, *Colossus: The Rise and Fall of the American Empire*, New York: Penguin Press, 2004; for a critique, see Vivek Chibber, 'The Good Empire', *Boston Review*, February, 2005.
2 Anthony Lake, 'From Containment to Enlargement', Speech at Johns Hopkins University, 21 September 1993.
3 See the report in Patrick E. Tyler, 'US Strategy Plan Calls for Insuring No Rivals Develop', *New York Times*, 8 March 1992.
4 Three basic sources on US strategy in the 1990s are Andrew Bacevich, *American Empire: The Realities and Consequences of US Diplomacy*, Harvard: Harvard University Press, 2002; Peter Gowan, *Global Gamble: Washington's Faustian Bid for World Dominance*, London: Verso, 1999; Noam Chomsky, *World Orders, Old and New*, Second Edition, New York: Columbia University Press, 1996.
5 The fullest study of this process is Patrick J. Hearden, *Architects of Globalism: Building a New World Order During World War II*, Fayetteville: University of Arkansas Press, 2002.
6 The process of expansion has been studied extensively, but the best general analysis, even forty years after its publication, remains Gabriel Kolko, *The Politics of War: The World and United States Foreign Policy*,

1943-1945, New York: Random House, 1968, and his successor volume, *The Limits To Power: The World and United States Foreign Policy, 1945-1954,* New York: Harper & Row, 1972.

7 George Bush and Brent Scowcroft, *A World Transformed*, New York: Knopf, 1998.

8 See the account in Andrew and Patrick Cockburn, *Saddam Hussein: An American Obsession*, Second Edition, London, Verso, 2002.

9 The indispensable source for understanding alignments within the Clinton administration on this issue is Kenneth Pollock, *The Gathering Storm*, New York: Random House, 2002.

10 Ibid., pp. 85-90, 98-99.

11 The reference is to Albright's infamous 1996 interview on the news show, *60 Minutes*, in which, when queried if she thought the half-million Iraqi deaths under the sanctions regime could be defended, she replied, 'we think the price is worth it'.

12 A central document on matters of oil, sanctions, and the choices open to the Bush administration is *Strategic Energy Policy: Challenges for the 21st Century*, a joint report by the James Baker Institute for Public Policy at Rice University and the Council on Foreign Relations, edited by Edward L. Morse and Amy Myers Jaffe, published in 2001. For the changed oil situation between 1990 and 2000, see pp. 13-20.

13 Ibid., p. 19.

14 Worries about the sustainability of sanctions had been expressed by Zbigniew Brzezinski, Brent Scowcroft and Richard Murphy in 1997, in 'Differentiated Containment', *Foreign Affairs*, May/June, 1997. See especially, pp. 20, 29.

15 Former National Security Advisor General William Odom advocated this line publicly and, we may assume, in closed policy circles.

16 See *Strategic Energy Policy*, p. 40.

17 Pollock, *The Gathering Storm*, pp. 94-95.

18 Ibid. For worries about regional consequences, see pp. 48, 70.

19 See also Gilbert Achcar, *The Eastern Cauldron: Islam, Afghanistan, Palestine and Iraq in a Marxist Mirror*, New York, Monthly Review: 2004, 'Introduction', esp. pp. 34-41. The introductory chapter to this book is an indispensable analysis of US Middle East policy in the 1990s and beyond. In addition, he locates the role of the second Intifada for the larger Middle East strategy after 2000, which I cannot do here.

20 For a revealing account of just how low terrorism actually was on the list of Bush's priorities after 9/11, see Noam Chomsky, *Failed States: The*

Abuse of Power and the Assault on Democracy, New York: Metropolitan Books, 2006, pp. 30-37.

21 For some material on how the US was able to parlay worldwide sympathy into longer-term concessions around the world, see Phyllis Bennis, *Before & After: US Foreign Policy and The September 11th Crisis*, New York: Olive Branch Press, 2003.

22 This was the title of an op-ed by Charles Krauthammer, which rejected the notion that there was a deep split within the Republican Party. See 'Fictional Rift', *Washington Post*, 13 September 2002.

23 Brent Scowcroft, 'Don't Attack Saddam', *The Wall Street Journal*, 15 August 2002.

24 *New York Times*, 25 August 2002.

25 Lawrence Eagleburger, Interview with Tim Russert, *Meet the Press*, NBC, 1 September 2002.

26 Richard Holbrooke, 'Do We Declare War? International Support will only come through International Means', *Contra Costa Times*, 1 September 2002. Emphasis added.

27 See James P. Rubin, Interview on *After Hours with Maria Bartiromo*, CNBC, 9 September 2002; for Berger, see his interview on *The News with Brian Williams*, CNBC, 15 November 2002.

28 Bill Clinton, Interview with Katie Couric, *NBC Today Show*, 11 February 2003.

29 Madeline Albright, 'Bridges, Bombs, or Bluster?', *Foreign Affairs*, September/October, 2003, p. 9. Emphasis added.

30 Bill Clinton, Interview with Katie Couric, *NBC Today Show*, February 11, 2003.

31 Bill Clinton, Interview with Katie Couric, *NBC Today Show*, 27 September 2002.

32 'Former President Bill Clinton and Charles Stewart discuss Clinton's induction into Arkansas Black Hall of Fame', *NBC News Transcripts*, 20 October 2002. Emphasis added.

33 Eagleburger, Interview with Tim Russert.

34 Zbigniew Brzezinski, 'The End Game', *The Wall Street Journal*, 23 December 2002.

35 Henry Kissinger, Interview, *Meet the Press*, NBC, 18 August 2002.

36 Ibid.

37 This was not just a slip, or off-the-cuff remark. Five weeks later, in testimony before the Senate Foreign Affairs Committee on September 25th, Kissinger used almost identical language to describe the First Gulf

War, and the basic logic of how displays of power could bring allies on board.

38 Holbrooke, 'Do We Declare War?' See also his comments in an interview with Brit Hume, *Fox News*, 1 September 2002, where he again clarified that, if the UN declines to pass the needed resolution, the US can move ahead with its allies and invade anyway.

39 Bill Clinton, Interview with Katie Couric, *NBC Today Show*, 27 September 2002.

40 Holbrooke, interview with Brit Hume; Zbigniew Brzezinski, interview with George Stephanopoulos, *This Week with Sam Donaldson and Cokie Roberts*, ABC, 1 September 2002. Brzezinski recommended the establishment of a 'very intrusive unilateral inspection' regime.

41 Holbrooke, interview with Brit Hume.

42 US Senate Committee on Foreign Relations, *Next Steps in Iraq: Hearing before the Committee on Foreign Relations*, 107th Congress, 26 September 2002. Berger, during these same weeks, made almost identical points in the public media: that Bush needed to make his case to the public, pull together a coalition, and then present a plan for post-invasion Iraq. Like Albright, he urged that the great utility of going to the UN was that it would buy time to complete the preparations for the invasion. See especially his interview on *CNN American Morning With Paula Zahn*, CNN, 14 November 2002, and his comments on *The News with Brian Williams*, CNBC, 15 November 2002.

43 In the same hearings, Henry Kissinger also presented testimony, in which he was more supportive of an invasion in the short term. When Albright was pressed whether she was rejecting outright the justification for an invasion, or even wanting to put it off for some years, she denied it, adding that 'we are probably not as far apart as it might seem. It is a matter of timing and, our favorite diplomatic word, nuance in terms of when we do things'.

44 Kagan, 'Multilateralism American Style', *Washington Post*, 13 September 2002.

45 US Senate Committee on Foreign Relations, *Next Steps in Iraq* (Albright testimony).

46 Brent Scowcroft, Interview with Judy Woodruff, CNN, 9 September 2002. Emphasis added.

47 Michael Isikoff and David Corn, *Hubris: The Inside Story of Spin, Scandal, and the Selling of the Iraq War*, New York: Three Rivers Press, 2006, pp. 125-28. It might very well be that the decision to support Bush's resolution was motivated by electoral worries. But it should be noted

that it was, for the most part, the elected officials in the party who were willing to take the fight to Bush – the very people who were most vulnerable to electoral worries; and it was non-elected leaders (with the exception of Gephardt) who pushed them to back Bush's resolution.

48 Clinton, in his February 11 interview with Katie Couric, advised: 'I don't think the President needs another Security Council resolution'. Holbrooke was even more categorical in September: 'There's got to be one resolution and one only. And if the Russians or the French or somebody try to water it down, then we'll pull out of the Security Council and go to our allies...'. Holbrooke, Interview with Brit Hume.

49 Dilip Hiro, 'How the Bush Administration's Iraqi Oil Grab Went Awry: Greenspan's Oil Claim in Context', 25 September 2007, available at http://www.tomdispatch.com.

50 Space precludes a fuller engagement with the 'oil grab' argument – but its flaws run deeper than I have been able to show here. For some recent analyses that are in line with the one I have offered see the excellent articles by Tom O'Donnell on Iran: 'The Political Economy of the US-Iran Crisis: Oil, Not Nukes, is the Issue', *Z Magazine*, 19(6), 2006, and 'Understanding the Washington-Tehran Deals', *Z Magazine* Online, April, 2008, available at http://www.zcommunications.org/zmag.

51 Andrew Bacevich, *American Empire*, Chapter 5.

52 On this, see Gilbert Achcar, 'Bush's Cakewalk into the Iraq Quagmire', *Counterpunch*, 5 May 2004, available at http://www.counterpunch.org. Achcar also emphasises, rightly, the role of Iraqi émigré intellectuals and politicians in propagating fantasies about a cakewalk.

53 This is the theme, inter alia, of Thomas Ricks, *Fiasco: The American Military Adventure in Iraq*, New York: Penguin Press, 2006; David L. Phillips, *Losing Iraq: Inside the Postwar Reconstruction Fiasco*, Boulder: Westview, 2005; Charles H. Ferguson, *No End in Sight: Iraq's Descent into Chaos*, New York: Public Affairs, 2008.

54 One such exception is Jonathan Steele, *Defeat: Why America and Britain Lost Iraq*, Berkeley: Counterpoint, 2008.

55 For the early plans, see Thom Shanker and Eric Schmitt, 'A Nation at War: Strategic Shift; Pentagon Expects Long-Term Access to Key Iraq Bases', *New York Times*, 20 April 2003. Its most recent incarnation was revealed by Patrick Cockburn. See 'Revealed: Secret Plan to Keep Iraq Under US Control', *The Independent*, 5 June 2008.

56 He has shifted from declaring a total withdrawal, to a withdrawal of 'combat troops', to more vague declarations of a need for flexibility. See

the revealing retrospective in Edward Luce, 'Obama Under Fire over Iraq Troop Pledge', *Financial Times*, 24 June 2008.

57 Ury Avnery, 'No, Obama Can't!', 10 June 2008, available at http://www.antiwar.com.

ON-SCREEN BARBARISM: VIOLENCE IN US VISUAL CULTURE

PHILIP GREEN

That is no country for old men. The young
In one another's arms, birds in the trees…
W.B. Yeats[1]

I

No country for old men: a land that once, for Yeats, was a place of sex, sensuality, and procreation, has now become, quite extraordinarily, a place of unremitting and inexplicable violence. This strange inversion of meaning and feeling is not the doing of the Coen Brothers (who may or may not have read Yeats in their college days) but of best-selling author Cormac McCarthy, who adapted Yeats's line (without citation) for his own version of portentous nihilism. Even the works of best-selling authors, though, are a special taste compared to the nation-wide appeal of hit movies; if *No Country For Old Men* is read through all eternity it will still not have been read by as many persons as saw the movie on its first smash weekend. So the point is not to ask how the change in Yeats's meaning came to McCarthy, but rather what it means now, that an entire culture (minus a huddle of serious poetry readers), invited to wallow for two hours in unmitigated and uninterrogated violence, shrugs its collective shoulders and accepts what it is being shown as reasonable, as a normal vision of 'the country'; as 'formally beautiful', as representing its makers 'at the height of their powers', as being an obvious candidate for a 'Best Picture of the Year' Oscar nomination. And its chief competition demonstrated a similarly strange trajectory, though in a different vein: Upton Sinclair's socialist, muckraking novel, *Oil*, transformed into Paul Thomas Anderson's cinematic 'masterpiece' (as it was hailed by critics), *There Will Be Blood. Oil* is not a great nor even a very good novel, but it is about what it purports to be about: the accumulation of capital that 'comes dripping from head to foot, from every pore, with blood and dirt'. The movie, contrarily, seems to start out as that story, but halfway through, overtaken by a loss of either nerve or interest, descends into a study of unmotivated, over-the-top and brutal individual psychosis, and loses whatever meaning it might have had.

If these films were unique there would be no need to ask questions about them; after all, there's an audience, even a mass audience, for almost anything. Contemporary US cinema, for example, also features movies about teen-age girls who ought to have abortions but instead have babies, virtually without thought or reason – but the existence of this genre signifies nothing ideologically except the power of what pollsters call 'intensity of preference', as wielded by the uncompromising body of 'Right to Life' opinion in the USA. But *No Country for Old Men* and *There Will Be Blood* are hardly unique. In just the past year, as I write these words, the big screen in the US has seen a parade of 'A' films, some of them even #1 at the box office, in which brutal and graphic violence explodes on the screen: *3:10 to Yuma, The Brave One, Eastern Promises, Transformers, 30 Days of Night, Jumper, Untraceable, We Own the Night, 300, Grindhouse, Sweeney Todd* (much more graphic, obviously, than the stage production), *Hostel 2, Saw 4, Rambo* (2008). These are not naturally violent films about the nature of warfare (*Saving Private Ryan, Syriana, The Valley of Elah, A Mighty Heart*), but are rather for the most part about nothing beyond themselves. Meanwhile, even in the much different world of smaller-screen network and cable television, where the general atmosphere of blood-letting that has come to pervade visual culture is of necessity somewhat attenuated, other developments in the kind of stories that TV prefers to tell are equally important to an understanding of what is happening.

There has been a sea-change, and we can describe it with some confidence. In cinema, the positioning of the mass audience, or at least a large sector of it, has been transformed from that of sympathetic identification to that of pure voyeurism; and thus from an approach centred on competing versions of moral behaviour to one centred on amorality, or more precisely, nihilism. This change, moreover, has taken place, as it only could, with the acquiescence or even participation of that audience. As one historian of Hollywood, David Bordwell, recounts, 'Researchers studying the reception of *Judge Dredd* (1995) found that fans were happy to list things they liked: "Lots of blood... Explosions... Good effects... Dead Bodies..."'.[2] So there is something happening on both sides of the producer/consumer transaction. But in any event we want to be able to do more than describe, or even indict, this change; we want to ask, why should this be; how did this come about?

Of course violence has always been a staple of cinema. The same historian, writing about the 'Hollywood style', for example, pays particular attention to the violent action movie, and to 'visceral violence' in movies. To be sure, the crime films and Westerns of the Sixties that he discusses follow a recognizable moral code, and besides were quite tame by twenty-first century standards.[3] But even horrific violence in cinema is hardly a recent discovery. *Night of the Living Dead* arrived in theatres in 1968, *The Texas Chainsaw Massacre* in 1974; and all 'slasher movies', of which the latter is one variant, are recognizably the progeny of Hitchcock's 1960 *Psycho*. But just the same there have been major changes in contemporary cinematic (and televisual) production.

In the first place, with rare exceptions, within the horror genre itself there are significant differences between these forerunners and their contemporary descendants, such as *Saw* or *Hostel* and their sequels (and imitators). As Carol Clover has argued, there has been a change in the sexual dimension: above all, perhaps, the horror story of the 70s and 80s films she discusses is told from the visual point of view of, alternately, the female victim, or the audience itself as victim.[4] This change from the misogyny of Hitchcock and his followers (e.g., Brian de Palma) to the sexual ambiguity and sometime gender subversion of the slasher genre was culturally significant; but so too, and perhaps now even more so, is the change from the genre as Clover then viewed it, to the contemporary horror film. The simplest way to put this is that *the slasher film has become a torture film*. It's not just that audience identification with a (usually female) victim has been replaced by audience *voyeurism*.[5] More, the standpoint of the camera is now neutral; very often, the camera is placed where no human being – at least none in the film – could possibly be, in order to make what we see as inhumane as possible. As two Netflix viewers of *Saw 3* and *Saw 4* (respectively) straightforwardly put it: 'Gore and torture is all you will know. The different ways of torturing a human being is unimaginable in this film. The gore level was very high, higher than any other *Saw*'; and 'this movie is nothing but sick and twisted ways of killing and torturing people for 90 minutes' – though that viewer and several viewers who made similar comments gave the movie five stars just the same.

Most striking, perhaps, is the comparison between two films in the serial-killer genre, 1991's notorious *Silence of the Lambs*, and last year's *Untraceable*. *Silence* was thought at the time to be particularly shocking, yet like the movies Clover groups under the rubric, 'Her Body, Himself', it features an active and aggressive female protagonist, Clarice Starling (played by previous Oscar winner Jodie Foster), who is the centre of the action much more often than the sadistic Hannibal Lecter (an Oscar-winning performance by Anthony Hopkins).[5] Sixteen years later, another A-list actress with Oscar-nominee credentials, Diane Lane, is reduced to the role of surrogate for audience voyeurism, spending most of her screen time merely watching (on her computer) the considerably more hideous activities of the serial killer who is pursuing her more than she is pursuing him. *Silence* is subtle and gripping – even, due to Foster's activism, for many female viewers. *Untraceable* has the subtlety of an attack with a sledgehammer – or a meat cleaver. The former could be fitted into Clover's text as containing subversive elements within the slasher genre; the latter, not at all.

To speak now of 'the pornography of violence', in other words, is to be literal. We, the viewers, are asked to watch a seemingly literal enactment: to watch, even if the 'money shot' of hardcore can't really be duplicated (or we'd be watching a snuff film), very convincing imitations of the most horridly graphic insults to the human body. Entrails seem 'really' to be yanked out of stomachs, eyes gouged out of their sockets, knives plunged deep into torsos, and so on. After this, hardcore porn would be a relief: though clearly, millions of viewers much prefer the sight of knives cutting into flesh.

The second significant difference is that, as the casting and marketing of *Untraceable* demonstrate, now the techniques and standpoint of the new horror film have leached into the mainstream. The movies from that era discussed by Carol Clover were indeed 'horror movies', conspicuously if informally labelled as such. It is when mainstream films, helmed by mainstream directors and more often than not aimed at that dominant demographic, '18 to 39 year old males', take on the appearance of sheer graphic and voyeuristic brutality that we have to take special notice. Only additional examples can make clear the novelty of what we're seeing.[6]

No Country for Old Men is the most obvious instance of this tendency, and it's particularly worth noting in this context that, film buffs and the dating partners of boys and men aside, it can be hard to find *a woman* who has actually seen this movie, or has any desire to see it. This is not a minor point: the difference between the 'chick flick' and the male action movie often seems to appear as the difference between two quite different versions of civil society, or even human life in general. But it is hardly unique. As Susan Faludi has pointed out, in the wake of 9/11 the unleashing of masculinity and its ideology, masculinism, has been like an earthquake in American cultural life. Manohla Dargis's comment on forthcoming (2008) summer movies, that 'In a summer stocked with he-men, women are left on the sidelines', is generally true of Hollywood's big-ticket movies, rain or shine.[7]

And if on the whole this represents a post-9/11 return of the repressed, the 'he' in he-men is often also a synonym for sadism.[8]

Another comparison with an earlier use of violence makes a similar point. *Eastern Promises* is a serious movie, directed by a serious Canadian director, David Cronenberg. Its most memorable scene is a graphic knife fight between the hero (though we're not yet aware of his true role) and two villains who are trying to kill him, all of them totally naked in a public bath-house. Knives flash and penetrate, blood jets and pours, and the battle goes on for almost ten minutes, with an absolutely total lack of credibility. The scene is reminiscent (perhaps deliberately) of an earlier battle to the death in Hitchcock's *Torn Curtain* (1966), in which Paul Newman spends an equal length of time desperately trying to save himself and kill his would-be killer with his bare hands. Hitchcock's point was to make us see how hard it is in fact to kill someone when you are not yourself a trained killer; blood, knives, torn flesh, etc., were absent from the screen, yet the scene is entirely mesmerising. Cronenberg's violence, on the other hand, makes no point. Nor do we need to look back into the sanctified past to make such comparisons. A recent British film, *London to Brighton*, is also built around a bloody scene, in which a young girl (or perhaps an older prostitute who is protecting her) somehow gets a knife away from a man who is torturing her and castrates him, after which he bleeds to death. We never actually 'see' either the torture or the castration; in fact we see nothing except his bloodstained clothing, yet the significance and shock of the event are perfectly clear, and every bit as powerful as the less narratively meaningful scene in *Eastern Promises*.

More instructively, perhaps, having recently seen a revival of the original (1954) *3:10 to Yuma* a few weeks after seeing the 2007 remake, I came away with the impression that here at last was a clear instance where aesthetic standards *are* applicable and comparisons possible: not just 'matters of opinion'. The original is a lovely movie and a joy to watch – even for the fourth time. The rhythm and pacing, from quietude or even silence to outbursts of violent action and then back again, the alternation between romantic nostalgia and cynical realism, produce pleasure in one of the best possible ways: by creating expectations, thwarting them, and then realising them, and thwarting them again, and finally realising them. The remake, contrastingly, has no rhythm and no pacing, but is merely an extended visual presentation of often incomprehensible and extraordinarily violent action, alternating extended gunfights in which an unlikely number of people are *not* killed (in addition to the many who are) in the course of the explosive violence, with a brutal massacre at the end making the same point the original made with a single killing.

The remake is 35 minutes longer than the original, and every one of those minutes is wasted in what appear to be repetitive and unnecessary (as well as unbelievable) attempts to explain 'motivation'. Why does the reluctant hero, Dan Evans, go through with his task of bringing in the murderous (though attractive) villain in the face of overwhelming odds, even after his employer has encouraged him to quit and guaranteed him his promised reward in any event; and why does the villain, Ben Wade, after Evans is killed, turns his gun on his own gang and voluntarily leap aboard the 3:10 to Yuma that will carry him to prison? The original, in which the two leap on the train together, did all that's necessary in two sentences: Dan Evans to his wife: 'The town drunk gave his life so people could live in peace and decency; how can I do less?' Ben Wade to Dan Evans: 'You saved my life back there; I don't like to be under an obligation'. Not exactly Hemingway, but getting the job done with perfect economy, in a film that can be seen and enjoyed multiple times. The remake leaves us baffled as to how so much additional viciousness, and so many additional deaths – including now the hero's own – could result in this conclusion. Nor is it possible to imagine re-seeing the remake – what would be the point of surrendering to its compulsive repetitions of dark and meaningless violence yet again?

What I found most interesting about this comparison, however, is that although the difference between low-key accomplishment and expensive junk seemingly could not be clearer, yet as I was about to leave the revival theatre, a man in a nearby seat – clearly a movie buff himself – said to his female companion, 'Yeah, I liked the remake more'. (She made no reply.) He is not alone; as of April 2008 the remake had grossed $55 million. Not exceptional, but enough to make us realise that there is something about this acceptance of the aesthetics of violence that has to be explained. How can it be, for example, that two versions of the science fiction classic *Invasion of the Body Snatchers* from 1956 and 1978, each of them a minor masterpiece of screwing tension up notch after notch by eschewing obvious violence, are succeeded in 2006 by an incompetent third version (*Invasion*) that destroys the whole concept, dissipating the tension with a seemingly endless and absurd chase scene in which Nicole Kidman manages to survive half a dozen violent attacks that would have wiped out the population of a small town, let alone one ordinary woman?

It is as though cinema can no longer be trusted to be cinematic, or to enthral its audience: movies, even movies for adults, must be turned into a version of the endlessly violent video games that are designed to retain the attention of adolescent (and not yet fully socialised) boys. So for example

1962's *The 300 Spartans*, a straightforward but occasionally inspiring movie about one of the most iconic battles in human history, is recycled into *300*, a contemporary version accurately described by (another) Netflix viewer: 'I don't think this should even qualify as a movie. It's really more like a testosterone soaked orgy of pointless gore and one-dimensional characters parading about and squawking catch-phrases for 116 minutes. You'll want it to be over long before it is'. I've said that the description is accurate, but so were the expectations of the film's makers: it is making big money on the video rental circuit.

What exactly is the problem here, though? We certainly should not want to accept the fatuous notion that our problem is the presence of 'gratuitous' violence. The unremittingly graphic sadism of *Hostel* is no more 'gratuitous' than is the unremittingly graphic sex of *Deep Throat*; the very subject matter of a work of art, or commerce, can hardly itself be 'gratuitous'. After all, if we advert for a moment to the other half of the culture warriors' tandem of trash, we perceive that the one genre in which 'sex' is *never* gratuitous is hard-core. That's what those movies are about, and they hardly fail to 'have a point': the feminist cultural theorist Linda Williams has written a whole book about the various scenarios of hard-core and their different meanings; the same could surely be done for violence.[9]

Nor do we want to fall into the grip of the Right-wing propagandists who use the argument that there is 'too much' violence today as a club with which to attack their phantom 'liberal conspiracy'; whereas earlier Hollywood cinema supposedly had somehow the 'right' amount of violence.[10] Actually, at no point in the history of movies have culture critics failed to deplore the allegedly deplorable amount of 'sex and violence' in Hollywood films. For example, this is how a recent book about Hollywood describes Bosley Crowther, the lead movie reviewer of the New York Times and most influential reviewer in the US for more than thirty years (and in fact a dedicated liberal in most other matters): '(as) far back as *The Killers* in 1946 and *White Heat* in 1949... [he] chided Hollywood for its eagerness to make movies about criminals and worried that the industry's emphasis on "malevolence" and "sadistic thrills" would generate "unhealthy stimulation" in moviegoers...'; moreover, the same writer goes on to point out, Sixties movies such as *The Dirty Dozen*, the Sergio Leone/Clint Eastwood 'spaghetti Westerns', *Bonnie and Clyde*, and *The St. Valentine's Day Massacre*, generated paroxysms of fury from him.[11]

Thus we do not want to fall into our own version of the nostalgia trap, by simply accepting the claim that there was a 'golden age' of cinema, compared to which contemporary films are mindless or vicious trash. The past is always a kind of golden age: it's when we were young, after all – it is no country for old men. Besides, many of the films we think of when we talk of today's cinema in the context of violence and brutality are in fact by some formal standards – of cinematography, pacing, ensemble acting – quite good films, well or even brilliantly made.[12] And since standards are incommensurable, it is useless to insist that contemporary standards are 'wrong' – that a movie should have been made one way rather than another, or had one subject matter rather than another. Having myself during the Sixties received several of Crowther's 'excessively violent' films as genuine and innovative works of art, and having immensely enjoyed all of them, I therefore have to repeat the necessity of avoiding any reductive notion of 'violence in cinema', before turning to a more nuanced explication of it.

II

At the same time, consideration of the development of commercial television in this age of torture gives added weight to the need both to avoid oversimplification of visual culture's presentation of violence, and yet to insist that a serious change has taken place in that culture. By its nature television is a much more intimate medium than cinema, and so the shock effects that Hollywood movies prize so highly are much more obtrusive in the bedroom or living room than they seem to be at the multiplex. The visual terrorism of *Psycho* can be isolated late at night on the premium or on-demand channels that give us, more or less, what we've requested and what we expect; in the prime-time schedule it could simply have no place. Even so, not just the serial-killing-as-good-clean-fun *Dexter*, but also 'law and order' shows such as *Medium, Criminal Minds, CSI* in its various incarnations, *Bones*, and some of *Law and Order's* spin-offs seem to be engaged in a constant quest to show the corpses of murder victims (and the reconstructions of their murders) in spectacularly unpleasant ways.[13] Add to this roster the several medical shows (most notably *Nip/Tuck*) that often treat close-up surgery as though imitating *The Texas Chainsaw Massacre*, and it's clear that developments in the movie theatres have hardly passed television by.

On most of these shows, moreover, violence indeed 'has a point': in the case of law and order, to show the depravity of the forces of evil and the concomitant virtue of the good guys. It's not clear, in other words, that we should we be especially happy when violence *does* make a point, as it more often does on television than in cinema. After all, the almost weekly scenes of torture in recent seasons of *24* have a point – as long as you accept that torture has a serious purpose, à la Alan Dershowitz or Richard Posner, rather than being the acting out of a psychosexual male fantasy. Even in that case it has a point, in that the ridiculously paranoid plot has been carefully calibrated to produce the maximum possible excuses for engaging that fantasy. If this 'point' is supposed to be somehow more constructive or uplifting than the hideousness of *Hostel*, we don't really want to hear the explanation as to why that might be so. And in any event, it is quite possible to make exactly the same point without turning us into witting or unwitting voyeurs: just as *London to Brighton* makes its point without graphic brutality, so in the 2008 series *Terminator: The Sarah Connor Chronicles*, in a scene where the future of the human race is arguably at stake, the necessary torture is committed by an android from the future – our contemporary heroine cannot bring herself to do it – and the camera tactfully turns away from the moment of violence.

But still, a new-found affinity for graphic violence is not the most significant aspect of contemporary commercial television. To understand what is happening to that medium, we have to understand a fundamental difference between television and cinema. Hollywood cinema is essentially an industry devoted to the production of visual pleasure, wherever that may take it. Contrastingly, commercial television, especially network television, is an industry devoted to the production and reproduction of *ideology*. As I have discussed at length elsewhere, the deep desire of those persons who control television production in the field of entertainment is always *to be* conventional while seeming to be daring or original.[14] In order to accomplish this feat, they most importantly have to navigate between different antinomies of American political culture: individualism vs. conformity, liberty vs. repression, tolerance vs. intolerance, inequality of real opportunity vs. the formal equality of the economic marketplace. At the same time they must try not to be partisan – that is, to allow implicit ideology to slide over into explicit propaganda – so as not to alienate too large a segment of the putative audience. The sum of these real if informal requirements has led to an institutionalised demand for 'balance' in every episode of every series, so that if anything potentially 'offensive' to an important audience segment is said on one side, its opposite must be said on the other. The result of trying to please everyone was called 'the door that swings both ways' by the cultural critic Judith Mayne, but in fact the door, however it swings, in most cases opens only in one direction, buffeted by a censorious and mobilising Right and a government agency (the Federal Communications Commission) that represents whichever wind blows the hardest.[15]

'Law and order' television – what I have elsewhere called 'Policeworld' – is the centre around which the right-ward swinging door pivots. 'Liberal' judges 'put rapists back on the streets'; defence attorneys are merchants of sleaze or dangerous demagogues; civil liberties exist only to get in the way of heroic policemen and prosecutors who are just trying to do their job, and so on: none of this needs to be subjected to the requirements of 'balance'. In the past, however, fragments of a different kind of consciousness could be found from time to time on the broadband; liberal individualism as critique of conventional order was underground but always emergent. *L.A. Law*, for example – the programmeme analyzed by Mayne in her discussion of 'the door that swings both ways' – did manifest a genuine balance, as defence attorney Harry Hamlin battled prosecutor Susan Dey for the right to have the last word; so too did its near-contemporary *Cagney and Lacey*, as seen most starkly in the sometime affair between hard-nosed cop Sharon Gless and ACLU attorney Steven Macht. But that world is gone; several developments mark its passing.

The first of these is the disappearance of what film historian Robert Ray calls 'the unofficial hero' or 'the outlaw hero', a convention with respect to which cinema and television were once quite closely linked. For a long time the unofficial hero was a significant presence in genre cinema (e.g., Humphrey Bogart, Jimmy Stewart and Gary Cooper in Anthony Mann's Westerns), and on TV as well. In particular, from the mid-1960s to the beginning of the Reagan era, what I've called the 'lonely town' genre was perhaps the single most recurrent plotline on all non-sitcom television (*The Rockford Files, Harry O, The Fugitive, Run for Your Life, Bonanza, Burke's Law*, among many others).[16] Based on the 1956 film *Bad Day at Black Rock*, it featured a protagonist who finds himself isolated in a small town where a terrible crime has apparently been committed, and is now being covered up (with everyone but the town drunk, or prostitute, or some other outsider, in on the cover-up). Invariably, the motive for the concealment was a theft of land or property from a missing victim, a theft upon which the well-being of the entire town now depends. Though the ostensible meaning of the story was ambiguous to the point of disappearance, in one way or another the story was always a variant of Marx's description of original accumulation; and told us that a representative American town – by extension, the American West itself – was founded on a primal crime of dispossession. In this way, during this entire period the Lonely Town was virtually the only evidence of critical social thought to be found in visual culture.

It was there to be found, though. Now it has disappeared, along with other versions of the unofficial hero: the incorruptible defence attorney (*Perry Mason, Matlock*, Harry Hamlin of *L.A. Law*), and the cynical private eye out of Dashiell Hammett and Raymond Chandler, who never believes that the whole truth is to be found in police stations or district attorneys' offices (*The Rockford Files, Harry O*). Now the unofficial hero is observable only in his absence from prime-time television; as of this writing only two women, Sarah Connor of *Terminator: the Sarah Connor Chronicles* and defence attorney Elizabeth Canterbury of *Canterbury's Law* were carrying out that traditional role.[17] Thus the traditional American cynicism about the law that was a constant of these genres in literature, film, and television, seems to have disappeared. And although this might seem a trivial matter, it in fact has major ideological ramifications, for what it really betokens is *the disappearance of the underdog as hero.*

The underdog hero represented liberal individualism (rarely socialism) as a critique of existing patterns of authority, and even of property ownership, as in the lonely town genre; and, when 'he' became a 'she' in the 1980s and '90s, of authority as patriarchy. Despite the fanciful critiques of entertainment television's 'trash' and 'sleaze' by the Right, the cop and the prosecuting attorney as hero, male or even female, now stand most of the time not for liberal individualism but for authoritarian populism, both in the omnipresent fictional narratives of 'police world' and in the more straightforwardly untrammelled world of 'real' cops (*America's Most Wanted*, et al.). The almost complete disappearance of the traditional private eye or defence attorney, as well as the more recently celebrated unofficial female hero or superhero (e.g., Xena, Buffy) underlines the privileged position of the forces of official coercion today. What this gradual and almost un-noticed ideological change in commercial popular culture signifies is the frightening disappearance, in public thought, of any limit on law: law itself has become the limit. *Beyond* the Law is what we call 'justice', or 'right'. The conflation of Law with Justice or Right, the excision of any independent notion of justice from public consciousness, or at least from the public sphere of communication, is as crucial a step toward barbarism as is the apotheosis of torture.[18]

III

We are now in a better position to describe a problem that is much more profound than 'too much violence'. After all, it would be quite possible to argue contrarily that movies – and above all television – once had not enough violence, that they sanitised, and often still do sanitise, its occurrences and especially its results. Opponents of the war on Iraq, let us remember, admire those non-American news programmes that show the carnage on the streets of Baghdad in all its graphic truth, and decry the conspiracy of American media to keep the reality of imperial war off our mental screens. And even with respect to fictional television, what was so satisfying about *The Sopranos*, to many viewers and critics alike, was the unflinching way in which it juxtaposed the Victorian morality of its gangster-protagonists with a truthful, seemingly unedited, look at their actual behaviour. How, then, to account for this apparent discrepancy in our expectations?

The answer lies in our apparent belief, however, pollyannish it may be, that knowing the truth can only improve our world; being immersed in lies can only degrade it. In the same way, understanding what is at stake when we must choose for or against violence can only elevate our public discourse, even if some of us will think that in a particular situation the wrong choice was made. Toward the beginning of the archetypal 1952 Western *High Noon*, newly-wed (and retired) Marshal Will Kane's Quaker and pacifist wife deserts him because he insists on remaining in their town and using violence to defend it against the outlaws who've returned to take revenge on him. At the climax of the film, having run back into town to be by his side, she shoots one of his would-be assassins – in the back. This scene, one of the most viscerally stunning in the history of American cinema (I involuntarily rose out of my seat the second time I saw it) has been subjected to much ideological criticism, as allegedly a covert endorsement of Cold-War anti-Communism and a repudiation of the ethic of non-violence.[19] That criticism misses the point, though: or perhaps it rather emphasises the point, in that the very act of making it shows us that there is something here for us to think about – even in the midst of such a shocking act of violence. A critique of pacifism is not necessarily an unprincipled endorsement of bellicosity, but has its own ethical content; even the American position in the Cold War was claimed by its most thoughtful proponents to rest on an ethical base of one kind or another (e.g., 'the national interest'), and when policies toward the Soviet Union seemed to them to depart from that base in the direction of mere anti-Communist ideology they – some of them at least – dissented.[20]

In this context, thinking back to the Cold-War era of *High Noon* and the original *3:10 to Yuma*, a time that is often referred to as belonging to the period of classical Hollywood cinema, we then become aware that in fact an extraordinary number of films from that period – and not only Westerns by any means – had precisely the same kind of narrative centre. That is to say, they centred on questions of individual moral choice. Should an individual follow the dictates of conscience or obligation, however uncomfortable or dangerous the direction in which they might lead, or rather follow the course of prudence or, just as often, disillusionment and cynicism about the possibility of engaging in moral behaviour at all? Does the concrete community in which a man is embedded, or the more abstract demands of individuality and conscience, have the more appropriate claim on his loyalties? *Casablanca*, *High Noon*, and *On the Waterfront* are the most famous examples of this kind of moral engagement, but the roster is virtually endless. Many, though hardly all, of these films were centred on an act of violence – as might be expected, since both the moral and emotional stakes are highest when life and death are at stake.[21]

Moreover, though there are many ways of providing content to the pleasure-for-profit machine that is American visual culture, the technological virtuosity of Hollywood, even on television, has always been most successfully adapted to emphasising the visceral elements of pleasure, from slapstick comedy to horror or action-adventure. It is only when these become as one-sided as they have begun to do, that we notice the difference. A movie, or even – though less so – a scripted television programme, is not a lecture but a series of visual images. No matter how it is framed by dialogue or narrative, in the visual world what you see is what you get. In other words, Hollywood's narrative fictions are visual fantasies; the question is, why *these* fantasies? Violence, it seems, is now more and more not being presented as a choice that may define our relationship to the social order or to ethical life. Instead, it is rather aestheticised – fetishised – as *nothing more than* a source of visceral pleasure; what we 'see' is the subordination of all other content to the fascination with sumptuous violence.

Yet aside from propaganda exercises like *24* (and even that is not really an exception), most commodities of visual culture have the same point: to make a profit, or at least return an investment. If showing scenes of violence is one way of doing that, then they have made their 'point'. The real problem is that scenes of violence, pointed or gratuitous, can be put in the service of any content. The aesthetic problem of visceral pleasure is that it can too easily be allowed to overwhelm all other sources of pleasure, but in and of themselves, visceral responses are as valid as any other, and we hardly want to read them out of visual culture – there go *Psycho*, *Jaws*, *Night of the Living Dead*, and a plethora of films, American and other, that have given pleasure to millions all over the globe. Whether we think of the chase scenes in *Bullitt*, *The French Connection*, or *Speed*; the fight scenes in *The Quiet Man* or *Crouching Tiger Hidden Dragon*; or the voyeuristic presentation of Rita Hayworth in *Gilda*, Elizabeth Taylor in *Suddenly Last Summer,* Sharon Stone in *Basic Instinct*, or Katherine Moennig in *The L Word*, these have in common that they convey the visual pleasures of fast action, athleticism, or sex appeal.

The question we rather want to ask, then, is whether a particular kind of imaginary violence has 'a point' other than fetishising, as well as implicitly justifying, our visceral taste for itself? It is as though a new and frightening version of 'pleasure' has been brought into the foreground of our visual culture. What is different about the contemporary delight in beheadings, torture, spattered gore, literal viscera, brains blown out by bullets seen in slow motion, or human flesh visibly exposed to the surgeon's knife, is that we are now being immersed in sights that are normally *un*pleasurable, that are, or ordinarily used to be, kept hidden. And the apparent purpose of these scenes is at best nothing more than to skilfully accomplish that kind of immersion in front of a mass audience; at worst, as in *24*, to accustom us to its malignant presence. Again, a comparison with pornography is instructive. As Linda Williams points out, violence against women is actually quite rare in hard core films, since the point they are trying to persuade us of is that the women are enjoying – taking pleasure in – the sexual encounters (the men's apparent pleasure being visual, the women's audible). With the contemporary film of violence, it's as though we were to become accustomed to seeing hard core films in which scenes of rape are so 'realistic' that we would feel – with some kind of enjoyment – as though we were watching an actual rape.

When Quentin Tarantino first introduced the notion, in *Reservoir Dogs*, that 'real' bloodshed could be enjoyed as a kind of spectator sport, that could be seen as an innovation in visual art. Now it is commonplace: including in his own work, as evidenced by the multiple on-screen beheadings in *Kill Bill Vol. 1*.[22] This dehumanisation of violence is the most far-reaching form of dehumanisation, in that after it there's nothing left. Once we have accepted torture, eye-gouging, flaying – what will we not accept? Here, the creators of on-screen barbarism merely replicate the barbarism in which the nation itself is engaged – without taking any responsibility for what they do. In this of course they take their cue from the real-time exponents of torture and brutality, or rather those who've authorised them. And the 'realistic' (if totally absurd) mise-en-scene of *24*, which does have a right-wing partisan as its creator, conveys this sense no more directly than does the apparently futuristic (but thoroughly contemporary) and equally well-reviewed made-for-TV-movie *Battlestar Galactica: Razor 2007*.

In this movie, the enemy of the human race, the Cylons, are only machines that have no purpose in making war other than to attack and conquer; no geopolitical explanations intrude on the purity of their evil. They are definitively non-human, having apparently neither 'women' nor 'children', and so in combating them no scruples need apply. As the commander of the Battlestar puts it, in fighting them 'we must be capable of setting aside fear, hesitation, even revulsion, and every natural inhibition that can make the difference between winning and losing... Then you're a razor; this war is forcing us all to become razors'. Meanwhile, on the radio the President (also a woman) announces the outlawing of abortion. It's not incidental that in this apparently futuristic fiction the most ruthless killers are women; ethical debate (so to speak: it consists only of asking how ruthless should we be toward our own side in pursuit of victory) seems to take place only among the men. Of course when you're fighting barbarians what can you be but barbaric? All you have to do is find a barbarian – that is, a non-human enemy, say Osama bin Laden – to fight. Though often in good liberal pluralist fashion attempting to find some contemporary real 'enemies' – i.e., Muslims – to humanise (see *The Kingdom*, *A Mighty Heart*, *Syriana*, *Redacted*, even on occasion *24*), the creators of our cultural products also let us see how we can treat an 'enemy' who is beyond that pale.

If we ask why this efflorescence of frightful violence in visual culture, it is obvious that political and ideological determinations are only a part of the picture. The arc of change and innovation within both technological capability and genre development certainly is a contributory factor. Script-writers or directors may have ideological messages they hope to get across, but their efforts to do so fade into insignificance next to the consuming need to *get it watched* – a need that over time manifests itself as the inescapable imperative, *be different! be new!* That is why, for example, the explosive, momentarily all-consuming descent of mass entertainment into the nether regions of bad taste known as 'reality television' has little to do with the mass audience's declining taste, real or alleged, and much to do with the playing out of the classic genres that film and later television have depended on throughout the twentieth century.

This imperative has combined with what has so far been striking progress in the technological capacity to produce, among other things, the hyper-realism in visual culture that the critics of its so-called bad taste are fixated on. Violence grows more graphic *of course*, for that development follows the same logic that depicts emergency room surgeries (or most grossly, the cosmetic surgeries of *Nip/Tuck*) in detail so precise that many viewers find the medical genre unbearably disgusting, or at best watch key scenes with their hands over their eyes, as though watching a horror movie. Critics want televised or cinematic violence to 'have consequences', a perfectly reasonable wish, but fail to understand that the chief consequence of producing images of violence, for better or worse, is to make them look more 'real', i.e. more brutal: surely as appropriate an outcome of violence as its supposed eventuation in lawful retribution. If visual fictions fail to give audiences that thrill of reality, after all, we can always turn to the local news; or Grand Theft Auto or Rock Star or Activision's latest version of mass slaughter. If the real is what we want, the days of 'shock and awe' showed that we can be getting all too much of it; or perhaps, as a nation, producing all too much of it. Moreover, the new technologies of film – the rise of computer graphics (CG) and other examples of green-screen technology; more powerful computers that can handle the demands of advanced editing capabilities such as the Final Cut programme; and digital cameras (24P, the Genesis, the Virgin), that marry the richness of film with the more flexible techniques of digitalisation – make it possible to carry cinematic and televised 'realism' to heights never before attained.

However, though technological determination does have consequences, it never operates entirely by itself; nor does any story that we might wish to tell require its latest apotheosis. A Quaker lady shooting a man in the back could not be any more morally or kinesthetically shocking if blood spurted from the screen all over the theatre. For brute technology to triumph as it has, some other potential avenue to meaning must be closed down. In the case of visual technology's triumph, what has correspondingly disappeared is the power of cinematic and moral imagination, as seen most clearly in our earlier reference to *There Will Be Blood*. It is an indicative film in that more and more Hollywood's film-makers seem unable to conceive that a story – even a violent story – might have meaning beyond itself; might have a serious moral or social dimension. To the extent that that is true, it is not a revelation about film-makers, but about the social order for which they create cultural commodities. In an era when the only politics remaining to American consumer/citizens is a politics of retrenchment on the one hand, and the unrestrained pursuit of naked power and wealth on the other, the growing fetishisation of violence no longer seems surprising, any more than does the loss of any critical purchase in mainstream television's typical narratives.

The dismissal of justice as limit is but the other side of the coin of the embrace of torture. That is to say, in this important arena of visual culture, contact with the ethical realm has increasingly been broken off. This may be seen as a tacit collaboration, unwitting as it may be, with the Bush Administration's project of ending all restraints on the use of force: what Hegel called, in a chilling phrase, 'the absolutely unfettered will'. This is what we mean by 'barbarism'.

NOTES

1 'Sailing to Byzantium', 1928.

2 See David Bordwell, *The Way Hollywood Tells It: Story and Style in Modern Movies*, Berkeley: University of California Press, 2004, p. 106.

3 Ibid., especially chs. 4 and 5.

4 In her definitive study of the traditional horror film and the 'slasher movie' that *Psycho* inaugurated, Clover argues that both have been 'subversive' of conventional cinematic and social values. Among the 'subversive' elements Clover finds in the slasher movies of the 1970s and '80s is the appearance, in response to the dynamic of 70s feminism, of the character of 'the Final Girl', who through 'her femaleness, however qualified', redefines the genre as 'a standard one of tale and epic', in which her point of view is a substitute for that of the traditional male rescuer, now 'either dismissably marginal or dispensed with altogether'. See Carol Clover, *Men, Women, and Chainsaws: Gender in the Modern Horror Film*, Princeton: Princeton Press, 1992, p. 48, n. 36.

5 See Elizabeth Young, '*The Silence of the Lambs* and the Flaying of Feminist Theory,' *Camera Obscura* 27 (September 1992), pp. 5-35.

6 For some statistically revealing studies, see Nick Browne et al., 'American Film Violence: An Analytic Portrait', *Journal of Interpersonal Violence*, 17(4), 2002, pp. 351-70; and David L. McArthur et al., 'Violence and its Injury Consequences in American Movies: A Public Health Perspective', *Western Journal of Medicine*, 173(3), 2000, pp. 164-68. The point about 'injury consequences', of course, is how rare or improbably minor they are.

7 See Susan Faludi, *The Terror Dream: Fear and Fantasy in Post-9/11 America*, New York: Henry Holt & Co., 2007. Dargis's comments are in the Arts and Leisure supplement on 'Summer Movies', *The New York Times*, 4 May 2008.

8 On Hollywood's flirtation with feminism from the '70s through the '90s, see Green, *Cracks in the Pedestal.*

9 Linda Williams, *Hard Core: Power, Pleasure, and the Frenzy of the Visible*, Berkeley: University of California Press, 1989.

10 See my *Primetime Politics: The Truth about Conservative Lies, Corporate Control, and Television Culture*, New York: Rowman & Littlefield, 2005, chs. 3 and 5, for a detailed critique of what I unapologetically call 'the Big Lie' of conservative media criticism.

11 See Mark Harris, *Pictures at a Revolution: Five Movies and the Birth of the New Hollywood*, New York: Penguin Press, 2008, pp. 338-39.

12 That *There Will Be Blood* and *No Country for Old Men* were both nominated for 'Best Picture of 2007', and that the former was, as noted earlier, hailed by many critics as a 'masterpiece', proves nothing in and of itself; but that fact at least forces us to contemplate the notion that there might be other criteria for attributing excellence than the ones by which those same critics likely rate *Citizen Kane*, *On the Waterfront*, or

Vertigo as 'masterpieces' as well.

13 I have Elizabeth Young to thank for this formulation.

14 See chapter 4 of *Primetime Politics*, from which this analysis is adapted. See also *Cracks in the Pedestal*, chs. 3 and 5.

15 See Judith Mayne, in '*L.A. Law* and Prime Time Feminism', *Discourse*, 10(2), 1988, pp. 30-47. The exception to this generalisation is the case of tolerance and intolerance; the latter on the whole gets short shrift in mass media, for total inclusion is their ultimate goal. Obviously who gets incorporated under the rubric of 'inclusion' has changed over time, but always in the direction of more rather than less. For an entertaining account of how 'balance' on TV is actually achieved, see Tad Friend, 'You Can't Say That', *The New Yorker*, 19 November 2001, pp. 44-49. My own analysis of 'having it both ways' is in *Primetime Politics*, ch. 4.

16 See Robert Ray, *A Certain Tendency of the Hollywood Cinema, 1930-1980*, Princeton: Princeton University Press, 1985. Rick Blaine in *Casablanca* can stand for all these heroes. I have analysed the 'lonely town' genre at greater length in *Cracks in the Pedestal*, pp. 131ff.

17 *The Sarah Connor Chronicles* was a brief off-season series on Fox in the spring of 2008. It is not yet known whether it will be renewed. As for defence attorneys, James Spader and William Shatner of the satirical – and often over-the-top – *Boston Legal* may be described with many epithets, but 'heroic' is not one of them. And Julia Margulies of *Canterbury's Law*, from the same short season as *The Sarah Connor Chronicles*, was more a bundles of neuroses and frantic sexcapades than Perry Mason or Matlock could have dreamed. (This was also true, though not quite as insistently, as the short-lived *Philly*, starring Kim Delaney as a defence attorney, of a few years back.) It's no accident that the only two unofficial heroes remaining on TV's schedule at this point were sexy women who, as such, can be slotted into typically 'masculine' roles even while ostensibly defying them.

18 As the late Iris Marion Young put it, writing about 'police brutality': 'The idea that the state is nothing but monopoly on the legitimate use of violence slides easily for many people into the idea that the use of violence by legitimate agents of a legitimate state is itself legitimate'. In *Global Challenges: War, Self-Determination and the Responsibility for Justice*, Malden: Polity Press, 2007, p. 98. On the necessary distinction between Law and Justice, see Drucilla Cornell, *The Philosophy of the Limit,* New York: Routledge Chapman and Hall, 1992, especially chs. 4-6.

19 This is a somewhat odd criticism, in that the screenwriter for *High Noon*, Carl Foreman, was blacklisted for refusing to testify about his alleged

Communist Party membership, and was about to go into exile in Great Britain. He thought he was attacking conformity and cowardice; he certainly did not think he was making a 'Cold-War liberal' statement. Nor did that larger-than-life non-liberal John Wayne miss the point, calling *High Noon* 'the most un-American movie' he'd ever seen (as can be seen on the DVD).

20 Among them George Kennan and Hans Morgenthau; see especially J. William Fulbright, *The Arrogance of Power*, New York: Random House, 1966.

21 A list will include not only the obvious Westerns, but also war movies, 'social problem' and political dramas, film noir, gangster movies, even a few comedies and children's movies. Among others: *The Wizard of Oz*, *The Ox-Bow Incident*, *Mr. Smith Goes To Washington*, *Red River*, *Rio Bravo* (Howard Hawks's and John Wayne's answer to the supposed 'anti-Americanism' of *High Noon*), *The Searchers*, *The Gunfighter*, *Along the Great Divide*, *Shane*, *Gentleman's Agreement*, *To Kill a Mockingbird*, *Man of the West*, *Born Yesterday*, *Gilda*, *From Here to Eternity*, *High Sierra*, *Knock on Any Door*, *The Hoodlum Priest*, *Twelve Angry Men*, *Spartacus*, *Viva Zapata!*, *Whistle at Eaton Falls*, *Run Silent Run Deep*, *Meet John Doe*, *The Informer*, *Command Decision*, *Twelve O'Clock High*, *Attack!*, *Uncertain Glory*, *The Rack*, *Young Mr. Lincoln*, *Decision at Sundown*, *Home of the Brave*, *The Purple Heart*, *It's a Wonderful Life*, *Out of the Past*, *The Fugitive*, *Force of Evil*... It should be noted that with fewer (literally) than a handful of exceptions, the bearers of urgent choice in these films are all white men. It is clearly a gain for liberal pluralism that in contemporary cinema women, and black men, are equally capable of being the protagonists of morally irrelevant narratives of violence; whether that change represents overall historical progress is another question entirely.

22 Hong-Kong martial arts cinema is generally credited with being the inspiration for Tarantino's approach, especially in *Kill Bill*; but one has to watch a number of those earlier films to see how different a sensibility he brings to his own version.

RACE, PRISONS AND WAR: SCENES FROM THE HISTORY OF US VIOLENCE

RUTH WILSON GILMORE

Moreover, the important question for the future in this case is not 'can it happen again?' Rather, it is 'can it be stopped'?[1]

What can be said about a political culture in search of 'infinite prosperity' that is dependent on a perpetual enemy who must always be fought but can never be vanquished? The United States ranks first in military power, wealth, war-making, murder rates, and incarceration rates. At the time of this writing in the summer of 2008, one in one hundred US adults was locked in a cage, and an additional two per cent were under the direct supervision of the criminal justice system. While the vast majority of people in custody did not kill or violently harm anybody, the centrality of violence to all aspects of US life helps explain the continuum from policing and prisons to war. Rather than rehearse well-known critical histories of stolen land, stolen labour, gender domination, and iron-fisted capital expansion, this essay uses them to historicise current events. It constructs a series of scenes from various periods that, in sum, are designed to demonstrate the persistence and convergence of patterns and systems. The resulting narrative arc is more cumulative than teleological, even though I believe with all my heart there's an end to violence in both senses of 'end': violence produces power, which under the grow-or-die culture of capitalism seems like a slightly erratic expression of self-interest; but violence does not produce *all* power, which means perhaps that its effectiveness might come to a finish.

SOUTHERN LOUISIANA: ARMED WHITE MEN

The violence wrought by Hurricane Katrina in September 2005 focused singularly shocked global attention on the naked, official, and organised depth of US racism. A global chorus – including many residents of the US – insisted they had not really known how bad it still is to be poor and of colour in the richest and most militarily powerful nation-state in the history of the world. The views of dead Black people floating in the floodwater, and living Black people huddled on roofs or in rowboats, or crammed into the hold of a troop transport ship in dry-dock, or into the vastness of the Sugar Bowl football stadium, either taught or reminded the world what it used to know about the United States: it is difficult and dangerous to be Black in this country. One particularly outstanding image, shot on both still and motion film from hovering helicopters, demonstrated in stark terms how the disaster was – and remains – a political rather than natural phenomenon. Picture: a line of armed white men pointing their Winchester rifles at a group of mostly Black people to keep them from walking across an interstate highway bridge from New Orleans onto the dryer ground of neighbouring Gretna. Professional and amateur pundits marvelled at this scene's explicitness. OK, they reasoned, perhaps unorganised neglect had allowed the levees to crumble, and perhaps the cumulative effects of flooding Black neighbourhoods to save white ones during previous hurricanes and floods stretching back across the century had increased the vulnerability of those locations. But how could anybody explain officers of the law stopping, rather than helping, people in obvious danger of dying? What is the continuity that produces and exploits group-differentiated vulnerability to premature death so casually, without fear of political consequence or moral shame?

Armed white men of Gretna figured in the media a century earlier, when a ready-to-lynch mob hit the streets one afternoon in the year 1900. A New Orleans newspaper account of the hunt concluded: 'The shots brought out almost everybody-white in town, and though there was nothing to show for the exciting work, except the arrest of the Negro, who doesn't answer the description of the man wanted, Gretna's male population had its little fun and felt amply repaid for all the trouble it was put to, and all the ammunition it wasted'.[2] This was a story of a non-lynching (although the 'man wanted' and others were slain that day) during the long period of Jim Crow rule committed to destroying Black self-determination. Had the 1900 Gretna gang caught its quarry everybody would still have had 'fun' – and used even more ammunition, since one favourite pastime of lynchers was to empty their Winchesters into the victim's *dead* body, to watch the bullets destroy whatever human form remained after burning, cutting, tying, dragging, flaying, disembowelling, dismembering had, in Ida B. Wells' words, 'hurled men [and women] into eternity on supposition'.[3]

Wells, whose *On Lynchings* was first published in 1892, used the pulpits of international organisations and the press to argue precisely how lynching combined the forces of both violence and ideology – or coercion and consent – to produce and consolidate power. She showed that this combination particularly provided the capacity to stifle association and competition, minimise ownership, and independence of thought and action, and therefore guarantee the extraction from Black communities of cheap labour (including sex) and profits from the sale of consumer goods. Her aim was not only to bear witness to the fact of each event – that someone died or nearly died – but also to testify to its context, to trace out the event's underlying or true cause. To achieve her end, she examined not only what people did, but also how the stories of their actions were narrated and used. Her exposition and analysis demonstrated the role of lynching in renovating racist hierarchy, gender subordination, and regional accumulation strategies. To do all this hard work every lynching was exemplary, which means it wasn't quick. Lynch mobs did not just take off after somebody with the intent of killing them extra-legally – albeit in most cases with the sanction of sworn state agents from sheriffs to governors to juries. Lynching was public torture, and both press and posse elites encouraged 'everybody-white' to get in on the fun. Mobs thrilled to participate in the victim's slow death, to hear agonised cries for pity and smell roasting human flesh, to shoot dead bodies to smithereens, to keep body parts – ears, penises, breasts, testicles, charred bones – as souvenirs, and to read detailed descriptions of torture in the newspapers. Mobs South, North, and West could usually count on the press to explain away the kidnapping, torture, and murder by invoking the naturalness of human sacrifice – particularly through the repetitive ascription of sub-humanity to the victim – and thereby to vindicate the torturers ('everybody-white') via the contradictory claim of supremacy.

If 'everybody-white' in Gretna were also the 'males' of Gretna, their violence ('fun' – in other words, its distance from 'criminality') cannot be legitimated in the same way for all males. But that's not an end but a beginning, because a dynamic society in which the victors present themselves as the pattern of human nature (in which *homo economicus* strips off his bourgeois haberdashery and becomes the imperially naked human nature in action), invites mighty struggles to establish who counts as masculine. Moreover, Ida Wells spelled out clearly that the 'usual crime' of rape pinned on lynch victims was a fiction, a lie known by everybody in the South. By publishing the open secret that white women had consensual, intimate, illegal sex with Black men, Wells dared name, in black-and-white, a persistent weakness in the hierarchy of entitlements and exclusions organising white supremacy. People then and now think race is natural because of the biology of reproduction, even though the biology of reproduction proves race is made of the social and political meanings assigned to it. And to complicate the issue, sex is not reproduction, while reproduction is always differentiation.

That's a lot to keep under control, and torture helped to perpetuate the normative view that there *should be* control. Thus it made no difference that most of the people tortured did not have illegal sex, consensually or not, with anybody. The convolution here is indicative of the paroxysms of thought and argument that stunningly establish a threshold of sanctioned torture (should non-consensual sex be so punished?) and thereby evade the question of how 'criminality' is naturalised by presenting it as the origin of the explosive horror of violence (the illegal sex) that then must be fought with the explosive horror of violence (the torture and lynching). Enshrouding this necessary convolution are the constantly renovated gender relations that give coherence to the rhetoric of vulnerability and perpetration. The rape of women of colour, and the pervasiveness of domestic violence in all kinds of households, speak both to the gendered hierarchy of racism and to the notion that masculinity is constituted through differentially legitimated force. Thus the spasmodically systematic application of violence to secure material and ideological domination over 'infinite prosperity' is a consistent practice of, rather than a rude eruption in, everyday life.

Representatives of and advocates for Black and poor people doomed, displaced or disappeared in the 2005 events in Gretna and New Orleans followed in Wells' footsteps, and carried grievances and demands for remedy before international bodies. When the United States showed up for its regularly scheduled interview at the United Nations Human Rights Commission in Geneva in 2006, commissioners asked questions about the usually suspect aspects of US life: Why are there so many poor people? Why are there so many prisoners? Why does racism persist in what Wells termed 'the organized life of the country'?[4] And in particular, why hasn't the devastation that slammed Black and poor communities where the Mississippi flows into the Gulf of Mexico been redressed?

Members of the Human Rights Commission struggled to understand how the United States could be lax in living up to the terms of treaties that it had helped to write,[5] but even though Article VI of the US constitution specifies that Treaties are part of 'the supreme Law of the Land', Native Americans do not puzzle over the question that (perhaps just for show) seemed to mystify the Geneva commissioners. The US has in fact consistently broken every treaty ever written with indigenous peoples, a habit of disregard unmodulated by a single wrinkle of official remorse, much less by redress for the slash-and-burn movement of white people across North America, from Virginia and New England in the seventeenth century, through coast-to-coast horrors of extermination committed in the name of god, lawgiving, freedom, and accumulation. Puritans described the screams of Indians being burned alive in torched villages as 'God laughing at his enemies'.[6] Indian-killers wore the body parts of those they had killed as jewellery, and made other useful and decorative objects from human remains. Through the violent dialectics of murder, dislocation, and disease, more than 95 per cent of indigenous Americans were hurled into eternity within the first few generations after contact with European colonisers.[7] The rest were removed, relocated, or 'terminated' – an astonishing word, meant to describe dispersal of people from reservations to cities. Weapons of various types, constantly improved to become like the rifles wielded in Gretna in 1900 and again in 2005, enforced indigenous agreement to treaties that consigned first-nation peoples to places and life-ways not their own, the alternative being straightforward extermination.

SOUTHERN NEW ENGLAND: THE MILITARY-INDUSTRIAL COMPLEX

I was born and raised in New Haven Connecticut, a small city dominated at first by tightfisted Puritans but then, over the centuries, shaped by Native Americans (many of whom passed as, or into, white or Black), free Black people, southern and eastern Europeans, and Puerto Ricans, Dominicans and most lately Chicana/os and Mexicans. It became a Catholic city with a significant Jewish population some time in the early twentieth century, during the height of the biggest immigration boom, in absolute numbers, in the history of the US. New Haven was ruled, first overtly and then behind-the-scenes, by WASPs, until they didn't care about it any more, when it ceased being a prosperous polity around 1980. The principle of 'dispersed inequality' that Robert Dahl famously and erroneously concluded in 1957 would be the future of the US multi-ethnic republic appeared to work well enough to warrant his book on New Haven politics during the post-world-war-II period, when the Elm City's two principal products of economic activity, guns and students, were being turned out in high quality and at high cost. But when things started to get bad, in New Haven and throughout the US, Dahl wisely repudiated his signature concept (even though US-trained political science doctoral candidates must, to this day, commit its error to heart).

Every New Haven schoolchild of the long twentieth century learned about the political and material marvels achieved by the white men whose names mark many of the city's major streets: Judges Goffe, Dixwell, and Whalley, who signed the death warrant for Charles I and fled to New Haven when Charles II took the throne; Eli Whitney, interchangeable parts innovator, wartime profiteer, and cotton gin engineer; and Oliver Fisher

Winchester, developer and manufacturer of the repeating rifle – the gun that 'won' the west. Youngsters toured their monuments, reported to each other on their accomplishments, and sang and danced their praise in dead-serious amateur musicals performed for elected and other elites.

Killing kings, mass-producing weapons, and framing accumulation as an inalienable right coalesced into white supremacy – the modern theory and practice that explains how, over the past few centuries, authority devolved from the person of the monarch to one, and only one, sovereign race. That race's divinely conferred and energetically exercised freedom to have, to take, to kill, to rule, and to judge when any of these actions is right or wrong – individually and in the aggregate – kept institutions like Winchester's arms factory and Yale University humming day and night.

Killing *somebody* has always been on the American agenda, and avoiding being caught in American crosshairs an ontological priority. For example, the lessons white supremacists violently offered to Black GIs after World War I can be summed up in a couple of imperatives: expect nothing, and don't wear your uniform. Lynching, which had minimally abated during the US's brief engagement in the war, heated up in the aftermath. There is always an increase in murder in the United States after the country goes off to war and wins – just as there is always a sudden spike after executions – which together form strong evidence that the 'state models behavior for the polity'.[8] 1919's bloody 'red summer', best known for the Palmer raids against leftist political and labour organisers, was simultaneously a time of intense racist lynching in the name of white supremacy. The class and race wars were related rather than coincidental. Not surprisingly, J. Edgar Hoover began his rise to power as the chief engineer of capitalist white supremacist policing by serving as technocratic overseer for many of the 1919 actions. He was still around as head of the FBI when over an 18 month period in 1969-71 federal and local police destroyed the Black Panther Party. In 1969, no less than in 1919, rhetoric about violence and violent action brought into view a perpetual enemy who must always be fought but can never be vanquished, presented as simultaneously criminal (acting outside the law) and alien (not belonging to the polity).

But when Black GIs came back after World War II they were not about to 'expect nothing' or hide their uniforms in the bottom of a trunk. Having heard from wives and fathers, sisters and friends, about the work radicals were doing stateside to advance the double-victory cause – the fight against US racism as part of the fight against fascism – many decided to fight to get well-paying blue collar jobs in factories. In New Haven, it was making guns. Winchester's was the biggest factory in the New England gunbelt, and the rifles used to kill indigenous people were still being produced long after the theft of the continent had been completed. Winchester's became the place where Black men went to work after doing their two or three or four years in the armed service – 'protecting' Berlin, South Korea, Okinawa, Thailand, Laos, South Vietnam. They knew how to shoot. They worked overtime on the assembly line. The wives worked at Yale in low-paying jobs. Their children sang and danced: when they were not rehearsing 'Jump Jim Crow' they warbled about superior inventions and modern points of view.

The modern point of view that sustained the social order was the relentless industrialization of killing, requiring fewer exertions of human physical and mental strength per person hurled into eternity. This was the military-industrial complex: the set of workers, intellectuals, bosses, boosters, places, materials, relationships, ideas, and political-economic capacity to organise these factors of production into the machinery of death. Eventually, President General Dwight David Eisenhower got nervous enough about the military-industrial complex to give it its name. He revered war; he loved capitalism. But did not like how war-making and profit-making had become so thoroughly intermeshed during the Cold War that, he argued, both entrepreneurial innovation and industrial policy would be shaped (and perhaps squeezed) by their might. His anxiety was about 185 years too late, though perhaps it is never too late to say you're sorry. The United States has never had an industrial policy other than the one cohering around warfare, although it became most fully operationalised with the establishment of the Pentagon and consolidated power of the Department of Defense's many constituents in the post-1945 era.

Winchester's New Haven arms factory was taken over by the Olin-Matheson corporation in 1963. After an employee buyout to forestall the factory's closure in 1981 failed, the factory was first acquired by a French holding company, then sold to a Belgian arms-making cartel. By the time the factory was completely shut down in 2006, prosperity had long since exited the city – along with nearly 25 per cent of its population. What was left in its wake were poor Black and Brown people, a spatially segregated arc of extremely well-to-do white households, and a shrunken middle-income stratum struggling to make public schools and services respond as they had in the earlier period. As has been the case across the United States, especially in places where wide gaps between rich and poor coincided with declining local economies, criminalisation became the preferred public response to the problems created by poverty. Young people from households which had been supported by guns produced and exported to kill other people's children now got their hands on imported guns to kill neighbours, family, and friends. Mostly, however, they were busy being poor.

The expansion of criminalisation is always explained away by reference to a secular rise in violent activity – rape, murder, child molestation are the unholy trinity. Highly rationalized, interpersonal violence did not account for the kinds of laws and techniques used to lock people up. But it served as an excuse, throughout the US, to shift infrastructural investment from schools and hospitals to jails and prisons. The same family that bought and later dumped Winchester's funds the Olin Foundation, which is among the principal sponsors of intellectual hacks who churn out racist reports and sound-bites proving that prison expansion is good for society. The war against the poor has thus oscillated between modes of incorporation (a job in a gun factory or a cot in a cage) that maintain the central force of racial capitalism.

FROM THE GREYHOUND STATION TO ABU GHRAIB: PRISONS AS MANIFEST DESTINY

'Criminal' has long been on the rise in the lexicon of putatively transparent or self-explanatory terms – like race or gender – used to designate fundamental (whether fixed or mutable) differences between kinds of people. Ida B. Wells saw the active connection between race-making and outlaw-making when she wrote: 'To lynch for a certain crime not only concedes the right to lynch any person for any crime but it is in a fair way to stamp us a race of rapists and desperadoes'.[9] The first public infrastructural accomplishment in post-Katrina New Orleans was to convert the city's Greyhound station into a jail; Burl Cain, the warden of the notorious Angola State prison – a post-civil war plantation where 85 per cent of prisoners are Black and an equal percentage serving sentences for the rest of their natural lives – was put in charge. In other words, the elites didn't start by burying the dead or feeding the living, but they did close a port – the bus station – in order to lock up as many as possible whose exit from the city had not yet been accomplished through dispersal or death. Of all sites, the bus station! In the US buses are symbolic of working-class mobility, and also – especially in the South – of the struggle, organised during the height of the long twentieth-century civil rights movement, to desegregate transportation no less than schools.

The conversion of the bus station into a jail occurred not long after Gretna's police blocked the public bridge, whose very existence symbolised the disinvestment in city centres in favour of the suburbanisation of the 1950s and 1960s. The failed levees of New Orleans themselves were, in their disintegration, symbolic not simply of urban abandonment but rather of a recalibration of (as opposed to a wholesale withdrawal from) the wealth-producing urban landscapes of the Big Easy, as New Orleans is familiarly called.

In the 25 or so years leading up to Katrina, a massive expansion of prisons and criminalisation spread across the United States, driven by different, but connected, processes of displacement, abandonment, and control. As was the case with kidnapped African labour and stolen indigenous land, a completely involuntary migration – this time around via conviction and incarceration – has once again resulted in the mysterious disappearance of millions of people. This ongoing disappearance is apparently not fully grasped, even in its accomplishment, to judge from the calmness with which most people in the US of all races receive the news that one out of every 100 of the country's adults is locked up in a prison or jail.

The rise of the cage as a large-scale all-purpose solution to problems is a relatively recent phenomenon in world history. Modern prisons were born and grew up with the United States, as impersonal but individualised sites of large-scale social control, in the long historical turn marked by the consolidation of the bourgeois nation-state as the world's fundamental political economic unit, the normalisation of capitalism, and the development of racist science and philosophy to explain it all. Although the reformist purpose of prisons was to end bodily torture, in the United States prison did not replace torture but rather complemented its role in securing social order. In the case of slavery prison was beside the point: there was no purpose in locking up a tool with life in it, while there was plenty of purposefulness in demonstrating to that and other living tools the imminence of premature death as the likeliest respite from endless suffering.[10] And in the case of land theft, there was no point in locking people up at public expense when those indigenous people who had not been slaughtered could be deported to reservations to fend for themselves. But what of others?

By the late 1840s, when various US political factions were debating the merits of permanently grabbing part or all of Mexico, the most clear-eyed proponents of 'Manifest Destiny' hesitated at the prospect of bringing into the union millions of Mexicans who, whatever they were, were not white. Supremacists claimed they had coaxed from (rather than forced into) the landscape a set of nearly identical, locally-controlled governmental institutions run by enfranchised white men. They were determined to maintain the absolute dominion of the sovereign race. Thus the anxiety was not just about having more not-white folks on US territory, but dealing with the problem of the vote – itself symbolic of their material delusion concerning local governance. If the Mexican-become-American men voted, then what of the union of free white men? The master-race republic sought to expand its wealth without diluting its distribution scheme. As we have seen, in the post-civil war period, public torture was pervasively used, even as the modern prison increasingly became part of rural no less than urban landscapes. Jim Crow, then, did not only work to suppress Black people; it was both template and caution for all who were not members of the sovereign race. That century's globalizing contradictions, characterized by indigenous extermination, wars of territorial expansion, socio-spatial segregation, racist science and eugenics, the redrawing of the world's imperial contours, and the spread of democratized blood-and-soil nationalism, coalesced at the time of the 1898 Spanish-American war, and these forces in sum gave both political and theoretical shape to the twentieth century's continuing human-sacrifice rampage.

The end of the nineteenth century was also defined by the development of the modern business corporation and the rise of engineering and a technocratic view of how to manage systems and structures – whether the DuPont Corporation, the city of Los Angeles, or the State of Mississippi. This combination of 'what' and 'how' formed the basis of 'Progressivism' – a movement misunderstood as an opening through which common people might democratically overcome racial capitalism and white supremacist imperialism. Rather, Progressives developed large-scale complex public and private institutions in order to guarantee the privatised extraction of value from land and other factors of production. As a result, it should not be surprising that Progressivism developed in the South and that Jim Crow was part of its original structure. Under the aegis of Progressivism, prisons became regulated by specialists and segregated by age and gender. This might not sound so bad – except for the fact that before the Progressive period few youngsters and few women were in any prisons anywhere.

Reform, then as now, opened the door to expanding prison under the guise of social improvement. At the same time, in the South the official end to the convict lease system took uncompensated labour (prisoners) out of competition with unemployed free labour; the struggle to end that system was resolved, in racist terms, by the formation of prison plantations for men (mostly Black) so that free workers (profiled white) could be assured of exclusive right to jobs, whether or not the work actually existed. In the late twentieth and early twenty-first century prison expansion has proceeded along these two fronts – as the necessary response to 'criminality', and as a reform of that response. The disfranchisement of prisoners gave George W. Bush the 2000 election.

The rationality underlying prison growth uses both rhetoric and practices of violence to make mass incarceration seem other than what it is – a machine for producing and exploiting group-differentiated vulnerability to premature death. The intellectuals who have figured out how to exercise racism without naming race have to work extremely hard to realise their goals, and they draw on a template and legacy of thought developed from and for the kinds of wars they imagine the US is fighting when it sends troops and materiel abroad. War and incarceration are supposed to bring good things to the places destroyed in the name of being saved; the devastation wrought overseas in Iraq and Afghanistan is both prefigured and shadowed by the history and current experience of life in the US itself. The convergence of theory and technique come into view in the construction of the perpetual enemy who must always be fought but can never be vanquished.

For the past twenty-five years the militarisation of everyday domestic life in the United States is acted out, in full dress, through, for example, the intensified criminalisation of kids, who in California in 1988 were officially named 'street terrorists'. Another example is the way that people in the US have gotten into the habit of wearing photo identification as though it were jewellery. Everyone expects to be stopped, but the expectation of what happens afterward diverges wildly. In such a milieu of battle-readiness and checkpoint-cheeriness it was remarkably easy for the lawyers defending the Los Angeles policemen who beat up Rodney King to argue, in spite of the visual evidence, that King was 'in control' of the situation. A millisecond of the globally circulated film of his beating shows King trying to get up as he is kicked and pummelled. This effort made King a violent desperado; and while the jury that acquitted the four cops probably would have let them go anyway, because the jurors came from a community of retired police and military and had a narrative of events on which to hang the cops' plea. 'Criminality' worked too well to fail in the courtroom.

The 1992 multicultural uprising against the verdict brought forth both spontaneous and systematic radical understandings of the internal racist logic of US institutions. It also gave a boost to the top-down development of legal and other machinery designed to suppress such opposition to racist policing. Although the Los Angeles police chief at the time was run out of his job, he has been replaced by a series of men for whom policing people of colour is the number one priority (Gretna in 1900 had a 'black detective' to help in that work, just as apartheid South Africa had Black police). Each has demanded a larger police force, arguing that every time something happens like Rodney King being beating up, or 13 year-old Devin Brown being shot dead because a policeman said he thought the kid, driving a stolen car, was 'a drunk' (which King was), the city will go up in flames if there isn't enough police power to keep it under control. They shop their techniques and demands around the world (getting rich as consultants along the way). Like the military, they want to surge. And as with contemporary warfare, they claim that what they do benefits the assaulted as well as the assaulter. The triggerman is safer and the target is precise. However, just as the outcome of what is called 'surgical strikes' in the era of increasingly capitalised warfare has meant that more civilians than ever die in each conflict, so it is the case with policing 'the war on the streets' at home.

The police and the military also act to guarantee their institutional role in the apparatus and activities of the state. On the one hand, for a nation conceived in the violence of indigenous extermination and chattel slavery, one might think that the governmental agents charged with 'defence' and 'internal pacification' would have nothing to worry about. But they do have things to worry about – ranging from the technical capacity to capitalise a lot of their individual human labour, to the fact that their opponents work around the clock to abolish policing, prisons, the military and capitalism. The constant agitation produces constant effort to shape both thought and action, and those in uniform use bodily violence as both rhetorical pretext and as disciplining practice in order to reproduce power.

The torture of prisoners by US military jailers at Abu Ghraib in Iraq in 2004 focused singularly shocked global attention on the naked and official depth of US racism. The revelation of the hidden spectacle that soldiers staged for themselves and the various audiences they sent pictures to, occurred a year before Katrina, and in retrospect the similarity of press and pundit reactions to the two outrages is rather compelling evidence of how successfully the production of power through violence works. Once the pictures came to light, one phrase, invoking a physical action, came up several times in English, French and Spanish language newspapers of varying political persuasions in both the 'first' and 'third' worlds: 'when Americans look away'. I can't tell you whether the phrase emerged in one place and then travelled, or whether it is a phrase commonly used to describe Americans' ADHD,[11] or something else. What does the phrase assume about 'Americans' and where they look? Were these newspapers right in assuming the real audience for the hidden spectacle, who happened to stumble onto it, could, as has happened historically, look and then look away – not out of denial, much less pity or shame, but rather with a deep and perhaps empathetic shrug for the *torturer*? The fact of torture consigns the tortured to a category of undifferentiated difference, an alien-ness underscored by religious or citizenship distinctions, but not reducible to them since both religion and citizenship can be changed. This suggests that the torture of prisoners today is about constructing racial categories no less than when white supremacy was being secured a hundred years ago.

Once the evidence of the outrage at Abu Ghraib was paraded before Congressional committees (and in art shows inviting 'public' comment in elegant books), the perpetrators were plucked out of the 'chain of command' and sent to prison. A lot was made of the fact that two or three of them had been stateside prison guards, and so what could one expect? Analytically, one could expect at least some critics to understand that what the guards did in both the US and Iraq was to help consolidate policing and prisons' institutional dominance. These institutions aspire to the same degree of security for their existence at the state and local level that the Pentagon enjoys at the federal level. This reduces questions of institutional reform to marginal squabbles over cost-benefits and better practices.

Such a devolution of criticism makes reformist reform very powerful in the way that neoliberalism operates.[12] But it is not only the current set of institutions structured in dominance that matter – though they do. The culture of capitalism – not the culture of *consumption* but of *capitalism* – informs all the tendencies laid out in the scenes depicted in this essay. 'Grow or die' works hand-in-hand with structural inequality to keep producing an outcome that people keep being shocked by. And yet, while being shocked, many are also persuaded of the naturalness of the system and are therefore vulnerable to accepting the proposition advanced by the man who coined 'manifest destiny' to describe Anglo Saxons' right to control the planet. As Charles Kingsley, the author of *Westward Ho* wrote in a letter to a friend in 1849: 'It *is* expedient that one man die for the people. One tribe exterminated if need be to save a whole continent. "Sacrifice of human life?" Prove that it is *human* life'.[13]

ABOLITION NOW

In the dream of advocates for people locked up in Guantánamo and other known and unknown US military-controlled prisons around the planet, the prisoners should be brought into the US criminal justice system where they can be charged, face their accusers, and be judged by their peers. This seems unlikely as a remedy for the real problem, which is violence, prisons, and warfare. It also proposes that things will cure things – better buildings (Bush's promise to remedy Abu Ghraib), training sessions (what US professional has not taken a harassment training session in the past two years?), handbooks, and new laws. Yet in regular US prisons and jails, where one out of every 100 US adults lives, torture and terror happen every day. In California every week a prisoner dies from medical neglect of easily-treatable maladies. Throughout the United States the households of prison guards, along with police and military, are more likely to experience domestic violence than households whose income is not organised around the willingness to use bodily violence.

The proliferation of new prisons in the US was followed by the proliferation of laws to guarantee their present size. And contemporaneously with domestic prison growth, there has occurred a US-led global production of a criminal class without rights, designed to evade rather than fulfil the terms of treaties – including the global prohibition against torture. The concept of a rights-less person is an indirect legacy of the 1857 Dred Scott Supreme Court decision that used race to define who counts as human and therefore who bears human rights. Today the world is full of activists who try to practice human rights as a science, bringing before courts and the 'organised life' of the planet claims of injury and demands for redress. Given the power that violence produces, it is perhaps time to pause and consider how the unfinished work of radical abolition might help us in practical as well as theoretical ways to get out of the trap of reformist reform. The violence of torture and official murder, toward the end of stealing labour, land, and reproductive capacity, have driven the history of the United States. If reform within that history is the pattern for change, it can only result in a 'changing same'.[14]

NOTES

1 David Stannard, *American Holocaust: The Conquest of the New World*, Oxford: Oxford University Press, 1992, p. xiii.

2 Ida B. Wells-Barnett, *On Lynchings*, Amherst: Humanity Books, 2002.

3 Ibid, pp. 48, 53.

4 Ibid, p. 48.

5 Rev. Daniel Buford, Untitled Report, CITY: Peoples Institute for Survival and Beyond, 2006.

6 Michael Mann, *The Dark Side of Democracy: Explaining Ethnic Cleansing*, Cambridge: Cambridge University Press, 2005, p. 84.

7 Stannard, *American Holocaust*, pp. ix-x.

8 D. Archer and R. Gartner, *Violence and Crime in Cross-National Perspective*, New Haven: Yale University Press, 1984.

9 Wells, *On Lynching*, p. 41.

10 Saidiya Hartman, *Scenes of Subjection*, Oxford: Oxford University Press, 1997.

11 Attention Deficit Hyperactivity Disorder – the condition so commonly attributed to children 'acting up'.

12 Ruth Wilson Gilmore, *Golden Gulag: Prison, Surplus, Crisis, and Opposition in Globalizing Capitalism*, Berkeley: University of California Press 2006.

13 Quoted in Reginald Horsman, *Race and Manifest Destiny: The Origins of American Racial Anglo-Saxonism*, Cambridge: Harvard University Press, 2002, p. 77.

14 LeRoi Jones, 'The Changing Same (R&B and New Black Music)', in Jones, *Black Music*, New York: William Morrow & Co., 1967, pp. 180-211.

STATE TALK, STATE SILENCE: WORK AND 'VIOLENCE' IN THE UK

JOE SIM AND STEVE TOMBS

If there is one principle that the modern state is organised around, it is its ability to resort to violence. As Walter Benjamin pointed out, not only are the boundaries of the legitimacy of violence established by law, but the power and authority of the state – indeed law itself – is necessarily and intimately bound to violence: 'Lawmaking is powermaking and to that extent, an immediate manifestation of violence'.[1]

That said, even in states of exception such as the contemporary 'war on terror', the process of hegemony-building shows clearly the existence of a complex dialectical relationship between consent and coercion. Thus, we would argue that to understand the *violence* of the modern state, we need first to reject any crude dichotomy between force and consent – for the articulation of state power always implies an intimate inter-relation in which both are inseparable. Thus, following Gramsci, Poulantzas, Hall et al., and others, a critical analysis of the state should move beyond narrowly focusing on the repressive apparatuses of state power, crucial though these are, to the ideological apparatuses of the state. This entails a series of analytical tasks, one of which is the extent to which the state talks, or remains silent on, apparently related social issues around violence. This is the focus of this essay.

In their cultural history of the British state, Philip Corrigan and Derek Sayer noted that '"the State" never stops talking'.[2] In making this important point about 'state talk', Corrigan and Sayer recognised that the power of the state in capitalist societies extended beyond its material role in confronting internal problem populations and external enemies, to the cultural and symbolic position occupied, and the interventions made, by the different institutions in civil society. They further noted that the state is involved in:

> ...*moral regulation*: a project of normalizing, rendering natural, taken for granted, in a word 'obvious', what are in fact ontological

> and epistemological premises of a particular and historical form of social order. Moral regulation is coextensive with state formation, and state forms are always animated and legitimated by a particular moral ethos.[3]

These insights provide a frame for the two issues around which this essay is organised. Each is concerned with violence, but violence of two quite different kinds. First, there is violence used *against* those who maintain state power, such as police and prison officers, and how this violence is socially and ideologically constructed as an affront to the state itself, and by extension, to a civilised social order. Second, there is the violence committed against workers in the routine processes of production – albeit denied the label of 'violence', and virtually legitimated by the state bodies which formally exist to prevent it.

This essay, therefore, presents two quite different stories of violent crime in contemporary Britain. One is a critical analysis of the loudly proclaimed dangers facing state servants, through a focus on what has been termed 'the victimised state'.[4] A second, quite different, tale is the silence associated with the mundane violence associated with working for a living, a form of violence for which there is, virtually, state-institutionalised impunity. While each is significant for understanding the ways in which contemporary state power operates, it is in their dialectical relationship that we find their real import: the pincer-like effects of their differing definitions is an important key to understanding what *counts* as violence in a neo-liberal social order – and, conversely, what does *not* count as violence within this social order.

THE 'VICTIMISED STATE'

The social construction of state servants as perennial victims of violence has become normalised to the point where it is now taken for granted by the majority of academics, politicians, media experts, policy makers and the public. This deeply-embedded, common-sense view of the everyday dangers faced by the police (and by other state servants such as prison officers) is immensely important for understanding the *ideological* role that violence plays in the reproduction of a deeply divided social order. This point becomes even more significant when considering the deaths of state servants. These events have a social and symbolic significance that extends far beyond the demise of the individual or individuals concerned. When police officers are killed on duty, as happened in England at Shepherds Bush in 1966, in Blackpool in 1971, in inner London in 1985 and in Manchester in 2003, these killings come to represent 'a potent symbol of lawlessness'[5] in a society that is alleged to be degraded and scarred by the hostility of the deviant to authority and order.

Thus, the undisputed claim to moral authority, and the symbolic position that police (and prison) officers command, has allowed their organisational representatives in the Police Federation to construct a clear and precise definition of the 'truth' about the normalised nature of violence and the risks and dangers faced by its members in their everyday working lives. The ideological power of this 'truth', which reproduces and reinforces a broader populist discourse concerning the difficult job that state servants do, is such that alternative definitions of social reality remain subjugated and muted. Indeed, those who attempt to articulate alternative definitions that challenge the nature and extent of violence experienced by state servants are, as has been noted elsewhere, 'insidiously position[ed] as heartless (they don't care about the officer who is victimised) and naïve (they don't live in the 'real' world)'.[6]

What are the theoretical and political implications of thinking about violence committed *against* state servants? There are five we wish to highlight here, which taken together can contribute to a fuller and, crucially, more critical understanding of the operationalisation of violence as a powerful ideological mechanism for reinforcing an inequitable and inevitably unjust social order.

First, the few state servants who die in violent circumstances become, for the many who follow their lives and deaths in the mass media, the embodiment of a set of mystical, eternal values to which the society should aspire. Thomas Mathiesen's brilliant insight into the panoptic *and* synoptic nature of contemporary power relationships is useful here. As he notes, contemporary forms of social control are not only built on a deeply embedded system of surveillance where the few survey the lives of the many but, in addition, as Mathiesen puts it, 'we have seen the development of a unique and enormously extensive system enabling *the many to see and contemplate the few...*'.[7] Thus the lives and deaths of individual state servants – the few – become a focus for the grief and outrage of the many. At the same time, the distorting and dislocating social divisions which remain integral to contemporary capitalist social relationships, and which underpin and give meaning to the violent activities of other individuals, organisations, corporations and states, are shunted to the ideological and political periphery as society expiates its guilt through focusing on the lone deviant individual who carried out what is invariably portrayed as an act of wanton barbarity. This solitary individual is situated at the centre of the gaze of the many by mass media whose capacity for engaging in the 'dramatisation of "evil"' has, if anything, intensified since Frank Tannenbaum coined the term over sixty years ago.[8]

Second, the 'ideological mystification'[9] surrounding violence against state servants operates through a dialectical process which is sustained by exaggerating the numbers who are assaulted and murdered, and overdramatising the seriousness of the violence against them. This process has allowed powerful moral entrepreneurs such as the Police Federation and the Prison Officers' Association to all but monopolise the debate about the violence and dangers faced by their members. This view of the matter, consecrated and blessed by the vast majority of the mass media and political spokespersons, has also been integral to the construction of a common-sense, populist discourse concerning what state servants do, and what is done to them on a daily basis by the dangerous.

However, a critical deconstruction of official discourse reveals a very different picture.[10] For example, between 1994 and 1998, 28 police officers died on duty. Twenty-one of these deaths, 75 per cent of the total, were due to the involvement of officers in road traffic accidents. Four officers were murdered. This represented 14 per cent of the total. The remaining three, 11 per cent of the total, died after, respectively, collapsing at work, having a heart attack while baton training, and being involved in a helicopter crash.[11] Furthermore, the claim that being a police officer generates a degree of stress which in turn accounts for the force's high rates of sickness is also more problematic than the advocates of the victimised state thesis recognise. As Mathew Norman has pointed out, the sick rate may be affected by a police culture which has had little to fear in terms of being held to account democratically, due to a 'protection racket' which has been 'slavishly' operated between the Police Federation and successive governments of both major parties.[12]

Third, violence committed *by* state servants is also mystified ideologically through complex processes involving *individualisation* and *circumspection*. This inevitably leads to a focus on the few 'bad apples' who are supposedly responsible for illegitimate violence by state officials, while simultaneously generating and constructing a highly restricted definition of the number, nature and extent of the physical and psychological violations committed against prisoners, who are, theoretically, in the care of the state. This construction distracts attention away from the institutionalisation of physical violence within the state, and also from 'something about which people seldom talk: namely, the *mechanisms of fear*',[13] both of which can be mobilised inside and outside places of detention such as police stations (and prisons), and on the streets, to discipline, regulate, oppress and even, in a number of cases, destroy those at the centre of the state's punitive gaze. In the four decades up to 2006, there were over 1,000 deaths in police custody. No officers have ever been convicted of causing any of these deaths.[14] Furthermore, between 1992 and 2005, 30 people were shot dead by the police. Again, there have been no convictions.[15] Thus, the *systemic* nature of the state's capacity for violence, and its institutionalisation, as well as the tacit and overt support for its use at all levels by its servants, is rarely if ever considered. This, in turn, is reinforced by a process of state and media-led *defamation* of those at the sharp, and often degrading, end of the state's interventions. As Simon Hattenstone notes, '"police sources" routinely vilify victims and excuse police officers'.[16]

Fourth, thinking critically about violence against state servants also raises a number of important issues concerning the concept of risk and how it has been theorised in contemporary criminology. Risk, and its impact on criminal justice policy, has dominated many of the recent debates in criminology, particularly with respect to the shift towards the 'new penology' and the social construction of the '*responsible' subject*.[17] It has also had a profound impact on the ideologies and practices of many criminal justice and mental health professionals.[18] However, there are serious conceptual and methodological problems in uncritically applying risk to the field of mental health and crime, particularly with respect to the issue of predictability.[19] Furthermore, a more comprehensive definition of what the concept means needs to be developed if it is to have any critical, analytical viability. In terms of academics, (and so-called 'practitioners'), this would involve shifting their professional gaze away from an overwhelming concern with, and concentration on, the behaviour of the powerless and the risks they pose, to considering the risks posed by the state to its citizens, offenders or otherwise. For example, can the concept of 'risk', as it is currently theoretically constituted, help to explain data from the Independent Police Complaints Commission which indicated that in 2004/05, 106 people died 'during or following police contact'? These included 3 fatal shootings, 36 in or following police custody, 23 during or following other police contact and 44 due to road traffic fatalities involving the police.[20] In the latter category, an investigation by the *Daily Express* (a newspaper not known for its sympathy towards liberal or radical causes) indicated that in 2005, thirty people were being killed each year in road accidents involving the police and that officers were involved in 'more than 55 crashes a day, but only a quarter of these happen when they are responding to an emergency'.[21]

Furthermore, developing a critical conceptualisation of 'risk' would also mean considering how the powerful have utilised and continue to utilise their self-referential propensity for being 'at risk' to justify political and policy clamp-downs. One effect of this analysis would be to belatedly turn the gaze of academics and practitioners upwards towards the powerful, and to identify how the discourse of the risks of violence faced by state servants has always been central to the legitimisation of their power and the implementation of authoritarian policies by the state.

Finally, the on-going construction of state servants as perennial victims reflects a more general contemporary political development which is tied in with the role of the *respectable victim* in the intensification of reactionary criminal justice and social policies. In the UK, this has been reinforced by the interventions of groups such as the Victims of Crime Trust and Protecting the Protectors (the protectors in this case being the police). These organisations are not only unconditionally supported by the main political parties but also have become a ubiquitous presence in the mass media. As in the US, the ideological cement for this support is the 'spectre of the predator criminal', which is the 'ever-present image'.[22] It is an image that is refined, articulated and disseminated by these pressure groups via the mass media, and, in a classic spiral of amplification, is reflected back to them by an increasingly fearful public whose idealisation of the past, and trepidation about the future, legitimates a further clamp-down in the present.

We now turn to another equally important issue which also has serious theoretical and political implications for thinking about violence and how it has been conceptualised: the question of violence related to the workplace.

VIOLENCE AT WORK

Despite the fact that most deaths and injuries caused by working in the UK result from infractions of the criminal law – the *Health and Safety at Work Act* (HASAW Act, 1974) being the principal criminal statute that applies here – such illegal killings of, and injuries to, workers remain unacknowledged as 'crimes', and are thus subject to gross under-enforcement. Indeed, thanks to the social-scientific commitment to defining violence both in terms of intention and as inter-personal – *neither of which is intrinsic to constituting violence* – such deaths and injuries are rarely even considered through the lens of violence.[23] Yet this type of organisational violence is much more widespread than is understood, and remains widely under-reported. Thus in the UK, for example, the most conservative estimates of occupational fatalities to workers typically stand at around 250 a year. Yet if we add to this 'headline' figure other official data on occupational deaths – notably, deaths of members of the public, and in particular road deaths to workers and members of the public resulting from incidents involving 'at work' vehicles – this increases the total of occupational deaths in 2006/07 from 241 to around 1,500. In other words, to obtain a more accurate figure of officially recorded occupational fatalities, we need to apply a multiplier of six or seven to HSE (Health and Safety Executive's) headline figure.

It is worth emphasising that the majority of these deaths result from crimes by employers – though they are rarely processed as such. Thus we know, through HSE's own research, that in a clear majority of workplace fatalities – in at least two out of three – there is *prima facie* evidence of violations of duties placed upon employers by the HASAW Act, and thus at the very least a criminal case to answer.[24] This general conclusion – based upon evidence indicating attribution of responsibility for the fatalities in question – also holds in the case of fatal injuries involving 'at work' vehicles, these being numerically the most significant omission from HSE's headline figure, and the site of most work-related deaths to workers and members of the public.[25] Here, the key factors in such fatalities include employers' failure to consider safer, alternative means of transport or indeed routes, the setting of unsafe schedules, journey times and distances, failures to maintain vehicles adequately, failures to invest in vehicles with additional safety features, and the lack of specialised training on offer for drivers.[26]

Non-fatal *injuries* data is subject to even greater levels of non-reporting: HSE's most recent study indicated that in only 32 per cent of cases involving employees, and only 13 per cent of cases involving the self-employed, who had suffered a reportable injury resulting in a hospital visit, had the injury, in fact, been reported.[27] Typically, according to official records, 30,000 major injuries are sustained by workers and 15,000 by members of the public each year in the UK (but not including injuries from accidents involving commercial or industrial vehicles).[28] Around 120,000 'over-three day' injuries to workers are typically recorded in any given year. Thus, occupational injury is far from an uncommon experience.[29] To gain an accurate estimate of the actual scale of injuries sustained would require multiplying the HSE's official figures by six or seven times.

Despite the problems involved in working with the available death and injury data, they do at least allow us to draw comparisons, no matter how crude, between violent crime recorded by the Home Office on the one hand, and occupational deaths and injuries on the other.

First, in terms of deaths, it is possible to compare the numbers of people killed at work with those recorded by the Home Office as homicides. This allows us to make several useful, if only indicative, observations. Initially it appears that one is twice as likely to be a victim of homicide in England and Wales than to die as a result of an acute, work-related incident. However, against this we need to bear in mind that the work-related fatality data here are for 'workers' only, and so capture only somewhere between one-sixth to one-seventh of occupational fatalities. On this basis, being a victim of a work-related fatality looks many times more likely than being a victim of homicide.

A similar, again simple but equally instructive, comparison, can be made in terms of occupational injuries. According to the 2006/07 British Crime Survey (BCS), there were a total of 2,471,000 violent offences in England and Wales, and 3.6 per cent of people experienced a violent incident.[30] Of these, 49 per cent resulted in no injury to the victim, about one in ten (12 per cent) required medical attention, and one in 50 (2 per cent) resulted in a hospital stay.[31] In absolute terms, this equates to some 49,420 BCS recorded incidents of violence resulting in a hospital stay. Now, we cannot disaggregate from HSE injury data those which similarly require a hospital stay. But we do know that the kinds of injures defined under the Reporting of Injuries, Diseases and Dangerous Occurrences Regulations (RIDDOR) as 'major'[32] are serious enough to warrant at least hospital treatment, while the definition of an injury to a member of the public is one that requires the injured person going straight to hospital. Thus, we can reasonably set against BCS data on violence resulting in a hospital stay HSE data for major injures to workers and injuries to the public which, for 2006/07, stand at 29,450 and 17,483 such injuries respectively. Combining these two figures produces a total – 46,933 – which is virtually the same as the figure for BCS recorded violence requiring a hospital stay. And this is not even to begin to estimate the numbers of over-three-day injuries – 114,222 in 2006/07 – which resulted in hospitalisation (nor, of course, to account for the high levels of under-reporting).

This comparison can also be expressed in percentage terms: again using data for 2006-2007, we find the percentage of workers experiencing a major injury stands at just under 0.1 per cent (0.097 per cent, or 97.1 in 100,000); this can be compared with the 0.072 per cent of BCS respondents (the 2 per cent of the 3.6 per cent who experienced violence) resulting in a hospital stay. Although such comparisons can only be broadly indicative, they do lead us to an inescapable conclusion, namely that work is more likely to be a source of violence in Britain than the conventional crimes recorded by the Home Office.

Yet 'safety crimes' are constructed as something to be acted on and counted, not by police forces, nor by the Home Office, but by regulatory agencies, and this crucially reinforces the idea that this category of crime, which involve violence towards, and the deaths of, many workers (and desperate impacts on their families) are not 'real' crimes. This institutional segregation of safety crimes by the state has profound implications for how we think about them and how we think about violence, so that we also need to examine what those agencies charged with responding to such offences actually *do*.

As we have already seen, processes of reporting and recording filter out the majority of deaths and injuries from the official figures. A second filter is apparent when there is a decision whether or not to investigate; almost 9 out of 10 major injuries that are reported to HSE are never investigated. A third filter is apparent when decisions are made whether or not to institute a particular type of enforcement action. When safety inspectors come across occurrences that breach the law *and* they decide to act on those breaches, prosecution is used much less readily than other types of enforcement action: the ratio of administrative (improvement and prohibition) notices to prosecutions is roughly 10:1.[33] And of the injuries that do get investigated, only 11 per cent lead to prosecutions.[34] In short, most safety crimes – including many of the most serious crimes – remain either undetected, or, if they are detected, are filtered out of the criminal justice system. And this also indicates that the separate treatment of safety crimes is rooted in the politics and practices of criminal justice rather than some intrinsic quality of such crimes. The 'filtering' processes can therefore only be fully understood within their political context. There are two tendencies within the current political context that are of particular importance in decriminalising safety crimes.

First, there has been the consistent erosion of HSE staffing resources which began under neo-liberal Conservative administrations and then, after a brief upturn in funding, became much more marked under the second Blair government from 2001 onwards. On 1 April 2002 there were 4,282 staff in post and on 1 April 2006 there were 3,991. Of those, 1,543 were deployed as frontline inspectors, compared with 1,625 on 1 April 2002. The steady erosion of HSE resources, from a low base, has certainly had an impact on the morale of the organisation and its confidence to lobby government for the resources it needs; HSE has, in recent years, refrained from making budgetary demands upon government.[35] It is difficult to imagine any police officer in any police force area in the country failing to ask for more officers and a larger budget – despite the fact that numbers of police officers are at an all-time high.

The second tendency within the political context that has influenced the decriminalisation of safety crimes is the post-1997 consolidation of the government's 'burdens on business'/anti 'red tape' agenda. New Labour established the *Better Regulation Task Force* in 1997, one of the key tasks of which has been to formalise a requirement that all proposed legislation affecting business must be accompanied by a 'Regulatory Impact Assessment' – the primary effect of which has been to pre-empt and minimise cost impacts upon business. This disciplinary process has formalised a pro-business/deregulation frame of reference for policy making across government.

Also since 1997 there has been a series of 'reviews' of regulation – always couched in terms of the need to reduce it – which reached their apogee in a new Regulatory Code,[36] published by the newly-formed Department for Business, Enterprise and Regulatory Reform. This sought to formalise existing, or set out new principles on how to handle what it calls 'the few businesses'[37] that break the law – all reducing the possibility of formal enforcement action. The document actually formalised the diminished goal of public protection when it emphasised that 'Regulators should recognize that a key element of their activity will be to allow, or even encourage, economic progress and only to intervene when there is a clear case for protection'.[38]

HSE, then, is under pressure on two fronts: first, from a real cut in resources that is clearly indicated by the reduction of staff in post; and, second, in terms of the momentum given to the 'burdens on business' agenda, and the moral undermining of HSE's remit. Unsurprisingly, then, the number of inspections has fallen, and recently very sharply: 41,496 HSE inspections in 2006/07 compared to 54,717 in 2005/06, a 24 per cent decrease. Thus in 2006/07 HSE-enforced workplaces could expect an inspection on average once every 14.5 years, compared to once every 7 years in 2001/02. Similarly, investigations are down: the proportion of major injuries investigated by HSE fell from 13 per cent in 2004/05 to 11 per cent in 2005/06.[39] Finally, the reduction in resources has affected levels of prosecutions, given that these are extremely resource-intensive, and so have always been historically few in absolute terms. By 2005/06, 840 convictions were secured by HSE (in 1,056 cases taken) – about half the figure of 1,616 convictions secured in 1999/2000 (in 2,115 cases).[40]

What is perhaps most remarkable about these processes is how they attract little or no popular, political, or academic attention; and just as remarkable here is the contrast between this deafening silence on the one hand and the ongoing moral panic that characterises social responses to most conventional violent crime on the other.[41] The latter attract censure, controversy, political dispute and priority, and, of course, criminal justice energy and resources built on coercive authoritarian policies. The former remain on the political margins, a muted but grim reminder of the dangers faced by workers, and the often violent impact on their lives engendered by contemporary capitalist labour processes.

VIOLENCE, IDEOLOGY AND MORALITY

We have avoided any attempt at a direct contrast between levels of death and injury sustained by the police and other groups of workers. Suffice to say that, in terms of relative exposure to risk, the assertion that police work is a dangerous occupation is more difficult to sustain than the police and their defenders recognise. If we examine major and 'over 3-day' injuries for police officers from the rank of sergeant and below for 2006/07, we find that no police officer died in an HSE-recorded occupational fatality; there were 763 major injuries and under 3,000 over-3 day injuries; of these, 186 (major injuries) and 561 ('over 3-day') injures were the result of physical assault; and the majority of injuries were as a result of 'handling' and 'slipping or tripping' at work. In the same year, there were 77 deaths of construction workers.[42]

That said, and strongly under-scoring the analysis presented in this chapter, such comparisons tend not to be made, since attacks on state servants, notably the police, are acts defined as violence, while those on workers are cast as accidents or, at best injuries. Thus while there is considerable under-reporting and attrition with respect to official injury data, the Home Office has in recent years put a great deal of effort into recording (through self-report surveys, as part of the British Crime Survey) 'violence' at work. Crucially, this exercise excludes corporate violence, since it defines violence in terms of a specific perpetrator: workplace violence incorporates 'All assaults or threats which occurred while the victim was working and were *perpetrated by members of the public*'. Further, violence from this source – as far as both the HSE and the Home Office are concerned – refers to 'any incident in which an individual suffers verbal abuse, physical abuse or threats in circumstances relating to their work'.[43] Once deaths and injuries to workers as a result of the routine processes of production are ruled out, and violence to workers is seen as committed only by people external to their work organisations – members of 'the public' who indulge in violent acts or threats to them – then the problem of violence can be officially defined as limited to a subset of occupations among which, not surprisingly, policing is the most vulnerable.[44]

There is a sense, however, in which such empirical comparisons are not as relevant as thinking about the state's response to, and representation of, violence against different groups of workers. This much is clear if we ask ourselves questions such as the following:

- Can we imagine the death of a police officer *not* being reported across a range of national media – while workers' deaths rarely rate more than a passing mention, if any, in local media?

- Can we imagine a police officer dying and this being immediately represented as an 'accident', which is the social, political and legal default position vis-à-vis occupational worker deaths?

- Can we conceive of a police officer dying on duty, or losing a limb or sight, and this not being investigated – though we know that only a small subset of occupational fatalities, and only about one-tenth of major injuries, are investigated?

- Can we imagine that with evidence sufficient to mount a prosecution following the death of a police officer, a prosecution would not proceed on the grounds that the better enforcement response is not to punish past wrongdoing but to find an underlying remedy and prevent re-occurrence?[45]

- Can we imagine that in the event of a successful prosecution being undertaken in such a case, the sanction applied to the perpetrator would be a fine (the most recent data on fines following successful prosecution show that the average fine for an occupational fatality in the UK is £29,867).[46]

The murder of a state servant, particularly a police officer, represents a profound, symbolic moment in the culture and politics of a society, triggering an outpouring of popular sentiment and political rage. Such deaths signify that the social body is on the brink of moral collapse and is therefore in need of an increased injection of law and order to revive it and inoculate it from the further spread of those diseased degenerates who threaten its healthy equilibrium. The fabric of the society has been so torn and desecrated by these deaths that it can only be repaired (and the death revenged) by weaving the thread of social control ever tighter through the sharp needle of authoritarianism. 'State talk', and the moral populism generated by this 'talk', thus plays a crucial discursive role in this repressive process through the mobilisation of a highly restricted definition of 'risk' that restricts it to the dangers confronting the consecrated guardians of the social order. Worker deaths, by contrast, are more or less invisible. Unless they arise from some multi-fatality incident, they invariably attract no media or political attention, and are unlikely even to lead to criminal justice processes. They are the silent, routine costs – literally, mere occupational hazards – of a certain set of social relations in a society in which 'risk' and 'entrepreneurialism' are increasingly validated, with very different distributions, not least comprehensible in class terms, of the costs and benefits of those activities. This is state-sanctioned violence.

However, the argument of this essay also suggests that critical social scientists need to think differently in order to develop a more nuanced approach to the question of state power and social control, not least in terms of the representations and functions of dominant definitions of violence. In particular, they need to reflect on the *moral* underpinnings of state interventions and the role that regressive visions of morality play in defining and redefining the nature of these interventions. In other words, when a police or prison officer is murdered, the plaintive iconography that is mobilised – these sanctified, incorruptible guardians of social order – justifies a further intensification of the state's clamp-down. This is a profoundly moral process as these deaths resonate with broader, hegemonic visions of terminal social breakdown which themselves are underpinned by a deep psychic anxiety about the nature and direction of the social order. In turn, they play a central discursive role in the reconfiguration of that order onto a more authoritarian terrain. Building a consensus around the essential benevolence of state institutions and their servants – particularly police and prison officers – while simultaneously socially constructing these same servants as living in perpetual danger from the degenerate and the desperate, has been central to this process.

This moral element of hegemony-building is also evident in the impunity with which businesses operate. For one of the key consequences of neo-liberalism has been that business has literally been granted a moral status, as intrinsic to the well-being and health of societies, and that it uses this as leverage, either explicitly or as an implicit resource, to address or pre-empt issues of stricter external control of its activities. Most crudely, then, the 'moral capital' attached to business activity has increased dramatically during the last three decades. Private enterprise, entrepreneurship, the pursuit of wealth, and the 'market' have all become valorised as ends in themselves. Just as the emergence of industrial capitalism was accompanied by a process in which paid work came to be invested with a moral meaning, somehow producing better people as a result of their engagement in it, now the institutions which organise and control work activity are increasingly represented as key moral agents. This elevation of private economic activity to the status of an intrinsically worthy end in itself coheres with a sustained attack on state, public and in particular regulatory activity, an attack cast in terms of the freeing of enterprise and the valorisation of risk, and helps make partial sense of the increasingly supine behaviour of governments in relation to capital.

Ultimately, for us, social science must be intimately related to social justice, and this means social scientists being aligned with social movements and recognising that we have some contribution to make to their struggles.[17] Part of this contribution is to engage in empirical and theoretical work which challenges orthodoxy, assumption or mystification – in order to contest the claim, for example, that workers are less innocent victims, undeserving of criminological attention, since they exchange their labour power (and thus exposure to risk) for a wage, or that the most dangerous occupations (exposed to 'real' violence) are those of state servants such as the police, prison officers and so on,[48] as opposed to the most vulnerable sections of the labour force. Further, this work must be, as Carlen says, part of an 'unfashionable crusade to bring "morals" back into public discourse'.[49] This would involve talking about social justice and democratic accountability, terms which correspond with Gramsci's notion of 'good sense' as opposed to state-defined discourses which engender a 'common sense' understanding of what violence means and how it should be responded to, in a society that remains scarred by grotesque levels of inequality and lacerated by social divisions which state institutions ultimately reinforce and reproduce.

NOTES

This chapter has benefited from the insights of Dave Whyte and Roy Coleman, to whom we record our thanks.

1 Walter Benjamin, 'Critique of Violence', in P. Demtz, ed., *Reflections: Essays, Aphorisms, Autobiographical Writings* (translated by Edmund Jephcott), New York: Schocken Books, 1921/1972, p. 295.
2 Philip Corrigan and Derek Sayer, *The Great Arch*, Oxford: Blackwell, 1985, p. 3.
3 Ibid., p. 4.
4 Joe Sim, 'The Victimised State', *Criminal Justice Matters,* 42, 2000/2001, p. 26.
5 Steve Chibnall, *Law and Order News*, London: Tavistock, 1977, p. 54.
6 Sim, 'The Victimised State', p. 26.
7 Thomas Mathiesen, 'The Viewer Society: Michel Foucault's "Panopticon" Revisited', *Theoretical Criminology*, 1(2), 1997, p. 219, emphasis in the original.
8 J. Robert Lilly, Francis T. Cullen and Richard A. Ball, eds., *Criminological Theory*, Newbury Park: Sage, 1989, p. 122.
9 Steven Box, *Power, Crime and Mystification*, London: Tavistock, 1983.
10 There are methodological issues here with respect to comparing different time-spans but the general point remains valid.

11 Personal communication to Joe Sim from Her Majesty's Inspector of Constabulary, 27 July 2000.

12 Matthew Norman, 'The Police and their Protection Racket', *The Independent*, 20 January 2006, p. 33.

13 Nicos Poulantzas, *State, Power, Socialism*, London: Verso, 1978, p. 83.

14 Norman, 'The Police and their Protection Racket', p. 33.

15 *The Independent*, 21 October 2005.

16 Simon Hattenstone, 'We cannot take them at their word', *The Guardian*, 18 August 2005, p. 18.

17 Malcolm Feeley and Jonathan Simon, 'The New Penology: Notes on the Emerging Strategy of Corrections and its Implications', *Criminology*, 30(4), 1992, pp. 449-74.

18 Nicola Gray, J. Laing and L. Noaks, 'Risk, the Professional, the Individual, Society and the Law', in Nicola Gray, Judith Laing, and Lesley Noakes, eds., *Criminal Justice, Mental Health and the Politics of Risk*, London: Cavendish, 2002.

19 Anthony Madden, 'Risk Management in the Real World' in Gray et al., eds., *Criminal Justice, Mental Health and the Politics of Risk*.

20 Rebecca Teers and Tom Bucke, *Deaths During or Following Police Contact: Statistics for England and Wales 2004/05*, London: Impendent Police Complaints Commission, 2005, p. 6.

21 *Daily Express*, 27 January 2005.

22 Ray Surette, 'News from Nowhere, Policy to Follow: Media and the Social Construction of "Three Strikes and You're Out"', in David Shichor and Dale Sechrest, eds., *Three Strikes and You're Out: Vengeance as Public Policy*, Thousand Oaks: Sage, 1996, p. 185.

23 Steve Tombs, '"Violence", Safety Crimes and Criminology', *British Journal of Criminology*, 47(4), 2007, pp. 531-50.

24 Steve Tombs, 'Health and Safety Crimes: (In)visibility and the Problems of "Knowing"', in Pamela Davies, Peter Francis, and Victor Jupp, eds., *Invisible Crimes: their Victims and their Regulation*, London: Macmillan, 1999, pp. 80-2.

25 Health and Safety Executive/Department for Transport, *Driving at Work. Managing Work-Related Road Safety. INDG382*, Sudbury: HSE Books, 2003.

26 Royal Society for the Prevention of Accidents, *Managing Occupational Road Risk*, Birmingham: RoSPA, 1998; see also Denis Campbell, 'Working Drivers "Responsible for 1,000 Road Deaths a Year"', *Observer*, 13 November 2005.

27 John Davies, Graham Kemp and Simon Frostick, *An Investigation of Reporting of Workplace Accidents under RIDDOR using the Merseyside Accident Information Model. RR528 Research Report*, London: HMSO, 2007.

28 Major injuries include fractures, other than to fingers, thumbs and toes; amputations; dislocations of the shoulder, hip, knee or spine; loss of sight (temporary or permanent); chemical or hot metal burn or any penetrating injury to the eye; injury resulting from an electric shock or electrical burn; injury leading to hypothermia or heat-induced illness requiring resuscitation or requiring admittance to hospital for more than 24 hours; and unconsciousness, via a series of specified causes. The vast majority of reported injuries to members of the public occur in the service sector, across education, shops, leisure and catering establishments, and healthcare; about half are injuries sustained as a result of 'slips' and 'trips', usually as a result of poor basic 'housekeeping'.

29 An over-3-day injury is one which is not 'major', but results in the injured person being away from work or unable to do their full range of normal duties for more than three days.

30 A self-report survey conducted by the Home Office, and now recognised as the source of the most reliable crime data in the UK.

31 Krista Jansson, David Povey and Peter Kaiza, 'Violent and Sexual Crime', in S. Nicholas, C. Kershaw and A. Walker, eds., *Crime in England and Wales 2006/07*, London: Home Office, 2007, pp. 49-72.

32 See note 28.

33 See Steve Tombs and Dave Whyte, *A Crisis of Enforcement: The Decriminalisation of Death and Injury at Work*, London: Harm and Society Foundation, 2008.

34 Unison/Centre for Corporate Accountability, *Safety Last? The Under-Enforcement of Health and Safety Law. Full Report*, London: Unison/ Centre for Corporate Accountability, 2002.

35 Tombs and Whyte, *A Crisis of Enforcement.*

36 'Regulator's Compliance Code' available at http://bre.berr.gov.uk.

37 Ibid., para. 8.

38 Ibid., para. 3.

39 'Just who does HSE Protect?', *Hazards*, 100, October-December, 2007, available at http://www.hazards.org.

40 http://www.hse.gov.uk/statistics/enforce/index-ld.htm#table1.

41 But not all – witness, for example, sexual and spousal violence (see the essay in this volume by Lynne Segal).

42 Internal data supplied by HSE Statistics Branch, written communication, 01/04/08.

43 Tracey Budd, *Violence at Work. Findings from the British Crime Survey*, London: Home Office/Health and Safety Executive, 1999, p. 2.

44 Peter Waddington, Doug Badger and Ray Bull, *The Violent Workplace*, Cullompton: Willan, 2006, p. 11.

45 These points are discussed more fully in Steve Tombs and Dave Whyte, *Safety Crimes*, Cullompton: Willan, 2007.

46 Health and Safety Executive, *Offences and Penalties 2004/2005*, available at http://www.hse.gov.uk.

47 Steve Tombs. and Dave Whyte, 'Researching the Crimes of the Powerful: Establishing some Rules of Engagement', in S. Tombs and D. Whyte, eds., *Unmasking the Crimes of the Powerful: Scrutinising States and Corporations*, New York: Peter Lang, 2003, pp. 261-72.

48 Joe Sim, 'The Victimised State and the Mystification of Social Harm', in Paddy Hillyard, Christina Pantazis, Steve Tombs and Dave Gordon, eds., *Beyond Criminology*, London: Pluto, 2004.

49 Pat Carlen, 'In Praise of Critical Criminology', *Outlines: Critical Social Studies*, 7(2), 2005, p. 88.

VIOLENCE'S VICTIMS: THE GENDER LANDSCAPE

LYNNE SEGAL

Twenty years ago, completing a book on changing patterns of masculinity, I welcomed the growing evidence of diversity in men's lives and their relations with women and children, while remaining aware of the resilience of so many aspects of gender hierarchy, both symbolically and socially.[1] Surveying the gender landscape today, one sees that the challenge to men's grip on power and privilege relative to women has continued, if haphazardly, with global capital itself sometimes seeming to support some of women's moves against traditional patriarchal precedents, although in narrowly defined ways that never disrupt the efficient workings of capital. Certainly, any shrinking of old gender hierarchies remains distinctly uneven, but women in the West are reaching higher levels in the labour market, even though legislation promoting equality between the sexes has failed to prevent women's average hourly wages still lagging well behind those of men, even in full-time work, while the gap is vastly greater in most sectors of part-time work.[2] Moreover, this level of economic progress for women in the richer western countries is accompanied by disturbing patterns in women's lives globally, with impoverished armies of women providing domestic or other underpaid, unprotected forms of personal service in countries far from their homes and families.[3] Above all, whatever may be agreed regarding women's progress on the bumpy road towards greater gender equality, many argue that any optimism vanishes once we turn our attention to progress in eradicating men's violence against women. This is surprising, one might think, when men's violence quickly became an issue of overriding importance to second-wave feminists whose hard-fought campaigns eventually succeeded in making it a key concern on social policy agendas ever since.[4]

CONFRONTING DOMESTIC VIOLENCE AND ABUSE

As I write, in February 2008, I notice that the UN Secretary-General Ban Ki-moon has just opened the 52nd session of the Commission on the Status of Women by launching yet another campaign to end violence against women, announcing that world-wide: 'At least one out of every three women is likely to be beaten, coerced into sex or otherwise abused in her life-time'.[5] Globally, levels of men's violence against women have not declined. Moreover, it was also over this issue of gender and violence that my own earlier work was most strongly criticised when first published, for its insistence on the importance of making an analytic distinction between masculinity and violence.[6] 'Masculinity', that wobbly, hybrid, historically contingent identity signifying manhood, I argued, did not have any necessary ties with violence. Nor, conversely, were acts of violence necessarily the deeds of men, performed to shore up or defend some sense of masculinity. Violence needed a more complex analysis. Masculinity too.[7] I would still suggest that, theoretically, these arguments are correct, although I suspect they remain contentious, when the gendered nature of violence, with men its prime perpetrators, has seemed to strengthen rather than decline in the 21st century. Strengthened the link may be, yet in my view analysing the connection between gender, victims and violence remains less straightforward than ever.

There are many ways in which the last few decades might be thought to have confirmed the importance of complicating the gendered analysis of violence. The development of Men's Studies has continuously highlighted the destructive effects of men's violence against women and children, adamant that men must join the struggle to eradicate it. Of course, we have long since learned that the low levels of reporting make statistics on violence against women unreliable.[8] Nevertheless, despite depressing global patterns (to which I'll return), where there have been serious efforts to tackle the problem evidence suggests some decline in patterns of domestic violence. For instance, following a ten-year government sponsored attempt to eradicate it in Australia, the number of recorded domestic assaults against women fell from 7.1 per cent of women reporting assaults in 1996 to 5.8 per cent in 2005. Again, where resources have been put into dealing with the problem, similar drops in its reported incidence have been recorded in the USA and Canada.[9] With men and women working together to end violence in the home, it remains important to insist that there is nothing inevitable about it. Indeed, such acknowledgement is all the more necessary when new forms of gender fundamentalism are regularly promoted that work to undermine any such hopes. We have seen this most forcefully in the popular reception attending evolutionary psychology, suggesting that men's proclivities to violence are biologically programmed, based on reproductive imperatives.

The American popular science writer, Robert Wright, for instance, suggests that feminism must falter from its own 'doctrinal absurdities', challenging its supporters to face up to the evolutionary basis for 'the "natural" male impulse to control female sexuality': 'Human males are by nature oppressive, possessive, flesh-obsessed pigs', he charmingly asserts.[10] Wright's book, *The Moral Animal: Why We Are the Way We Are*, was a best-seller for many years in the 1990s.[11] Inspiring such views, the psychologists Martin Daly and Margo Wilson are two leading psychologists using evolutionary theory to account for homicide and male violence in the USA. They argue, for instance, that evolutionary psychology can explain why husbands are far more likely to murder their wives than their biological children (because of the lack of genetic closeness – the corollary of their 'kin selection' hypothesis), and also why a child is much more likely to be murdered, or physically abused, by a step-parent than a child living with two biological parents.[12] What is typical about such bizarre explanations is that what their theory fails to explain so greatly exceeds what it claims to explain: not just the overwhelming number of cases of adoption that do not result in child abuse, but the immense discrepancies in spousal homicide and violence rates between poorer and richer cities, even within the USA. Moreover, it is now well known that midwives in both the USA and Britain have been reporting for many years that violence against women often *begins* when that woman is pregnant with a man's baby; the latest figures reported in the UK estimate this to be true for one-third of women who are attacked.[13] If one must take seriously these psychologists' frequent boast of the 'evolutionary rigour' on display in their explanations of male aggression (in line with competitive reproductive fitness), then one has to point out to them that it is precisely when they are pregnant to their live-in partners that 'females' cannot be impregnated by rival males. This is the time when they most fully 'obey' the so-called 'Darwinian' rules for 'kin-selection': when they are carrying a child with 50 per cent of the aggressor's genes.[14]

WOMEN'S VIOLENCE

Interestingly, however, in line with what many feminists have seen as a backlash against their calls for more resources to combat men's violence, Wilson and Daly have also stressed that, at least in the USA, 'women kill their husbands almost as often as the reverse', with 75 women killing their husbands, to every 100 husbands who kill their wives.[15] Here again these two evolutionary psychologists are swimming with, and helping to swell, a popular tide, joining over 200 pieces of research over the last few decades concluding that 'women are as physically aggressive, or more aggressive, than men in their relationships with their spouses or male partners'.[16] In my book *Slow Motion* I thought it was important to recognise that women can be the initiators of physical violence. This acknowledgement was unpopular with most feminists working against men's violence who, at the time, collected their data in ways that definitively excluded women's violence in intimate relationships and who, even now, have tended to mention it only in passing, or in other ways to treat it as insignificant. One of the very few feminist scholars whose important historical research I could draw on was that of the socialist feminist Linda Gordon. In *Heroes of Their Own Lives* (1988) she also thought it important to note that, in certain circumstances, women were quite as likely as men to use physical violence against partners or children, although with less injurious effects. In another move unpopular with many feminists working on violence (often more identified with radical feminist perspectives), Gordon also stressed that poverty and other forms of material deprivation and cultural dislocation were associated with, though not on their own responsible for, patterns of domestic violence.[17]

Today it is surely clear that it was right to raise the issue of female violence when tackling the more destructive outcomes of men's violence. But how then do we confront those who, just as feminists feared, have used any such admission to dismiss feminists' calls for more resources for women confronting men's violence? Michael Kimmel is just one of the gender theorists currently attempting to do this, seeing the importance of acknowledging some women's involvement in intimate partner violence, while also noting the many studies indicating that significant gender differences still remain, with women far more likely to be seriously injured.[18] Richard Gelles, the very man whose research is usually cited by Men's Rights groups as first emphasising that men too can be victims of violence (and who was often attacked by feminists for saying so) presents a similar argument. Although he believes that men and women may hit one another in roughly equal numbers, this *must* be qualified by the knowledge that, women are seriously injured at more than 'seven times the rate of men':

> Thus, when we look at injuries resulting from violence involving male and female partners, it is categorically false to imply that there are the same number of 'battered' men as there are battered women. Research shows that nearly 90 percent of battering victims are women and only about ten percent are men. Movie portrayals of the vengeful, violent women notwithstanding... there are very few women who stalk male partners or kill them and then their children in a cataclysmic act of familicide. The most brutal, terrorizing and continuing pattern of harmful intimate violence is carried out primarily by men.[19]

Despite the greater visibility of women's own manifestations of violence nowadays, in both heterosexual and lesbian relationships (making feminist arguments about violence less legitimate if we ignore the issue), it is quite safe to conclude that it is still women who are overwhelmingly more likely to be seriously injured by men's anger and attempts to control them.[20]

The point is that admitting the existence of women's aggression does not in any way contradict the cultural reality that 'masculinity' is signified in terms of practices of physical strength, assertiveness and dominance over women. As gender theorists have been illustrating for decades, in different ways, appearing authoritative and powerful is what men must do if they feel in need of proving their 'manhood'; it is inculcated from infancy.[21] One doesn't have to be a fully-fledged Lacanian to notice that it comes with language itself. Despite quite significant cultural variations, it is not hard, therefore, to highlight a very particular gender dynamic triggering, and indeed often sustaining, forms of men's aggression, and the greater degrees of violence it often entails. Since 'masculinity' is supposed to confer a certain status and authority on its 'owner', men are more likely to feel entitled to maintain a sense of their manhood through controlling women, and to depend psychologically on the sense of empowerment which women's submissiveness can give them. Moreover some men have also lived in highly gender-differentiated contexts, which are often the most steeped in patterns of male violence. There are thus multiple gendered configurations, always interacting with aspects of social deprivation and complex cultural differences, which determine which boys, and which men, are most prone to violence, while themselves also being at greatest risk of being harmed by other men from their own social milieu, i.e. those furthest from achieving the everyday respect and social status that masculinity was supposed to confer on them.

It is interesting how relatively little concern there is with the way in which boys and men suffer greatly at the hands of other men. If we fail to point out the horror of this, as though men's violence is only really 'violence' if directed at women or gay men, we pass over another way of highlighting the pathologies so often associated with dominant conceptions of masculinity. As those who study the interactions of poverty, social dislocation and general stress have found, these factors do not directly explain men's violence, but they do indicate something about its likely occurrence and its most frequent victims.[22] The way in which the assertion of some sense of masculinity can, in certain times and places, become ensnared with routine practices of violence emerges even more clearly if we turn specifically to rape, and men's use of sexual coercion.

RE-ASSESSING RAPE CONTROVERSIES

Second-wave feminism emerged out of the civil rights, anti-war and sexual liberation politics of the 1960s, as women activists began to link their marginal place within movement struggles to the ever more blatant sexism of the Sixties alternative press. 'Liberate socialist eminences from their bourgeois cocks!', was the slogan unfurled at a German SDS conference in 1968, as Helke Sander and other women addressed their male comrades in the radical student movement.[23] However, all too soon the initial feminist desire to define and enjoy sexual pleasure and relationships in new ways brought the predicament of some men's sexual incontinence and coerciveness to the fore. (Men's sexual coerciveness, of course, also includes their sexual abuse of children, however, involving as it does a related but rather distinct set of controversies, I simply have not the space to cover this topic here.[24]) From the beginning, then, feminists were forced to tackle the jumbled incoherence of rape myths, which so regularly dismiss and disparage the female victim. Susan Brownmiller's *Against Our Will: Men, Women, and Rape* (1975) was the most influential feminist text on rape to emerge from the 1970s.[25] However, although seen as emblematic of feminist thought, aspects of the analysis of rape offered by this New York based radical feminist activist were always controversial, even within feminist thought. Those who then identified themselves as socialist feminists usually favoured a more complex analysis of sexual violence, rejecting Brownmiller's totalising account of rape's unchanging, transhistorical nature ('nothing more or less than a conscious process of intimidation by which *all* men keep *all* women in a state of fear').[26]

It is fortunate that Joanna Bourke has recently provided a comprehensive update of the history and contemporary nature of rape, again focusing on the perpetrators of sexual violence.[27] Based on meticulous research on data from Britain, the USA and Australia, she copiously illustrates how commonplace it was till very recently to be told that no woman could be raped against her will. The earlier juridical platitude that it was impossible to 'sheath a sword into a vibrating scabbard' evolved in the twentieth century into pop-Freudian banalities that female rape victims in some way invited their own violation. Yet, complicating this picture, even as the world was warned of the multitude of women falsely crying 'Rape', the same chauvinistic imagination broadcast the ubiquitous dangers women faced from 'the lecherous brute that leaps forth out of the darkness and drags defenceless woman to her ruin'. As Bourke reveals, there were underlying continuities in these clashing mythologies, both in the location of putative innocence and that of always anticipated guilt. Some fictions revolve around encounters between the young and unsullied white virgin (always innocent) in need of protection from the black man or swarthy foreigner in our midst.[28] Other myths entail that women with little power or protection, especially servants and working-class women, can always be seen as inviting 'their own rape', and indeed be attacked for deviously accusing men of the crime. Indeed, what triggered Bourke's own recent research into the nature of rape was her anger at the continuing abysmal failure to prevent or punish its perpetrators. At least in the UK, this is a situation that has deteriorated rather than improved over the last thirty years since feminists highlighted the problem: the higher the incidence of reported rape, the lower the conviction rate, falling from one in three case of reported rape in the 1970s to one in twenty today[29] – which interestingly is not paralleled in the USA, where conviction rates have been steadily rising.[30] Nowadays, rape ideologies often arrive packaged in respectable scholarly wraps. The most provocative of these is once again that of evolutionary psychology, another pair of whose leading exponents, the Americans Randy Thornhill and Craig Palmer, offer their own 'natural' history of rape, arguing that the male of the species (from insects upwards) is born with a 'rape-adaptation' mechanism, an inherited proclivity to use violence to spread his seed, if denied access to suitable females.[31] As I, and others, have pointed out many times elsewhere, the theory is hardly worthy of critique.[32] Based on Thornhill's anthropomorphic research on a dung beetle, the scorpion fly, this supposed explanation that rape proclivities are innate because they 'confer reproductive advantage' on the perpetrator fails to explain almost all known facts about human rape practices: it is usually performed by men who have sexual partners; it rarely results in conception; women who are too young and too old to conceive are also victims of rape; there is a high prevalence of rape between men.[33]

However, although it is probably the most pernicious, evolutionary psychology is not the only theoretical perspective on rape that has served, to greater or lesser degrees, to oversimplify or misrepresent the complexity of sexual assaults. At least until very recently psychiatrists, especially informed by unsophisticated versions of psychoanalysis, have also played a part over the years in excusing the crimes of rape perpetrators. Bourke quotes, for example, from the US psychiatrist Warren Willie's studies of rapists in the 1960s, pointing to the culpability of female rape victims: 'as often happens in these cases, the victim reveals some features in her behavior that hint of unconscious desires to be the victim of assault'.[34] With grim humour, we can also read his fellow Californian psychiatrist, Sheldon Kardener, arguing in 1975 (when women's liberation was in its heyday) that feminists were actively seeking their own sexual violation, dressing provocatively, unconsciously wanting to fulfil their 'worst expectations by demanding that the man force his attentions on her', enabling her to 'self-righteously scream "rape"'.[35]

CONFRONTING THE CULTURAL SCAFFOLDING OF RAPE

While recording the historical persistence of sexual violence, and the dismal failure of Western societies to eliminate it, Bourke uses her research to insist that there is nothing natural or inevitable about it. It exists in the form and magnitude we know it, she concludes, because rape is still being culturally incubated and tolerated. Her book takes us through the institutions that have spawned or sheltered rapists, beginning, as with much domestic violence, within marriage. In different surveys, 8 per cent to 14 per cent of wives report instances of spousal rape, with some studies reporting, contrary to received belief, that wives sustain more physical damage than other rape victims.[36] Marital rape was finally accepted as a crime throughout Britain in 1992, but still (despite media fears) remains one of the hardest forms of abuse to prosecute.

A better-known site of sexual torment is located within military cultures. The mass sexual mutilations in the fields of Vietnam have entered collective historical memory, having been replayed by Hollywood. However, there is far less awareness of the systemic cementing of manliness to sexual coerciveness that is routine in military training. It is not just the incitement to aggression in times of battle that explains the gang rapes that occur in zones of conflict, Bourke suggests, but also men's sense of their own vulnerability and weakness, in particular their fear of being labelled 'chicken' or 'queer'. Another institutional site of sexual violence can be found in certain prison cultures. The sexually abused bodies of women in wartime find their echo in the fate of many men in prison cells and corridors, especially in the USA, where male on male rape is not only endemic, but often involves prisoners being repeatedly raped by gangs of inmates.

All men are not rapists, but downplaying the sexual violation of men helps conceal the reality that men are indeed rapeable. They can be quite as vulnerable as any woman, at least inside cultures that tolerate the notion that to affirm manhood is to 'penetrate' another's body, or to seek 'active' sexual pleasure and control over them, by whatever means. Paradoxically, as Bourke depicts, while prisoners generally despise convicted civilian rapists, the opposite is true for prison rapists: 'If you raped someone [in prison] it was like a feather in your cap'.[37] That this is indeed primarily a cultural affair, one condoned by the relevant prison authorities, is confirmed by British prison surveys which suggest far lower levels of male rape victims than in the US. (It is also quite certain that any increase in rape convictions in the USA do not factor in prison rapes, which are rarely reported). Far more than with instances of women's domestic violence, the huge reluctance to acknowledge that men are also victims accompanies discomfort over defining women as rapists. Lynndie England, sexually abusing men in Abu Ghraib, is not the only woman who might teach us that some women enjoy sexually abusing men (or perhaps women). Only 1 per cent of incarcerated rapists are women. However, lesbian gang rape and individual assault is reported from prisons in the USA, while in various surveys of boys and men reporting sexual molestation between 6 per cent and 24 per cent of the reported sexual abusers were female. Whatever the precise incidence rates, however, the cultural imaginary that likes to confirm the dichotomy of masculinity as active and femininity as passive does not apply. Women apparently have their own distinctive patterns of humiliation. Again as Bourke illustrates:

> While male guards stomped on male prisoners with boots and threatened to bugger the men in the showers and poked phosphorous lights up their rectums, the women threw menstrual fluid and slowly stripteased. The sexualization of abuse carried out by women had distinctive characteristics, drawn from the arsenal of feminine strategies of romance and seduction. We must take seriously the idea that female perpetrators are not simply imitating men, but living out their own feminine fantasies about power and sexuality.[38]

Bourke's comprehensive survey of the diversity of methods, victims, perpetrators and locations of bodily violation, is itself exemplary of the ways in which the meanings of 'rape' itself have shifted, leaving it a far more open and contested category today. Notions of rape as enforced penile penetration of the vagina always misconstrued much that happened in forced sexual encounters, even in the most standard rape scenario.

As those trying to understand sex crimes began to stress some decades ago (in response to feminist perspectives), rape is a hybrid phenomenon.[39] Sexual abuse can serve many purposes: release of sexual excitation; forms of identity maintenance and fears of weakness; expressions of anger, aggression, revenge; desires for power and control; differing combinations of any or all of these, and more. Certainly, however, the overwhelming predominance of male perpetrators to female perpetrators tells us also that sexual coercion as a perverse form of identity-maintenance connects with particular male obsessions with manliness, even as it undermines other men's narratives of manhood in terms of self-control, responsibility, kindness and concern for others, especially for those who are vulnerable. Understanding the gendered complexities of violence, therefore, means first of all challenging any and all definitive ties of 'masculinity' to 'power' or 'dominance', fundamentally enshrined in sexual assertiveness, with 'femininity' condensed into its symbolic opposite. It is this ideological trope which provides the basic 'cultural scaffolding of rape' which Nicola Gavey analyses, yet again, in surveying contemporary continuities in the discourses and imagery of the submissive young woman, always willing and waiting to be overpowered by the pressing sexual demands of any passing man.[40] No wonder so many men can now be found imagining they suffer from that new disease, 'erectile function disorder', keeping Pfizer's profits soaring.[41]

However, if we want to challenge the impact of such gendered identity scaffolding, with its habitual indifference to concomitant problems of sexual coerciveness, it is necessary to question all forms of reductionism that ignore the cultural underpinnings of rape. This includes, as we saw, myths about male 'biology' and fabled reproductive 'imperatives', which actual men find so hard to live up to, as well as any excuses diverting attention away from the perpetrator onto the victim, or some other 'guilty' female, such as the mother. However, it also means tackling myths perpetrated by certain feminist anti-violence advocates as well. Along with Bourke, I would argue that it is simply false to claim that 'all men are either rapists, rape-fantasists, or beneficiaries of a rape-culture', though many feminists have promoted this outlook, from Susan Brownmiller yesterday to Catharine MacKinnon and the many people she influences today.[42]

Why this position needs to be challenged, along with other rape mythologies, is that it perversely endorses rather than challenges the gender binary it is so crucial to question: most men are not rapists, a few women have raped and remain potential rapists, men and women are equally rapeable; why suggest any inexorable pattern behind such abusive practices? Picking up the torch from her former companion at arms, Andrea Dworkin, MacKinnon likes to pretend that, from an authentic woman's perspective, there is little to distinguish desired heterosexual encounters from strictly coercive ones: 'What looks like love and romance in the liberal view looks a lot like hatred and torture in the feminist view'.[43] Against such bizarre claims, which make any celebration of heterosexual pleasure impossible, we need to keep noting that manifestations of sexual violence vary hugely across time and place. The chief risk factor for women is without doubt the level of gender inequality in her social milieu, which is usually associated with notions of male sexual entitlement and high tolerance for men's sexual coercion. The second most important risk factor is poverty and social dislocation, often accompanying specific cultures of violence. Cultures of violence, however, reach their apex on battlefields, or similar sites of sanctioned cruelty towards others.[44] It is through understanding the historical contingencies and diverse social locations inciting practices of rape that Bourke herself is led to remain optimistic that it is possible for men to join feminists struggling to forge futures free from sexual violence. I think she is right, although, sadly, I see many of the obstacles we must confront looming larger, rather than shrinking, in this new century.

VULNERABILITY AND VIRILITY IN THE GLOBAL DOMAIN

Globally, we have less cause for optimism than for gloom when assessing the shifting patterns of interpersonal violence. On the one hand, as we saw above, over the last fifteen years there has been widespread cultural condemnation of interpersonal violence, with numerous campaigning groups, NGOs, web-sites and other public facilities and resources put into promoting awareness of men's violence against women, combined with innovative training programs for combating it.[45] On the other hand, inequality has been deepening globally, vastly increasing the numbers of men who feel insecure and resentful.[46] Moreover, under the current imperial hegemony of the USA, the beginning of the twenty-first century has ushered in an era so far presenting us with spectres of endless war.[47] Civil unrest and militarism are known to be invariably associated with the lauding of more violent expressions of masculinity, remorselessly coupled with an increase in intimate abusive practices. This has been painstakingly recorded by earlier explorations of the effects of being within, or returning from, war zones, for instance, in the work of Susan Jeffords, Cynthia Enloe and, most recently and chillingly, in UNESCO reports on the tough and aggressive masculinities emerging from battlefields and beyond.[48]

Off the battlefields, but gearing up for them, Susan Faludi has just published her latest book, *The Terror Dream* (2007), surveying the US media's frenzied reaction to the al-Qaeda-inspired '9/11' attacks on the USA (in September 2001).[49] This produced, as she demonstrates, widespread calls for the restoration of true American manhood, in need of nurturing by women contentedly embracing their separate role as wives and mothers. The immediate aftermath in much of the mainstream media was apparently to blame feminists, in headline after headline, for 'softening up' US manhood. In all the standard conservative media, on Fox News, in the *Weekly Standard* or *National Review*, psychologists such as David Gutmann were wheeled out to explain what happens 'when we go soft', with spokesmen for Bush, including William Bennett, quickly identifying the new culprit, 'feminists': 'Our culture has undergone a process that has aptly been termed "debellicization"... Having been softened up, we might not be able to sustain collective momentum in what we were now being called on to do'.[50]

If only! What 'we were now being called on to do' was quite explicitly said to include legitimising torture and mercilessness: 'It was time to think about torture', Jonathan Alter declared in *Newsweek*, adding, 'we'll have to think about transferring some suspects to our less squeamish allies, even if that's hypocritical'. Forget the 'human rights weenies', it was time to start 'flouting the Geneva Convention', *Time* columnist Charles Krauthammer agreed; both were writing in 2001, before the USA was officially at war with anyone.[51] It's not, of course, that such barbarous activities have not been practised before by Western nations, but what does seem new here is the willingness to boast about it, in the name of restoring American virility.

Any woman, such as Susan Sontag, daring to raise an alternative voice, was instantly subject to extreme vilification. After 9/11 Sontag wrote in the *New Yorker*, 'Who doubts that America is Strong? But that's not all that America has to be': for this she was labelled an 'ally of evil' and called 'deranged' by Andrew Sullivan in the *New Republic*; said to be subject to 'moral idiocy', in the *New York Post*, and accused of dressing the nation in girl's clothing: 'the same people urging us not to blame the victim in rape cases are now saying Uncle Sam wore a short skirt and asked for it', was columnist Jonathan Alter's weird reaction in *Newsweek*. At much the same time, for writing in the *Nation* that she wished the American flags waved after '9/11' could stand for 'equality and justice and humanity' rather than 'jingoism and vengeance and war', Katha Pollitt was variously charged with 'lunacy', 'idiocy', 'facile insipidities', and more, across the spectrum of the US media, with 'The *Chicago Sun-Times* summing up the overall reactions in one article "Oh, Shut up! We're at war, sweetheart"'.[52] It is possible to hope that this manic surge of machismo may have somewhat subsided now, given the catastrophe attending George W. Bush's race to war. Nevertheless, it is hard not to fear that the good attending the visibility of public campaigns against violence in the personal domain remain overshadowed by the harms threatened from current disorders and ongoing militarism in the global arena.

Staying in the gloomy global domain, any source of optimism again tends to be beaten back when men's sexuality, however varied or reformed in some sites, is placed alongside evidence of men's unsafe sex practices in other places. Today there is ample proof of men's refusal to use condoms in contexts where HIV/AIDS is rampant, which as the Panos Institute has documented is most prevalent in sites of greatest poverty, and especially in parts of Africa, where rates of rape are also the highest in the world.[53] At the same time, we are seeing hugely increased sexual trafficking in women, again coming mainly from countries ravaged by poverty, or destabilised by ethnic conflict and war, as Vesna Nikolic-Ristanovic and many other researchers report from post-communist and war-affected nations.[54]

It is here, however, that some anti-sexist men, along with feminists and other human rights activists, have once again been working hardest to promote new sexual agendas which refuse to define men's sexuality simply as violent, involving men globally in addressing and educating boys and men generally to resist the aspects of dominant masculinities that exploit and harm women.[55] It is also true that globalisation's ruthless disruption of local patriarchal cultures can, at times, serve to generate new spaces for more progressive forms of gender and sexual relationships.[56] Nevertheless, those men who are receptive to change and to sharing power and responsibilities with women in their public and private lives are nowadays having to work even harder against reinforced virile metaphors in a global conjuncture characterised by their states' ruthless wars. It is hard to get the balance sheet right, somewhere between optimism and despair, when surveying men's divided interests in the disorders sewn by corporate capital's ongoing economic and military imperialism. No-one, however, has worked harder at attempting this than R.W. Connell, one of the very earliest and most persuasive scholars of masculinity, today still surveying men globally as they come into focus, recklessly 'scrambling in the ruins of patriarchy'.[57]

MEN, WOMEN AND WAR

Unsurprisingly, however, it has continued to be feminist scholars and women peace activists who have most consistently studied the reactionary rhetoric of gender in warfare. Most influentially, the books of the American peace activist Cynthia Enloe have analysed the 'masculinist' postures and practices of warfare, detailing their effects on the women caught up in them.[58] In the UK, Cynthia Cockburn has been equally visible, organising with women globally in conflict zones and expressing their outrage against all forms of 'masculinist' violence in the silent vigils of Women in Black.[59] It is also noteworthy that only 52 per cent of American women under twenty-five initially supported the (second) US war in Iraq in 2003, compared with 82 per cent of men.[60] Nevertheless, neither today, nor yesterday, have there been consistent links between women and opposition to militarism – even among feminists. In general, the majority of women have supported the wars their leaders have waged in their name – men at war fighting to protect women (and children) back home. Directly and indirectly women have played a crucial role in wartime: usually, in their loyalty to men in uniform and their scorn for those who refuse to fight; sometimes, in their support for military dictators; periodically, when allowed to appear on the battlefield, in their enjoyment of joining what they see as the quintessential world of men.[61]

Today, there are more women than ever before active in the various military services. Hence for some women, including feminists, the battle is to improve the conditions for female soldiers, not to confront the practices of warfare itself. In the USA it is now estimated that one in seven soldiers is a woman, and between 2003 and 2007 more than 160,000 women had already served in Afghanistan and the Middle East. As Helen Benedict's research highlights, the single main problem these women soldiers report is their fear of harassment, rape and violence from the men who serve with them, with little, if any, protection provided by the army itself.[62] One of many studies underlining this problem, conducted during 1992-3, reported that 90 per cent of female veterans of the first Gulf War claimed to have been sexually harassed in the military, ranging from rape to relentless teasing and constant intrusive staring. Serving in Iraq with the National Guard in 2005, Mickiela Montoya told Benedict that she carried a knife with her at all times: '"The knife wasn't for the Iraqis", she told me, "it was for the guys on my own side"'.[63] More bizarrely, Colonel Janis Karpinski, commander of Abu Ghraib during the scandal over the sadistic torture of male prisoners there and the only high ranking officer demoted for her role in it, has recently become a strong critic of the military's negligent treatment of the extreme perils faced by female recruits.[64]

Nevertheless, despite some women's support for or involvement in warfare, it is also women who have repeatedly organised against militarism and committed themselves to working for peace. Often they have fought for peace in their self-identification as mothers and nurturers, sometimes they have opposed wars from political commitments to justice and equality as socialists or feminists, or perhaps as Quakers, or from other spiritual or religious belongings. The particular group of feminist peace activists whose outlook and tactics I know best, who are daily busy trying to tease out the complex relations between gender and militarism, are the women who helped found New Profile, an Israeli feminist, anti-militarist organisation formed in 1998. New Profile's goal is to 'civil-ise' Israeli society, knowing that their country is not only one of the most highly militarised societies in the world, but one of only two countries that demands mandatory conscription for women. This is sometimes presented as an expression of women's equality in Israel. However, New Profile highlights the costs of the militarised nature of Israeli society, exposing the very permeable boundaries between the Israeli military (IDF) and civil society. New Profile also offers support for 'Refuseniks' and their families, assisting those who refuse to serve in the IDF, or at least in its occupied territories.[65] The IDF's regular violence against Palestinians, their daily humiliation of them at the hundreds of check-points undermining civil society in the West Bank, the current brutal closure and blockade of Gaza, all necessary to maintain Israel's forty-year occupation and enclosure of Palestinian territories, inevitably seeps into the fears and practices of everyday life in Israel. A significantly higher percentage of Israeli women are murdered or beaten by male partners when these men are serving in the IDF than at any other time.[66] Studies also suggest that eighty per cent of Israeli women soldiers say they have experienced some form of sexual harassment, with little public or official concern.[67] The feminist message of New Profile is thus not only their passionate condemnation of the damage Israel's continued military expansion brings to Palestinians, but its destructive effects on its own citizens.

Meanwhile, the high rates of suicide and stress experienced by Israeli boys and men in the IDF also go unreported. It was only through reading Rela Mazali, one of the founders of New Profile, that I learned that during the years preceding Israel's most recent war in Lebanon, 'the number one cause of deaths among Israeli soldiers was suicide, and large numbers of veterans are disabled by depression and drug abuse'. Over a decade ago, Mazali was already protesting about the medical profession's suppression of the high incidence rates of post-traumatic stress disorder among troops, but with little response.[68] Over the last decade a general paralysis appears to have descended on much of the broader Israeli peace movement, following Israel's continuing use of its military might as a measure of first resort. In the face of Israel's unrelenting military escalation, alongside fears of Palestinian retaliation against Israeli civilians, one of Israel's largest blocs, Peace Now, has been only sporadically active since 2000. Notwithstanding the grim failure to achieve its goals, however, the Israeli women's peace groups have often proved the most resolute in their refusal to accept the seeming inevitability of conflict.[69]

Whether in Israel, or anywhere else, of course, there have always been peace campaigns led by men, alongside historical evidence of the courage of individual men conscientiously refusing to kill or injure their alleged enemies. Not all women are peacemakers, nor are all feminists pacifists, but it is surely right to suggest that applying a gender analysis to warfare is one indispensable tool for critiquing militarism and its endless cycles of war, at least in the world as we have known it. The rhetorics of domination, and the training in the uses of coercion necessary for producing military cadres, still connect us almost immediately with images of men and masculinity. It is men who remain associated with all that is tough, assertive, stoical, obedient, heroic. Moreover, men's traditional monopoly of institutionalised force, whether in the military or the police, has helped secure their dominance over women, as well as maintaining existing hierarchies between nations and between differing classes and ethnic groups.[70]

However, as I've already mentioned, what most feminists, at least up until now, have said less about is the ways in which men too are the constant victims of the violence of other men, overwhelmingly so in times of conflict, when men are also more likely to suffer sexual humiliation, rape and other forms of bodily fragmentation and abuse. Men too have tended to remain silent about this. The Canadian academic Adam Jones is one observer of wars and genocide who does stress the importance of a broader gender frame in studying the causes and effects of conflict, including the gendered targeting of men, both as the anticipated perpetrators and as the constant victims in the staging of violence. The demonisation of out-group males was a key feature of the propaganda discourse instigating the three classic genocides of the twentieth century, of Armenians in Turkey, Jews in Europe and the Tutsis of Rwanda.[71] In the most recent atrocities in Rwanda, for instance, Jones emphasises the inordinate stress placed upon maintaining traditional masculine gender roles stemming from years of economic crisis and resource scarcity, with young Hutu boys and men systematically targeted in order to focus their anger on the Tutsi menace.[72]

Clearly, it is not only in sensational atrocities, from genocide to the torture of prisoners in Abu Ghraib, or the indefinite detention of Islamic captives in Guantanamo Bay, that we need to ponder the ways in which men suffer hideously, primarily at the hands of other men. Men become victims all the time, whether in schoolyards, workplaces, football terraces, prisons or battlefields. There is certainly a gendered story in play here, but it does not simply reduce to a male/female, terrorizer/victim scenario, as women join men in the work of objectifying and psychologically annihilating the 'enemy', finding ways to 'effeminise' him, if he is a man. Again as Bourke argues, the point to note is that there is always a very *particular* story to tell about violence, specific to its own time and place, including the ambiguities of its gendered dynamics. Such stories are never merely the operation of universal truths or inevitabilities, whether seen as biological, cultural or psychological. I can easily imagine more androgynous combat units in the very near future, which might well deploy women and men equally in operating the latest technologies of warfare. In my view, what we need to stress is that in military combat men actually experience fear, trauma and bodily shattering, much like a woman, which is why so much work goes into denying this. As Judith Butler argues in *Precarious Life*, we should begin with the premise that all human bodies are fundamentally dependent and vulnerable.[73] Our common condition is precisely this shared helplessness, which is as evident in the susceptibility of our desires and attachments to rejection, humiliation and loss, as in our life-long physical injurability. Studying, and yet also attempting to undo, never to reinforce, the cultural mythologies of gender is another way in which we all need to think and argue counter-intuitively when addressing the gendered landscape of violence.

NOTES

1 Lynne Segal, *Slow Motion: Changing Masculinities, Changing Men*, London: Palgrave, 2007 [1990].

2 In the UK, in full-time public sector jobs women earn just over 13 per cent less than men; in part-time private sector jobs women's wages are still an appalling 45 per cent lower than men's. Equal Opportunity Commission, *Sex and Power: Who Runs Britain?*, Manchester, 2006.

3 See, for example, Barbara Ehrenreich and Arlie Russell Hochschild, eds., *Global Woman: Nannies, Maids and Sex Workers in the New Economy*, London: Granta Books, 2003.

4 Some of the best known texts include, Jocelyne Scutt, *Even in the Best of Homes: Violence in the Family*, Ringwood, VIC: Penguin Books, 1983; Diane E.H. Russell, *Sexual Exploitation*, London: Sage, 1985; Jalna Hanmer and Mary Maynard, eds., *Women, Violence and Social Control*, London: Macmillan, 1987; Liz Kelly, *Surviving Sexual Violence*, Cambridge: Polity Press, 1988.

5 UN speech, 'We "cannot wait" to end violence against women – Secretary-General Ban', available from http://www.un.org/news.

6 See Sue Lees, *Ruling Passions: Sexual Violence, Reputation and the Law*, Buckingham: Open University Press, 1997; Jeanne Gregory and Sue Lees, *Policing Sexual Assault,* London: Routledge, 1999.

7 The development of Men's Studies has continuously highlighted the destructive effects of men's violence against women and children, influencing more men to seek out creative ways of dealing with the problem. See Michael Kaufman, *Cracking the Armour: Power, Pain and the Lives of Men*, Toronto: Penguin, 1993; Michael Flood, 'Engaging Men: Strategies and Dilemmas in Violence Prevention Education among Men', *Women Against Violence: An Australian Feminist Journal*, 13, 2002-2003;

Robert Connell, Ingeborg Breines and Ingrid Eide, eds., *Male Roles, Masculinities and Violence: A Culture of Peace Perspective*, Paris: UNESCO Publishing, 2000; Jeff Hearn *The Violences of Men: How Men Talk About and How Agencies Respond to Men's Violence to Women*, London: Sage, 1998; Michael S. Kimmel, 'The Gender of Violence', in Michael S. Kimmel, ed., *The Gendered Society*, Oxford: Oxford University Press, 2000.

8 See Kelly, *Surviving Sexual Violence.*

9 Michael Flood and Bob Pease, 'The Factors Influencing Community Attitudes in Relation to Violence Against Women: A Critical Review of the Literature', Victorian Health Promotion Foundation, Melbourne, 2006; J. Brzozowski, ed., *Family Violence in Canada: A Statistical Profile* 2004, Catalogue no. 85-224-XIE, Ottawa: Statistics Canada, 2004.

10 Robert Wright, 'Feminists Meet Mr. Darwin', *The New Republic*, 28 (November), 1994, pp. 34-36.

11 Robert Wright, *The Moral Animal: Why We Are the Way We Are: The New Science of Evolutionary Psychology*, New York: Pantheon, 1994.

12 Martin Daly and Margo Wilson, *Homicide*, New York: Aldine de Gruyter, 1988.

13 *Why Mothers Die: The Confidential Enquiry into Maternal Deaths, HMSO*, November, 1998, reported in Sarah Boseley, 'Abuse Risk Higher During Pregnancy', *The Guardian*, 24 November 1998, p. 7.

14 For example, Randy Thornhill and Craig Palmer, *A Natural History of Rape: Biological Bases of Sexual Coercion*, Cambridge: MIT Press, 2000; Lynne Segal, 'Nature's Way?: Inventing the Natural History of Rape', *Psychology, Evolution & Gender*, 3(1), 2001.

15 Margo Wilson and Martin Daly, 'Who Kills Whom in Spouse Killings? On the Exceptional Sex Ratio of Spousal Homicide in the United States', *Criminology*, 30, 1992.

16 Martin S. Fiebert, 'References Examining Assaults by Women on their Spouses or Male Partners: An Annotated Bibliography', *Sexuality & Culture*, 8(3-4), 2004, p. 140.

17 Linda Gordon, *Heroes of Their Own Lives*, New York: Viking, 1988. Gordon's analysis was in agreement with mainstream sociological research on the topic, such as Murray Strauss, Richard Gelles and Suzanne Steinmetz, *Behind Closed Doors: Violence in the American Family*, New York: Doubleday, 1980 and most subsequent sociological overviews, including P.C. McKenry and S.J. Price, eds., *Families & Change: Coping with Stressful Events and Transitions*, Thousand Oaks: Sage, 2005.

18 Michael S. Kimmel, '"Gender Symmetry" in Domestic Violence: A

Substantive and Methodological Research Review', *Violence Against Women*, 8(11), 2002, p. 17.

19 Richard J. Gelles, 'Domestic Violence: Not an Even Playing Field', http://thesafetyzone.org/everyone/gelles.html. See also Richard J. Gelles, 'The Hidden Side of Domestic Violence: Male Victims', *The Women's Quarterly*, 22, 1999.

20 See John Archer, 'Sex Differences in Aggression Between Heterosexual Partners: A Meta-Analytic Review', *Psychological Bulletin*, 126, 2000; Sandra Lundy, 'Abuse That Dare Not Speak Its Name: Assisting Victims of Lesbian and Gay Domestic Violence in Massachusetts', *New England Law Review*, 28(Winter), 1993; Teresa Scherzer, 'Domestic Violence in Lesbian Relationships: Findings of the Lesbian Relationship Research Project', *Journal of Lesbian Studies*, 2(1), 1998; Lori B. Girschick, *Woman-to-Woman Sexual Violence. Does She Call it Rape?*, Boston: Northeastern University Press, 2002.

21 From several thousand possible references, let me single out R.W. Connell's definitive texts, *Gender and Power*, Cambridge: Polity Press, 1987 and *Masculinities*, Cambridge: Polity Press, 1995.

22 B. Pressman, 'Violence against Women: Ramifications of Gender, Class and Race Inequality', in M.P. Mirkin, ed., *Women in Context: Toward a Feminist Reconstruction of Psychotherapy*, New York: Guilford Press, 1998; R. Carillo and J. Tello, eds., *Family Violence and Men of Color: Healing the Wounded Male Spirit*, New York: Springer Publishing Company, 1998; C.K. Ho, 'An Analysis of Domestic Violence in Asian American Communities: A Multicultural Approach to Counseling', in L.S. Brown and M.P. Root, eds., *Diversity and Complexity in Feminist Therapy*, New York: Haworth Press, 1996.

23 Reported in Renny Harrigan, 'The German Women's Movement and Ours', *Jump Cut: A Review of Contemporary Media*, 27(July), 1982, pp. 42-44.

24 For those interested, see, for example, Anne Cossins, *Masculinities, Sexualities, and Child Sexual Abuse*, Boston: Kluwer Law International, 2000.

25 Susan Brownmiller, *Against Our Will: Men, Women, and Rape*, New York: Simon and Schuster, 1975.

26 Ibid., p. 15. For my own criticisms, see Lynne Segal, 'The Belly of the Beast 11', in Segal, *Slow Motion*; and Lynne Segal, *Straight Sex: Rethinking Sexual Pleasure*, Berkeley: California University Press, 1994.

27 Joanna Bourke, *Rape: A History from 1860 to the Present*, London: Virago, 2007.

28 Ibid., pp. 95-6.

29 Liz Kelly, Jo Lovett and Linda Regan, *A Gap or a Chasm? Attrition in Reported Rape Cases*, Home Office Research Study, 293, London, 2005.

30 US Department of Justice Bureau of Justice Statistics, *Crime and Justice in the United States and in England and Wales, 1981-96*, available from http://www.ojp.gov/bjs.

31 Thornhill and Palmer, *A Natural History of Rape.*

32 Segal, 'Nature's Way?'.

33 Ibid.; J. Burr, 'Review Essay: "Sex, Lies and Scorpionflies. The Problem of Evolutionary Psychology in Understanding Rape"', *Psychology, Evolution & Gender*, 2(2), 2000.

34 Bourke, *Rape*, p. 138.

35 Sheldon Kardener, 'Rape Fantasies', *Journal of Religion and Health*, 14(1), 1975, p. 55.

36 Patricia Weiser Esteal, 'Survivors of Sexual Assault: An Australian Survey', *International Journal of the Sociology of Law*, 22(4), 1994, pp. 337-8; A. Myhill and J. Allen, *Rape and Sexual Assault of Women: The Extent and Nature of the Problem – Findings from the British Crime Survey*, Home Office Research Study, 237, London, 2002.

37 Bourke, *Rape*, p. 348.

38 Ibid.

39 See, for instance, A. Nicholas Groth with H. Jean Birnbaum, *Men Who Rape: The Psychology of the Offender*, New York: Plenum Press, 1980.

40 Nicola Gavey, *Just Sex: The Cultural Scaffolding of Rape*, London: Routledge, 2005; Meika Loe, *The Rise of Viagra: How The Little Blue Pill Changed Sex in America,* New York: New York University Press, 2004.

41 Loe, *The Rise of Viagra.*

42 See Bourke, *Rape*, pp. 7-8.

43 Catharine MacKinnon, 'Not a Moral Issue', in MacKinnon, *Feminism Unmodified: Discourses on Life and Law*, London: Harvard University Press, 1987, p. 149.

44 See, for example, E.G. Krug et al., eds., *World Report on Violence and Health*, Geneva: World Health Organization, 2002.

45 See, for example, David Morgan and Monica Wilson, 'Working with Men who are Violent to Partners – Striving for Good Practice', in Hazel Kemshall and Jacki Pritchard, eds., *Good Practice in Working with Violence*, Philadelphia: Jessica Kingsley Publishers, 1999; Margaret Cameron, 'Young Men and Violence Prevention', Trends and Issues in Crime

and Criminal Justice No. 154, Australian Institute of Criminology, Canberra, 2000.

46 Christine Adler, 'Explaining Violence: Socioeconomics and Masculinity', in D. Chappell, P. Grabosky and H. Strang, eds., *Australian Violence: Contemporary Perspectives*, Canberra: Australian Institute of Criminology, 1991.

47 Carolyn Nordstrom, *Shadows of War: Violence, Power, and International Profiteering in the Twenty-First Century*, Berkeley: University of California Press, 2004.

48 Susan Jeffords, *Remasculinization of America: Gender and Vietnam*, Bloomington: Indiana University Press, 1989; Cynthia Enloe, *Maneuvers: The International Politics of Militarizing Women's Lives*, Berkeley: University of California Press, 2000; Ingeborg Breines, Robert Connell, and Ingrid Eide, eds., *Male Roles, Masculinities and Violence: A Culture of Peace Perspective*, Paris: UNESCO, 2000.

49 Susan Faludi, *The Terror Dream: What 9/11 Revealed about the American Psyche*, London: Atlantic Books, 2007.

50 Ibid., pp. 28-30.

51 Ibid., p. 155.

52 All quotes from and about Sontag and Pollitt, in ibid., pp. 28-30.

53 Panos Institute, *Young Men and HIV: Culture, Poverty and Sexual Risk*, London: Joint United Nations Programme on HIV/AIDS (UNAIDS)/ The Panos Institute, 2001; Michael Flood, 'Lust, Trust and Latex: Why Young Heterosexual Men Do Not Use Condoms', *Culture, Health, & Sexuality*, 5, 2003.

54 Vesna Nikolic-Ristanovic, *Social Change, Gender and Violence: Post-Communist and War-Affected Societies*, Boston: Kluwer, 2002. See also Liz Kelly, 'Wars Against Women: Sexual Violence, Sexual Politics and the Militarised State', in S. Jacobs, R. Jacobson and J. Marchbank, eds., *States of Conflict*, London: Zed Books, 2000.

55 Michael Kaufman, 'The AIM Framework: Addressing and Involving Men and Boys To Promote Gender Equality and End Gender Discrimination and Violence', UNICEF, March, 2003.

56 See, for example, Manuel Castells, *The Power of Identity*, Cambridge: Blackwell Publishers, 1996, p. 165.

57 R.W. Connell, 'Scrambling in the Ruins of Patriarchy: Neo-liberalism and Men's Divided Interests in Gender Change', in Ursula Pasero, ed., *Gender – From Costs to Benefits*, Wiesbaden: Westdeutscher, 2003, 58-69.

58 Cynthia Enloe, *Does Khaki Become You? The Militarization of Women's*

Lives, London: Pandora Press, 1988; *Bananas, Beaches and Bases: Making Feminist Sense of International Politics*, Berkeley: University of California Press, 2000; and *The Curious Feminist: Searching for Women in The New Age of Empire,* Berkeley: University of California Press, 2004.

59 Cynthia Cockburn, *The Space Between Us: Negotiating Gender and National Identities in Conflict*, London: Zed Press, 1998; *The Line: Women, Partition and the Gender Order in Cyprus*, London: Zed Press, 2004; and *From Where We Stand: War, Women's Activism and Feminist Analysis*, London: Zed Press, 2007.

60 The Pew Research Center for the People and the Press, 'War Concerns Grow, But Support Remains Steadfast', 3 April 2003, available at http://people-press.org.

61 Sandra Gilbert, 'Soldier's Heart: Literary Men, Literary Women, and the Great War, *Signs*, 8(3), 1983; Lynne Segal, *Is the Future Female*, London: Virago Press, 1987, pp. 162-303.

62 Helen Benedict, 'The Private War of Women Soldiers', *Salon*, 7 March 2007, available from http://www.salon.com.

63 Ibid.

64 Janis Karpinski, *One Woman's Army: The Commanding General of Abu Ghraib Tells Her Story*, New York: Mirimax Books, 2005.

65 I have written elsewhere of the disaster the Israeli-Palestinian conflict has had on the lives of Palestinians, especially on those in Israel's occupied territory, many of whom remain doubly dispossessed. See Lynne Segal, *Making Trouble: Life and Politics*, London: Serpent's Tail, 2007, ch. 7.

66 Madelaine Adelman, 'The Military, Militarism, and the Militarization of Domestic Violence', *Violence Against Women*, 9(9), 2003.

67 Rela Mazali, 'And what about the Girls?': What a Culture of War Genders out of View', *Nashim: A Journal of Jewish Women's*, 6, 2003.

68 Rela Mazali, 'Raising Boys to Maintain Armies', *BMJ*, 311, 9 September 1995.

69 These groups include: Bat Shalom, MachsomWatch (women monitoring soldiers' conduct at checkpoints), Women in Black, Women Against The Wall, Women and Mothers for Peace, Women's Coalition for Peace and B'tselem, a highly active campaign combating human rights abuses in the territories, mainly led and staffed by women peace activists.

70 John Tosh, for instance, has pointed out that military values have often served to justify and enforce male dominance. Nevertheless, this 'patriarchal dividend', or gender privilege, has also placed so many young

men in danger of serious injury and death. See Tosh, 'Hegemonic Masculinity and Gender History', in Stefan Dudink, Karen Hagemann and John Tosh, eds., *Masculinities in Politics and War: Gendering Modern History*, Manchester: Manchester University Press, 2004, p. 55.

71 Adam Jones, ed., *Gendercide and Genocide*, Nashville: Vanderbilt University Press, 2004, p. 2.

72 Ibid., pp. 98-99.

73 Judith Butler, *Precarious Life: The Powers of Mourning and Violence*, London: Verso, 1994.

GIRLS AS DISPOSABLE COMMODITIES IN INDIA

BARBARA HARRISS-WHITE

A novel by the Lebanese writer Amin Maalouf, *The First Century after Beatrice*, tells of the rumour of an Egyptian scarab whose powder has the property, when taken by men, of screening out females at conception. A drug with the same property is developed by a multinational corporation and marketed under the name and aura of the scarab. It starts to get around. But its impact is irreversible. Throughout what Maalouf calls the 'South' a generation overwhelmingly consisting of boys is produced. The result is unexpected and horrific: the proliferation of men deprived of full social identity, mass violence, terrifying insecurity for a minority of girls, a new kind of traffic in women, widespread physical reprisals against the 'North', a global descent into economic autarky. Not the answer to the population problem, the scarab instead catalyzes a demographic and economic disaster strewn with violence, beside which our own era of degenerate capitalism appears as a golden age.

In India real life has begun to mimic science fantasy. Females are being screened out as foetuses before birth, and as children afterwards. It is done through a violent but insidious process of gender cleansing that takes place in the bosom of the family, often with the complicity of women. While girls are very far from being as scarce as in Maalouf's narrative, their current scarcity has started to produce anecdotal and symptomatic evidence of the kind of reactions described in the novel. India's gender imbalance both reflects and feeds on kinship patterns, and on caste and class inequalities that are woven into the fabric of everyday social life.

This is graphically seen in sex ratios that track the relative number of females to males. Whereas the world average sex ratio was 990 in 1991, the number of females per thousand males of all ages in India was only 929 – which reflected a sharp decline over the course of the 20th century (down from 972 in 1901). While it recovered slightly to 933 in 2001, we have to factor into the rise in relative female status an increase in adult male deaths from tobacco, alcohol and sex-biased diseases like TB. By reducing the male denominator, the relative gains to women are exaggerated.[1]

According to the 2001 census, however, the sex ratio *at birth* was 892; by the time of the interim Sample Registration Surveys of 2002-4 it had deteriorated to 882 – seven per cent under the world-wide ratio of 950.[2] World-wide more boys than girls die in infancy so that the initial surplus of boys tends to decline towards parity with increasing age in childhood. But from the final decades of the last century, the sex ratio tracking the mortality of Indian children under the age of six (the Child Sex Ratio, CSR) has started to behave in alarming ways. While the overall ratio of females to males in India's population was slowly improving, among children it declined, and at a faster rate. From 945 in 1991 it dropped to 927 in 2001.

The all-India average also conceals an epidemic of deterioration in the northwest of the subcontinent, which has been spreading to the south; and it is worst in urban areas, among upper castes and the rich.[3] It appears to bear no relationship to the differing levels of human development achieved in India's states.[4] While the maximum deterioration is found in the states of the northern poverty belt, the lowest CSRs are actually found in the most economically developed states of the North West. By 2001, the CSR was below 850 in Haryana (770 by 2004), below 800 in Punjab and 760 in the most affluent metropolitan suburbs of south Delhi – only three girls for every four boys. Even in the most egalitarian state, Kerala in the south, the CSR fell over the last quarter century as it did even more seriously in Left Front-ruled West Bengal.[5]

Girls in certain relatively advantaged castes and communities such as Jats, Sikhs and Jains are thought to be most at risk. One field study of 6,500 households is reported to have discovered a low of 300 among upper caste Hindus in the Fatehgarh Saheb district of Punjab in 2007 – just one girl for every three boys.[6] In nearby Haryana the CSR was recently found to be 541 among the richest segment of the population; it was over 1000 among the poor.[7] It is highest in mountainous and/or tribal regions. There you may be indigent and 'backward' but if you are a girl child you have the highest chances of staying alive in contemporary India. Even so, the more female siblings you have, the higher your chances of death.

How are these girls and female foetuses killed? There are three kinds of proximate mechanisms – culling in childhood, infanticide and sex-selective abortion. For Malini Bhattacharya, member of India's National Commission for Women, 'This is a demographic disaster… Women are so devalued that their birth must be prevented'.[8]

Neglect is likely to be by far the major culler of girl children. Already by the 1980s there was substantial evidence of lethal combinations of undernutrition and health neglect, broadly in parallel to the regional and socio-economic patterns of excess female mortality. Gender-biased health spending persists, and is significantly associated with the deaths of girl children.[9]

Infanticide is thought to be common in certain regions of India but restricted to certain castes. In the state of Tamil Nadu, for example, a central 'spine' of infanticide has been identified in districts characterised by rapid agrarian change and upwardly-mobile low castes.[10] Female foeticide has long been known but until the last decade it was thought to be a costly luxury unaffordable by the rural masses.[11] Knowledge of it was largely confined to small case studies and anecdotes until 2007 when the *Lancet* published the first conclusive evidence of a connection between amniocentesis, sex selective abortion and the sex ratio, in a paper claiming that half a million girl foetuses were being destroyed in India each year.[12]

While certain social commentators refer to these deaths in terms such as 'extreme and reprehensible violence', the idea that these deaths are a form of violence, or murder, or a crime is always widely denied – even in a society attuned to phrases like 'silent violence' and 'structural violence' to describe routine oppression and exploitation.[13] Culling by default through underfeeding and/or neglectful health care when faced with accidents at birth, or with upper respiratory tract infections or diarrhoeal disease, is certainly not regarded as a form of violence. Infanticide does not require active smothering, starving, drowning or herbal poisoning: it may be done passively by exposure at birth. Abortion is also rationalised as an indicator and instrument of female autonomy, and of a woman's right to choose.

The idea that these deaths are a distinctive aspect of capitalist modernity is also widely rejected. That there is a long social, economic and political history to the sex ratio is undeniable. Alice Clark's research on upper-caste reproductive behaviour in early 20th century Gujarat showed how the practice of hypergamy (marrying upwards in status terms) carried the consequence of eradicating the women of the highest-ranking castes. Land could be retained within a tight circle of kin while lower-caste bride-givers paid dowry for the privilege of connecting themselves upwards. Here it was assets that were being protected, rather than the specific logic of capitalism at work.

Equally, the longstanding debate about the relative roles of economic and cultural drivers of female disadvantage has been resolved in favour of culture. Satish Agnihotri has shown conclusively that the practice of paying a dowry (which makes girls a burden) and the kinship practice of village exogamy (which isolates brides) spread southwards from northern India in the last part of the 20th century and are not directly related to macro-economic indicators. My own work on small-town business elites in south India confirms the significance of culture. It shows that there is no sense in which dowry could be said to be either punitive or a form of pre-mortem inheritance on a par with male legacies,[14] yet the under-15 sex ratio was 784 in the mid-1990s. It is clearly, as Agnihotri has concluded, a result of the vicious cultural expression of female subordination and male supremacy;[15] so much so that a woman researcher commented that 'the criminals are within us'.[16] It is not only men who are pressured to kill girls, it is even more women who have internalised their own patriarchal oppression so deeply that they perpetrate and condone these crimes in hegemonic complicity.[17] A preference for sons long predates capitalism, a son being an essential insurance in old age, a legitimator in Hindu death rituals and the link between past and future generations. Son-preference may even be intensified by fertility decline and by the state's more or less voluntary two-child policy, since the accident of two daughters is starting to be displaced by 'crafted' combinations involving at least one son.[18] Last but not least, the violence expressed by the CSR is part of a rise in the pervasive violence against women which exceeds the fabled rates of growth of services. 'This violence has always been there, it is being re-invented' says Malini Bhattacharya.[19]

Nevertheless, I wish to argue that the killing of girls in the 21st century does have a great deal to do with capitalist modernity and that the practice has been 're-invented', at least in part to regulate and respond to the market economy. There are three aspects to the argument.

First, in the informed political imagination, it is from the reforms initiated in 1991, the year of the nadir of the aggregate sex ratio, that the deterioration of the CSR may be dated – and, for many, a cause-effect relationship may be established. But the argument goes both ways and is hotly debated. On the one hand, the political economist Jayathi Ghosh exemplifies those for whom it is a demographic response to poverty and vulnerability, exacerbated by state neglect.[20] Her argument is nuanced: with liberalisation new barriers prevent access to public services; utilities are privatised and commodified; infrastructural investment is neglected; health, education and social services are starved of resources. Work in the wage-labour force is being replaced by even more insecure and disguised wage-work in petty commodity production, trade and services. Women enter domestic service on a large scale. Eighty per cent of wage workers earn less than Rs 20 ($0.50) per day. It is this insecurity, these poverty wages, and significant male-female differentials in wage rates, that are thought to trigger violence against those who are already vulnerable. Why rear a child who will earn lower wages and returns and also bring shame on your family if you cannot afford the costs of a conventional marriage for her?

By contrast other scholars date the era of liberalisation to a much earlier time, with no 'kink point' either in economic growth or in the evolution of the institutions which form the social structure of accumulation.[21] For them, the key trigger for the new wave of violence against girl children is not so much the increases in insecurity, and the persistent gendered differentials in wage-rates, as the acquisition of property. In south India, for example, whereas increases in the incomes of *landless* agricultural labourers are not found to be associated with a deterioration in the CSR, for rural households *with* landed property there appears to be a clear inverse relationship between income levels and the CSR.[22] India's landholding structure is being progressively miniaturised: 95 per cent of rural households currently own under two hectares of land – and have expenditures exceeding income.[23] Capitalist development in India is creating a huge space for debt-ridden petty production in the agricultural and the non-farm 'informal economy', and the acquisition of the smallest amount of property leads to the mass imitation of the male-biased inheritance practices that protect its transfer across the generations.

Second, the cultural politics of the dowry have a lot to answer for. Since the turn of the century recorded dowry deaths (murders of brides for lack of a full dowry) are running at 7-8,000 per year, and dowry suicides at 3-5,000.[24] The dowry has been reworked to serve the interests of accumulation. Historically vested in the bride and composed of movables (notably jewellery), it formed a private security fund. It is now commonly vested in the groom's family. In the business class it has for long been a carefully-calibrated component in the cross-generational transfer of assets. In the new middle classes, based in finance, trade, services and the professions, and defined through consumption, lifestyles are shaped by advertising and the media. Grooms can be 'auctioned' and brides turned into commodities; auspicious marriages (and pre-marriage ceremonies) are festivals of ostentatious consumption, and dowries take the form of money, property and consumer durables. What Shahid Pervez has called the 'consumption-oriented reproductive journey' is expressed in other one-sided exchanges through a woman's life-time of reproductive rituals and is now fast being generalised among the rural masses where expenditure exceeds income.[25] If the dowry is understood as a response to insecurity then it has rebounded adversely on the gender it began by favouring, and has increased the security of families that produce sons. When reproductive practices make daughters into such economic burdens, the threat of having to amass dowry is motive enough to dispose of 'female commodities'.[26]

Third, the process of culling has been medicalised and commodified. The aborting of female foetuses – 'death before birth'[27] – has started to become a field of accumulation in its own right. Referring to ultrasound scans in the era of liberalisation Malini Bhattacharya, the member of the National Commission for Women quoted above, admitted that 'one has to allow freedom of choice to the service seeker and the freedom to sell by the service provider' – together with the freedom to advertise openly in the print media.[28] For the service seeker, an ultrasound scan is available for $8, equivalent to a week's male wages. Foeticide may cost a family one to two months' earnings, while dowry requires the mobilisation of several years' income; for the service provider, the *Wall Street Journal* reports that since 2000 ultrasound technology sales have increased at about 10 per cent per year – in 2006 the sector turned over $77m.[29] UNICEF estimates that the turnover of the foeticide industry 'downstream' of the ultrasound machines has now reached $244m.[30]

The technology itself caters for a differentiated market: a machine can cost anything from $7,500 to $100,000. There are now some 30,000 *registered* clinics. How does this relate to general health-sector coverage? There are about 84 million married women in the reproductive age group, so there is one diagnostic clinic per 2,800 married women, while there is one general physician per 1,666 people. If each ultrasound clinic has just one qualified practitioner then in a population well in excess of a billion already roughly one in twenty doctors are making specialist profits from demand for foetal sex information. But in India's huge informal economy, there is also an unknown number of *unregistered* clinics – increasingly based in small towns or operating as mobile services – profiting from the market in second-hand, refurbished or onward-sold new machines. In a study in Maharashtra in 2004 75 per cent of ultrasound centres were found to be neither owned nor managed by trained medical personnel.[31] Elsewhere there is a widely reported systematic transfer of responsibility: scans are under-enumerated; results are indecipherable on paper; records are manipulated or not kept at all. (In Hyderabad, in a rare audit in 2006, only 16 per cent had adequate details of patients).[32]

General Electric took the lead in the new wave of foreign corporate investment able to enter India in the 1990s. It dominates a market of 15 companies in a joint venture with Wipro, the outsourcing company, taking advantage of the latter's distribution and service network and linking up ('partnered') with local banks to aid instalment purchases. The oligopoly includes Siemens AG, Philips Electronics NV, Mindray International Medical Ltd (from China) and Erbis Engineering, an agent for Japan's Toshiba. The companies are unable to prevent the unlawful use of the ultrasound machines they sell.[33] As a result, amniocentesis has been described by the senior Indian Administrative Service official and scholar of the sex ratio, Satish Agnihotri, as a 'weapon of mass destruction' – misused even in some government health facilities as well as in private ones.[34] The proliferation of private commercially-run medical colleges has also facilitated the production of doctors available for commercial female foeticide. In a unique sting operation in 2007, 70 per cent of medically qualified owners of scanning facilities were found to be prepared to carry out sex-selective abortions as late as the seventh month of pregnancy.[35]

This violence against girl children is in theory prohibited by law. In this sector as elsewhere India is festooned in progressive, regulative and protective law. But while the Pre Natal Diagnostic Techniques Act of 1994, made more stringent in 2003, restricts prenatal scanning to the detection of foetal genetic abnormalities, in the real world just being female counts as a genetic abnormality. And the Prohibition of Dowry Act of 1962/5 is honoured in the breach. In 2005 the Hindu inheritance laws were reformed to enable women to inherit, on the argument that the right to property empowers women. But in practice this is thought to increase the fear in joint families that their land will pass on inheritance to their girl children at a stage when the latter are married 'out' of the family (and sometimes out of the locality) and into rival families who will then assume control. In April 2008, the Indian Prime Minister called for a 'clamp down'.[36] But lack of legal literacy, lack of access to justice (implicating the police and the judiciary),[37] surprisingly low conviction rates,[38] and lack of sufficiently deterrent penalties[39] means that the law is hardly ever enforced. At its best the law serves as a goal for aspirations, at its worst a discursive mask for a nexus of criminal interests and 'passivists'.[40]

What is being done? Nation-wide state-led campaigns for the adoption of girls have clearly failed.[41] Certain states, Tamil Nadu for instance, have offered incentives to mothers of girl children – though these incentives have been criticised as inadequate even for the routine expenses of pregnancy. Midwives are paid for childbirth but these payments are thought to be ten times less than the rate for midwives assisting infanticide. In the parts of society that demand infanticide there will be relatively large financial incentives for midwives' complicity. Area-based projects in high-risk areas have had patchy success. One of them brought the local female infanticide rate down by 90 per cent during the 1990s through a set of stages: first crèches for working women, next a mother-and-child welfare project, and finally monitoring and counselling women at high risk. But responses that are focussed on targets perceived to be at 'high risk' – whether regions or couples

– miss the routine culling that takes place by neglect.

The National Commission on Women monitors legal and constitutional protection but it too neglects the culling of girl children, focusing instead on rape and sexual assault. The Commission's draft bill on these kinds of violence lies un-presented to Parliament and un-incorporated into the 11th Plan. The Commission's amendments to the Acts outlawing trafficking are also 'lying with' a Government that has shown much more energy in easing the regulations for export, finance and services than improving the conditions for labour, let alone enforcing existing law.

Concerned academics and investigative journalists have played an important progressive role in researching, explaining and publicising the dynamics of this violence.[42] A huge number of NGOs have lately mobilised public awareness of the issue in ways that are often idiosyncratic and hinder the formation of a coherent movement. Oxfam has organised a coalition of 400 of them under the slogan 'We Can', and an India-wide network has brought together 3,000 more under the acronym FORCES.

They have work to do. First all culling – including neglectful, 'benign' practices as well as the deliberate acts – have to be recognised as violent. Second this violence must be 'denaturalised', which is a sensitive issue for women, linked as it must be to a larger fight against religious obscurantism. It faces opposition even from elements within the medical profession (where it is also depoliticised, as a 'public health problem'), and despite publicity it has hardly registered in the media, where ridicule and shame are recognised tropes in other progressive causes.[43] Third, this practice, and the larger issue of violence against women, has to enter national politics.

Currently the complex of problems of violence against women is neglected by all major political parties: the low status of women is an intrinsic part of India's party politics. 'When there are debates in Parliament on the Pre Natal Diagnostic Techniques Act or even the Domestic Violence Act, the presence of parliamentarians is minimal' commented Malini Bhattacharya of the National Commission on Women.[44] Invisibly low on all these agendas are debates over the status of women as sellers of their labour: on the issues of sex-neutral minimum wages, work rights and women's control over their own incomes – not to mention the de-commodification of their work via income guarantees, pensions, social security, or the structures of violence in which all this takes place.

The killing of girls, violence against women and the growing markets for ultrasound and sex selective abortion are terrible indicators of capitalist development with Indian characteristics. While the domestic sphere and the process of biological reproduction have always been dangerous for women, it is the desire for upward mobility in an era of renewed primary accumulation and rampant commodification, combined with the oppressive market for labour and the absence of decent state-mediated social security, that make the home and the womb such increasingly violent places.

NOTES

A small extract used in this essay was earlier published in 'Gender Cleansing: The Paradox of Development and Deteriorating Female Life Chances in Tamil Nadu', in R. Sunder Rajan, ed., *Signposts: Gender Issues in Post-Independence India*, New Delhi: Kali for Women, 1999. I am grateful to Shaheed Pervez and Aseem Prakash for their help with recent academic literature and statistics.

1 These gains are due to slow but steady improvements in the life expectation of girls who reach 5 years of age together with a deterioration in male mortality in adulthood.

2 Between Censuses, demographic information is collected from very large samples by the National Sample Survey Organisation (NSSO); for data for 2004 see Randeep Ramesh, 'India to Crack Down on Doctors Aborting Girls', *The Guardian*, 25 April 2008.

3 Urban areas have CSRs lower than the national average; rural areas of prosperous states have very low CSRs; but because of the generally better sex ratios in rural areas the overall sex ratio is higher is poorer states. See L. Visaria, 'Improving the Child Sex Ratio: Role of Policy and Advocacy', *Economic and Political Weekly*, 22 March 2008, pp. 34-37.

4 The Human Development Index, the standard indicator of well-being, normalises and summarises life expectancy, literacy, education, standard of living, and gross domestic (state) product per capita.

5 Most recent data for the 1991 and 2001 censuses shows Kerala's CSR increasing by 2 per thousand while West Bengal's deteriorated by 7. UNICEF, 'Child Sex Ratio', available at http://www.unicef.org.

6 'Preference for Boys Further Skews India's Sex Ratio', *Express India*, 13 December 2007, reporting an ActionAid study. For other quantitative information in this paragraph, see Census of India, 2001; R. Bhagat, 'Slaughter in the Womb', *The Hindu*, 19 March 2007.

7 Staff Reporter: 'Caution over Skewed Child Sex Ratio in Andhra Pradesh', *The Hindu*, 8 September 2003; S. Agnihotri, 'Missing Females: A Disaggregated Analysis', *Economic and Political Weekly*, 19 August

1995, pp. 2074-84.

8 Quoted in T.K. Rajalakshmi, 'Reinventing Violence', *Frontline*, 24(25), 2007/2008, pp. 18-19.

9 B. Harriss, 'Differential Female Mortality and Health Care in South Asia', *Monograph 1*, Centre for the Study of Relief Administration, New Delhi, 1988; and 'The Intrafamily Distribution of Hunger in South Asia', in Jean Dreze, Amartya Sen and Athar Hussain, eds., *The Political Economy of Hunger*, Oxford: Clarendon Press, 1994, pp. 224-98.

10 Piramalai Kallars and Vellalar Gounders; V. Athreya and S.R. Chunkath, 'Fighting Female Infanticide', *The Hindu*, 17 March 1996; S. Pervez, 'Death before Birth: Negotiating Reproduction, Female Infanticide and Sex Selective Abortion in Tamil Nadu, South India', PhD Thesis, Edinburgh University, 2008.

11 For instance the density of sonography and of sex selective abortions in Maharashtra correlates closely with purchasing power and is concentrated in the rich sugar belt. R. Bhagat, 'Slaughter in the Womb'.

12 For case study evidence see *The Guardian*, 25 July 2007; see also *The Lancet*, 8 January 2007.

13 On 'quiet violence', see B. Hartmann and J.K. Boyce, *A Quiet Violence: View from a Bangladesh Village*, London: Zed Books, 1983; for the same idea, see Tony Beck, *The Experience of Poverty: Fighting for Respect and Resources in Village India*, London: ITDP Books, 1994; Mike Watts gave us the phrase 'silent violence' in 1983: *Silent Violence: Food, Famine and the Peasantry in Northern Nigeria*, Berkeley: University of California Press, 1983; for structural violence, see Johan Galtung, 'Violence, Peace, and Peace Research', *Journal of Peace Research*, 6(3), 1969, pp. 167-91, for 'objective violence' see Slavoj Zizek, *Violence*, London: Profile Books, 2008 (see also Bernstein, Leys and Panitch, in this volume). The naturalisation of this violence survives injections of proselytizing, anti-abortion Christian advocacy, sometimes funded from US evangelising organisations.

14 Estimates of the business assets per son (net of the dowries paid out on daughters) have been compared with estimates of total dowries per daughter from key elite informants willing to divulge these sensitive details; B. Harriss-White, *India Working: Essays on Society and Economy*, Cambridge: Cambridge University Press, 2003, pp. 128-30.

15 S. Agnihotri, *Sex Ratio Patterns in the Indian Population: A Fresh Exploration*, London: Sage, 2000; see also T. Dyson and M. Moore, 'Kinship Structure, Female Autonomy and Demographic Behaviour: Regional Contrasts within India', *Population and Development Review*, 9,

1983; Harriss-White, *India Working,* chapter 5.

16 Bhagat, 'Slaughter in the Womb'.

17 See N. Kabeer, *Reversed Realities: Gender Hierarchies in Development Thought*, London: Verso, 1994.

18 R. Kaur, 'Dirty Sex', http://downtoearth.org.in, 20 December 2007; In Shahid Pervez' ethnographic research in Tamil Nadu, the two-child norm is socially pervasive but experienced in class specific ways: Pervez, 'Death before Birth'.

19 Malini Bhattacharya, reported in Rajalakshmi, 'Reinventing Violence', p. 18. Reported crimes against women are rising at rates exceeding the expansion of the service economy – 10 per cent or more – most especially crimes of family cruelty, notably burns and rape of women under 20. Dalit women are disproportionately at risk. Trafficking thrives in camps of developmentally displaced people and migrant labour. In recent times, women have been compelled to enter the migrant labour force in significant numbers. Rajalakshmi, 'Reinventing Violence'; V. Venkatesan, 'Lacunae in Law', *Frontline,* 24(25), 2007/2008, pp. 20-23. There is reported to be a close association between the CSR and other forms of violence against women. *The Hindu*, 8 September 2003. On gender based violence in the capitalist peripheries, see G. Terry and J. Hoare, eds., *Gender-Based Violence*, Oxford: Oxfam, 2007.

20 J. Ghosh, 'Structures of Insecurity', *Frontline*, 24(25), 2007/2008, pp. 27- 30.

21 C. das Gupta, 'State and Capital in Independent India: From Dirigisme to Neoliberalism', PhD Thesis, School of Oriental and African Studies, 2008, presents evidence of the period 1965-80 (that others have identified as one of industrial deceleration) as being rather one of institutional flux in which practices of early liberalisation and Indian FDI were being established at the same time as structures of dirigisme were being used and challenged.

22 P. Nilleson and B. Harriss-White, 'Life Chances: Development and Female Disadvantage', in B. Harriss-White, S. Janakarajan et al., eds., *Rural India Facing the 21st Century*, London: Anthem, 2004, pp. 328-49.

23 Ministry of Finance, *Report of the Expert Group on Agricultural Indebtedness*, Government of India, 2007.

24 S. Saxena, *Child Marriage in South Asia: Brutal Murder of Innocence*, New Delhi: Concept, 2004; T.K. Rajalakshmi, 'Woman as Victim', *Frontline*, 24(25), 2007/2008, pp. 4-8.

25 Ministry of Finance, *Report of the Expert Group on Agricultural Indebtedness*;

Pervez, 'Death before Birth'.

26 The alliance between the upper caste, urban Hindu beneficiaries of capitalist modernity and right-wing cultural politics (not confined to the Hindu nationalist BJP but at work wherever Hindu political sentiment is courted) is associated historically with – and arguably also at work on – the Child Sex Ratio. The relationship involves the media – e.g. patriarchal soap operas – religious discourse, and cultural practices reinforcing the male-centric social order (see Vanaik, this volume).

27 Pervez, 'Death before Birth'.

28 Malini Bhattacharya in Rajalakshmi, 'Reinventing Violence', p. 26.

29 P. Wonacott, 'India's Skewed Sex Ratio puts GE Sales in Spotlight', *The Wall Street Journal*, 19 April 2007; Reuters, 13 December 2007.

30 http://www.unicef.org/india/media_3285.htm.

31 L. Bavadam, 'Fear of the Unknown', *Frontline*, 24(25), 2007/2008, pp. 9-17.

32 P. Wonacott, 'India's Skewed Sex Ratio'.

33 Ibid.

34 S. Thapar, 'Save The Girl Child', *The Hindu*, 19 March 2007; K. Sharma, 'No Girls, Please, We're Indian', *The Hindu*, 29 August 2004.

35 Thapar, 'Save the Girl Child'; *The Guardian,* 25 July 2007.

36 Randeep Ramesh, 'India to Crack Down on Doctors Aborting Girls', *The Guardian*, 25 April 2008.

37 See Brinda Karat, CP(M) Rajya Sabha member, in interview with T.K. Rajalakshmi, *Frontline*, 24(25), 2007/2008, pp. 24-26.

38 UNICEF reports no convictions in 22 of the 33 states by 2006; and of the few doctors booked under the PNDT Act – 422 by 2007 – only 2 have been convicted and according to Ramesh ('India to Crack Down') by April 2008, one was back in business.

39 Cases have been registered against GE, Wipro and Erbis for knowingly selling to unregistered clinics, the penalty for which in 2008 was a fine of Rs 50,000 ($1,250 or £625) and 3 month's jail. Ramesh, 'India to Crack Down'.

40 Informal norms are at variance with, and much more powerful than, the law. Deviance from informal norms – a dowry-less marriage for instance – receives social punishment while the criminal breach of the law goes almost entirely unpunished by the state.

41 Ramesh, 'India to Crack Down'.

42 While it may be invidious to identify individual examples, it is important to note the tireless efforts of the demographic sociologist Sabu George, in relating his field research to public interest litigation against

the misuse of reproductive technology; of demographer Leela Visaria, of economist Venkatesh Athreya and of civil servants and scholars Satish Agnihotri and Sheela Rani Chunkath (as above). See T.K. Rajalakshmi, 'Sex Selection and Questions of Law', *Frontline*, 17(21), 2000. *Frontline* and *Economic and Political Weekly* have played important roles in raising the awareness of elite intellectuals.

43 Visaria, 'Improving the Child Sex Ratio'.

44 Quoted in Rajalakshmi, 'Rethinking Violence'.

INDIA'S PARADIGMATIC COMMUNAL VIOLENCE

ACHIN VANAIK

What is referred to as communalism – intolerance and tensions between religious communities – would seem to be part of a worldwide phenomenon of religious resurgence and the rise of religio-political movements and groups of all kinds, amidst an even broader emergence, over the last three decades, of various kinds of cultural exclusivisms.[1]

Capitalist modernity is characterised by the permanence of change, of constant flux. Contrary to early Enlightenment assumptions and hopes, the certainties of tradition and custom (religiously-based or otherwise) have not been replaced by the new certainties of reason and knowledge but by uncertainties. Modernity institutionalises as never before the principle of radical doubt. Modernity constantly disrupts and revolutionises everyday life, imposing social and psychological costs, even as it also creates the more self-reflexive personality (a more dynamised self in a more dynamised society, as compared to the relative inertia of self and society in the pre-capitalist past) for whom existential dilemmas can be more intense because there are no longer any easy answers. The devastation of older values, ways of life and forms of belonging (even if these were relatively recently acquired) is traumatic. These costs are compensated for and made more bearable by the promise of collective amelioration and better times – by the notion of steady and cumulative progress.

But the advent of neoliberalism has seen still further transformations, greater social disorientation, loss of dignity and male self-respect, creating fertile ground for the rise of all kinds of aggressive self-assertions, religious or ethnic, that can serve as some form of consolation and whose affirmations (the more negative forms of identity politics) are a balm for social despair.[2] It is the failed promise of modernity, both in its current neoliberal version and in its previous socialist version, that has led to the cultural intolerances of today whose forms vary geographically, preceded as they have been by different histories, rooted in different combinations of the old and the new. When the present is unsatisfactory and the future looks bleak it is the unchangeable past that appears to provide a source of security and certainty.

Here it can be legitimately asked what difference does the emergence of a neoliberal phase make to the lives of the vast majority of Indians, for whom poverty and insecurity have been long enduring features? The fact that there is a rich and continuous history of struggles from below, and that unlike in other bourgeois democracies there is no electoral apathy – indeed not only are voter turnout rates high, and relatively higher for marginalised sections of the population, but they become progressively higher as one descends from the national level to the state and then to the municipal and panchayat levels – this fact is testimony to the expectations and hopes of progressive change that persist among the most downtrodden. However, where these popular aspirations once faced a self-declared 'developmental state' that saw itself as in some way answerable to the public for its developmental failures, such hopes now have to deal with a state that sees itself and its role in quite different terms. The Indian state now sees itself as a 'competitive state', with little responsibility for ensuring development for all, whose role is instead to establish the conditions for the emergence of a globally competitive economy driven by private wealth. Losers must now blame themselves and should no longer make unwarranted demands on the state. Nor must they be allowed to become too socially and politically disruptive. The Indian state has become ideologically and politically more ruthless and uncaring.

This global spread of neoliberalism – understood as a general economic direction, not an achieved 'state of affairs' – can only take place, moreover, via the states system. The stability of neoliberalism necessarily rests on non-economic structures – political, social, cultural and ideological. It is states, above all, that provide the legal, regulatory, infrastructural and institutional framework in which neoliberalism can operate and flourish. It is states that police capital-labour relations in favour of the former. It is states that manage macro-economic tensions and are the means, especially if they are electoral democracies, of legitimising elite rule. There is thus both a transnationalism as well as variant nationalisms associated with the stabilisation of neoliberalism. At the geopolitical level there is the issue of coordination of the states system to be provided by a 'hegemonic stabiliser', single or collective. Posed in Marxist terms, this is a debate about ultra- or super-imperialism and the cross-country elite alliances that follow from these alternative global arrangements, now that it is evident that in this latest phase of capitalism, inter-imperialist competition must be played out in an altogether different register, marking a decisive break from its militaristic past. At the nation-state level, the rightward shift represented by neoliberalism could only be sustained because it was accompanied everywhere by a rightward shift of politics (internal and external) and of ideology, whose forms have, however, always been determined by national specificities. Indeed, the sources, patterns and rhythms of this fusion of the national and the geopolitical are invariably distinctive. In India the key factor has been the rise of Hindu nationalism or, more accurately, of Hindutva (the 'politics of Hinduness') and its transformative impact – including its impact on the paradigmatic form of violence in India – communalism. Before concentrating on communal violence, however, we need to take into account the fact that violence is in fact an all-too-normal feature of the country's modern history.

VIOLENCE IN INDIA: ANYTHING BUT ABNORMAL

Since independence India has always posed something of an enigma. Barring the two year interlude (1975-77) of Emergency Rule – and even then the Indian state was less authoritarian and ruthless than the average Latin American or African dictatorship of those times – India stands out as a developing country exhibiting, at the macro-level, a remarkable durability and stability of democratic institutions and processes. Yet at the meso- and micro-levels, few developing countries can match the frequency, scale and intensity of either routinised or episodic violence that exists in India. This structural coexistence raises disturbing questions about the relationship of such violence to, and its functionality for, the existing political, economic, social and cultural order. Any comprehensive study of violence in India must therefore operate on an extraordinarily wide terrain of interacting relationships, recognising its multiple forms and sites. Amidst the welter of different typologies of violence and of approaches towards understanding it, from the socio-psychological to the most abstractly structural-functional, this essay will mainly limit itself to addressing Hindu communal violence against Muslims, and the rise of Hindutva with which it is connected – the violence that has done most to reshape the trajectory of Indian politics and the behaviour of the Indian state.

Nevertheless, one's point of departure even here must be an awareness of just how pervasive violence is in Indian society and polity and just how inadequate the mainstream political discourse is in recognising this, in understanding its sources, and in evaluating its consequences. A brief if schematic listing of the types of violence prevalent can perhaps help drive home this point. There is 1) criminal and gang violence; 2) sectarian intra-group violence, e.g., Shia versus Sunni; 3) patriarchal violence; 4) inter-ethnic violence, e.g. between Kuki and Naga tribes; 5) socio-economically motivated violence associated with class oppression, resistance and struggle; 6) ethno-national, i.e., secessionist violence; 7) communal violence; 8) officially-sponsored and directed violence, executed by the apparatuses of the state at the central, provincial, district, city and lower administrative levels, arising from declared or undeclared policy and simultaneously reinforcing caste, class, gender, and ethno-national oppressions.

These categories are ideal types, and in real life the forms of violence are invariably mixed. Secessionist trends characterise movements and groups in Kashmir and in the northeastern region, currently divided into seven states. These tensions are partly the legacy of the artificial administrative boundaries created by colonial expansion and rule, connecting a northeastern region with no strong historical or cultural ties to 'plains India'. But post-independence central government behaviour is also to blame. Of the various ethnically-based insurgency movements that once demanded independence all have been tamed or marginalised barring the Naga resistance which has persisted for several decades. But here a combined policy of bribery (provision of substantial financial largesse to be controlled by select local elites, and the incorporation of educated youth into central bureaucracies) and ruthless repression (by Indian armed forces enjoying special powers violative of basic democratic norms) has succeeded in creating a stalemate. The result is that a war-weary Naga leadership now seems prepared to settle for greater autonomy within the Indian Union, though mutual suspicions continue to bedevil early prospects of a negotiated settlement.

The Kashmir issue has from its inception remained hostage to relations between India and Pakistan, with both sides insisting that any resolution of the issue must exclude the possibility of a fully independent and secular Kashmir. In the Indian-occupied part, which was pressured to formally accede to the Union in 1948, its autonomy was to be constitutionally guaranteed by Article 370. In reality this commitment to maximum autonomy has been systematically eroded over time. Indeed, no state has been more frequently subjected to President's Rule, i.e., the temporary suspension of provincial rights and powers as well as of a range of civil liberties. By the late 1980s for the first time genuine indigenous movements emerged in the Kashmir Valley. A secular trend demanded complete independence for all of occupied Kashmir and an Islamist trend demanded either a separate Islamic state or merger with Pakistan. Ever since, sections of the Pakistan establishment have supported cross-border militant Islamist groups to fish in these troubled waters. This has understandably been condemned by India but it is necessary to recognise that the troubled waters were created by the Indian government. By New Delhi's own reckoning these Islamist groups have never numbered more than 4,000 militants, yet India stations around half a million army and para military personnel to control a population that has now become substantially alienated from the brutalities of both the Islamist groups and the Indian armed forces. The soldier-civilian ratio at 1 to around 13 makes the Valley one of the most militarised regions anywhere in the world.[3]

While caste and class relations are essentially vertical, gender relations are both horizontal and vertical. Violence against women has a scale, depth and frequency that is simply unmatched by any other kind of violence. While caste and class violence also have a normalised and quotidian character, gender violence is uniquely pervasive. It is not just episodic and collective but has a distinctive familial, individualised and privatised character. It also traverses all boundaries, and all other forms of political violence also express themselves in specifically gendered ways – rape, beating and humiliation of women being part of the process of establishing the authority/dominance of class, caste, ethnic group or government. What is more, violence against women is intimately connected to the more collective forms of periodic violence. The human emotions that lead to such 'sudden extremes' simmer in the cauldron of everyday social relations and practices.[4] Yet the very universality, pervasiveness and constancy of female oppression in and across all social relations tends to deprive it of the more specific charge and power whose accumulating force in particular historical circumstances can significantly alter the political trajectory of a state and society. The gravamen of this essay is that this is precisely what the accumulating forces of Hindutva since the early 1980s have been able to accomplish.

What of caste and class violence? The strong overlap between lower caste and lower class occupations in town and country means that often the motivations and purposes behind the perpetration of violence by upper layers is not neatly separable along straightforwardly class or caste lines. The same can be said of resistances from below. This is not to say that distinctively caste-motivated violence against Dalits ('outcastes'), or specifically anti-tribal violence, is not widely prevalent. It most certainly is. Atrocities (including murder, rape, arson, injury, etc.) against Dalits are routine, as also are gender-related crimes like dowry deaths and rape. Figures for violence against these social groups outstrip those for communal violence and are certainly underestimates of the actual scale. For example, the average annual figure for atrocities against Dalits between 1997 and 2001 was 25,587. For tribals in the same period it was 4,285. Recorded dowry deaths in 1991 were 5,077 and for rape the figure was 9,793; by 1998 recorded dowry deaths were 6,917 and rape cases had risen to 15,031.[5] These figures testify to the caste and patriarchal nature of Indian state and society.

But one of the brighter aspects of the evolution of Indian society over the last several decades has been the political and electoral upsurge of Dalits and lower castes. Overall the impact has been positive, if mixed. The ideological foundations for legitimising caste hierarchies have been weakened. For the purposes of political mobilisation and putting effective pressure on policy-making authorities, newer and larger agglomerations of lower and middle castes and of Dalits (cutting across their own respective caste sub-divisions) have emerged. But non-Dalit lower castes have not so far established an independent political presence. They have provided a large constituency of support for forces representing more the interests of the upper sections of the middle or 'backward' castes. Reservation policies for Dalits in government jobs and educational institutions have created a significant middle class which has not only provided leadership and resources for further mobilisation but also shaped its general direction. This is reformist rather than radical or revolutionary, both in the goals sought – raising the social status and power of Dalits through accession by their own elites to the higher echelons of governmental structures – and in the means used – seeking electoral alliances with various political parties and forces even if some of these represent the upper castes and classes.

As a result the material conditions of rural Dalits (the majority) remains much the same. The contemporary paradox is this: the majority of Dalits belong to the agricultural proletariat but the majority of agricultural proletarians are not Dalits. It is the unification of this rural proletarian layer behind appropriate demands for land reform, liveable wages and assured employment that has the potential to revolutionise Indian society. The current Dalit leadership and the politics they are pursuing have no such perspective of forging a rural cross-caste class alliance from below. The dominant upper layers of the 'backward castes' are themselves landowners highly resistant to any such demands. Unsurprisingly, despite the rise of the 'backward castes' and Dalits there has been little positive impact on the scope and scale of episodic and quotidian violence inflicted on Dalits and lower castes.

The segment of the population whose condition has improved the least are the 'tribals' of central India. It is in these forested regions that the influence of armed Naxalite groups (above all the Communist Party of India-Maoist), as the foremost expression of rural class struggle from below, is strongest, although it is also expanding elsewhere. Indian Maoism has strong roots in some 76 districts (out of a total of slightly over 600 districts in the whole country) spread over the nine states of Bihar, Jharkhand, Chhattisgarh, Uttar Pradesh, Maharashtra, West Bengal, Orissa, Madhya Pradesh and Andhra Pradesh; and it has a meaningful presence in some 50 other districts. Indian Maoism has become more Indian and less Maoist, and has therefore not only survived but grown. But it is nowhere as strong as made out by the Indian government, whose officials sometimes claim that Naxalism has spread to nearly 200 districts. Naxalites are being deliberately demonised. It is notable that the only other form of demonisation is of Muslim militants. Both are being defined as terrorists who must be wiped out.

Terrorism is properly understood as a technique, a tactic, and a method, and a working definition suitable for most cases is that it is any act causing or threatening to cause physical injury to innocent unarmed civilians. It can be and is used by a host of agents, ranging from individuals and non-state combat groups to the apparatuses of the state. This is not to deny that Naxalite groups resort on occasions to unacceptable forms of terrorist violence. But in India by far the greatest number of civilian fatalities and injuries are caused by the terrorist actions of official bodies controlled by and answerable to either the state governments or the Central government.

The demonisation of the Naxalites has been ramped up by the Congress-led government elected in 2004. In 2006 Prime Minister Manmohan Singh declared them to be the single biggest national security threat; and soon followed that up by calling them a 'virus' needing to be 'eliminated'. Such demonisation serves multiple purposes. It aims to justify the retention of repressive 'anti-terrorist' and 'security' laws which rationalise arbitrary arrests and prolonged detentions/incarcerations without legal access or adjudication. It allows many state governments to obtain greater resources from the Centre in the name of fighting Naxalism, which can then be used for other purposes. It shifts the focus away from police brutalities and from the political collusion that allows armed gangs hired by richer landowners and forest contractors to assault and subdue the landless and tribals who constitute the main social base of Naxalism. It also aims to justify the setting up by some state governments of the Salwa Judum or 'Peace Campaign', which are armed groups comprising Maoist defectors, volunteers and 'lumpens' who are paid a salary and have been given special policing powers. They, in effect, act as an 'outsourced' vigilante arm of the state, which does not wish to control their atrocities and criminal activities so long as they help fight and weaken the 'higher' danger posed by the Naxalites.

Yet despite the clear evidence of how structurally rooted are the causes of such multiple forms of violence, the conventional political discourse continues to celebrate Indian democracy and insists quite wrongly on seeing violence as an abnormality or disease, the antidote for which is supposed to lie in 'improving' the existing democratic structures, processes and spaces in state and civil society. The rule of law, proper monitoring of electoral behaviour, the judiciary, parliament, governmental bureaucracies, the press, lively civic associations, etc., are perceived as the mechanisms whose healthy functioning is supposed to determine the overall health of the liberal democratic order. Alongside this effort at improvement, conventional wisdom adds that it is necessary to purge the main sources of the disease of violence – Naxalites, Muslim terrorists, secessionist militants, communal elements. By succeeding in these endeavours the body politic can be expected to be well on the way towards full recovery.

Absent from this conventional diagnostic and prescriptive discourse is the sense that capitalist modernisation in its uneven and combined character of development necessarily creates its own (though variable) sources, conditions, stimuli and forms of violence. Missing also is the realisation that there is, as a consequence, in very many societies including India's, a culture of violence, a kind of low-intensity violence taking routinised, ritualised, normalised and accepted forms in everyday life, which under specific circumstances are highly conducive to the eruption of more congealed and denser forms of episodic violence. Nor is such a conventional discourse capable of recognising how the changing neoliberal character of India's political economy is associated with a changing landscape of political violence. Certain kinds of periodic violence become more prominent. New definitions of what constitutes violence appear. New notions of what is acceptable or unacceptable emerge. New priorities on what kinds of violence to deal with – or not deal with – are set.

HINDUTVA: THE KEY FACTOR

Since the early seventies Indian politics has been in deep flux, reflecting an endemic crisis of bourgeois political leadership. The Emergency was a failed attempt at resolving this dilemma through an authoritarian stabilisation.[6] But over the last two decades a significant acceleration has taken place in the dynamics of uncertain socio-political contestation. This accelerated phase broadly overlaps with the neoliberal economic turn and the dramatic surfacing of an ugly religious nationalism. Democracy is redefined as Hindu majoritarianism, and secularism as a false and anti-Hindu, minority-favouring construct – ideas that have secured substantial and growing resonance in Indian society.[7]

This endemic crisis of bourgeois political leadership has been reflected in a political instability (encased within a framework of considerable systemic durability) that has gone through two phases. From 1971 to 1989 general elections had a referendum-like character. Major swings in electoral behaviour were actually testimony to the fact that no serious contender for Central rule could rely on sufficiently stable electoral support. Ironically, during this phase large parliamentary majorities in wave-like elections were not an indication of overall political stability but of the very opposite. It was in this period that the Congress won its greatest ever number of seats (in 1984), only to fail dismally the next time around. This was the period when two elected non-Congress centrist alternatives – the Janata Party of 1977-80 and the V.P. Singh government of 1989-91 – achieved power, yet neither was able to last a full term. From 1989 onwards a new phase appeared, first of minority governments and then of coalition rule. Increasingly, the overall uncertainties of the polity had come to be reflected in parliamentary instability.

The landmark political event after the Emergency was the implementation by the V.P. Singh minority government in 1989 of the Mandal Committee's recommendation to reserve 27 per cent of jobs in Central government for the 'other backward castes' or OBCs.[8] Since less than 50,000 jobs overall were affected, the significance of the step was symbolic, but nonetheless politically powerful, expressing as it did the new assertion of the middle castes or OBCs who make up the majority of caste Hindus and comprise a wide spectrum of their own, from the poorest MBCs ('most backward castes') to the upper ranks of OBCs that are still demarcated from the 'forward castes' and Brahmins at the top. This sparked large-scale demonstrations in Western and Northern India, led by middle class-upper caste students, and even self-immolations by some individual students.

This was soon followed, moreover, by an even more dramatic landmark event, the Ram Janmabhoomi campaign carried out by the Sangh Parivar, aiming to unite Hindus against the 'Muslim Other' – faced with the Mandalisation of Indian politics which threatened to institutionalise caste divisions among Hindus. The Sangh Parivar is a 'family' of organisations that make up the organised Hindu right. The 'father' organisation is the RSS or Rashtriya Swayamsevak Sangh (National Volunteer Corps), a cadre-based force of over a million whose spinal cord is made up of ascetic full-timers who are supposed to remain unmarried as a mark of total devotion to the cause. The Bharatiya Janata Party or BJP is the electoral wing. The VHP or Vishwa Hindu Parishad (World Hindu Council) is the substantially autonomous cultural front, while the members of the Bajrang Dal (Lord Hanuman's Army) are the lumpenised storm-troopers. The Sangh also controls a major trade union federation and has its own students' and women's wings. The Ram Janmabhoomi campaign culminated in the destruction of the Babri Masjid mosque on December 6, 1992 – a calculated act of defiance of the Supreme Court as well as a deliberate assault on the Indian Constitution's commitment to secularism. The month-long campaign had itself aroused communal sentiments and hatreds on a massive scale, and it led to widespread communal violence that took over a thousand Muslim lives.

The next landmark event was not so much the formation of the BJP-led coalition government in 1998 as the manner in which its decision to conduct nuclear tests was taken – and received. While the unelected and publicly unaccountable RSS was privy to the decision, the coalition partners were kept in the dark –- a fait accompli that was soon enough accepted by all parties (including the Congress) except for those of the left. The shadowy but powerful role played by the RSS in Indian politics reached its climax with the pogrom against Muslims in Gujarat in February-March 2002 in which at least 2,000 Muslims were killed and tens of thousands displaced from their homes and businesses. This was easily the worst communal pogrom since the Partition holocaust.[9] Not only did the then Prime Minister, A.B. Vajpayee, subsequently rationalise this, but the pogrom could not have taken place without the private sanction of the Chief Minister of Gujarat, Narendra Modi (who had served in the RSS for about a decade-and-a-half, before being made General Secretary of the BJP's Gujarat unit in 1988). Far from Modi and his senior political, bureaucratic, judicial and police cohorts being held criminally responsible, he actually profited politically. His re-election with an increased majority in the December 2002 state elections testified to the normalisation of communalism in Gujarat. Modi was then re-elected for an unprecedented third time in December 2007. Frighteningly, he is now widely tipped to eventually become the leader of the BJP and thus a possible Prime Minister in a future BJP-led coalition government at the Centre.

Each of these landmark events since 1989 is associated practically and/or symbolically with violence. One should not interpret the BJP's possible electoral plateauing over the last two general elections as reflecting a political-ideological decline of the Sangh Parivar.[10] The violence and repression carried out by the Sangh Parivar in most of the landmark political events discussed above caused no lasting damage to its political credibility, its ability to forge alliances with other regional parties, or to its cultural, ideological and institutional influence in civil society. The Hindutva train – in reality it is several trains, on multiple tracks – has already covered enormous ground and continues to move forward, albeit at varying speeds and with stops, occasional reverses, and restarts. Of course, the forward march of Hindutva is a socio-political process which interacts with other important socio-political processes, not only the ongoing forward march of the OBCs, the unprecedented assertiveness of Dalits (outcastes), and ongoing Muslim ferment, but also the regionalisation of the Indian polity and the rise of a massive Indian 'middle class' (not actually a median category, but the top 15 per cent-20 per cent of the Indian population) that provides the social foundation for the stabilisation and growth of right-wing reactionary politics, both secular and communal. The highly complex way in which all these processes interweave establishes the contours within which Indian politics today and tomorrow are playing themselves out.

COMMUNAL VIOLENCE IN INDIA

In terms of sheer numbers Hindutva is the biggest religious nationalist movement in the world. For nearly three decades after independence, Hindutva's salience remained low. The horrific legacy of the Partition genocide, the assassination of Mahatma Gandhi by a Hindutva devotee, the political and ideological dominance of the Congress party (claiming to uphold the principles of socialism, secularism, democracy and nonalignment), the defeat and dismemberment of Pakistan in 1971, all contributed to this reality. From the 1970s onwards the process of Congress decline and growing disillusionment with the principles that the first prime minister, Jawaharlal Nehru, had done so much to establish became unmistakably obvious. There did emerge new forces, which failed however to re-establish a stable non-Congress form of centrist rule. All this began to pave the way for the rise of Hindutva. It is not a coincidence that parallel to this emergence that (a) there was a fairly dramatic escalation in Hindu-Muslim riots; (b) the overwhelming majority of victims (deaths and injuries) were Muslims; and (c) the police and paramilitaries were among the principal perpetrators of the violence.

The officially-recorded figures speak for themselves. Between 1954 and 1963 the average annual number of Hindu-Muslim riots was 60.6 and the average annual number of deaths was 34.4 persons. Between 1964 and 1979 the respective figures were 319.2 riots and 260.2 persons. Between 1980 and 1988 the figures were 534.1 riots and 416.6 persons. In the six years after 1988 for which figures are available (1989-93, plus 2002) we still get an annual average of 528 deaths.[11] The emergence of lower caste and women's movements have at least made the high recorded figures of atrocities against them something of an embarrassment for higher political authorities and forced some kind of acknowledgement of failure on their part. But when it comes to the predominantly Muslim victims of communal violence there is no such acknowledgement from the culpable state authorities or parties (i.e. the Sangh).

Paul Brass's argument that 'riots are dramatic productions, creations of specific persons, groups and parties operating through institutionalised riots networks within a discursive framework of Hindu-Muslim communal opposition and antagonism that in turn produces specific forms of political practice that makes riots' is entirely correct.[12] In other words, whatever the triggers, communal riots are organised and not spontaneous phenomena. Moreover, the most developed and organised perpetrators are the Sangh Parivar and other militant Hindu organisations. Brass outlines the three phases through which the organisation of communal violence passes: preparation/rehearsal, marked by the presence of 'fire-tenders' who keep inter-group tensions stoked; activation/enactment undertaken by 'conversion specialists' who are the on-the-ground mob mobilisers and leaders; and finally, the aftermath of communal violence events, whereby the 'blame displacers' – comprising politicians, intellectuals and media people – help shift the discourse away from the suffering of victims to 'problems of governance', and who implicitly or explicitly justify the violence. Little wonder then that the perpetrators invariably avoid prosecution even when they are identified. Deaths in such riots/pogroms are caused by mob frenzy and police killings as well as by individuals carrying out cold-blooded brutalities independently of collective action.

The spur for much of this communal violence, as Steve Wilkinson has shown, is electoral competition.[13] His empirical work on state and town variations in the incidence and duration of ethnic and communal riots comes to the conclusion that minorities will be protected only when it suits ruling or aspiring political parties at the state level to woo the Muslim vote. In the south of India where there have been strong backward caste movements and therefore greater intra-Hindu competition, the Muslim vote becomes more important and they are safer. But Wilkinson's belief that intra-Hindu competition will increase, as a result of the Dalit and OBC upsurges in the north, and that this will lead to an eventual decline of Hindu-Muslim riots, is over-optimistic to say the least. Current statistical trends on communal violence belie this, while the growing communalisation of the general political-ideological environment in the north has created popular expectations that such violence will repeatedly occur and should occasion no great alarm or surprise. This is apparently because there is to some degree or other a 'pampering' of minorities, especially Muslims, in the search for their 'vote banks'. So, it is claimed, there is no fundamental flaw in Indian democracy but an understandable 'Hindu resentment' that basically *reacts* against this alleged pampering, even if the reactions are sometimes 'excessive'. In other words, as both Brass and Wilkinson understand so well, it is the political dimension that is decisive, namely the role played by the Sangh Parivar and the success it has had in making its ideological constructs a spreading public 'common sense'.

The police and para-military forces are invested with all necessary legal powers to prevent riots from taking place through pre-emptive action, and when riots start, to bring them swiftly to an end. If despite this there are frequent and sustained communal riots, it is because the police, at the behest of the political leadership in the states concerned, have either remained silent spectators or even participated in the riots. While many a prominent spokesperson from the Muslim community has called for a more religiously mixed police force, this is really of very limited value. At most a more diverse police force can create a somewhat less prejudiced atmosphere in police ranks, but widespread and strong biases reflecting the existing prejudices and stereotypes among the general population remain. No wonder then that despite low Muslim representation in the army, Muslim leaders have much greater trust in it and repeatedly call for army deployment during riot situations. The structure of the police is like that of Indian society – a tiny national ruling elite, a comfortable regional middle class, and a mass of the poor – 90 per cent of all police are constables or head constables.

Having a more religiously mixed police force is not the answer. In Andhra Pradesh, the Muslim percentage among the police is 16 per cent or about double the percentage of Muslims in the state. Yet in every major riot since 1978 the police have exhibited partisan behaviour against Muslims. In Kerala and West Bengal, where the proportion of Muslims in the police is far below their proportions in their respective state populations, the frequency of riots is low and police behaviour impartial. In West Bengal, this is because the Communist Party (Marxist) or CPM-led Left Front (which also includes the other big mainstream left party, the Communist Party of India or CPI) has been in power for the last 30 years. In Kerala it is because these two Left parties and the Muslim League factions feature in coalition governments. In Bihar and Uttar Pradesh, where the police are notoriously communal, they have behaved impartially when the highest civilian authorities like Chief Ministers Lalu Prasad Yadav and Mulayam Singh Yadav have demanded it.[14]

THE GUJARAT POGROM

On February 27, 2002 the Sabarmati Express, jam-packed with Hindutva activists and supporters returning from Ayodhya had one of its passenger cars burnt by Muslim locals just as it pulled out of Godhra station in Gujarat. Fifty-eight people, including women and children, died. Days earlier, on their onward journey to Ayodhya – the site of periodic agitations calling for the construction of a Ram temple to begin – Hindutva activists had already raised the communal temperature by their anti-Muslim sloganeering and generally hooliganish and intimidatory behaviour. Similar behaviour on their return journey had raised tensions to a high pitch among local Muslims along the train route. According to eyewitnesses at Godhra station, the molestation of a Muslim girl on the platform and the terrorisation of a Muslim tea-vendor lit the spark that led to the torching of the car. But while this was a spontaneous event by unidentified locals, what followed was the most awful – and politically serious – pogrom in post-independence India.

Over the next few days and weeks the Gujarat state government headed by Chief Minister Narendra Modi, a rabid Hindutva ideologue belonging to the RSS and the ruling BJP, carried out a massive pogrom and reign of terror. Mobs numbering in the thousands were unleashed while the police were told to remain aloof. At least 2,000 Muslims were butchered. Muslim-populated localities in cities, towns and villages throughout much of the state as well as Muslim-owned shops and businesses were torched and destroyed. Over 150,000 people were displaced and had to take refuge in makeshift camps set up by a few Muslim and non-Muslim civic associations. Pregnant women were skewered, others gang-raped and then burnt to death. The scale of violence was enormous, but always selective and carried out with remarkable speed. This was only possible because of several months of prior preparation and planning. Muslim homes and businesses had been geographically identified. Transport had been made ready and gas cylinders and other combustible materials stocked. Distribution of venomous and hate-spewing pamphlets had long been taking place.[15]

And several years later, rehabilitation and compensation remains incomplete and inadequate. The Gujarat police, judiciary and government have shown more alacrity in arresting 'suspects' and charging them for the Godhra 'conspiracy' than in pursuing those involved in the pogrom that followed. The higher echelons of the police and bureaucracy are unpunished, while the top leaders of the Sangh Parivar responsible for the carnage have never been touched. The Congress, the main opposition party in Gujarat, played a negligible role in providing succour to the victims when most needed. Neither at the state or national level has the Congress since 2002 dared to carry out a genuine and serious campaign highlighting this horror or vigorously declaring its opposition to Hindu communalism, or warning how Gujarat has become a laboratory for the kind of violence that can be unleashed elsewhere. Leaving to one side the debate about whether or not the Sangh Parivar constitutes a fascist force, and whether or not India has been facing or will face the danger of a fascist takeover and transformation, there is no dispute within the left about the fact that the Sangh has fascist characteristics. This is most evident in the way it organises mass violence as a spectacle, and how for its devoted cadres and supporters such ethnic cleansing is experienced as cathartic and celebratory. But the Sangh also speaks in different voices to different audiences, often skilfully using the language of democracy.

The Sangh's exercise of periodic communal violence has played an important part in the expansion of its popularity and influence. But it also has its down-side. Its greatest gains socially have been upwards, among the Indian 'middle class', especially among professionals and those with college credentials. This section is comfortable with the Sangh's anti-Muslim sentiments but it is also worried by the 'disturbances' created by riots and the possibility of 'retaliatory' violence.[16] Future violence by the Sangh must be contextually sensitive, that is, calibrated to best achieve anticipated gains in social terrains that have been carefully surveyed and properly prepared for. Such violence must be occasional, controllable and as far as possible presented as reactive to some issue or event, and therefore more easily justifiable.

THE CLASS PROFILE

So what is the social background of the Sangh activists and cadres, of those who willingly participate in such collective brutalities? And what of the general social profile of those who support the Sangh? The Sangh is a flexible constellation whose organisational components enjoy variable measures of autonomy, but with the RSS as the overall guardian at the hub. The RSS provides trained and experienced activists and full-timers to the other affiliates and makes sure that the BJP in particular does not go too far in the direction of programmatic compromises because of electoral or administrative compulsions. The cadres of the RSS, men who usually first make contact with the organisation as adolescent youths, come overwhelmingly from urban Hindu upper castes and middle and lower-middle class backgrounds. That this is the main recruiting ground of the RSS is overdetermined by the fundamental nature of the Hindutva credo. This claims that India is a Hindu nation that needs to overcome its historical weakness caused above all by earlier Muslim rule and by the persisting 'unfairness' and 'danger from within' represented by today's 'pampered' and 'unbending' Muslim minority. Therefore a new militarised Hindu unity must be created.

There is an external principle for forging unity – hostility to the 'threatening Muslim Other' – which has the advantage of more easily transcending caste and class divisions among Hindus. But there must also be an ideological principle of unification internal to Hindus and Hinduism, for which the only viable candidate is a loose and accommodating Brahminism. But by being a Brahminism nonetheless, it has much more difficulty in transcending caste, class and regional cleavages. Hence Hindutva's much stronger attraction for the upper castes, especially those sections that for various reasons also feel more vulnerable and insecure.

But right-wing Hindu communal violence also finds other class supporters because such riots all too often have a real economic functionality. Indeed, one of the more important background conditions that are conducive to many such riots breaking out where they do is the existence of economic competition between entrenched Hindu entrepreneurs, traders and contractors and a rising layer of Muslim entrepreneurs, small proprietors and investors. Many such Muslims are beneficiaries of steady remittances from abroad or are returnees who have accumulated savings from work in the Gulf States and elsewhere. Time and again, the consequences of communal riots have been the economic devastation of such Muslim competitors. There is a Hindu propertied class that benefits from such violence and has every reason to give solid political as well as financial-material support to Hindutva forces. Asghar Ali Engineer, perhaps the single most diligent observer, chronicler, analyst and commentator on communal riots in India, has repeatedly pointed out that such riots take place in towns where there is a substantial percentage of Muslims, well above the national average of 13 per cent but also well below a majority or near-majority of the local population. Such violence hardly ever takes place where Muslims constitute such a small proportion that they cannot pose any kind of economic or political challenge.[17]

However, the greatest class advantage for the Sangh is undoubtedly the new acceptability and legitimacy it has gained in the eyes of big capital. The BJP governing at the Centre is seen as no different from the Congress in being committed to promoting the interests of big capital in the name of creating a strong India. True, the Sangh's willingness to carry out anti-Muslim violence is a matter of unease, but only that. Protection of profit-making is far more important than protection of Muslims. Little wonder, then, that even after the Gujarat pogrom one of the premier bodies representing the collective interests of the Indian capitalist class – the Confederation of Indian Industry (CII) – had no hesitation in inviting Narendra Modi to address the chieftains of Indian capital, while Gujarat remains a favoured destination for investment by Indian and foreign capital.

As for the BJP, it has overtaken the Congress as the most favoured repository of votes for the upper castes and upper classes. In the last 2004 general elections, 43 per cent of the upper castes voted for the BJP compared to 21 per cent for the Congress. Among peasant proprietors 25 per cent voted for the BJP compared to 23 per cent for the Congress. Among OBCs the vote share was approximately the same, while among Dalits, Adivasis, Muslims,

Sikhs and Christians, the Congress did consistently and significantly better. Among the upper middle class the BJP secured 31 per cent of votes compared to 26 per cent for the Congress; among the lower middle class the Congress secured 28 per cent to the BJP's 25 per cent, while among the poor and very poor the Congress did considerably better.[18]

COMBATING HINDUTVA

The Indian state defines as its principal enemies the Naxalites, the secessionist currents and the internal terrorists who are presumed to be influenced by or connected with al-Qaeda-like transnational bodies, or with Pakistan-based Islamist groups with a focus on Kashmir. Hindutva is not seen as anywhere near as serious a threat. No doubt one reason for this is that whereas secessionism threatens the territorial 'sovereignty of the state', and Naxalism the 'authority' that goes along with such a notion of sovereignty, communal violence in the name of the religious majority does not. Indeed Hindu communalism disguises itself as a form of national unity, expressing the 'popular' sovereignty that the state is supposed to represent and embody. The demonisation of Islam and Muslims also neatly fits into the wider global effort to use the ideological banner of the 'global war on terror' as the way to win greater acceptance of US imperial behaviour.[19]

Hindutva also operates quite comfortably within the parameters of Indian democracy. The first-past-the-post electoral system benefits it once a threshold of popular support is surpassed. The privatised associations of civil society, much celebrated by a certain strand of democracy theorists, present no barrier to Hindutva. More than any other political force the Sangh straddles and connects the domains of civil society and the apparatuses of the state. More than any other force it is rooted in the pores of civil society and possesses a density of structures that should be the envy of every other political force in the country – schools, recreational bodies, religious and cultural institutions, a plethora of associations catering to different groups from retired armed forces personnel to housewives – with some 40,000 RSS shakas or cadre-led branches in cities and small-town India providing support mechanisms for addressing the problems of everyday life.[20]

One of the most important aspects of the Sangh's success over the last two-and-a-half decades has been not merely its own expansion but also its contribution to the transformation of the character of the main opposition party, the Congress. The longer-term stabilisation of what can be called 'authoritarian democracy' is ensured when the programmatic differences between two main contending forces for electoral supremacy in a bourgeois system have so greatly narrowed that the political centre of gravity remains firmly on the right, no matter who wins. This is clearly the case in the US between the Republicans and the 'New Democrats'; between the Conservatives and 'New Labour' in the UK; and between the strong saffron of the BJP and the pale saffron of the Congress in India. What has occurred over the last 25 years is not so much the Congress-isation of the BJP as the BJP-isation of the Congress. The latter should no longer be seen as some kind of bourgeois centrist party, but as a clearly right-wing party.

Regardless of whether there is a Congress-led or BJP-led coalition government at the Centre, the essential direction of Indian economic policy (neoliberalism) and of its foreign policy (strategic partnership with the US) will, apart from minor qualifications, remain the same. Nevertheless, it also remains the case that the distance between the Congress and BJP is significantly greater than that between the major contending parties in any liberal democracy anywhere in the world. The BJP is not the equivalent of the Republicans or of West European Christian Democracy. It is a considerably more dangerous political phenomenon and will remain so as long as its umbilical cord to the RSS and the other organisations of the Sangh remains intact, which there is every indication it will.

Clearly, the struggle to defeat this pernicious force can only be a long-term project. To overcome communalism and its concomitant forms of violence (quotidian and periodic) we need to fight against more than communalism. Given the powerful connections between neoliberal globalisation, imperial aggrandisement, cultural exclusivisms, ecological despoliation and social and economic inequalities of various kinds, this struggle must be waged at all these levels. This task is made all the more difficult because no country is as crisscrossed by different lines of cleavage as India – regional, urban-rural, linguistic, tribal, caste, class, religious, and all of these are further crisscrossed by differences of gender, skill, income and wealth. Despite sectoral movements of sometimes remarkable scale and scope, these have never coalesced to the point where the Indian state has been unable to somehow manage these multiple yet separated pressures. The task for Indian progressives is thus clear: to find a way of generating a politics of the universal that can appeal to and incorporate the politics of the singular – to make that coalescence.

With only some 7 per cent of the workforce in the 'organised' sector of the economy, which is bound by regulations and rules governing employment practices, and only around 3 per cent unionised, it is hardly surprising that progressive politics is dominated by a range of single-issue groups (including the best of the NGOs) taking up basic developmental concerns, and by sectoral social movements taking up the causes of women, tribals, lower castes, displaced persons, slum-dwellers, etc. But there is also a diverse set of left forces and parties that are well organised and enjoy considerable regional influence. Maoism has come to power in Nepal and has sustained itself, even grown, in India. Admittedly, the mainstream left parties – the CPI and CPM – are, for all their rhetoric, essentially social-democratic in nature. But they still remain, like the Maoists, among the more intransigent opponents of communalism.

Insofar as Hindutva is rooted in the pores of Indian civil society, the building of secular, democratic, welfarist and justice-seeking counter-institutions on the same terrain is absolutely vital. To some extent this does take place through the actions of the multiplicity of broadly progressive groups, movements and parties that exist. But unlike in the case of the Sangh, here there exists no organisational mechanism or any overarching (even if minimal) form of ideological agreement that can, however loosely, unify their actions and orientations against Hindutva. In other words, what is most needed is some kind of counter-constellation of all these progressive forces, a 'Left and Democratic Front' whose coordinating structures will of course have to be internally far more democratic than that of the Sangh. This is most likely to emerge from the very experience of sustained collective struggle and joint actions; while also central to the construction of such a Front would have to be the preparation of a holistic and common political programme. This would encompass specific concerns and demands but would above all convincingly express an inspiring alternative vision of a far more humane, ecologically viable and socially just order beyond the barrenness of today's capitalism.

NOTES

1 Eric Hobsbawm, 'Whose Fault-Line Is It Anyway', *New Statesman & Society*, 24 April 1992, p. 26.

2 It is in this context that studies of mass psychology, of crowd behaviour and mob frenzy typical of communal riots or pogroms are most illuminating. Useful and important studies of this type include those by Elias Canetti, *Crowds and Power*, New York: Farrar, Strauss and Giroux, 1984; Gustave Le Bon, *The Crowd: A Study of the Popular Mind*, New York: Viking Press, 1960; and for ethnic violence in South Asia, S.J. Tambiah, *Levelling Crowds: Ethnonationalist Conflicts and Collective Violence in South Asia*, New Delhi: Vistaar Publications, 1997.

3 For the extent to which the Indian government is responsible for human rights violations, see the Amnesty International Report, *Torture and Deaths in Custody in Jammu and Kashmir*, January 1995.

4 See the fine compilation by Amrita Basu and Srirupa Roy, *Violence and Democracy in India*, Kolkata: Seagull Books, 2007. For an important study that explores the relationship between women and Hindutva, either as victims or allies, see Tanika Sarkar and Urvashi Butalia, eds., *Women and the Hindu Right*, New Delhi: Kali for Women, 1995. The very low female to male sex ratio in India is testimony to the extraordinarily institutionalised character of women's oppression. Barbara Harriss-White devotes a specific study for this volume.

5 See K.S. Subramanian, *Political Violence and the Police in India*, New Delhi: Sage Publications, 2007, pp. 156 and 196.

6 See my *The Painful Transition: Bourgeois Democracy in India*, London: Verso, 1990. While in a macro-political sense the Emergency was not comparable to many dictatorships, it must not be forgotten that the government carried out a terrible campaign of forced sterilisations that was the single greatest reason for creating deep unpopularity in north India with Emergency Rule.

7 Some empirical evidence for this is given in a post-2004 election survey which showed how Hindutva through over two decades of sustained communal propaganda and practice has gained substantial adherence from the middle and upper sections of society to a 'new common sense' characterised by 'a) a majoritarian viewpoint, b) high expression of religiosity, c) insistence on maintaining group boundaries, d) lack of sharp awareness or knowledge about blatantly communal events, e) mild approval of minority interests, and f) a weak association between these and partisanship as far as support to the BJP is concerned'. According to this survey, more Hindus vote for the BJP than for the Congress (in 2004, 40 per cent as compared to 35 per cent) and this support is stable, i.e., the BJP does not require communal campaigns to sustain it. See Suhas Palshikar, 'Majoritarian Middle Ground?', *Economic and Political Weekly*, 18-24 December 2004.

8 These are the intermediate or backward castes which, according to the last census of 1931 that enumerated castes, constitute 52 per cent of the Indian population. The Mandal Committee (named after B.P. Mandal, who chaired the Committee) came out with its report in 1978 recommending such reservations in Central government jobs and educational institutions. It was only partly implemented (education was excluded) in 1989. In April 2008, the Supreme Court ruled that 27 per cent reservations must now be given to OBCs in central government educational institutions but excluding the 'creamy layer'. This is an upper layer among OBCs whose income and educational status presumably

disqualifies it from getting reservations. But the criterion for identifying this creamy layer has still to be clarified. Since the southern states had historically witnessed strong anti-Brahmin caste movements even before independence, OBC gains there had already taken place with some states having significantly more than 27 per cent reservations in state government and educational institutions. The 27 per cent figure was arrived at because approximately 23 per cent reservations already exist at the central level for Dalits (untouchables) and for indigenous peoples (referred to as tribals or Adivasis) at 15 per cent and 8 per cent respectively. To obviate legal challenges total reservations at the Central level were to be kept at 50 per cent.

9 While the 1984 anti-Sikh pogrom in the wake of the assassination of Prime Minister Indira Gandhi by her Sikh bodyguards took some 3,000 lives there remains a profound political difference between the two. That took place in a context of secessionist (the movement for Khalistan or separate Sikh homeland) tensions where the killing of Mrs. Gandhi was an act of vengeance for the prior assault by the Indian army on the holiest of Sikh shrines – the Golden Temple in Amritsar – where the leader of the Khalistan agitation, Sant Bhindranwala had taken final refuge. The assassination in turn triggered the pogrom. That this was a one-off event has been confirmed by the relative ease with which harmonious Hindu-Sikh relations have been re-established. The Khalistan movement has completely faded away and never at any time enjoyed more than a small minority support from Sikhs. Hindu-Sikh relations are simply not comparable to that of Hindus and Muslims, while the Hindu right is more prone to seeing the Sikh community as the historical sword-arm against Muslims and as a natural ally than as any kind of hostile opponent.

10 For a description of how deeply rooted the Sangh is in Indian civil society, see among many sources, C. Jaffrelot, *The Hindu Nationalist Movement and Indian Politics: 1925 to the 1990s*, New Delhi: Penguin Books, 1999 and C. Jaffrelot, ed., *The Sangh Parivar: A Reader*, New Delhi: Oxford University Press, 2005.

11 Compiled from the Table of 'Hindu-Muslim Riots and Resulting Victims' given on page 556 in Jaffrelot, *The Hindu Nationalist Movement*. I have changed the 1993 figure of 558 to 874 to include victims in the March riots of that year in Mumbai and added the rough estimate of 2,000 for deaths in the Gujarat pogrom of February 2002 before taking the annual average.

12 See P. Brass, *Forms of Collective Violence*, New Delhi: Three Essays

Collective, 2006; and his *The Production of Hindu-Muslim Violence in Contemporary India*, New Delhi: Oxford University Press, 2003.

13 See S.I. Wilkinson, *Votes and Violence: Electoral Competition and Communal Riots in India*, Cambridge: Cambridge University Press, 2004.

14 Omar Khalidi, *Khaki and Ethnic Violence in India*, New Delhi: Three Essays Collective, 2003; and K.S. Subramanian, *Political Violence*.

15 The most detailed account of what happened was given by the Concerned Citizens' Tribunal in its two-volume Report called *Crime Against Humanity: An Inquiry into the Carnage in Gujarat – Findings and Recommendations*, Mumbai, 2002. The official National Human Rights Commission subsequently endorsed the principal findings of this Report after making its own inquiry.

16 In the last couple of years there is some evidence that for the first time Indian Muslims may have become involved in public bomb blasts as well as becoming recruits to transnational terrorist groups.

17 See A.A. Engineer, ed., *Communal Riots in Post-Independence India*, Hyderabad: Orient Longman, 1984. For an acute analysis of the material background to the Gujarat pogrom of 2002, see Barbara Harriss-White, *India's Market Society*, New Delhi: Three Essays Collective, 2005. She points out that in eastern Gujarat villages, poor tribals attacked Muslim moneylenders on behalf of the Sangh. Economic exploitation alone does not explain this since elsewhere it is Hindu middlemen who exploit tribals. But local implantation of Hindutva activists and sustained communal propaganda against Muslims could combine with economic resentments to create such brutalised tribal behaviour.

18 See Yogendra Yadav, 'The Elusive Mandate of 2004', *Economic and Political Weekly*, 18-24 December 2004.

19 In this regard Europe, with an anti-Muslim/anti-Islam racism on the rise, as well as Russia (Chechnya), China (Xinjiang) and India (Kashmir) all facing insurgencies in Muslim populated regions, are to some extent willing accomplices in this demonisation and lend unwarranted legitimacy to this fraudulent 'global war on terror'. For a critique of the 'software' of the US imperial project and its use of variant ideological banners, see A. Vanaik, ed., *Selling US Wars*, Northampton, MA: Olive Branch Press, 2007.

20 Jaffrelot, *The Hindu Nationalist Movement* and *The Sangh Parivar*; also Basu and Roy, *Violence and Democracy in India*.

REFLECTIONS ON INDONESIAN VIOLENCE: TWO TALES AND THREE SILENCES

TANIA MURRAY LI

TWO TALES

In June 2001 I visited the Napu highlands of the Indonesian island of Sulawesi together with colleagues from a local NGO advocating recognition of customary land rights. We were attempting to understand why land held by indigenous, Christian highlanders under customary tenure was falling rapidly into the hands of migrants. The migrants were mainly Muslim, members of the Bugis ethno-linguistic group that predominates in the southern part of Sulawesi. The atmosphere we encountered was very tense: every day, truckloads of Christian refugees arrived from the coast, while Muslim/Bugis families fled to the coast from the hills, leaving their houses, stores, farms and mosques behind them. In the coastal town of Poso, and the surrounding countryside, less than a hundred kilometres away by road from our study site, Muslims and Christians were in the midst of a violent confrontation that left about 1,000 dead, 4,000 houses destroyed and at least 90,000 people displaced.[1]

In subsequent months, news reports described Poso as a ghost town. Barracks built to house returning refugees were repeatedly torched. Muslims moved about with some security, but Christian government officials could report for work only by paying for armed guards. Both sides organised militias for attack, retribution, and 'religious cleansing', and received support from rogue elements in the army and militias outside Sulawesi. Military forces were eventually increased, and a peace accord brokered which included the disarmament of both sides, and the expulsion of non-Sulawesi militias. Yet the accord did not stop the violence. There were 'mysterious shootings' of pedestrians on city streets and farmers in their fields, assassinations of religious leaders, and more than 47 bombings in the next five years. A new militia arrived from Java and operated for several years before the police dislodged it. By 2008, the segregation of territory along religious lines was entrenched, as refugees from both sides, unable to return to their formerly mixed towns and villages, were obliged to settle where they were. Sadly, the Sulawesi case was not unique: violence and mass evictions along ethnic or religious lines broke out in five provinces in the period following President Suharto's ouster in 1998, after 32 years of military-inflected rule.[2]

How can such violence be explained? In 2001, a young man from one of the highland villages we were studying, a university graduate with responsibility for village 'peace and security', offered this account of the crisis. In 1998 Habibie, a national figure closely identified with the organisation of Islamic intellectuals (ICMI), had replaced Suharto as president. Soon thereafter, Muslim migrants started to arrive in large numbers, buying up land in the hills with money supplied to them by Habibie through various state-linked religious foundations. In his view, the Muslim Bugis influx was part of a plot, the purpose of which was a Muslim takeover of the largely Christian highlands. So what, he asked me, was the western (Christian) world going to do about their situation? Surely they had some responsibilities? If not for the Dutch missionaries who Christianised the highlands in the colonial period, this conflict would not be occurring, as the highlands would be Muslim too. Meanwhile, he was concentrating his efforts on calming the Muslims still remaining in the village, organising a 'communications' committee to intercept and counter inflammatory rumours, and preparing for village defence.

Preoccupied by different questions, but highlighting the same dates, I offered a different explanation for the migrant influx. In 1998, Indonesia's currency collapsed, and producers of world market crops priced in dollars enjoyed a massive windfall of cash. Bugis farmers from the south with already established cocoa stands poured into highlands, renting buses to tour the countryside looking for additional land on which to grow this 'brown gold'. Thousands more would-be cocoa farmers followed suit, supplying labour to Bugis patrons while saving to make their own land purchases. Enticed by cash offers greatly exceeding normal land prices, and intimidated by local authorities which refused to recognise their customary land rights, many villagers had sold up. As the new cocoa went into production, they found themselves looking with envy at new Bugis houses, complete with satellite TVs. In my tale, religious and ethnic tensions were grounded in a major agrarian transformation in which land was becoming commoditised and new classes of landowners and landless wage labourers were emerging. So what, I asked my interlocutor, could the highlanders do to hold onto their remaining land in the face of this migrant influx?

The numbers were indeed striking. A survey conducted in 2001 found that, in the Napu village of my interlocutor, Bugis outnumbered highlanders and comprised 63 per cent of the total village population, and about 30 per cent of the subdistrict as a whole. About 40 per cent of local households had sold land to incoming migrants within the last five years.[3] The arrival of Muslim foundations linked to President Habibie was also confirmed. In 2000 the three senior executive positions in Poso District were occupied by prominent members of the Habibie-linked association for Muslim intellectuals, ICMI.[4] Not confirmed was the link my interlocutor drew between Muslim foundations, and the rapid and recent arrival of a large number of Muslims buying up land in his village.

The land issue was not, of course, news to villagers. Although they lacked aggregate numbers, they were aware of the trend. I knew from my reading that the Sulawesi cocoa boom echoed the trajectory of previous booms (and busts) in West Africa and elsewhere. The displacement of indigenous populations by migrants, the sequence of crop diseases, dependence on chemical inputs, indebtedness and continuing expansion into new forest zones to profit from 'forest rent', were wholly anticipated by agricultural historians, although they took the Sulawesi highlanders by surprise. Conspiracy scenarios were not news to me. Tales in which prominent figures in the political, administrative and military machine manipulate people to further their own ends – be it profit, or a religious cause – are common in Indonesia, continuously circulated through, and generated by, the local rumour mill. Note also that both our tales included regional, national and transnational elements, making connections across time and space. It was not the case that I invoked global processes, while my interlocutor focused on local ones.

The main difference between our two explanations was their affective load, and the consequences that follow from them. For the highlanders, feeling besieged and vulnerable, it was crucial at that moment to recognise proximate enemies and potential allies. Their analysis of the role of Islamic foundations in sponsoring the migrant influx enabled them to identify at least one concrete mechanism behind their social and economic marginalisation. The idea that these foundations were directly linked to the new president confirmed their worst fears: behind the talk of economic development for the highlands lurked an Islamist agenda, of which Bugis migrants were both the instruments and the intended beneficiaries. For me, on the other hand, a political-economic emphasis was vastly more acceptable, more attuned to my academic and political sensibilities, than one which reduced the problem to a dualistic divide (Christians versus Muslims), or limited it to the exposure of a conspiracy. I was concerned that he and his village security committee might identify conspirators, and violently expel them, while leaving the broad, systemic, class-forming processes directly connected to land tenure unaddressed. He shared a concern to avoid violence: although he expressed his suspicions to me, and was monitoring the Bugis as closely as he could, he did not organise an attack.

More generally, I would argue, accounts of violence need political economy to counter the simplifying culturalism of so much popular analysis. Describing Indonesia, journalists readily elaborate on the impossibility of peace and unity across '13,000 islands, roiling with an untamed mix of cultures, ethnic groups, rivalries, gods and spoken tongues'.[5] Anthropologists have sometimes fuelled popular stereotypes of exotic tribal practices, mob mentalities, or an Indonesian proclivity to run *amuk* – not least when their analysis is reduced to media sound bites. Thus Clifford Geertz in an interview with the *New York Times* on the eve of Suharto's fall stated that Javanese people seem polite, deferent and controlled until 'all hell breaks loose'.[6] What a reader might take away from this comment is a generalising, ahistorical model of Javanese culture which begs the questions why here? why now? why these targets? why these forms? why not everyone? – and so on. This is the gap that a historically-grounded, political-economic analysis helps to fill.

An emphasis on culture and meaning, on the other hand, is needed to counter the crude materialism of neo-Malthusian accounts, both popular and academic, that attribute conflict to the pressure of people on resources, radically under-specifying the diverse forms and mechanisms of this 'pressure', and failing to account for populations under extreme economic stress who nevertheless establish conditions of tolerance and peace.[7] Similarly, an emphasis on culture modifies the hasty turn to economic globalisation to explain the increased prominence of religious or ethnic identifications, a turn which psychologises a presumed 'need' for community and begs the question of why economic insecurity should not be addressed through other forms of mobilisation, such as unions or political parties.

While polemical encounters sometimes require a simplifying emphasis on the cultural or the material, the risk of such polemics is to re-establish a dichotomy that scholars building on the legacy of cultural Marxism have worked hard to dissolve. In a conflict zone such as highland Sulawesi, a form of analysis which attempts to grasp the materiality of cultural understandings, and the simultaneity of material and symbolic struggles seems especially important. The causes of violence are unlikely to be reducible to either material or cultural, and much is obscured by a crude binary framing. To delve deeper, we need to break three silences which cloud popular understandings of violence: a silence about history, about geography, and about agency.[8]

HISTORY

The phrase 'divide and rule' captures a prominent element of colonial practice. But the creation and maintenance of the social boundaries upon which colonial rule depended was not a seamless or mechanistic process: it was hard work. We need to account for the conditions under which particular racial, ethnic or religious divides inscribed by colonial regimes became *popular*. To do this, we must explain how they were able to make use of ideas already present in society, including residual histories and memories, to form the kind of unspoken common sense sometimes described as hegemonic.

In Indonesia, in contrast to many other (post)colonies, ethnic identities have never been legally inscribed. The Dutch instituted a racialised legal and administrative system based on three categories: European, Foreign Oriental (mainly Chinese), and Native. They did not further divide the Native population in the way the British did in India, with long lists of castes and tribes, or in Africa, where indirect rule through African chiefs meant that individuals carried an ethnic/tribal label on their identity card. To this day, the Indonesian national census does not collect data on ethnic identity, although in various years it has recorded rough proxies such as home language and province of birth. Ethnic prejudice and stereotyping do exist, of course, both within and outside the state machinery, but they have not been institutionalised in legal or administrative codes. Religion, in contrast, was an axis of divide-and-rule deliberately used by the Dutch when they attempted to limit the gathering strength of Islam as a unifying, anti-colonial force, by sending Christian missionaries into the highlands of Indonesia's many islands to create loyal, Christian bastions. In the Sulawesi conflict, the highland town of Tentena, which was the headquarters of the colonial mission, became the centre for Christian militias and refugees and expelled its Muslim population, while the coastal zone and the city of Poso became identified with Islam as the Christian population fled to the hills.

In the Napu highlands, my interlocutor was tasked with maintaining a fragile peace among indigenous Christians and the migrant Muslim population. He also had to restrain his fellow villagers from their desire to go to Poso to help defend Christians and take revenge. In Napu, at a moment of extreme tension, religion became a short-hand for two overlapping divides: Christian/indigenous versus Muslim/migrant. In other parts of Indonesia, the divides do not align so neatly: migrants and locals might all be Muslim, for example. Coincidentally, the divide highlighted by my interlocutor lined up with the emerging class divide between successful migrant farmers busy acquiring land for cocoa, and local farmers who sold up and lost out. On inspection, the overlap turned out to be less than complete: there were

Christian highlanders with significant landholdings, often village officials, who had not sold their own land, but profited by acting as brokers for incoming migrants. There were poor Bugis migrants who arrived with no money, looking for work with Bugis patrons, knowing it would take years to acquire land. Yet my interlocutor was not interested in these details. He was convinced the Bugis migrants came with money from Muslim foundations, and land for cacao was incidental to their agenda.

GEOGRAPHY

Village homelands

The central and agreed fact in both the tales with which I began is the influx of Muslim migrants into the Sulawesi highlands. The effects of this influx on the spatial organisation of daily life were stark. When we asked the headmen of villages in Napu and neighbouring sub-districts to provide us with their lists of current residents, a standard instrument of village administration, they admitted that their records were hugely inaccurate. So many new people had moved into the area in the past two years, they were unable to keep track. Very few of the newcomers had reported to the headman with details of their household membership, their place of origin, and their intention to take up permanent residence in the village. One village secretary had just completed the pre-count for the national census, and found that the village population had doubled, with the new 'half' comprising Bugis migrants, few of whom he had ever seen before. Many of them, he noted, spoke only the Bugis language so he could not communicate with them in Indonesian. They were living in barracks or crammed into the houses of relatives, three or four households per unit. Most of them were concentrated in a separate hamlet on the periphery of the main village settlement, building their houses on farm land acquired by a Bugis broker and sold off to clients recruited through kinship and place-based networks. In one village, where the Bugis population was still small, a large new mosque had been built: that, said a resident, is for all the new people who are about to move in to start planting cocoa on the thirty hectare plot recently acquired by their leader.

A sense of belonging in the village was not so obvious for the highland population either. Sulawesi's highland villages should not be imagined as intact tribe-like communities, fixed in their current locations since time immemorial. They were formed through the forced resettlement of diverse groups from the surrounding hills to a river valley or plateau where colonial and contemporary rules could monitor, tax and 'improve' them.[9] Depending on when and where they converted, villagers belong to several distinct Christian congregations. They speak multiple languages. There are often tensions between earlier and later settlers over issues such as land and village leadership. People have kin in other villages, and sometimes also in the original hill-top settlements which were never completely emptied. The unintended consequences of this imposed historical mobility have played out in land dealings between highlanders and Bugis migrants: individuals who had sold their valley land to migrants were looking to their ancestral lands on the hill slopes as a refuge, a place to which they could withdraw and start their economic enterprises, and their communities, over again.

A few Muslim Bugis, mainly traders, were resident in the highlands for decades before the conflict erupted, living peacefully among the Christian population. In 2001 most of these old time Muslim residents left their homes in the Napu highlands, a departure their Christian neighbours found insulting. My interlocutor, responsible for village security, set great store by his ability to reassure Muslim residents that Christian villagers had no violent intentions towards them, and were committed to peace and mutual respect. Thus he was hurt when his next door neighbour, a small-time Bugis merchant with whom he had grown up and attended elementary school, left one night with his wife and children, without even saying good bye. 'It makes you wonder', he said, 'what is really in their hearts'. In saying this, he repositioned his neighbour from a distinct individual, whose personal history he knew, to a member of a group. All Muslims became duplicitous, not just the newcomers he thought had been sent by the Muslim foundations.

A place in the nation

From the perspective of Indonesia's coastal and urban zones, the highlands are unruly frontiers, marginal to national life. Their imputed marginality is rooted in a set of place-myths that serve to exaggerate the social distance between the highlanders and the coastal and urban populations among whom they aspire to live and work. Once again the example of my young interlocutor is instructive. Why was he, a university graduate, back in his home village underemployed, busying himself with the local defence committee, and dreaming of making a fortune in cocoa? He was there only because he had been unable to find a government job in the city of Poso. The Christian population of the highlands, although often well educated as the result of several generations of mission schooling, is still despised and excluded by urban and coastal Muslims who associate them with the heathen past, and with practices such as headhunting.

In recent years Christianity itself has come to be defined as increasingly marginal to national life. In the latter decade of President Suharto's rule and continuing with his replacement, Habibie, the neutral stance towards diverse organised religions promised by the constitution was undermined by an intensified connection between Islam and state power.[10] Suharto's answer to the criticism of the urban middle classes angered by the corruption and greed of his family and cronies was to offer support to some of the more strident Islamist groups in return for their political loyalty. He also used state funds to support missionary efforts directed mainly towards secular Muslims, and inflected all state institutions with a more assertive Islam, demonstrated in practices such as the use of Muslim blessings to begin and end official events.

These shifts in central government policy and practice towards different religious groups resonated loudly in Poso town, and also in the surrounding hills. The three major rounds of violence in Sulawesi in 1998-2001 all began in Poso town, and involved struggles over Poso District senior political or administrative positions in which Christian and Muslim candidates were in competition. At the time, Poso District had a relatively even split in its population: 57% Muslim, 40% Christian. The Suharto regime had managed mixed districts such as this by deliberately engineering a balance: if the district head was Christian, the deputy would be Muslim, and in the next round of appointments they would switch.[11] Post-Suharto democratisation meant that senior politicians would be elected, not appointed, and candidates in many parts of Indonesia responded by mobilising constituencies along ethno-religious lines. Further, the economic stakes of public office became much higher when legislation for administrative decentralisation went into effect in 2001, giving the regions more autonomy, more control over local assets (minerals, forests), and direct access to central government funds that they could spread among their clients and allies. In all the islands where violence broke out in 1998-2001, the cities were heavily dependent on government spending, with 20-30 per cent of the working population employed by the government.[12] Young men like my interlocutor saw their chances of government jobs diminish as a Muslim-dominated district administration reconfigured patronage networks to favour Muslims. The tight links binding Islam, the ruling regime, and the administrative apparatus at every level also affects rural matters such as development contracts, licences and land allocation. Muslim foundations funded by President Habibie to take over the hills in which Christians predominate were, for my interlocutor, the outcome of this hostile plot.[13]

Indonesia's radical Islamist groups draw the spatial boundaries of their struggle quite differently from the Christian minorities. For them, Christians are representatives and reminders of the colonial power which prevented the emergence of an Islamic state a century ago, blocked it at independence, and still stand in its way. Christians are tainted by their association with the colonial power, and are seen as alien Others. Worse, foreigners are still interfering: Islamists see the mission planes that fly into remote highland areas as a massive Christianisation project.[14] They accuse Christians of harbouring plans to declare independence for their islands and enclaves, with the support of international forces: my interlocutor's assumption that I would have Christian loyalties hinted in this direction. But while he identified his enemy in the militant Muslim foundations, brotherhoods and militias infiltrating his neighbourhood, radical Islamists interpret the entire apparatus of international aid and finance as evidence of a very powerful conspiracy supporting Christian interests.[15] US military action in Afghanistan, and the search for terrorists networks allegedly lurking in Indonesia and the Philippines, heighten the sense that both Islam and national sovereignty are threatened by the white/Christian/Zionist 'West'. Presented as a unified package, and declaimed at Friday prayers across the nation, the threat to Indonesia's Muslims can be made to seem very grave, despite the fact that they make up 86 per cent of the population. Yet most Indonesian Muslims, who practice a moderate form of Islam, do not subscribe to a view of the West as alien and hostile.[16] Their sense of the nation, and their own place within it, also has global coordinates. In 2001, 10,000 Indonesians of all faiths signed a petition opposing religious extremism and defending 'the Indonesian way of life, which is to live together in tolerance'. The organisers hoped to dispel negative images of Indonesia that circulated in global media during the street rallies protesting US bombing in Afghanistan. Their vision of modernity rejects violence, and the shame of living in a violent land.

AGENCY

Locating agents

To understand communal violence, one has to be able to account for its popularity – why, that is, large numbers of ordinary people become involved as perpetrators or supporters. The view of Indonesian government officials and activists alike is that people become involved because they are manipulated by political elites who use ethnicity or religion as tools to divide and mobilise people, inciting them to commit violent acts.[17] They label the perpetrators puppets, and the 'intellectual leaders' puppeteers. I find this approach problematic, because it treats ordinary people as dupes, incapable of acting on the basis of their own critical assessments. In my experience, these assessments include cynicism about the greed, corruption and self-serving ambition of political and other elites, and detailed knowledge of their misdeeds. Thus it seems unlikely to me that they would be so easily led. More important is the role of the actual and aspiring middle classes – people like my interlocutor – who are often overlooked in studies of violence, especially when it is assumed to reflect economic duress. It is lower level professionals, or the would-be professional classes, excluded from power and advancement, who have been leaders on both sides of the conflict in Poso and in the other islands: religious leaders, parliamentarians, businessmen, bureaucrats, retired soldiers, academics, NGO activists, and students.[18]

A unique feature of the conflict in Sulawesi was the resonance between the concerns of would-be urban elites and struggles over land taking place in the countryside. The cocoa boom set up an unusually acute tension among the aspiring middle classes in rural areas: among people who had been unable to obtain government jobs, or who recognised that export oriented agriculture offered much better returns, especially in the context of high export prices designated in dollars, inflation in the cost of basic goods, and low government salaries. The new crop offered, for the first time, an opportunity to make serious money and attain a comfortable middle-class life style in the mountainous hinterlands that coastal Muslims had hitherto despised, and that educated Christians routinely left behind. But the potential of cocoa was discovered and monopolised by Bugis migrants who bought up land at low prices before the highlanders caught on. It was expanding opportunity, not a Malthusian resource crunch, which made tensions in the countryside so very high, and helped to supply the conflict's popular base.

Cruelty

To explain the context of violence, we must recognise the political economic tensions, and the material stakes of high office, government jobs, and access to land for cocoa. But there is more work to be done before we can make any sense of the intimate agency of direct personal attack. At this point, it is useful to draw a distinction between conflict, which we can understand as being 'about' or 'over' valued material or symbolic goods, including high ideals and contending visions of the good life, and the phenomenon of cruelty: forms and degrees of violence which are excessive, savage, sadistic and which we tend to label, at the risk of tautology, irrational. A striking example of such cruelty and excess occurred in another Indonesian island, Kalimantan, in March 2000, when the indigenous Dayak population set about evicting migrants on a massive scale. In one incident, 118 terrified refugees on a bus leaving the province were stopped and massacred in a field.[19] In the logic of a conflict over resources and the reclaiming of place, the perpetrators had already achieved their goal – the migrants were leaving. Why make the decision – because decision it was – to stop the bus and kill them? Note that cruelty is not only a phenomenon of hinterlands and forest frontiers, witness the frequent lynch-mob killings of petty thieves in the capital city Jakarta, some of them extracted from police stations and taken out to be burned alive.

In all Indonesia conflict zones in 1998-2001, the violence included dismemberment, the tearing of foetuses from pregnant women, the disembowelling of children, mutilation and torture, horrors so intimate that the term cruelty cannot be avoided. In the Sulawesi highlands during my visit, the talk circled endlessly around acts of cruelty reported to be taking place in Poso town: the rape and murder of two young girls by their next-door neighbour, and so on.

Although the motivation that leads one person to disembowel another, or even just shoot him in the back, exceeds the logic of conflict and defies analysis in economistic terms, it is possible to make some sense of its forms and effects. The French scholar Etienne Balibar offers a hint when he points to the role of 'residues' of history returning, decontextualised, as distorted or exaggerated memories, and deployed in the condensed and truncated form of a fetish or exhibited as an emblem.[20] Such an emblem capable of expressing extraordinary, polyvalent power was reported in Poso, where a pig was found pinned to a wall in crucified form, under the caption 'Jesus is a pig'. This may well have been an urban legend. I find it unlikely that Muslims, the presumed perpetrators, would be prepared to grapple with this (to them) unclean animal in order to create this fetish. Moreover, while Christians would indeed be insulted by the charge that the son of god is an animal, the emblem of the pig is much more poignant to Muslims. Whether or not the pig existed, the image of its crucified form together with the caption presented an impossible conundrum, an overdetermined and highly potent sign. This sign took its meaning from the long history of religious identity formation I have described, but it took its peculiar force from the absurdity and distortion of the fetish itself. Without reading a motive into the sign, we can examine its effects: to communicate that the world you most feared, one characterised by the impossible and unthinkable, has come to pass. This is the message that circulated in the hills, as people discussed the crucified pig.

Other condensed and fetishised symbols deployed in the Sulawesi conflict included hills and forests as places of disorder; mutilation and decapitation of weak and defenceless people; and the communist party (PKI). All three appeared in a report in *Kompas*, the most respected national daily newspaper, about one horrific incident. There were thirteen Muslim victims, including the elderly imam of the local mosque, a pregnant woman and young children. They were living in a mountain village in the Poso interior. Their attackers disappeared into the forest, an area so vast and inaccessible that the police could not hope to apprehend them or offer protection. The police chief described the action as 'extremely sadistic, even more so than the PKI'.[21] The incarnation of the communist party as a fetish symbolising extreme violence was the deliberate work of the Suharto regime, which engineered the massacre of half a million alleged communists in 1965 yet insisted that the violence was the work of the 'communists' themselves. Note that communists were assumed to be godless and at home in the hills, like the savage headhunters whose memory the reporter simultaneously invoked. To the police, the reporter, and the newsreading public, these associations are not deliberate manipulations – they simply confirm the reality of the phenomenon they have learned to suspect and fear.[22]

The burning of houses and public buildings, and the cutting and burning of cocoa trees, also merits this kind of scrutiny. At one level, the destruction of cocoa trees can be seen as the reclaiming of territory. If the expelled population has no more trees, they will be less tempted to return, and someone more deserving can occupy the vacated space. But there is a problem with this logic: Indonesia's national and customary law recognise that a person who has planted trees has a legitimate claim on the land, and sooner or later the person who destroys the trees will have to pay compensation. It would be more rational, in the short run at least, to leave the trees standing and harvest the fruit, worth a fortune in the local farm economy. In 2001, journalists reported that some trees are indeed being harvested by 'thieves'. But tens of thousands of productive trees, as well as houses, schools and other buildings of high value were also destroyed, sending a powerful message: economic logic of the kind that might be thought of as shared did not apply.

Retrospectively, the violence looked different. By the time I interviewed Muslim and Christian refugees in 2003, they were much less ready to point fingers at 'proximate enemies', individual or collective. Indeed, they did the opposite: they echoed the official view, that they had been manipulated by unknown forces. 'We always got on fine with our neighbours, there was nothing between us' was one refrain, followed by 'we don't know who the perpetrators were, or how this could happen'. This kind of statement could be interpreted as a rhetorical device to deflect blame and avoid future reprisals – we are not violent, these acts of cruelty were not committed by us, it was other people. Certainly, this version of events is less terrifying than the recognition that neighbours turned on each other. Yet in the period 1998-2001, thousands of 'ordinary' people – Christians and Muslims – were involved in direct confrontations, usually in the form of a mobilised mob, enraged at news of atrocities committed by the other side. The militias that formed had assistance from outside the region, but they recruited locally. When police launched an attack on a well-entrenched militia in 2008, allies and sympathisers from across the province mobilised in its support.[23]

AGAINST VIOLENCE

In the highlands of Napu, my interlocutor and his colleagues in the village security committee creatively revised the task of looking out for stray 'communists', their official remit in the Suharto period, and carried out a twenty-four hour watch for miscreants of either faith. They adopted the Suharto-era rhetoric which described combatants as youthful hotheads, using this fiction to draw together a coalition of Muslim and Christian elders with the common task of keeping their respective hotheads under control. During my visit, when a rumour emerged that the members of a Muslim prayer group had gone home after their evening worship to fetch their weapons, the communication committee sprang into action to verify that this collective arming had not occurred, and thus prevented a pre-emptive strike. Even at the height of the Poso conflict, the Suharto-era proscription of the mobilisation of people along the lines of SARA – an acronym that stands for ethnicity, religion, race or class (*suku*, *agama*, *ras*, *antargolongan*) – still had a great deal of resonance in the hills, where many people agreed that SARA was a bad thing, and a disruption of peace and development.

Ironically, but unsurprisingly, violence and its control may also strengthen ruling regimes. The populist President Sukarno was obliged to form an alliance with the army in order to suppress the separatist and religiously-oriented rebellions that threatened to break up Indonesia in the 1950s. Memories of this violent and disrupted period encouraged many Sulawesi villagers to favour a firm, controlling state. As I noted earlier, the Suharto regime helped to engineer violence on a massive scale (half a million alleged communists killed) and then based its legitimacy on its capacity to prevent violence among the ignorant masses (who were cynically blamed for *their* excesses!).[24] In the 1998-2001 period, a series of post-Suharto presidents were ineffective in preventing violence, but they were active in brokering peace agreements between warring groups, lecturing citizens about how to behave, managing flows of refugees and providing for their needs.

In the wake of the violence, the field of 'conflict management' took the place of economic development in amplifying and consolidating the role of government at every level. Government officials pontificated on the psychological deficiencies of the masses who run *amuk*, and need 'mental guidance' (*pembinaan mental*), especially the youth, who were said to be easily led.

International aid donors located the cause of the violence in the weak development of 'civil society', a problem they sought to rectify by lavishing funds on NGOs, and creating a new industry in mediation and 'conflict transformation'. I find the donors' diagnosis inaccurate. Indonesia has a 'thick' civil society, with dense sets of social relations connecting individuals beyond the household, and thousands of more or less formal groups dedicated to culture, sports, religion, etc. Sadly, some of these groups were involved in the violence, when youth clubs doubled as militias. But there is nothing wrong with Indonesian capacities for organising a rich social life, or for analysing the world around them. The deficiency, in my view, lies elsewhere: in the lost art of engaging in critique, and working out differences by non-violent means, i.e. the practice of politics.

The practice of politics

For thirty-two years of Suharto's rule the regime suppressed the practice of politics in favour of the obsessive logic of development. It curtailed party organisation, elections, claims for regional autonomy, and unions; it banned popular mobilisations over matters such as land reform. It defined politics negatively, as a disruption of progress. It urged the people who did not benefit from development to await their turn. Suharto presented himself as the Father of Development, and this image had some traction. In 1996 I was struck, watching TV news in the home of a member of the Sulawesi village elite, by the emotion expressed on the death of Suharto's wife Ibu Tien, 'She was the mother of the nation, the mother of us all'. No talk there of the scandals, corruption and greed of Ibu Tien, matters which the cynics in Java, rich and poor alike, endlessly discussed. In 1998, the year Suharto was deposed, I was again surprised at reactions to scenes of protestors in Jakarta setting fire to shopping centres and destroying bank machines. 'Why do those people in Jakarta want to spoil their nice things – if we had those things here, we would take better care of them'. Yet uneven development did produce some trenchant critiques, in Sulawesi and elsewhere, and a renewed demand for political engagement.

A young man in the Sulawesi hills – not the one I cited but another, similarly educated, also back home in his village – described to me how he had 'learned to conduct politics' (*belajar berpolitik*). By this he meant learning to figure out for himself what was wrong and right in the world, and how to carry that assessment forward to bring about change. His epiphany occurred a few years earlier, when an NGO began helping the people of his village resist the construction of a hydro-electric dam that would flood their land and force them to leave. Home from Java where he had worked and studied for some years, he was sent by the village headman to observe the activities of this NGO, and report back on what kinds of trouble they were fomenting. So he started to attend their meetings, listening from the back, and came to the gradual realisation that much of what they said about the importance of livelihoods, the environment, and the legitimacy of customary land rights made perfect sense. In contrast, the more he listened to government officials promoting the dam as a step towards 'development' in the province as well as a better future for the villagers, the less credible he found them.

The campaign against the dam occurred under the Suharto regime, when individuals who had critical insights shared them frequently in the form of cynical jokes and asides, but not in more systematic forms directed towards collective action. NGOs defending villagers' rights to land and livelihood were threatened by the authorities, and accused of being communist. But seeing the dedication of the NGO's young staff, and absorbing some of their intellectual energy, this young man became convinced that learning to conduct politics was a positive step. He described his feeling as one of awakening from a long and lazy sleep. He began to look with new eyes at the people around him in his village and in the provincial government who did not understand, or were too afraid to engage in, political process. When I met him in 2001, after the fall of Suharto, he felt the possibilities for 'learning to conduct politics' had opened up, but people were very slow to grasp them. They had to unlearn habits of quiescence cultivated through three decades of Suharto-era double-think and double-talk, and start to think of politics positively, as an entitlement.

Throughout the struggle for independence and especially in the period 1945-65, until the army-led coup which ushered in Suharto's rule, many Indonesians had been active in the practice of politics, and vigorous in debating the shape of the nation. There were mass mobilisations of workers, peasants, women, youth, regional and religious communities, all engaged in struggles over the distribution of resources *and* the recognition of differences (cultural, historical, regional, religious) that linked and cross-cut each other in complex ways. But the first president, Sukarno, retreated into the paternalism of 'Guided Democracy', and the Suharto regime referred to the populace as a 'floating mass' incapable of politics, for whom the moment of political maturity was indefinitely postponed. Conjuring up the spectre of a communist threat, the regime enjoined this 'mass' to support the Suharto regime since it alone could secure a stable state of non-politics in which nothing 'untoward' or 'excessive' would happen.[25]

Some Sulawesi highlanders wish for a return to those quiet days, and believe that the post-Suharto violence was caused by an excess of 'politics', understood as intrinsically disruptive. Others now recognise the eerie stillness created by the *absence* of politics as the key problem to be redressed. Suharto-era mal-development, and the greed of Suharto's cronies and corrupt officials, have been exposed, but they were obvious enough and easy targets. The much harder task of (re)learning how to live with differences between groups has only just begun. This requires more than democratic elections and the rule of law. In requires the strengthening of situated individual and collective practices of reaching settlements under conditions in which conflict, dissension, and pluralism must be regarded as permanent. Cultural and religious identifications, whatever the processes through which they were formed and embedded, cannot be wished away, and they are especially intractable in situations where people have acted violently in their name. Procedures for living together in difference are the best that can be achieved. From this perspective, the most significant element in the genealogy of the current violence is not primordial identity or religious persuasion, nor the failure to reach some imagined end-point of mutual understanding and consensus, nor is it the existence of conspiracies or even material inequalities but the surprisingly effective anti-politics of the Suharto regime. It is the loss of capacity in the practice of politics which fosters the shift from conflict, a normal condition of human life, to cruelty and excess.

NOTES

1 Lorraine Aragon, 'Communal Violence in Poso, Central Sulawesi: Where People Eat Fish and Fish Eat People', *Indonesia*, 72, 2001; Human Rights Watch, 'Breakdown: Four Years of Communal Violence in Central Sulawesi', Human Rights Watch, New York, 2002.

2 Gerry van Klinken, 'Communal Conflict and Decentralization in Indonesia', in *The Australian Centre for Peace and Conflict Studies Occasional Paper Series*, University of Queensland, Brisbane, 2007; Tania Murray Li, 'Ethnic Cleansing, Recursive Knowledge, and the Dilemmas of Sedentarism', *International Journal of Social Science*, 173, 2002.

3 Gunter Burkard, 'Stability or Sustainability? Dimensions of Socio-Economic Security in a Rain Forest Margin', STORMA Discussion Paper Series No. 7, Palu, September, 2002, pp. 4, 6.

4 Arianto Sangaji, 'Rumput Kering Di Balik Anyir Darah: Konteks Ethno Religus Dari Trajedi Kemanusiaan Poso', Yayasan Tanah Merdeka, Palu, 2005, p. 24.

5 Seth Mydans, 'Indonesia's Identity Crisis', *The New York Times,* 11 September 2001.

6 Philip Shenon, 'Of the Turmoil in Indonesia and Its Roots', *The New York Times*, 9 May 1998.

7 See, for example, Thomas Homer-Dixon, *Environment, Scarcity and Violence*, Princeton: Princeton University Press, 1999.

8 See the account of these silences in the genocide in Rwanda by Mahmood Mamdani, *When Victims Become Killers: Colonialism, Nativism, and the Genocide in Rwanda*, Princeton: Princeton University Press, 2001.

9 Tania Murray Li, *The Will to Improve: Governmentality, Development, and the Practice of Politics*, Durham: Duke University Press, 2007.

10 Robert Hefner, *Civil Islam: Muslims and Democratization in Indonesia*, Princeton: Princeton University Press, 2000.

11 In the period 1971-1982, the ratio of Christian to Muslim members of the ruling Golkar party in Poso District was 29:24. In 1997-2004 it was 29:43. See Sangaji, 'Rumput Kering', p. 17.

12 Klinken, 'Communal Conflict'.

13 Many Christians assessed the government's official transmigration program that moved a predominantly Muslim population from Java into Christian areas as a plot to make them a minority in their own homeland. See Sangaji, 'Rumput Kering', p. 17.

14 Ibid., p. 22.

15 ICG, 'Indonesia Backgrounder: Jihad in Central Sulawesi', International Crisis Group, Jakarta/Brussels, 2004.

16 Hefner, *Civil Islam*.

17 An NGO identified twenty-four senior regional government officials who were involved as 'puppeteers' and 'provokers', and documented the role of rogue elements in the army who set one group against another by, for example, placing a mutilated Muslim corpse where an already-heated mob would find it and become enraged. See WALI II, 'Kronologi Kejadian Poso', Wahana Lingkungan Hidup Indonesia, 11 June 2001. See also Sangaji, 'Rumput Kering'.

18 Klinken, 'Communal Conflict', p. 6.

19 ICG, 'Communal Violence in Indonesia: Lessons from Kalimantan', International Crisis Group, Jakarta/Brussels, 2001, p. 109.

20 Etienne Balibar, 'Violence, Identity, and Cruelty', *New Formations*, 35, 1998.

21 Anon, 'Sebanyak 13 Warga Muslim Poso Ditemukan Tewas', *Kompas*, 3 July 2001.

22 See James Siegel, *A New Criminal Type in Jakarta: Counter-Revolution Today*, Durham: Duke University Press, 1998. He offers striking insights into the mass-mediated process through which murder, fraud and

other crimes come to shape a distorted public sphere. He describes how monstrous, shocking and unnatural actions, including those labelled sadistic and inhuman, serve to concentrate an otherwise amorphous, alien power, and reinscribe the state as the guarantor of security.

23 ICG, 'Indonesia: Tackling Radicalism in Poso', *Asia Briefing*, 75, 2008.

24 The main killings, concentrated on the island Java, were coordinated by the army but perpetrated by Muslim youth groups, and experienced by Java's highlanders as a Muslim attack. The consolidation of separate political streams or pillars (Islam, nationalism, communism) in the Sukarno period made these identities strong enough to command the loyalty, and evoke the killing power, of their members. See Hefner, *Civil Islam*. He describes the distress still experienced by Muslim youth group members when they reflect on their role.

25 John Pemberton, *On the Subject of 'Java'*, Ithaca: Cornell University Press, 1994, pp. 4, 6.

COLOMBIA: OLD AND NEW PATTERNS OF VIOLENCE

ULRICH OSLENDER

The peace of the rich, is a war against the poor
Graffiti on a wall in central Medellín, 2003.

On 15 October 2005, Orlando Valencia travelled with a group of nine other people on a dirt track road in Colombia's north-western Chocó Department. Near the small town of Belén de Bajirá their car was stopped by police. Orlando and two fellow travellers were taken to the local police station for interrogation. This most likely did not come as a great surprise to him. His outspoken activism against the unlawful, forcible implementation of African Palm plantations in his native Curvaradó region had seriously annoyed the agro-industrial companies eager to exploit the lands in this tropical rainforest environment. As a recognised community leader, Orlando had indefatigably denounced the impunity with which right-wing paramilitary groups at the service of these companies threatened local populations and killed community leaders. He had been invited by the US-based human rights NGO Lutheran World Relief (LWR) to address their Partnering for Peace conference due to be held in Chicago on 21 October that year.[1] However, the US Embassy in Bogotá had refused him a visa. So he returned to the Curvaradó region, accompanied by fellow community members and a representative of the Montreal-based activist group Projet Accompagnement Solidarité Colombie (PASC). The latter – together with volunteers from International Peace Brigades – provides an international presence in three 'humanitarian zones' set up in the region to protect Afro-Colombian civilians against murder, kidnapping and torture by military and paramilitary forces. This protection was not to be enough for Orlando that day in October 2005. Shortly after he left the police station, he was forced onto a motorbike by persons known to be paramilitaries. Ten days later his lifeless body was found with a bullet in its head. His hands had been tied. He leaves behind his wife and their seven children.

As shocking as this cold-blooded killing was, it is unremarkable in the wider Colombian context. Cases of extreme violence – including massacres and torture – have become so common that their extraordinariness is hardly questioned anymore. As Daniel Pécaut, one of the best known experts on violence, or *violentólogos* – argues, violent events in Colombia are so varied and diverse that organised and random violence have entered into a reciprocal relationship that has led to a state of generalised violence.[2] Violence is in fact so ingrained in the very constitution of society, from national governance to everyday lives, that it may appear trivial, or banal. In Pécaut's view, this 'banality of violence' tends to obscure the existence of situations of real terror.[3] We may be shocked by events of extreme violence. But we are not surprised (any more). The cold-blooded murder of Orlando Valencia is shocking, all the way from its conception to its execution. But it is only another tip of the iceberg of the all-pervasive, systematic regime of terror that many local populations are subjected to in Colombia. Since 1996, Orlando's native Curvaradó region, for example, has seen 13 instances of the forced displacement of entire communities as a result of paramilitary terror, intimidation, selected killings and massacres. At least 115 community members have been assassinated or 'disappeared' over the last ten years.

Orlando's case is representative of the wider strategies of oppression with which dissent is dealt with. As Nazih Richani says, the 'dominant economic groups look upon violence as an efficient mechanism with which to crush the opposition. This attitude has shaped the political behavior of the dominant social groups toward the working classes, the peasants, and Left-wing political parties'.[4] Violence meted out to labour unionists, for example, has reached truly apocalyptic dimensions – every second trade union leader assassinated in the world each year is Colombian. This 'death of trade unions' is symptomatic of the relationship between neoliberal deregulation, state policy and paramilitarism.[5] The persecution of labour unionists by paramilitary groups, the outlawing of labour unions in the public sector, and the deregulation of the labour market all pursue the same strategy. Its aim is the weakening or disappearance of organisations that resist policies friendly to transnational capital.

It is this link – the *political economy* of violence and the way it is played out on the ground in specific locations – that I want to focus on in this essay. The armed conflict in Colombia is usually portrayed as one of Marxist rebels versus right-wing militias and the Colombian army, with the civilian population caught up in the crossfire. Discussions of the political and economic dimensions of the conflict often look at the role played by the illegal drug trade and natural resources such as oil and how they fuel the conflict by providing economic opportunities for the diverse armed actors.[6] Yet these debates often fail to examine the wider global forces that significantly shape the violence and terror on the ground. I think it is important to examine the Colombian conflict within these wider strategies of globalisation, one of which is the expansion of a global economy of expropriation. For David Harvey, for example, the contemporary moment of 'new imperialism' is characterised by new cycles of 'accumulation by dispossession'.[7] According to his analysis, one strategy for capital to overcome the crisis of overaccumulation (a condition whereby capital surplus lies idle with no profitable outlets in sight) is to seize common assets and turn them to profitable use. Today, then, we witness a new wave of 'enclosing the commons', pushed through by 'policies of dispossession pursued in the name of neo-liberal orthodoxy'.[8]

These processes are also responsible, in my view, for the escalation of the armed conflict in Colombia in regions that had hitherto been at its margins. The Pacific coast is one such region that was until recently considered a haven of peace, insulated from Colombia's cartography of violence, but has now become fully integrated into it. Below I examine this region as a lens through which the wider context of violence can be viewed and understood. I want this to be an 'embodied' narrative, in which the voices of the victims are heard. I do not claim impartiality in this account. I emphatically side with those whose lives are being destroyed by the logic of a capitalist world order in which nothing is unconnected. As a researcher interviewing dozens of activists in Colombia, who have been subject to all kinds of violence, I became committed to making their struggle known, albeit through my own interpretations and with my limited ability to convey it. This essay, then, does not provide yet another historical account – nor an all-encompassing explanation – of how violence developed over the last two centuries in Colombia.[9] Instead I want to focus on current trends and particular manifestations of violence, and how they illustrate and may explain the wider underlying patterns of domination and repression that provide the structural context for all kinds of violence on the ground. The first section will briefly introduce the wider perspective in which violence has become shaped in Colombia over the last decades. I will then outline some of the contemporary patterns of violence, particularly those against organised labour. The remainder of the essay will then look at the Pacific coast region as an arena in which ethnocidal violence against Afro-Colombians is linked to capitalist expansion and development policies.

LA VIOLENCIA IN PERSPECTIVE

Most narratives of violence in Colombia refer at some point to the notorious period of bi-partisan-induced national slaughter between 1946 and 1966 that has become known – for lack of a more fitting expression – as *La Violencia.* It cost the lives of over 200,000 Colombians, predominantly in the rural areas. La Violencia began as a sectarian conflict between the Liberal and Conservative parties, with campesinos constituting the majority of combatants and casualties. It saw the most brutal killings and massacres imaginable. People were cut in pieces with machetes, or burned alive. Pregnant women had their bellies slashed, their foetuses thrown into the air and pierced on bayonet points. 'Don't leave the seed', was the order of the day. New modes of killing were practiced, such as the infamous *corte corbata* (the 'necktie cut'), in which the victim's tongue is pulled through the slit throat and left to hang like a tie.

Maria Victoria Uribe has studied at length the technologies of terror deployed during La Violencia, which she interprets as sacrificial displays aimed at dehumanising the victims.[10] For those who can stomach it, she provides an inventory of techniques of manipulation perpetrated on the victims' bodies. She has since traced the same techniques in the killing sprees committed by paramilitary groups today. The collective assassination of unarmed and defenceless people, she argues, has in fact become a recurrent cultural practice in Colombia, infused by the semantics of political terror:

> The obsession with manipulating the Other's body characteristic of La Violencia has now been replaced by a faunalization that mimics the industrial slaughter of cattle, entailing a diminution of the meanings ascribed to the Other's body. Acts of barbarity, shamelessly publicized in television news broadcasts and newspapers, have transformed Colombians into beings filled with fear: fear of war, of violence, of blood, of losing one's own family, even of watching the news on television.[11]

These acts of barbarity have also transformed entire regions into landscapes of fear, where the armed groups' impact is visibly inscribed. Violence leaves its traces, and its manifestations can be read off these landscapes. Houses are burnt down or riddled with bullets, their doors kicked in, windows smashed and roofs torn off. Dead and dismembered bodies lie in fields, float in rivers, or get stuck in mangrove swamps. Villages have been abandoned by their frightened inhabitants and transformed into empty, eerie spaces devoid of life, let alone laughter.[12] The effects generated by acts of barbarity are not coincidental but intended and planned. Extreme violence is aimed at producing terror and unmanageable fear in the targeted population. One may argue that terror is not so much aimed at the victim to be killed but at the family, friends and neighbours who witness the public spectacle of torture and dismemberment. Terror is a communicative strategy of armed groups to send a powerful message to the survivors of a massacre as a method of controlling these populations.[13] As a prominent black activist in Colombia told me in November 2004:

> Terror has always been a terrible exemplary strategy in this country, all that one heard during La Violencia: the *corte de franela* [literally 'T-shirt cut', by which arms and head of the victim are cut off], which was not just to kill someone but to send a message to the remainder of the population. Or playing football with severed heads. Or what you now hear in some areas that they force families to eat the meat of their relatives. These are powerful messages so that people don't organize themselves ...When they [the armed groups] enter a village and kill 10, then 50 others panic and flee. Those who stay, do so in a situation of absolute submission under the dominion of the armed group that plays out its own logic and rules. This is a concrete strategy, well thought out and impeccably administered throughout the country.

While the cruelties and atrocities of Colombia's internal conflict seem to surpass all imagination, one must remember that civil war, armed uprisings and bloody repression have a long tradition in Colombian history. In fact, Colombia in the 19th century has been described as a 'country of permanent war'.[14] Following the Wars of Independence from Spain there were fourteen civil wars, countless small uprisings, two international wars with Ecuador and three coups d'état. Responsibility for these wars lay with the Liberal and the Conservative parties that were formed in the mid-19th century and polarised Colombian society. Mobilised by powerful bonds of personal allegiance, the rural poor fought and died for the rival causes of a bipartisan land-holding oligarchy. The wars never ended in decisive victories but merely provided short breathing spaces before renewed fighting took place. As Gonzalo Sánchez has argued, these were 'unfinished wars' without clear victors or vanquished: 'What was at stake ...was not the takeover of the state, a change in the system, the replacement of one class with another, ...but simply the participation of occasionally excluded forces in the bureaucracy, their incorporation or reincorporation into the institutional apparatus'.[15]

The bipartisan oligarchy shared political power and monopolised wealth in this way while the vast majority of Colombians lived in poverty. These tensions became explosive in the mid-1940s, when the populist Liberal candidate for presidency, Jorge Eliécier Gaitán, mounted a challenge that went beyond party politics to confront the class conflict and the elitism of Colombia's 'oligarchic republic'.[16] Gaitán's mass politics found wide-spread popular support. When he was assassinated during a rally in Bogotá on 9 April 1948, people spontaneously rose up in a collective fury in what is known as *El Bogotazo*. Violence spread into the countryside and people took up arms, virtually running amok. After ten years of unremitting national bloodletting, a political solution was sought through a party pact that created the National Front in 1958. Under this pact political power would alternate every four years during a period of 'peaceful coexistence' until 1974. This hegemonic power-sharing arrangement, however, did not open up any space for political participation beyond the two dominant parties. The criminalisation of social protest forced resistance increasingly underground, building the basis for what were to become, in the mid-1960s, armed guerrilla groups. The most important ones still dominating the national scenario today are the Revolutionary Armed Forces of Colombia (FARC) and the National Liberation Army (ELN). Whereas the ELN was heavily influenced by the ideas of the Cuban revolution, basing their strategy on the *foco* theory of guerrilla warfare, the FARC arose in 1964 as a direct response to government and army repression of peasants. FARC's longer-term regional structure of social welfare for peasants explains the deep loyalty that the guerrilla group enjoys, and their strong support base in many regions otherwise abandoned or neglected by a weak state to this day. Despite a number of peace initiatives involving the FARC and the ELN, they both still form part of the violent political landscape in Colombia.

PATTERNS OF CONTEMPORARY VIOLENCE

Reflecting on the possibilities of an emerging civil society articulating itself within this context of armed struggle, Eduardo Pizarro, another renowned *violentólogo,* argued in 1993: 'The guerrilla movement has not been a suitable instrument for social and political change, nor has it contributed to the expansion of democratic spaces. On the contrary, in Colombia the "chronic rebellion", perceived by the elites as a potential threat, real or imaginary, has served as a justification for the maintenance and even the increase of democratic restrictions throughout decades. Internal war and authoritarian restrictions have mutually reinforced one another'.[17]

This analysis still seems valid. The economic, political and social inequalities that came to be addressed in the 1960s by a number of guerrilla organisations still remain intact. As long as the oligarchy feels that it can sit out the conflict without having to concede to rebel demands, it will do so. This is all so much easier, of course, with significant support from the United States, which feels it cannot afford to 'lose' Colombia in the way that Venezuela has been lost in this century. This wider geopolitical context explains the continued US commitment in Colombia, where the 'war on drugs' functions as a convenient pretext for intervention.

The economic elite have never had it so good, one may argue, now that an authoritarian president is in power who enjoys significant popular support. Forrest Hylton has done a good job of grasping the extraordinary character of the oligarchy in Colombia, listing the kinship ties of its modern presidents and mapping the topography of oligarchic clientelism. To him, this is Colombia's 'evil hour' – an allusion to one of Gabriel García Márquez's first novels, *La Mala Hora* – when with Álvaro Uribe's inauguration as President in 2002, 'the outlaws have become the establishment'.[18] Uribe's authoritarian restrictions – nicely clad in the postmodern political discourse of his 'Democratic Security' campaign – are the worst seen for decades in Colombia. As Gisela Cramer argues in a recent, exhaustive review of Uribe's security policies, these 'rely, to a far greater extent than in previous years, on the use of force'.[19] At the heart of these policies lies a significant increase of the state's coercive capacity. This includes the modernisation of the military and the police in an effort to regain full territorial control within the country's borders. To achieve this, Uribe's administration has resorted to a heavy-handed approach that has widely been criticised by human rights groups in and beyond Colombia. Particularly worrying have been the mass detentions of suspected guerrilla sympathisers or collaborators, often without proper arrest procedures and based on flimsy evidence by paid informants. Basically, anyone who might be remotely considered critical of the regime has to fear some kind of retribution. Internal war and authoritarian restrictions still mutually reinforce one another.

The brunt of authoritarian repression is borne by social movement leaders, teachers, university professors and organised labour. Colombia has for decades been the most dangerous country in the world for trade unionists. The figures are simply staggering. Since 1986 the National Labour School (Escuela Nacional Sindical), a prominent labour rights group in Colombia, has recorded more than 2,500 killings of trade unionists – with no convictions of these murderers in 98 per cent of the cases. This trend continues despite claims made by the Uribe administration that levels of violence have dropped. Not only are homicide rates in Colombia still amongst the highest in the world, but since Uribe came to power in 2002 nearly 400 trade unionists have been killed, with only 10 cases resulting in a conviction.[20] According to the International Trade Union Confederation (ITUC), 78 trade unionists were murdered in Colombia in 2006 alone – more than half of the 144 trade unionists killed worldwide in that year.

In a significant deviation from the normal pattern of impunity for such murders, August 2007 saw four soldiers from Colombia's 18th Army Brigade sentenced each to 40 years in prison for the killing of three trade union leaders in 2004. This notorious army brigade received counterinsurgency training from the US Special Forces to protect an oil pipeline that is partially owned by US-based Occidental Petroleum in the state of Arauca. The soldiers' conviction became the most high-profile case of all Colombian trade union murders, as it so clearly demonstrated the active involvement of the Colombian military – protecting US interests – in the killing of trade unionists.

The president of Colombia's mineworkers union Sintraminercol (Sindicato de Trabajadores de la Empresa Nacional Minera), Francisco Ramírez Cuellar, has powerfully outlined 'the relations between the mining industry, the Colombian government, the Colombian military, the paramilitaries, the US government, US multinationals, the US military, US agencies, and the web that all of these have spun to protect foreign investments' in the following terms:

> During the last few decades and in the context of the imposition of the neoliberal economic model, they have manipulated bilateral and multilateral agreements in their own interest, they have acted as consultants in the drafting of new legislation, and, most seriously, they have participated openly in the Colombian state's military response against the strong popular resistance that has arisen among Colombians who oppose the process of globalization. The popular organizations challenging the imposition of this model suffer from methods of state terrorism that include extermination, genocide, forced displacement, and every conceivable kind of violation of human rights, in the defense of the interests of the powerful and to protect foreign investment in Colombia.[21]

It goes without saying that such outspoken denunciations resulted in death threats and attacks against Sintraminercol union leaders.

VIOLENCE AND CAPITALIST DEVELOPMENT IN THE PACIFIC COAST REGION

Most of my fieldwork over the last 15 years has been carried out in the Pacific coast region in Colombia. I was initially interested in this tropical rainforest area because of the international attention it had received as one of the planet's biodiversity hotspots. Travelling extensively the Pacific lowlands in 1994, I quickly realised that Afro-Colombians, who make up some 90 per cent of the population in this region, were mobilising over territorial, cultural and socio-economic rights. In fact, in the early 1990s, the Pacific coast basin was at the centre of a legislative initiative that redefined relations between black populations and the Colombian state. Building on inclusionary declarations in the 1991 constitution which defined the nation as multicultural and pluriethnic, Law 70 was passed in 1993, granting collective land rights to rural black communities in the Pacific region.[22] Many black leaders regard this legislation as a 'small constitution' for Afro-Colombians, 'because it recognizes a group of persons whose country ignored them throughout its history'.[23] While black activists had long lobbied for such recognition, it was also in the state's interest to empower these communities territorially and enlist them in the task of preserving the rich ecosystems that they had traditionally inhabited and which were threatened by the overexploitation of natural resources such as timber and alluvial gold deposits.[24] Moreover, encouraged by a global awareness over environmental destruction – signalled by the UN's Brundtland Report in 1987, and the Rio Summit in 1992 – the Colombian government was keen to present the Pacific coast region as a laboratory where such global concerns could be channelled into a regional development strategy based on biodiversity conservation. The early 1990s, then, attested to a convergence of interests between governmental institutions and black organisations to work towards more sustainable ways of developing the Pacific coast region.

This optimistic outlook was to change dramatically, however, in the mid-1990s. In late December 1996, just 4 days before Christmas, a combined army and paramilitary offensive dubbed Operation Genesis attacked the local population in the municipality of Riosucio in the north-western Department of Chocó. Supported by army helicopter gunships, paramilitary search troops killed and 'disappeared' hundreds of peasants. One of the survivors, Marino Córdoba, remembers the 'tragic dawn' of 20 December 1996:

> Five o'clock in the morning of a day that seemed quiet as usual. Nobody expected at that time the terror that suddenly woke us

> up. We were stunned by the screams of those who tried to flee. There were bursts of gunfire. With their butt rifles they knocked down the doors that we didn't open out of fear. It was madness. Confused we screamed and ran because we saw men armed to the teeth. …'The paras have arrived', one of the armed men shouted. That was when we realized who it was. …The victims were paraded through the village in underwear; they were brutally beaten, hands tied behind their backs, and then they were taken away and disappeared. Those of us who could see what was happening managed to jump into the river and hide among the reeds. We stayed for two days submerged with the water up to our necks, without food, desperate. …At 8 am helicopters of the Army's Boltígero Batallion arrived. They circled over the village and then dropped off troops. We were still submerged in the water among the reeds and thought that things had changed at last. But to our great surprise the helicopters began to bomb the area. The paramilitaries gave orders by radio to those in the helicopters and these sprayed us with machinegun fire, bombs and grenades. We couldn't believe what was happening. This was not a game, this was death that was very close. Many of my friends were killed by the gunfire; it was horrible to see them die without being able to do anything.[25]

Estimates put the number of deaths at 500 during the (para)military operation. Over 20,000 people fled in its aftermath. Marino Córdoba eventually managed to escape to the capital of Bogotá. Shortly afterwards he founded the Association of Displaced Afro-Colombians (AFRODES), which aims to provide support to the thousands of black peasants and fishermen who have been forced to flee their homes. Yet as an outspoken community leader, Marino's life was also threatened in Bogotá. After a number of failed attempts on his life he fled in January 2002 to the United States, where he was granted asylum. He has received many peace prizes and as AFRODES's spokesperson in the US he continues to denounce what he and others call an 'ethnocide', or 'the second genocide', against the Afro-Colombian population. As a displaced female black activist told me in an interview in December 2004:

> After slavery this is the second time we are being uprooted. First we were expelled from Africa; our ancestors had to come to America to serve as slaves. They gained their freedom eventually, but now, in full twenty-first century, we are banished from the lands that we

> have obtained and made ours since the abolition of slavery. And we are pushed into the cities to fill up the slums, where they turn us into beggars.

Reflecting in hindsight on the events of 1996 in Riosucio, Marino is sceptical of the official claim that the military incursion was aimed at routing out FARC guerrillas from the region (and the army never admitted to the massacres committed by paramilitary groups): 'If the combined action of paramilitaries and army in Riosucio aimed at forcing the guerrilla from the region, why were we all bombed, massacred and displaced, if our only weapons were the tools with which we work the land to feed our families? ...Or was their aim really to drive away all the people living in this area?'[26]

As another prominent black leader explained to me in an interview in Bogotá in November 2004: 'The displacement in the Pacific coast region is not a consequence of the armed conflict, the way in which the government wants to portray it to international public opinion. No. The displacement is a strategy of the conflict. The armed conflict uses the strategy of displacement to empty those lands that are needed to develop their megaprojects'.

At the heart of this unprecedented paramilitary incursion into the Pacific coast region lies a changing rationale for developing the region. The conservation strategy of the early 1990s has been abandoned and replaced by a return to the logic of exploitation and extraction, to capitalist accumulation and land dispossession. One recent overview of capitalism's long historical process of enclosure and attack on the commons actually captures the current deterritorialisation trends in the Colombian Pacific coast with chilling accuracy:

> The great work of the past half-millennium was the cutting off of the world's natural and human resources from common use. Land, water, the fruits of the forest, the spaces of custom and communal negotiation, the mineral substrate, the life of rivers and oceans, the very airwaves – capitalism has depended, and still depends, on more and more of these shared properties being shared no longer, whatever the violence of absurdity involved in converting the stuff of humanity into this or that item for sale.[27]

This development can best be illustrated with the rapid expansion of African Palm plantations that are established with national and transnational capital on lands collectively owned by rural black communities.

THE 'VIOLENCE OF ABSURDITY' IN AFRICAN PALM CULTIVATION

African Palm was first introduced to Colombia in 1932, but it was not until the late-1950s that it became of commercial value, mainly for the use of palm oil in the production of soaps, vegetable oils and animal feeds. The area under African Palm cultivation grew tenfold, from 18,000 hectares in the mid-1960s to 188,000 hectares in 2003. Estimates put the current area under production at around 300,000 hectares, making Colombia the fourth largest palm oil producer in the world, after Malaysia, Indonesia and Nigeria. And much more is to come. On repeated occasions President Uribe has identified palm oil production as one of the principal export strategies for the future, for which six *million* hectares are to be put under cultivation by 2019. This staggering figure can be explained in part by the current world-wide hype over the production of biofuels into which palm oil can be converted, and which Uribe clearly wishes to exploit.

The African Palm industry had already received an important boost as part of the 'Economic Opening' development strategy in Colombia under the government of Cesar Gaviria (1990-1994). A strategic development alliance was established between the government and the National Federation of African Palm Companies (Fedepalma) and a fund was created (Fondo del Fomento Palmero) to support the commercialisation of oil palm products. Under President Pastrana (1998-2002) African Palm plantations were promoted as an alternative to illegal coca crops, with funding under Plan Colombia, the largely US-sponsored drug eradication campaign, a strategy also pursued under Uribe's policy of Democratic Security.

Yet in the Colombian Pacific region this development model has encountered significant resistance. First, the planting of a monoculture such as the oil palm is considered detrimental to the environment and the biodiversity in the region, which Law 70 was meant to help conserve. Second, the forcible establishment of African Palm production runs against the kind of development envisaged by black communities, who are also nominally protected under the same legislation. One state-sponsored method of overcoming resistance has been the cooptation of individual members or entire villages through the establishment of 'strategic alliances' between palm companies and Afro-Colombian communities. These alliances give incentives to local people to cooperate and provide land and labour for cultivation. They have been partly successful, and have driven a wedge into many communities, where individual members may see immediate personal benefits through the employment promised by the palm companies. But where cooptation does not work, coercion is applied. Many are the reports that have denounced the forced sale of lands by peasants under pressure from armed groups. As an Afro-Colombian lawyer and activist put it very simply, in an interview in November 2004: 'You know that when the power comes with a gun in hand, basically people end up collaborating'.

In order to break the organisational capacity of black communities, their leaders are targeted by paramilitary death squads. Some are forced to leave their homes, towns, or, as in the case of Marino Córdoba, even the country. Others are silenced by killing them, as is the case of Orlando Valencia. Moreover, it is not just the individual who is intimidated and chased, but, for maximum effect, their families are also terrorised. When I met Ana María (not her real name), a displaced activist from the Pacific region, in a cafeteria in Bogotá in November 2004, she told me how hard it was for her to part with her home, after paramilitaries had turned up at her door one day and left a message with her mother, giving her 24 hours to leave: 'This was so difficult to swallow. Because you just have to leave. It's not a decision that you take. No, you have to leave because they are going to kill you. So you just leave. And it is not just yourself, your family is in this also and everyone around you runs the same risk because of what you do'.

Another activist, whom I interviewed a few days later, was about to return to his native river basin where he had been at the forefront of organising local communities. He was determined not to give in to the armed groups, despite the killings of several of his family members:

> In September 2000, paramilitaries stormed into the house of one of my sisters in a neighbourhood in Buenaventura. I had entered a few minutes earlier, but they didn't realise that I had left through another door. They opened fire on everybody who was in the house and killed seven people then and there, cousins and nephews of mine. I got away by a few minutes. Then, in another neighbourhood of Buenaventura, they shot dead one of my brothers. Two more of my nephews were killed at the home of my other sister. ...On 11 May [2004], paramilitaries disappeared another nephew of mine, also in Buenaventura. ...This just shows the intensity of the threat and the persecution that we have been subjected to. Because the first thing they ask my family is: where is this relative of yours?

CONCLUSIONS

I needed this essay to conclude the way it began – with a personal story. These lived experiences are often absent in the waves of analysis offered by *violentólogos* proper. But in my eyes they form an important part in our understanding not only of the physical manifestations of violence in particular places, but also of the wider underlying structures of domination and oppression. Trade unionists and social movement leaders bear the brunt of systemic state violence directed against all voices of dissent. Their personal experiences show the real nature of the dominant power structures and the way in which patterns of oppression are played out on the ground. Moreover, the voices of the activists interviewed and cited give a raw dimension to the narrative that disrupts the moral high ground and the very possibility of detached armchair analysis, in the face of the lived experience of terror and violence. They add urgency to efforts to break the cycles of violence. Black leaders, for example, internationalise or globalise their struggle by stressing the link between palm oil production in Colombia and the global demand for biofuels, holding 'us' in the West directly co-responsible for the massacres and the forced displacement of black peasants so that their lands are planted with African Palm trees. They also remind us that in the early 1990s global concerns were largely responsible for the Pacific coast region being temporarily transformed into a laboratory for biodiversity conservation. Biofuels or biodiversity? The wrong answer to this question will continue to see rural black populations terrorised.

This essay makes no claim to analyse the complex phenomenon of violence in Colombia as a fully comprehensible, transparent phenomenon. I agree with Pécaut, who argues that 'no single coherent intellectual or political framework or category is able to explain this violence'.[28] The framework I have applied here draws on Marxist insights into the capitalist imperative of ceaseless expansion and accumulation. It insists on a global dimension that is often absent from debates that stress the peculiarity of Colombia as a 'poster child for studies of violence'.[29] Of course the precise ways in which violence is carried out are particular to the geographical and historical context, and draw on the specific historical repertoire of violence in Colombia. The barbarities committed by paramilitary groups today, for example, are clearly linked to forms of torture, massacre and mutilation practiced during La Violencia. Yet, focusing on the exceptionality of this 'poster child' it is easy to forget the global dimensions of an expanding drive of capital, pushed through by violent means, which lies at the heart of current patterns of displacement and dispossession in Colombia and elsewhere. The Pacific coast region is only one of the latest instances of the age-old tendency for peasants to be forcibly pushed off their lands. A new round of primitive accumulation has gripped the capitalist globe, and as we (should) know, capitalism's capacity for ceaseless re-structuring and its thirst to penetrate the most hidden corners of unchartered terrain knows no end (as yet).

NOTES

Thanks for research support are due to the EU's Marie Curie International Fellowship and the UK's Economic and Social Research Council.

1 For info on the conference, see http://www.lwr.org/colombia/convention.
2 Daniel Pécaut, 'From the Banality of Violence to Real Terror: The Case of Colombia', in K. Koonings and D. Kruijt, eds., *Societies of Fear: The Legacy of Civil War, Violence and Terror in Latin America*, London: Zed Books, 1999, p. 145.
3 Ibid., p. 142. When Pécaut talks of the 'banality of violence', he wishes to stress the ordinariness, or triviality, with which violence is perceived and enacted. He does not refer to the Arendtian notion of the 'fearsome, word-and-thought-defying banality of evil' that stared Hannah Arendt in the face at the trial of Nazi Obersturmbannführer Adolf Eichmann in Jerusalem in 1961. In fact, he doesn't mention Arendt at all. See Hannah Arendt, *Eichmann in Jerusalem: A Report on the Banality of Evil*, Harmondsworth: Penguin Books, 1977 [1963] p. 252.
4 Nazih Richani, 'The Political Economy of Violence: The War System in Colombia', *Journal of Interamerican Studies and World Affairs*, 39(2), 1997, p. 67.
5 R. Zelik, 'Gewerkschaftssterben in Kolumbien: über den Zusammenhang von neoliberaler Deregulierung, staatlicher Politik und Paramilitarismus' [The Death of Trade Unions in Colombia. On the Relationship between Neoliberal Deregulation, State Policy and Paramilitarism], *Prokla*, 33(1), 2003, pp. 51-75.
6 See, e.g., Alexandra Guáqueta, 'The Colombian Conflict: Political and Economic Dimensions', in K. Ballentine and J. Sherman, eds., *The Political Economy of Armed Conflict: Beyond Greed and Grievance*, London: Lynne Rienner, 2003, pp. 73-106.
7 David Harvey, *The New Imperialism*, Oxford: Oxford University Press, 2003, pp. 137-82. See also David Harvey, 'The New Imperialism: Accumulation by Dispossession', *Socialist Register 2004*.
8 Ibid., p. 148.
9 There is an enormous body of literature on violence in Colombia. Excellent introductions are Catherine LeGrand, 'The Colombian Crisis

in Historical Perspective', *Canadian Journal of Latin American and Caribbean Studies*, 28(55-56), 2003; and Charles Bergquist, Ricardo Peñaranda, and Gonzalo Sánchez, eds., *Violence in Colombia: The Contemporary Crisis in Historical Perspective*, Wilmington: Scholarly Resources Inc., 1992. For a detailed analysis of the period known as *La Violencia* (especially its second half), see Gonzalo Sánchez and Donny Meertens, *Bandits, Peasants, and Politics: The Case of 'La Violencia' in Colombia*, Translated by A. Hynds, Austin: University of Texas Press, 2001. Its impact in the Antioquia region has been excellently documented in Mary Roldán, *Blood and Fire: La Violencia in Antioquia, Colombia, 1946-1953*, Durham: Duke University Press, 2002. The political crisis of the 1980s is covered in Francisco Leal Buitrago and León Zamosc, eds., *Al filo del caos: crisis política en la Colombia de los años 80*, Bogotá: Tercer Mundo Editores, 1991. The decade of the 1990s – including peace negotiations – is analysed in Bergquist, Peñaranda, and Sánchez, eds., *Violence in Colombia*. See also Nazih Richani, *Systems of Violence: The Political Economy of War and Peace in Colombia*, Albany: State University of New York Press, 2002.

10 María Victoria Uribe, *Matar, rematar y contramatar: las masacres de La Violencia en el Tolima, 1948-1964*, Bogotá: Cinep, 1990.

11 María Victoria Uribe, 'Dismembering and Expelling: Semantics of Political Terror in Colombia', *Public Culture*, 16(1), 2004, p. 81.

12 Elsewhere I have conceptualised these effects of violence on landscapes and on people's changing sense of place as 'geographies of terror' in a critical attempt to recover the complexity of the concept of terror from the mind-numbing dominant geopolitical 'war on terror' discourses. See Ulrich Oslender, 'Another History of Violence: The Production of "Geographies of Terror" in Colombia's Pacific Coast Region', *Latin American Perspectives*, (forthcoming October 2008), and 'Spaces of Terror and Fear on Colombia's Pacific Coast: The Armed Conflict and Forced Displacement among Black Communities', in D. Gregory and A. Pred, eds., *Violent Geographies: Fear, Terror, and Political Violence*, New York: Routledge, 2007.

13 On torture as communicative strategy, see Michael Taussig, 'Culture of Terror – Space of Death: Roger Casement's Putumayo Report and the Explanation of Torture', *Comparative Studies in Society and History*, 26(3), 1984. See also Michael Taussig, *Law in a Lawless Land: Diary of a* Limpieza *in Colombia*, Chicago: University of Chicago Press, 2005.

14 Gonzalo Sánchez and Ricardo Peñarando, eds., *Pasado y presente de la violencia en Colombia*, Bogotá: Cerec, 1986.

15 Gonzalo Sánchez, 'War and Politics in Colombian Society', *International Journal of Politics, Culture and Society*, 14(1) [special issue: 'Colombia, a nation and its crisis'], 2000, p. 21.

16 Jenny Pearce, *Colombia: Inside the Labyrinth*, London: Latin America Bureau, 1990, p. 45.

17 Eduardo Pizarro, 'Colombia: hacia una salida democrática a la crisis nacional?', in C.I. Degregori, ed., *Democracia, etnicidad y violencia política en los países andinos*, Lima: IEP/IFEA, 1993, p. 156.

18 Forrest Hylton, 'An Evil Hour: Uribe's Colombia in Historical Perspective', *New Left Review*, 23, 2003, p. 51.

19 Gisela Cramer, 'Democratic Security in Colombia', in L.S. Gustafson and S.R. Pattnayak, eds., *National and Human Security Issues in Latin America: Democracies at Risk*, Lewiston: Edwin Mellen Press, 2006, p. 110.

20 Data gathered from reports by Human Rights Watch, 'Colombia: New Killings of Labor Leaders', 2007, available at http://hrw.org, and US Labor Education in the Americas Project (USLEAP), 'Impunity Rate Abysmal for Colombian Trade Union Murders; Only Three Convictions in First Half of 2007', 2007, available at http://usleap.org. The International Centre for Trade Union Rights (ICTUR) provides detailed information on the killings of trade unionists via its quarterly 'Colombia Bulletin', available at http://www.ictur.org. See also the reports published by the International Confederation of Free Trade Unions (ICFTU), http://www.icftu.org.

21 Francisco Ramírez Cuellar, *The Profits of Extermination: How US Corporate Power is Destroying Colombia,* Introduced and Translated by A. Chomsky, Monroe: Common Courage Press, 2005, pp. 29, 32.

22 For details on this legislation and its impact, see Karl Offen, 'The Territorial Turn: Making Black Territories in Pacific Colombia', *Journal of Latin American Geography*, 2(1), 2003; Peter Wade, 'The Cultural Politics of Blackness in Colombia', *American Ethnologist*, 22(2), 1995; and the special issue of the Journal of Latin American Anthropology, 7(2), 2002.

23 For an illuminating interview with leaders of the Afro-Colombian displaced community, see http://www.safhr.org/refugee_watch20_voic-es.htm.

24 On the history of alluvial gold deposit exploitation, see Robert West, *Colonial Placer Mining in Colombia*, Baton Rouge: Louisiana State University Press, 1952, and this US geographer's seminal work on the

region: Robert West, *The Pacific Lowlands of Colombia*, Baton Rouge: Louisiana State University Press, 1957.

25 Marino Córdoba, 'Trágico amanecer', in M. Segura Naranjo, ed., *Exodo, patrimonio e identidad*, Bogotá: Ministerio de Cultura, 2001, pp. 249-50.

26 Ibid., p. 252.

27 Retort, *Afflicted Powers: Capital and Spectacle in a New Age of War*, London: Verso, 2005 pp. 193-94.

28 Pécaut, 'From the Banality of Violence to Real Terror', p. 142.

29 Diane Davis, 'The Age of Insecurity: Violence and Social Disorder in-the New Latin America', *Latin American Research Review*, 41(1), 2006, p. 182.

THE COMMODIFICATION OF VIOLENCE IN THE NIGER DELTA

SOFIRI JOAB-PETERSIDE AND ANNA ZALIK

Over the past four years, the Niger Delta has come to be widely portrayed as a quintessential site of oil-related conflict. The contemporary insurgency in the riverine area clearly emerges from historical and contemporary extraction of oil from that territory and the social relations that have come to facilitate it. These armed groups make direct claims on oil revenues – seeking contracts with private companies, payments from competing politicians, and control over the proceeds of trade in 'bunkered' (contraband) oil. Concurrently, an apparently mounting 'criminality', in the form of gang and cult activity in urban areas, unfolds alongside this insurgency. Competitive security provision for the oil industry and for rival politicians shapes a protection racket prosecuted by armed militias. While these 'gangs' simultaneously act as security agents for, as well as a threat to, the oil industry the key victims of the resulting violence are not foreign oil workers but the local resident populations – the Niger Delta's so-called 'oil minorities'.

The mounting violence in the Delta thus expresses a competitive struggle over land around industrial installations that is linked to both party politics and control over various aspects of the oil trade – whether licit or illicit. What remains contested are the various frames through which the violence is to be explained: competitive thuggery (as represented by various youth gangs fighting for dominance in enclaves); commodified insecurity of industrial installations (in the form of kidnappings for ransom); or regional sovereignty and resistance (as expressed by MEND – the Movement for the Emancipation of the Niger Delta, the predominant armed resistance movement at present). Militia activity taking each of these forms surfaced in the aftermath of a period of relatively non-violent resistance in the previous decade. Indeed, in the 1990s, the Niger Delta's global expression was shaped particularly by the struggle of MOSOP (the Movement for the Survival of the Ogoni People) and the formation of the Ijaw Youth Council (IYC), alongside a range of other minority movements. Through the 'judicial murder' of Ken Saro-Wiwa, and organised state violence against popular resistance, peaceful protests against military rule, transnational oil industry domination, and for minority recognition were largely crushed.

In the post 9-11 period, unpacking the competing representations of mounting violence in the Delta is both a sensitive matter and crucial to critiquing the foreign militarization of the Gulf of Guinea. The representation of the Niger Deltan crisis in the global media is not unrelated to speculative profiteering on oil futures markets, which is receiving increased criticism from regulators.[1] Consequently, although our main focus here is the rise of contemporary militia activity in Rivers State and the competitive political violence related to it, we wish to make a series of linked arguments concerning the region's representation. First, the spotlight on the state in Nigerian academic analysis of the Delta crisis manifests broader disputes over federal control and territorially-embedded resources (oil, agriculture, palm oil, labour) in which the region's social movements have been central actors. Historically, these movements formed part of regional and tribally-identified resistance groups that emerged through decolonization, manifesting the crystallization of ethnicity under indirect rule.[2] But focusing on the Nigerian federal state tends to lead to *inattention* to global speculative exploitation and tends to confirm the private oil industry's own representation of the 'risks' it faces in the Niger Delta. The violent context permits the corporations to make windfall profits, even while they claim it causes them 'losses'. If one were to employ, instead, the late Charles Tilly's reading of the state as an organised criminal syndicate,[3] the Nigerian state's role as facilitator of global capitalist windfalls in the transnational oil market might receive the attention it deserves.

We also wish to suggest that resistance against the authority of the federal government echoes with contemporary global struggles (e.g. in Latin America) for resource sovereignty, but in a form that is masked by the crystallization of ethnicity as the lynchpin of socio-political organization. Ethnicity was central to attempts to achieve consent under British indirect rule, and is cemented today through various forms of decentralization and 'social capital' promotion. This 'compromised modernity' has served to obfuscate in the Western imagination the way in which contemporary 'criminal activity' and youth violence in the Delta is equally an expression of what may be called late capitalism's 'anti-economy of social exclusion'.[4] The economic exclusion of marginalised youth as a result of state-capitalist developmentalism and, more recently, of structural adjustment policies,[5] has also served to constitute not so much a reserve army as active armies of young people that have become involved in the competitive appropriation of oil wealth. These activities at times overlap with more 'conventional' criminal activity: theft, the drug trade, commercial sex work, and kidnappings for ransom. But the competition to provide 'security' for both legal and contraband oil extraction, while prompting periodic *in*security in the Niger Delta's urban centres, has thus come to serve a functional purpose for global capital.

This provides a challenge to oppositional social movements in terms of how to represent militia activities in a context of rapid change, as even those purporting to act in the interests of Deltan sovereignty are drawn into turf wars and/or collaboration with political elites seeking to maintain a fragile grip on power. As one social movement leader put it following the 2003 elections (which an environmental rights organization referred to as an 'armed struggle'),[6] in the Nigerian climate the ability to lead security operations for politicians means 'you can go from being a nobody to an everybody overnight'.[7] The 2007 elections were less violent in the Delta (although not in the rest of the country) than in 2003, but in their immediate aftermath marauding armed militias, unhappy with token compensation for the 'security services' they had provided politicians, instilled fear throughout Port Harcourt. Against the ruling-class controlled media's conscious 'attempt to criminalise the struggles of the masses of the Niger Delta', Godwin Frank, a Nigerian political and environmental rights activist, endorsed a Human Rights Watch report as follows:

> demonstrating that the past and on-going violence in the Niger Delta in general and Port Harcourt in particular, is a specific outcome and an expression, albeit more virulent, of the dynamics of primitive accumulation by the Nigerian ruling class.
>
> A situation in which various fractions, segments and alliances of a ruling class, consciously and decidedly cultivate lawlessness & general violence and promote atomization & destruction of organizations of the masses, in an attempt to assume vantage positions in the business of unbridled looting of public wealth. Our capitalists do not set up industries to compete amongst themselves for market share; they set up and foster gangster-organizations to compete for public-wealth. The size of their loot is proportional to the level of violence they are able to unleash on the masses. No doubt, we are in the vice-grip of VIOLENCE LAISSEZ-FAIRE!![8]

Internationally, the layering of resistance activities over pre-existing ethnic militias, and disputes between rival 'security providers', have led to an official depiction from Washington, DC think-tanks of a criminalised, terror-prone Niger Delta. To challenge this discourse, this essay focuses on the factors that gave rise to the contemporary militias, showing how misleading it is to describe their activities in terms of 'terror'.[9] As we will see, the commodification of political violence, which has become increasingly widespread since the transition from military rule, may be depicted, ironically, as a kind of 'democratisation of violence'. Support among youth for attacks against politicians reflect the general sense of disenfranchisement from the oil wealth that political elites are presumed to have monopolised. This distrust is palpable in communities throughout the Delta, as youth accuse chiefs of having 'chopped' (eaten) payments from the oil companies. Through competitive electoral processes that provide paid employment for youth excluded from extractive modernity, these same youths arm themselves, challenging any monopoly over force in the so-called 'ungovernable' creeks. Their activities thus further compromise and privatise the federal state, while facilitating their ability to make claims on political elites, even while their activities are at times harshly repressed. Locally, this results in violence and intimidation against civilian populations by both militias and state security forces, while creating a climate of alarm, which yields heightened risk-returns for multinational investors. An examination of these dynamics alongside an emerging territorial insurgency shows that to perceive the contemporary Niger Delta through the lens of terrorism further consolidates the 'Slick Alliance' between global capital and the Nigerian state that oppresses the Delta's resident oil minorities.

SOCIAL EXCLUSION ON THE NIGER DELTA

The Niger Delta region, located in the southernmost region of Nigeria, encompasses some 70,000 sq. km, nine states, and a population of over 28 million. The predominant sites of petroleum extraction, where densely forested, maze-like wetlands shape the geography surrounding oil installations, are Rivers, Delta and Bayelsa states. Ethno-linguistically there may be over 100 dialects spoken in the Delta, from at least five language groups, and in the riverine area villages within 15 minutes of one another may speak different ones. Together, the population of these states is estimated at close to 10 million. Neighbouring Akwa Ibom State to the east of Rivers State is less conflictual, not only because of the particular history of the Ibibio people that are that state's main inhabitants but also because the oil installations there are primarily in the deep offshore. The residents of Delta, Rivers and Bayelsa states, in contrast, have mounted organised resistance against government and the oil industry, with the Ogoni inhabitants of Rivers State prominent internationally as a result of the movement led by Saro-Wiwa until his execution in 1995.

The contribution of oil wealth to the Nigerian polity makes clear why this region is of key strategic significance to the country's economy and stability, and also suggests why Nigeria exemplifies the 'resource curse'.[10] Between 2002-4, oil revenues accounted for about 50 per cent of Nigeria's GDP; almost 80 per cent of all government revenues; and 97 per cent of its foreign exchange earnings.[11] This stands in sharp contrast with the region's deepening socio-economic problems. Indeed, in Port Harcourt, unemployment may be as high as 30 per cent – a reflection of the income effects of a boom and bust, enclave industry. As the prominent political economist Okechukwu Ibeanu details in a recent study:

> available figures show that there is one doctor per 82,000 people, rising to one doctor per 132,000 people in some areas, especially the rural areas, which is more than three times the national average of 40,000 people per doctor... While 76 per cent of Nigerian children attend primary school, in the Niger Delta the figure drops appallingly to between 30 and 40 per cent.[12]

The leading industrial operators in the petroleum sector are Shell, Chevron-Texaco, Total, and Agip in conjunction with the Nigerian National Petroleum Corporation, as well as Exxon Mobil in the offshore of Akwa Ibom State. As the 'first-mover'[13] in the Nigerian oil industry, Shell's influence on socio-political relations throughout the country is palpable. Given the relative absence of federal infrastructure in the Delta, Shell is at times a *de facto* state in the region. The social history of the Nigerian oil industry is rooted in the regional identity and territorial struggles of the late colonial and early independence period in the Niger Delta. Oil explorations were initiated in the 1930s by Shell, with the first successful well drilled near Oloibiri in today's Bayelsa state in 1956. The 'minorities' of the Niger Delta were already identified as a marginalised set of social groups in the period leading up to decolonisation.[14] Six years after Nigerian independence in 1960, the continuing regional tensions led to the Biafran Civil War in which the Igbo east attempted to secede. The war partially concerned the control of oil-producing regions and their associated revenues, the British siding with the Nigerian Federation and the French with Biafra, while Shell surreptitiously fuelled both sides.[15]

This period also saw the emergence of sovereignty movements in the Niger Delta, especially among the Ijaw. In January 1966 Isaac Adaka Boro, then a university student in the east, led a revolt and guerrilla movement against the Nigerian state (referred to as the 12-day revolution), proclaiming a Niger Delta People's Republic. With a hundred and fifty-nine volunteers, Boro established the first post-independence ethnic militia in the Niger Delta. The echo of his movement figured in the ongoing regional pressures for an autonomous Rivers State, ultimately established in May 1967. As the new state was seen as strengthening the Southern minorities vis-à-vis the Ibo southeast in the federation, it was among the factors prompting Igbo/ Biafran secession. Boro's legacy remains central to Ijaw national identity and contemporary Deltan resistance movements, in particular in their armed variety. Boro's army, the Niger Delta Volunteer Force (NDVF), resonates in the names subsequently taken by today's militias in Rivers State.

The period after the civil war saw a series of military dictatorships in Nigeria, with a brief period of democracy in the Second Republic which, alongside broader global downturns and the impact of structural adjustment policies, ravaged the Nigerian economy in the 1980s and '90s. The Niger Delta witnessed deepening socio-environmental degradation, marginalisation and impoverishment. Particularly notable was the infrastructural isolation of the rural and riverine villages to which roads, water systems and electricity were not extended despite numerous 'plans' by federal development commissions. This context was worsened by ecological degradation resulting from the oil industry's presence, including ubiquitous unprotected pipelines and huge surface flares of associated gas. An agrarian and fishing socio-economy has persisted in riverine communities accessible only by boat, although there is an ongoing outmigration from them into sporadic oil enclave employment.[16] In the urban areas, an acute housing shortage has led to the springing up of squatter/slum settlements along the waterfronts.[17] A context of 'relative deprivation' is therefore evident in both the Delta's isolated swampland communities and its urban slums, alongside the highly securitised, gated residential facilities of the oil industry.

COLONIALISM, ETHNICITY AND COMMODIFICATION

The Delta was a site of global resource extraction – of slaves, rubber and palm oil – long before petroleum was discovered. Palm oil lent its name to the 'Oil Rivers' by which the Delta fluvial system came to be known. The slave trade under Portuguese and Dutch control, from the 15th to the 19th century, was followed by British 'maxim gun' diplomacy and its translation into legal relations of commercial dominance.[18] Overseas commerce was established with the emergence of Niger Deltan city states in the 18th and 19th centuries. As Peter Ekeh has argued, the involvement of the local population in the trans-Atlantic slave trade was among the key factors strengthening the role of kinship/tribal identification as a central provider of human security, while central state war-making was directly associated with predatory violence against the local population.[19]

The bone of contention between the traditional political leadership and the colonial state was the local rulers' commercial and political rights, which were threatened by the economic activities of the Royal Niger Company.[20] Stronger settlements developed a protection racket on the waterways in the form of the *comey,* a security tax on the movement of goods – not altogether unlike the money paid by oil companies for security today.[21] A century after the formal abolition of slavery, the establishment, expansion and consolidation of the Southern Nigerian Protectorate between 1900 and 1913 – which incorporated the Southern Nigerian 'Oil Rivers Protectorate' established in 1885 – was accomplished by brute force using protectorate troops and police.

Under British and Royal Niger Company control, local merchants were able to trade with other local merchants only by smuggling, with interesting parallels to the bunkering of oil today. But although Britain subjugated the Niger Delta City States militarily, it did not destroy their chieftaincy institutions. Traditional political institutions were adapted under the policy of Indirect Rule which shaped the contemporary politicisation of cultural ties, through the promotion of the warrant chiefs of the colonial era. Today, oil industry 'host community' policies reproduce these localised, divisive relations through competition for development funds and promises of labour and security contracts, the price of which is determined by the 'value' of the oil installations of which a given village is deemed the 'landlord'.[22] Chiefs claim compensation from the multinationals for oil prospecting activities in the community, based on a provision in the Land Use Act which states that compensation for surface rights over land acquired for oil activities is to be made to Traditional Rulers to disburse as they deem fit on behalf of their communities.[23] Such practices made certain chieftaincies and territorial claims highly lucrative and contentious; both state institutions and oil companies treated chiefs as their primary interlocutors with the local communities. The geographical boundaries between the oil communities have likewise become deeply contested, with oil industry mapping and naming practices leading to violent conflicts.

Since the mid-1990s, the youths of communities in Rivers State have aggressively demanded the dismantling of hierarchical traditional leadership structures in favour of more horizontal arrangements. The companies, in turn, have been compelled to make payments to the youths, who have accused the chiefs of corruption, for access to their facilities or to ensure the security of their operations.[24] Due to the gulf between traditional authorities and the youth who are the 'security' providers, Community Development Councils (CDCs) – a revolving governance structure functioning alongside the councils of chiefs – are of increasing salience. In certain cases, the CDCs have been taken over by youths following major intra-community conflicts in which armed groups have expelled the traditional authorities.[25]

The establishment of new states and Local Government Areas in the Nigerian Federation has also led to complaints over unclearly defined boundaries. Although intended to serve as a route toward sub/minority group and local participation in development, this both reflects and prompts inter-ethnic clashes over the ownership of oil-fields, farmlands and waterways.[26] In some of these conflicts, state security forces watch while violence rages, especially where intelligence reports indicate that the state's business interests are not threatened. This creates civil insecurity that has in turn stimulated the rapid privatisation of security. Prior to 1999, under a military government in which the state was very much 'a force to be feared', most neighbourhoods in Port Harcourt organised self-defence or vigilante groups. Over time, these private policing initiatives became counter-productive, as small arms provided for collective security resurfaced in intra-community disagreements, ultimately exacerbating violence. This occurred in the 1999 democratic process, though in a mild form, due to the presence of the military which was there to facilitate the transition to democratic rule.

But what has emerged since 1999 is a political culture where elites win power through violent competition. Competitive electoral politics has taken on a ruthless character in which it is assumed that the winner takes all. Central to this is the use of militias by the political parties, either as part of their campaign cadres or directly to control the electoral outcome. Concurrently, and despite the formal outlawing of company 'standby' payments to community youths, the employment of local and private security forces by the industry remains commonplace, contributing to a protection racket where territorially-dominant armed groups act as both security and threat to industry.[27]

The frequent vandalising of oil facilities, the opposition to construction of new facilities, the blockades of oil rigs, the kidnapping of local and international personnel, and the attacks on and shut-downs of facilities have led to arrests, the detention and trial of activists (sometimes on trumped-up charges) and the deployment of military forces. These deployments are reminiscent of the military regimes of Babangida and Abacha, when forces were sent in against a variety of protesters and/or 'criminals', leading to the destruction of villages and the deaths of unarmed civilians.[28] The military's approach to the Niger Delta has been described as 'maximum force at the slightest hint of insecurity'.[29] A series of security operations with names like 'Fire for Fire' and 'Operations Flush 1, 2, 3' are examples of high-profile security initiatives. Although these demonstrate the ongoing securitised, repressive attitude of the state, the increasing availability of small arms and attacks contribute to the 'terrorist' discourse employed by security-affiliated think-tanks.[30] It is in this context that the proliferation of ethnic militia groups in Rivers State needs to be understood. As we shall now see, uncovering the origins of this discloses the conjoint fuelling of armed groups by politicians, oil industry security contracts, and the trade in bunkered oil.

VIOLENCE AND ITS REPRESENTATION

The ethnic militias in the area surrounding Nigeria's 'oil capital', Port Harcourt, the capital of Rivers State, are rooted in competitive social relations arising from both electoral contests and the trade in contraband oil. The dispute between the *Niger Delta People's Volunteer Force* (NDPVF) led by Asari Dukubo, and the *Niger Delta Vigilante* (NDV) led by Ateke Tom, gained international notoriety in 2003-4. In reaction to the turf-warfare and commodified violence that increasingly characterised their dispute and various others, the Movement for the Emancipation of the Niger Delta (MEND) emerged with the aim of reappropriating and reshaping the public representation of armed resistance in the Delta.

In examining the dynamics shaping both the rise of NDV and NPDVF and the subsequent emergence of MEND, global and 'local' perceptions of resistance and protest against industry are highly salient. In 2002-3, many residents of the Niger Delta riverine and peri-urban area, including women and youth, would refer to any shut-down of an installation as 'violence'. Presumably they had adopted the corporate language that describes as 'violent' all facility occupations. This was particularly notable at Shell's Women's Peacebuilding Forum in Yenagoa in Bayelsa State in 2003, attended by hundreds of women from that company's host communities. Ironically, this went hand in hand with a tendency to place responsibility for 'social breakdown' in the Niger Delta crisis on women as mothers at the Forum. The internalization of the equation between popular protest against the oil industry and the criminalisation of resistance has not only been accepted by the courts, but by the affected populations themselves.

The violence between Asari- and Ateke-affiliated militias in the Port

Harcourt area reflects the range of interests involved in the Delta's 'protection business'. Port Harcourt and Warri are the two key oil towns in Nigeria. While Warri had been a central site of inter-ethnic violence for various decades, especially pronounced in the late 1990s and leading to massive displacement in 2003, armed conflict in Port Harcourt emerged particularly in the democratic transition period, with 2003 a major watershed. The rivalry between Asari and Ateke may be best understood as a conflict between rival gangs seeking territorial control, a form of 'competitive thuggery'. But both Asari and Ateke were also providers of 'local security' services, in contests for chieftaincy stools where territorial authority entailed access to oil industry payments. Their ability to gain adherents among a range of youth results from the widespread disaffection of youth gangs in the slums alongside the relatively advantaged classes drafted into increasingly violent cult fraternities on university campuses. In wrangling over chieftaincy titles and political posts these alienated youth were also exploited by those desperate for power.

Asari Dokubo, from a politically important family of the Kalabari area, and Ateke Tom, from Okrika, both belong to clans with significant commercial and political histories in Rivers State and the Niger Delta generally. In the constitution of an Okrika community defence force, those charged with prosecuting an ongoing rivalry with the neighbouring Eleme clan over the land base of the Port Harcourt Refinery were known as the Bush Boys/ Peacemakers, while Ateke was first armed as the leader of the young men charged by the Okrika Divisional Council of Chiefs with security of the community's mainland. But following the height of Okrika's conflict with Eleme, Ateke was accused of employing violence and intimidation against his own community and was, for a time, expelled from Okrika by the Bush Boys. The latter would later become allies of Asari. While Ateke and Asari had served as local security in these areas, in the 2003 elections their militias came to be patronised by the ruling PDP (People's Democratic Party) under Governor Odili. Their increasing access to arms before, during and after the election, was among the factors that allowed them to compete for and assert control over sites in the contraband oil trade in the Cawthorne Channel area. It was with the support of PDP state representatives, whose central position in funding the violence of the 2003-4 period is now under investigation by the Rivers State Truth and Reconciliation Commission, that Ateke's position as a regional gang leader solidified. He was also employed to support leadership factions in the Kalabari area to which Asari Dokubo was opposed, another key contributor to their dispute.

Asari Dokubo's rise to prominence was similarly associated with clan and political sponsorship. But both his relatively advantaged class position and the broader movement of the Ijaw Youth Council (IYC) that he led from 2002 placed him among Niger Deltan 'civil society' in a way that set him apart from Ateke. He was installed as president of the IYC in 2002, in elections orchestrated by Governor Odili and marked by a heavy state security presence. Established as a politically-autonomous branch of the Ijaw nationalist movement at Kaiama in Bayelsa State in 1998, the IYC was considered an organic social movement and highly democratic. The organisation's founding document, the Kaiama declaration, protested the economic exclusion and political marginalisation of the Ijaw by the state and transnational oil companies.[31] The PDP's role in IYC elections tarnished the legitimacy of Asari's presidency, however, and a portion of the IYC leadership affiliated with Deltan social justice organisations distanced themselves from him.

Although Asari later came to represent more militant tendencies in the IYC, he was reportedly not present at Kaiama in 1998. But by 2004 his ability to command a range of Deltan youth brought him international notoriety. Coupled with his identity as a convert to Islam, the international media coverage squared well with the discourse concerning threats to global freedom and energy security that accompanied the US invasion of Iraq.[32] The portrayal of Asari as a warlord leading young African men toting sophisticated weapons conformed to neo-conservative 'failed state' perspectives on 'chaos' in West Africa.

Partially due to the criticism from sovereigntist branches in the IYC, Asari disassociated himself from Odili and the PDP following the elections. His militia adopted the name the Niger Delta Peoples Volunteer Force (NDPVF), informed by Isaac Boro's movement of the 1960s, while Ateke's militia became the Niger Delta Vigilante. But concurrent with Asari's increasing criticism of the political elite and the Nigerian State, his conflict with Ateke mounted and took on the characteristics of a turf war. This came to a head in November of 2003 in a major clash at Buguma, the Kalabari capital and Asari's hometown.

The heightening of the violence between the two leaders must also be understood in the context of struggles to control the profits from the bunkered oil trade. Contraband oil bunkering in the Niger Delta has a complex history. Cartels of oil bunkerers initially established armed gangs to patrol creeks during operations, ward off non-associated state security, and escort the product to the high seas. They tapped directly into the oil industry's pipelines or wellheads, connecting the pipes to large barges hidden where the mangrove forest provides cover. The 'asphyxiating and unfriendly terrain comprising thick mangrove forests and swamps',[33] criss-crossed by creeks, rivers and canals, is a unique feature of the Niger Delta that makes it possible for illegal bunkerers to evade state control.[34] The industry has made a concerted effort to mark bunkered oil as 'illegal' (see for instance, the website legaloil.com), especially as it is exchanged on global spot markets alongside 'legitimately' extracted oil. As recently described in the *Financial Times*: 'Smaller ships ferry back and forth to fill up tankers on high seas. The tankers often come with guns, exchanged as part payment for oil. The oil is then transported to third parties, often to refineries in Central Asia and eastern Europe, which buy at a discount to market price, refine the oil and sell it on the world market'.[35]

By 2003, the leaders of the militias had become both marketers of 'security' and bunkerers, since they had acquired the infrastructure and technical skills to operate autonomously. This is a direct assertion of local 'resource control', reminiscent of struggles for commercial power in the late 19th century. Various armed groups, including Asari's NDPVF, the FNDC (Federated Niger Delta Communities) of the Western Delta – a region encompassing Western Bayelsa and Delta States – and the currently prominent MEND, came to employ a sovereigntist discourse to describe the trade. Local militias' success at bunkering derives from better organisation, superior equipment, more funds and growing linkages with state political actors.

With the rise of NDV and NDPVF, drug gangs in Port Harcourt quickly aligned with one of the two militia groups to consolidate their trade zones. Consequently the Asari and Ateke dispute came to implicate gangs located in the urban slums, as well as cult groups that had arisen in the college/university system.[36] In the case of both gangs and cults, a quest for social mobility motivates participation in organised crime, encompassing drug dealing, robberies, car theft, and extortion. Despite an absence of stable hierarchies or long-established leaders capable of controlling all of these activities, the cult groups – whose leaders are paid to provide security protection for drug traffickers – have managed to direct the drug trade, carving the metropolis of Port Harcourt into distinct territories.

As a result of the increasing violence between their adherents, which affected the broad Port Harcourt area, various domestic and international NGOs were enlisted to 'resolve' the Asari-Ateke conflict. The mediation included meetings held outside the Delta (for instance in Jos, Plateau State) to which large numbers of young men from rival militias were bussed in. The push to resolve the Asari and Ateke rivalry coincided with Asari's distancing himself from Odili, openly critiquing the Nigerian political class and the state, and his assumption of the mantle of Deltan freedom fighter. It was reportedly through the advice of some of Asari's critics in the IYC leadership that he moved toward an anti-marginalisation platform. From the perspective of Ijaw youth, the resort to arms among one branch of the movement both anticipated future repression and led to the development of a more militant consciousness. While Asari was portrayed in the global media as a tough gang leader, within the Delta he came to be seen as an important freedom fighter. Long before his arrest on treason charges in 2005, which led to a huge groundswell of support for him in the Delta, he had started to employ the language of anti-apartheid movements in South Africa to describe the Deltan struggle. As he put it in an interview in July 2003: 'Rivers and Bayelsa are all Bantustans'.[37] Following his release from federal detention, and in contrast to his position in the 2003 elections, in 2007 Asari in fact offered to mediate in the conflict between Ateke and other Port Harcourt gang leaders.[38]

Unlike the rise of the NPDVF and the NDV, MEND's leadership structure is less defined and perhaps better understood in terms of Ike Okonta's description as 'an idea rather than an organisation in the formal sense of the word'.[39] MEND emerged in 2005-6 as a kind of umbrella for a dispersed collection of armed groups. Following attacks on facilities, MEND would claim responsibility, citing as causes the marginalisation of the Delta and its youth, the lack of productive employment, and the deterioration of the ecology of the region's fishing and farming subsistence base – in essence exclusion from both the formal oil economy and its agrarian alternative.[40] With regard to the attacks on oil facilities attributed to MEND, conflicting accounts of its activities demonstrate the crucial and sometimes hazy role of MEND's spokespeople in shaping public perception of a Niger Deltan insurgency. An event that occurred as this essay went to press highlights the significance of such divergent accounts for the representation of MEND as a broader social movement. Reports of an attack on the Bonga Offshore platform on June 19, 2008, the first deep offshore project in Nigeria, Shell-operated and highly strategic, prompted a flurry of international wire coverage of the Delta that led to a surge in prices. It also prompted fears that apparently secure, deep (i.e. on the high-seas) offshore installations could be as vulnerable to attack by militant groups as the onshore. But a week after the reported attack, a story in a Nigerian daily with roots in the Delta region, the *Vanguard*, offered an alternative account linking it to a labour dispute between Shell and its private security contractors:

> The alleged militant attack on the floating production storage and offloading vessel led to the shut-down of 225,000 per day crude oil output and rise in world price of crude. An American, Capt Jack

> Stone who works for an oil services company was alleged to have been kidnapped but later released... But a new twist has entered into the story, bringing with it an argument on who actually carried out the attack... (A)uthoritative sources told Saturday Vanguard that the attack and shut-in of the flow station were actually carried out from within the vessel, and not by MEND. "It was not a militant action at all", the sources revealed.... saying that the incident occurred when about 55 security personnel who are staff of a private security outfit operated by a retired senior military officer... forcefully shut the floating station in protest of Shell's maltreatment. Their anger, the military source continued, was that for the past three months, in spite of having worked under severe and dangerous conditions to secure the multi-billion dollars investment, Shell refused to pay them their salaries... MEND maintained they had attacked the facility to prove (they) have the capacity to attack anywhere in the Niger Delta to press for the release of its leader, Henry Okah as well as fight for the development of the Niger Delta region. "Shell thinks that we are fools. The company sacked a lot of Niger-Deltans from their employment when we are asking for more jobs for our people under the guise of restructuring. But the truth is that they are taking their production off shore, where they think that the military will protect them, that is part of the reason we went there to tell them that no place is safe for them in the Niger-Delta except they realize that they have to give jobs to our people and provide us with development incentives. We are telling them that we know their game plan and that it will not work..."[41]

The parties involved in providing these conflicting accounts of the Bonga incident include not only MEND and the former military – now privately-operated contractors to the neoliberalised state – but also Shell itself. The location of the Bonga field, offshore facing the contentious city of Warri, evokes memories of the 'evacuation' of the area facing Bonga by Chevron in 2003 during inter-communal election violence related to conflict over Local Government Area boundaries. The airlift of the residents by Chevron received the US Secretary of State's 'Corporate Award for Excellence' in November 2003. This evacuation occurred less than a year after a series of sit-ins at Chevron installations in the same area, where women residents of the riverine oil industry 'host communities' threatened to disrobe on a Chevron platform.[42] These women's protests gained international media sympathy and evoked fears among the multinationals of another Ogoni-style 'peaceful' uprising, much more likely to win the sympathy of global audiences than armed youth attacks. Five years later many of the 'evacuated' communities remain largely abandoned.

'DEMOCRATISED VIOLENCE'?

Much contemporary analysis of violence in the Delta locates the root of the region's insurgency exclusively in competition for the rewards of oil bunkering, attributing the motivation for conflict to economic-resource predation and 'greed'.[43] True, 'resource predation' is the rebel organisations' essential means of finance: the payment of operational allowances to combatants, the running costs of the camps, the payment of instructors and the purchase of weapons by NDPVF and NDV – all these are provided out of the proceeds of oil bunkering. But none of this accounts for the emergence of the NDPVF and the NDV. The 'resource predation' interpretation perceives their activities as 'organised crime', obscuring how militancy derives from grievances against the state and capital.

Since 2003, armed youth groups and militias in Rivers State have rapidly evolved from appendages of Delta political life to major political institutions in their own right. This was a consequence of the political elites' inability to control the militia leaders, a central contradiction of the commodification of violence. In part, this followed from the growing financial capacity of the groups to acquire sophisticated weapons on their own, as the presence of a small arms market in the region escalated inter-militia conflicts. The deepening contradiction assumed the form of splits and the formation of new alliances and counter-alliances between armed groups, either to secure compensation from the state or to fight among themselves to secure the highest bidder in the volatile democratic process. While this has contributed to weakening traditional and formal forms of authority, it does not fully explain the erosion of social deference to these authorities.

The ability to use arms also shapes a locally-mediated protection racket, which is now central to the political economy of both violence and oil industry security in the Delta. Although militia attacks serve as a major threat to extractive security, they have in fact been a boon to oil traders and security-operation profiteers, allowing speculative accumulation by corporate insiders. This dynamic is partially determined by the complex socio-cultural geography of the riverine area, which facilitates a regionalization of violence distinct from other parts of Nigeria. The goal of a violence-free Delta remains elusive both because the criminal acts are endorsed, rationalised and defended on the terrain of party politics, creating incentives for the ongoing reproduction of violence, and also because a local market has emerged in security/insecurity. The dynamic is shaped not only by ongoing rivalries for commercial dominance, control over territory, and domination of 'protection rackets' for politicians and bunkerers, but also by relations of subjugation that in fact encourage the rise of 'illicit' trade in the first place.

Whatever its representation, the trade amounts to a just claim against 'accumulation by dispossession'.[44] Relations of subjugation in the Niger Delta are in part a legacy of the trans-Atlantic trade and colonial rule, but are also shaped by the particular properties of oil as a territorially-embedded resource. The way the oil industry allocates the benefits from oil extraction to local actors and communities as 'hosts' to installations has served to further divide and rule the Delta's 'oil minorities' and has given rise to groups of armed youth now deeply involved in commodified practices, both political and commercial.[45] Given these circumstances, Godwin Frank's closing words concerning the 2007 post-election violence are worth noting:

> All said and done, what is most important to note is that we are at a cross-road; either we reclaim and rebuild our mass-based democratic organizations, position them for a focused struggle for a new and better society, or we nose-dive into unmitigated barbarism! Social history is never static! It is becoming increasingly clear that retrogression is gaining an upper hand over progression!! Let's act now!!![46]

As the violence perpetrated by some of the gangs and cults does indeed generate fear among the population, it partially legitimates the ongoing presence of both state and private security forces, which in turn reproduces relations of insecurity and distrust. Significantly, the nonviolent demands for reform made in the 2001 women's war against Chevron were considerably more threatening to that company's global reputation than the activities of marauding youth militias, of which the multinationals in the Delta now come to present themselves as victims.

NOTES

1 J. Chung, 'Soros Sounds Alarm on Oil "Bubble"', *Financial Times*, 3 June 2008; N. Cohen, 'Analysts Split on Upside to Oil Prices', *Financial Times*, 28 May 2008; Jeremy Grant et al., 'Futures Watchdog Investigates Oil Market', *Financial Times*, 29 May 2008.

2 C. Ake, *Political Ethnicity and State-Building in Nigeria in Global Convulsions: Race, Ethnicity and Nationalism at the End of the Twentieth Century*, Albany:

State University of New York Press, 1997; M. Mamdani, *Citizen and Subject: Contemporary Africa and the Legacy of Late Colonialism,* Princeton, Princeton University Press, 1996.

3 For instance, Tilly writes: 'But consider the definition of a racketeer as someone who creates a threat and then charges for its reduction. Governments' provision of protection, by this standard, often qualifies as racketeering. To the extent that the threats against which a given government protects its citizens are imaginary or are consequences of its own activities, the government has organized a protection racket. Since governments themselves commonly simulate, stimulate, or even fabricate threats of external war and since the repressive and extractive activities of governments often constitute the largest current threats to the livelihoods of their own citizens, many governments operate in essentially the same ways as racketeers. There is, of course, a difference: Racketeers, by the conventional definition, operate without the sanctity of governments'. Charles Tilly, 'War Making and State Making as Organized Crime', in P.B. Evans, D. Reuschemeyer and T. Skocpol, eds., *Bringing the State Back In,* Cambridge: Cambridge University Press, 1985

4 See P. Idahosa and R. Shenton, 'The Africanist's "New" Clothes', *Historical Materialism,* 12(4), 2003, and A. Cameron and R. Palan, *The Imagined Economies of Globalisation,* London: Sage, 2004.

5 See K. Shettima, 'Ecology, Identity, Developmentalism and Displacement in Northern Nigeria', *Journal of Asian and African Studies,* 32(1-2), 1997; O.O. Ibeanu, 'Exiles in their Own Homes: Conflicts and Internal Population Displacement in Nigeria', *Journal of Refugee Studies,* 12(2), 1999.

6 As described by Environmental Rights Action in a posting in Nigeria's Guardian newspapers. See also Isaac Osuoka, 'Nigeria: Oil, Elections and the International Community', 29 April 2007, available at http://www.zmag.org and Anna Zalik, 'Armed Struggle as Election? Social Protest, Extractive Security and the De/Legitimation of Civilian Transition', available from the author.

7 Personal interview, August 2003.

8 Godwin Frank wrote this in a personal email attached to his distribution of the report, 'Politics as War: The Human Rights Impact and Causes of Post-Election Violence in Rivers State, Nigeria', *Human Rights Watch,* 20(3), 2008.

9 That this remains necessary, when various of our colleagues have been

making the point for over a decade, only underlines the importance of social construction to shaping military intervention in the Niger Delta. See Ike Okonta 's 2000 article: 'The Lingering Crisis in Nigeria's Niger Delta and Suggestions for a Peaceful Resolution' available from http://www.cdd.org.uk.

10 M. Watts, 'Resource Curse? Governmentality, Oil and Power in the Niger Delta, Nigeria', *Geo Politics*, 9(1), 2004.

11 UNDP, 'Niger Delta Human Development Report', New York: UNDP, 2006.

12 O.O. Ibeanu, 'Introduction', in CLEEN Foundation, *Civil Society Organizations and Conflict Management in the Niger Delta – Scoping Gaps for Policy Advocacy*, Ikeja-Lagos: CLEEN Foundation, 2006, p. 3.

13 George Frynas, Matthias P. Beck & Kamel Mellahi, 'Maintaining Corporate Dominance after Decolonization: The "First Mover" Advantage of Shell in Nigeria', *Review of African Political Economy* 27 (85), 2000, pp. 407-25.

14 Willinks Commission, *Report of the Commission Appointed to Enquire into the Fears of Minorities and the Means of Allaying Them,* London, Colonial Office, Nigeria, 1958.

15 See Ike Okonta, *When Citizens Revolt: Nigerian Elites, Big Oil and the Ogoni Struggle for Self Determination*, Trenton: Africa World Press, 2008 and Anna Zalik, 'Petro-Violence and Partnership Development', *Review of African Political Economy*, 31(101), 2004.

16 A speedboat ride from these communities to Port Harcourt, Yenago or Warri may take 2 hours and cost upwards of $10 US dollars for a one-way trip. By market boat, the trip takes some days.

17 Yomi Oruwari, 'Planners, Officials and Low Income Women and Children in Nigerian Cities: Divergent Perspectives over Housing and Neighborhoods', *Canadian Journal of African Studies,* 37(2/3), 2003, pp. 396-410.

18 B. Ibhawoh, 'Stronger than the Maxim Gun: Law, Human Rights and British Colonial Hegemony in Nigeria', *Africa*, 72(1), 2002, pp. 55-83.

19 P. Ekeh, 'Social Anthropology and Two Contrasting Uses of Tribalism in Africa', *Comparative Studies in Society and History*, 32(4), 1990, pp. 660-700 and 'Colonialism and the Two Publics in Africa: A Theoretical Statement', *Comparative Studies in Society and History*, 17, 1975, pp. 91-112.

20 Under the British, those successful rulers most likely to assert their commercial dominance versus imperial interests were also displaced: the defeated, deposed or subjugated included King Jaja of Opobo

(1887), Nana of Itsekiri (1892), Overnarame (1897), King Ibanichuka of Okrika (1896), and Koko of Brass. See T.N. Tamuno, *The Evolution of the Nigerian State*, Longman: London, 1972.

21 E.J. Alagoa, 'Long Distance Trade and States in the Niger Delta', *Journal of African History*, 11(3), 1970 and 'The Development of Institutions in the States of the Eastern Niger Delta', *Journal of African History*, 12(2), 1971.

22 Bill Knight and Chris Alagoa, 'Sharing the Akassa Process: 5 Years of Building Partnerships and Seeking Sustainability in the Niger Delta', Conference on Health, Safety and Environment in Oil and Gas Exploration and Production, Kuala Lumpur, Malaysia, March 2002.

23 C. Dule and C. Nwankwo, 'Land, Oil and Human Rights in the Niger Delta: A Tale of Criminal Abuses', Niger Delta Channel, Port Harcourt, January, 2001.

24 J.S. Peterside, 'Ethnic Associations and Crisis of Human Rights Enforcement in the Niger Delta', Ph.D Thesis, Department of Sociology, University of Port Harcourt, 2001.

25 See D.V. Kemedi, 'Community Conflicts in the Niger Delta: Petro Weapon or Policy Failure?', Berkeley Workshop on Environmental Politics Working Papers, Berkeley, 2003; and Watts, 'Resource Curse?'.

26 A. Efemini, 'Managing Conflicts in the Niger Delta Region of Nigeria', *CASS Newsletter*, 1(1), Centre for Advanced Social Science (CASS), Port Harcourt, 2005; Knight and Alagoa, 'Sharing the Akassa Process'.

27 Private security of this kind is in fact sanctioned through the Voluntary Principles on Security and Human Rights, a joint US-UK initiative to which various oil companies and NGOs are signatories.

28 A highly criticized case was the destruction of Umuechem in 1990, in which numerous unarmed civilians were killed by the military following Shell's request for government protection from protesters. Among the most notable of such military invasions in the past 10 years was the sacking and burning of the town of Odi in Bayelsa State in 1999.

29 O. Douglas, 'Environmental Security in the Niger Delta', *CASS Newsletter*, 12(3&4), Centre for Advanced Social Science (CASS), Port Harcourt, 2004.

30 E. Cesarz, J.S. Morrison, and J. Cooke, 'Alienation and Militancy in Nigeria's Niger Delta', *CSIS Africa Notes*, 16, Centre for Strategic and International Studies, Washington, 2003.

31 See Patrick Naagbaton's '9 Years after the Kaiama Declaration', *The Port Harcourt Telegraph*, 12 December 2007, available from http://www.

thephctelegraph.com.

32 Western analysts emphasize Asari's identity as Muslim and his links to Libya, where he spent some time. His followers are not Muslim, as the Ijaw population largely practices Christianity or traditional religions. Nevertheless, his adoption of the title Alhaji and later Mujahadid served dominant Western anti-Islamic discourse.

33 Charles Ukeje, 'Oil Communities and Political Violence: The Case of Ethnic Ijaws in Nigeria's Delta Region', *Terrorism and Political Violence*, 13(4), 2001, p. 21.

34 As demonstrated in press coverage of the Soku gas plant, near previous Asari strongholds, the oil industry 'tolerates' bunkering as part of its concern with the security of its installations.

35 Dele Cole, 'Why Choke the Goose', *Financial Times*, 24 June 2008. Cole is a businessman and politician from Rivers State who was a founding member of the PDP and a former special adviser to President Obasanjo.

36 The first university fraternity, Pyrates, was founded in 1952 by Wole Soyinka and others at the University of Ibadan with the objectives of promoting social awareness and fighting social injustice. However, the intentions of these fraternities shifted as they spread to other Nigerian universities. Contests for influence between fraternities since the 1980s have resulted in violent clashes in which small arms are freely used.

37 Personal interview, 2003.

38 It should be noted that Asari's current position has been criticised, as some see his criticism of arrested MEND leader Henry Okah as seeking to curry favour with the federal government.

39 See Ike Okonta, 'Niger Delta: Behind the Mask', 26 October 2006 and 'MEND: Anatomy of a Peoples' Militia', 2 November 2006 in *Pambazuka News*, available from http://www.pambazuka.org.

40 MEND's kidnappings of oil workers in the Niger Delta have similar purposes. Although MEND's hostages have generally been released unharmed, an August 2006 kidnapping ended tragically, with 10 youth involved in negotiating the release of a Nigerian worker – who also died in the incident – gunned down by the Nigerian military. These deaths received minimal international coverage. As a colleague in the oil town of Warri wrote in a personal communication: 'The question we are now asking is, would the youths have been fired at if the rescued Shell official was white?'.

41 E. Amaize et al., 'Attack on Bonga: MEND Reveals How its Men Carried Out Raid', *Vanguard*, 28 June 2008. See earlier statement by

MEND spokesperson Jomo Gbomo, 'MEND Releases Hostage and Claims Responsibility for Shell's Bonga Offshore Oil Fields Attack', 19 July 2008, available from http://saharareporters.com.

42 Interviews with oil industry staff 2003 and 2006. MEND's emergence in the Western Delta followed the marginalisation of these well-publicised women's occupations of Chevron's Escravos facilities in 2002. The villagers' ongoing calls for resettlement and for fulfilment of these agreements were ignored and in February 2005 another protest launched from Ugborodo bordering on Chevron installations was answered brutally, with at least one protester killed. See 'Chevron Nigeria – Assault on Protestors' available at http://www.amnestyusa.org. Due partially to the evacuation, and conveniently for the company, Chevron's community development commitments made in response to the women's protests were not carried out and depopulation of the villages meant that local protests could hardly be sustained over time. In a public forum in 2006, a Chevron official stated that the company had no reason to fulfil development commitments made with the Warri women protesters since 'the communities' had not fulfilled their end of the bargain – to provide a peaceful operating environment.

43 P. Collier, *Economic Causes of Civil Conflict and their Implications for Policy*, Washington: World Bank, 2000.

44 D. Harvey, *The New Imperialism*, Oxford: Oxford University Press, 2003.

45 But it must be noted that these incentives toward the reproduction of violence serve not only those who fight. Indeed, an entire 'conflict' industry of peace-making and peace-keeping specialists, Nigerian and expatriate, has emerged to 'resolve and re-mediate' the bloodshed, who would clearly be out of a job if the crisis was allayed, while, as noted at the outset, the violence has also been a boon to oil traders and security-operation profiteers.

46 See note 8.

REVOLUTIONARIES, BARBARIANS OR WAR MACHINES? GANGS IN NICARAGUA AND SOUTH AFRICA

STEFFEN JENSEN AND DENNIS RODGERS

Images of urban gangs as the embodiment of a modern-day barbarism are commonplace, particularly in policy-making circles,[1] among law enforcement officials,[2] as well as large swathes of the general population.[3] More often than not fuelled and underpinned by the sensationalist media depictions of the phenomenon,[4] such portraits tend to represent gangsters either as evil and deranged sociopaths,[5] or as the exemplification of the ever-growing spread of anomic and senseless violence in a world that is increasingly characterised by the loss of traditional socio-political reference points.[6] In his classic anti-colonial manifesto *The Wretched of the Earth* Franz Fanon famously proposed an alternative vision, however. Although he acknowledged that the gangster was often 'a thief, a scoundrel or a reprobate', he also contended that when the gangster's violence was directed against colonial authority, it became imbued with popular legitimacy through a process of 'automatic' identification, and the gangster as a result 'lights the way for the people'.[7]

The post-colonial transition notwithstanding, this view of gangs as proto-revolutionary vanguards has continued to inform the analyses of many gang researchers over the past few decades.[8] During the course of our own research on gangs in respectively a poor neighbourhood in Managua, the capital city of Nicaragua, and a coloured township in Cape Town, South Africa, we have found considerable empirical resonance between Fanon's vision and the real-life discourses of many of the gangsters that we have interviewed and spent time with. Although narratives of fighting with the authorities, only stealing from the rich (or the racially dominant), and protecting local communities and neighbourhoods have long been features uncovered by research on gangs,[9] we found these to often be actively framed in explicitly revolutionary terms. Nicaraguan gang members, for example, frequently compared their behaviour with the actions of the *Sandinista* revolutionary regime, while gangs in post-Apartheid South Africa explicitly justified themselves as ANC-inspired forms of resistance against institutionalised racism.

Such clear-cut discourses by the principal actors involved seemingly make the idea that contemporary urban gangs are proto-revolutionary vanguard social forms highly appealing, but a more fine-grained analysis suggests that the reality is much more complex. Although drug gangs in Cape Town in the late 1990s, for example, often undoubtedly constituted important economic resources for township inhabitants – as one beneficiary put it, 'in the townships there are no banks, only the merchant [drug dealer]' – their territorial occupation of townships was premised on a violence which, despite their own representations, was often turned against local inhabitants. Similarly, while many living in Managua's myriad poor neighbourhoods during the 1990s considered that their local gang 'protects us and allows us to feel a little bit safer, to live our lives a little bit more easily', in the 2000s the same people simultaneously saw gangs as precipitating a 'state of siege' which made it 'impossible to live'. In the face of such ambiguity, the notion of gangs as revolutionaries – no less than barbaric sociopaths – misses the point.

Instead, we wish to propose that gangs are a phenomenon better viewed through Deleuze and Guattari's concept of the 'war machine'.[10] This captures not only the ambiguities of gangs, but also the underlying similarities between gangs that have emerged in very different contexts, each with their own localised histories of accumulation and marginalisation. In doing so it allows us to better understand what it is that gangs and their violent practices really represent, and what relation they have, if any, to revolution.

GANGS AND REVOLUTION: MANAGUA

There exists a direct relationship between the contemporary rise of Nicaraguan youth gangs and revolution. Although the phenomenon has roots that can be traced back to the 1940s, it only emerged as a significant social factor in the early 1990s, following the demobilisation of thousands of young men from the ranks of the Sandinista Popular Army (the age of military conscription was sixteen).[11] Gang members from this period systematically mentioned three basic reasons for joining a gang. First, the change of regime in 1990 led to an abrupt devaluation of their social status, which as conscripts defending 'the Nation', had previously been very high; becoming gang members had seemed a means of reaffirming themselves vis-à-vis a wider society that seemed to rapidly forget them. Second, becoming gang members had been a way of recapturing some of the dramatic, yet formative and almost addictive, adrenaline-charged experiences of war, danger and death, as well as of comradeship and solidarity which they had lived through as conscripts, and which were rapidly becoming scarce commodities in polarised post-war Nicaragua. But third, and perhaps most important from the point of view of the link with revolution, becoming gang members had seemed to many a natural continuation of their previous role as conscripts. The early 1990s were highly uncertain times, marked by political polarisation, violence, and spiralling insecurity, and these youths felt they could better 'serve' their families and friends by joining a gang than attempting to 'protect' them as individuals.

By the mid-1990s, however, what could perhaps be characterised as an incipient form of vigilantism had become institutionalised via a process of local territorialisation based on forms of gang warfare that through their semi-ritualised nature provided a sense of predictability for local inhabitants within a wider context of chronic insecurity. The first battle of a gang war typically involved fighting with fists and stones, but each new battle involved an escalation of weaponry, first to sticks, then to knives and broken bottles, and eventually to guns, mortars and AK-47s. Although the rate of escalation varied, its sequence never did – i.e. gangs never began their wars with firearms. The fixed nature of gang warfare constituted something of a mechanism for restraining violence, insofar as escalation is a process in which each stage calls for a greater but definite intensity of action, and is therefore always under the actors' control. It also provided local neighbourhood inhabitants with an 'early warning system', such that gang wars can be conceived as having been 'scripted performances' that offered local communities a means of circumscribing what Hannah Arendt famously termed the 'all-pervading unpredictability' of violence.[12] The motivation offered by gang members for this particular behaviour pattern was imbued with a definite political ideology: they repeatedly claimed to be 'the last inheritors of *Sandinismo*', contending that they had joined the gang and engaged in violence due to their 'love' ('*querer*') for their local neighbourhood. One gang member called Miguel claimed: '*Así somos, nosotros los bróderes pandilleros* [that's how we are, us gang member brothers], we show our love for the neighbourhood by fighting other gangs'; another called Julio said that 'you show the neighbourhood that you love it by putting yourself in danger for people, by protecting them from other gangs... You look after the neighbourhood in that way, you help them, keep them safe'.

A conceptual parallel can be made here with the 'love' that Ernesto (Che) Guevara saw as the mark of 'the true revolutionary'.[13] Guevara, however, was referring to an abstract 'love of the people', while gang members were clearly motivated by a much more narrow, localised form of affection. This was expressed very clearly by the gang member called Julio, as he cleaned up a local graffiti extolling the virtues of the Sandinista youth organisation, which a person or persons unknown had crudely painted over in bright red – the colours of the anti-*Sandinista* PLC (*Partido Liberal Constitucionalista*) – the night before. Julio angrily berated the '*hijos de la setenta mil putas Somocistas*' ('sons of seventy thousands Somocista whores') who had done this:

> Those *jodidos* [assholes] don't respect anything in the neighbourhood, Dennis, nothing! OK, so they don't like *Sandinismo*, that's how it is, I don't like their politics either, but this is more than just a *Sandinista pinta* [graffiti], it's a part of the neighbourhood history. Our history, *bróder*! It's something that belongs to the community, to all of us; it shows us who we are, where we come from, how *Sandinismo* built our houses and made us into a community. It shows what the neighbourhood is, and people should therefore respect it, whatever their political opinions.

To this extent, Julio's revolutionary sympathies can be said to have reflected less a revolutionary ideology than his local neighbourhood's historical associations with *Sandinismo* (it had been a hotbed of anti-Somoza activity during the insurrection, as well as the pilot neighbourhood for the new revolutionary government's urban reconstruction programme in the early 1980s).[14] Certainly, there also existed a revealing discrepancy between gang members' political rhetoric and the concrete reality of their political practices. Although Julio and other gang members for example all actively volunteered to help with Daniel Ortega's campaign for the October 1996 elections, putting up banners and distributing flyers in their neighbourhood, for example, this support remained exclusively local in scope. None of the gang members volunteered to help outside the neighbourhood, even when Ortega's campaign tour stopped at the nearby market, where they often spent much of their time. Nor did any of the gang members make any efforts to go to the Sandinista party's campaign closing rally in downtown Managua, despite it being widely publicised, with free buses laid on to boost attendance. Ultimately, the parallels between gang activities and revolutionary action in Nicaragua in the 1990s proved largely circumstantial, as was highlighted dramatically when gang dynamics changed radically between the mid-1990s and the early 2000s. In particular, gangs evolved from being motivated by a sense of social solidarity with their local community to being predatory institutions focused on regulating an emergent cocaine-based drug economy, to the exclusive benefit of their members who dominated the drug-dealing 'labour market', so to speak.

Although drugs were by no means unknown to gang members such as Julio or Miguel in the mid-1990s, their main drug of choice at the time had been marijuana and they had not been involved in any regular form of trafficking. Cocaine dealing developed in the neighbourhood from mid-1999 onwards; initially on a small scale involving just one individual but rapidly expanding into a three-tiered pyramidal drug economy which by mid-2000 solely involved gang members and ex-gang members.[15] The potential rewards of the drugs trade were substantial at all levels of its pyramidal economy, ranging from around $450 per month at the lowest street-selling level to upwards of $1,100 per month for the middle level, and clearly much more for the top tier (about which precise information was less easy to obtain). In a neighbourhood where about half of the economically active population was unemployed, and a further 25 per cent underemployed, and where in 2002-03 those who did work earned a median monthly income of about $105, such sums were extremely significant. A gang member called Kalia made this clear during an interview in February 2002: 'What the fuck do you do when you don't have any food and there's no work to be had? You have to find some other way to look out for yourself, that's what! That's where selling drugs comes in, they're the only thing that's worthwhile doing here in the neighbourhood'.

Overall some 40 per cent of households in Kalia's neighbourhood seemed to be benefiting either directly or indirectly from drug trafficking. Most obviously, many of the previously ramshackle, mainly wooden, washed-out, monochrome houses had undergone a very visible process of infrastructural amelioration, with a significant proportion now bigger, (re)built in brick and concrete, often painted in bright pastel colours, and in some cases even two stories high (a rarity in earthquake-prone Managua). The changes inside many of these houses were just as impressive and extensive, as they now displayed tiled instead of dirt floors, fitted kitchens instead of gas burners, and (local) designer furniture instead of second-hand, as well as luxurious appliances such as wide-screen televisions with cable services, mega-wattage sound systems, Nintendo game consoles, and in one exceptional case a broadband-connected computer. The inhabitants of these new houses generally wore better-quality – often brand-name – clothes than had been the norm previously, displayed ostentatious jewellery and expensive watches, had the latest model mobile phones (in a neighbourhood where only a dozen households had had land lines) and ate imported food which they often bought in supermarkets rather than the local open-air market.

At the same time, however, the local neighbourhood drug economy was violently regulated by gang members who frequently brutalised local inhabitants in order to precipitate a generalised state of terror and ensure that their dealing could occur unimpeded. As one woman lamented during an interview in February 2002, specifically contrasting the situation with the mid-1990s, when the neighbourhood gang had an ethos of social solidarity:

> Before, you could trust the gang, but not anymore… They've become corrupted due to this drug crack… They threaten, attack people from the neighbourhood now, rob them of whatever they have, whoever they are… They never did that before… They used to protect us, look out for us, but now they don't care, they only look out for themselves, for their illegal business… People are scared, you've got to be careful what you say or what you do, because otherwise they'll attack you… We live in terror here, you have to be scared or else you're sure to be sorry…

Despite this clearly very different relationship with the local community, gang members nevertheless frequently continued to invoke the neighbourhood's historical association with *Sandinismo* in order to justify their actions. Indeed during an interview in February 2002, Bismarck, an ex-gang member turned middle-level dealer, directly compared the drug trafficking to the neighbourhood reconstruction programme promoted by the revolutionary government of the 1980s. Sitting in his plush new home built with drug money, he asked:

> 'So, Dennis, how do you see the barrio now? It's been what, almost 5 years since you were last here? Things have changed, haven't they? What do you think of my house, do you remember how it used to be a wood shack with cardboard instead of window panes?'
>
> 'Yes, I mean, wow, it's absolutely incredible how it's changed, Bismarck! All this concrete, these brick, these tiles, and this electronic equipment… It's all because of drugs?'
>
> 'That's right! You wouldn't believe how much money you can make selling that shit!'
>
> 'Well, it's certainly impressive, I have to admit. I never thought I'd see anything like this, last time the barrio seemed to be completely regressing…'

'So it was, but now it's been rebuilt like after the Revolution, except that instead of *Sandinismo*, it's the market that's been helping us!'

'I guess you could put it that way, Bismarck, but don't you think there's also a big difference between *Sandinismo* and the market? I mean, the drugs aren't helping everybody, are they? Sure, there are lots of nice, new houses in the barrio now, but some of these new houses are better than others. Yours is much nicer than Kalia's next door, for example, although he also sells drugs, and there are also many houses in the barrio that haven't changed at all since I was last here. There's lots of inequality now, which wasn't the case before, and that can't be a good thing'.

'Well, you can't help everybody, you know. Life is hard here in Nicaragua, Dennis, and you've got be clever and try to survive by hook or by crook. Kalia's just plain dumb, he uses his profits from selling drugs to smoke up, and then loses his head and can't sell properly. And those who don't have the drugs to sell, well, that's just the luck of the draw. It's like the lottery that attributed the houses in the rebuilt barrio to everybody, some people got bigger and better located houses than others, but nobody complained because it was all random, and everybody had the same chances to start off with'.

Of course, not everybody had the same opportunities, insofar as drug dealers were all gang members or ex-gang members, whose monopoly over the use of violence in the neighbourhood was what enabled them to sustain and regulate drug dealing. Instead of promoting a sense of inclusion and universal protection, gangs in urban Nicaragua in 2002-03 could now more plausibly be seen as engaged in localised 'primitive accumulation'. Gang members violently constituted themselves as a nascent local 'narco-bourgeoisie' in a context of otherwise extreme poverty and acutely limited alternative economic opportunities. By 2007, the situation was even starker, as the gang had become professionalised and drew members from a variety of neighbourhoods. To this extent, even if members of contemporary Nicaraguan gangs still compare their behaviour to the actions of the *Sandinista* revolutionary regime, they now effectively embody an ideology that clearly mirrors Nicaragua's broader post-revolutionary political economy of ever-increasing levels of inequality and iniquitous governance.[16]

GANGS AND REVOLUTION: CAPE TOWN

As in Nicaragua, there are obvious links between gang culture and revolution in South Africa, i.e. the ANC-led struggle against the notorious apartheid regime, known simply as 'the struggle'. This is especially the case among African[17] gangs in and around Johannesburg, where African urban male subcultures developed along ethnic lines as a general consequence of the expansion of the mining sector in the 1930s and 1940s.[18] While initially similar to other urban gangs that have developed in contexts of rapid urbanisation and social change around the world,[19] these groups became increasingly directed against dominant white society following the social devastation produced by the forced resettlement of Johannesburg's African population to townships in the 1950s. Resettlement set the scene for the gangs' militarisation and their embracing the struggle following the Soweto uprising of 1976, which constituted a turning point in the fight against apartheid.[20] From this moment on gang subculture became subsumed within the larger framework of the struggle.[21] A clear indication of their new revolutionary ethos was the fact that the gangs which had developed in Soweto township after the forced removals in the 1950s changed their name from '*tsotsi*' (hooligan or thug) to '*comtsotsi*' (a combination of 'comrade' and '*tsotsi*').

A similar link between gangs and revolution also existed in Cape Town, where gangs in coloured townships were instrumental in the widespread consumer boycotts called by the ANC against the apartheid regime. For example, a local township activist called Gadidja described how she had enticed the gangs to participate in the boycotts: 'I'd tell Dessie, the leader of the gang, do you know that the white man's trucks are coming in through Modderdam Road? And Dessie would go to the road and order the trucks looted'. Another activist, however, suggested that 'the gangs actually exploited the struggle. It gave them freedom to commit crimes; they would exploit it and hijack the meat truck, the furniture truck, anything. At the time, it was acceptable because it was a part of causing havoc amongst the whites. [...] We saw this as being part of the campaign, but not realizing that these guys were actually exploiting the whole situation'.

Certain ex-gangsters interviewed some 13 years after the end of the struggle would often comment on the involvement of gangs with some amusement: 'Yeah, those were glorious days. But you know, we were actually protecting the community'. This claim is by no means implausible. As a former township activist said regarding the looting of trucks, 'then there was chicken for everyone'. There existed a definite sense in which gangsters adopted something of a 'social bandit' role,[22] re-distributing some of the gains from their criminal proceedings, which helped make them a symbol of the struggle for many in the townships. Gangsters furthermore patrolled and policed the boundary between the townships and dominant society, contributing to the former's reputation for being 'ungovernable', which arguably minimised the apartheid state's everyday intervention.

To this extent, coloured gangs in Cape Town can be said to have been active in the struggle, but their commitment as well as their genesis varied markedly from that of Johannesburg gangs. This is partly because Cape Town gangs did not emerge as a response to migration to the mines, but were rather a product of the waves of coloureds and poor whites who migrated to the city as a result of the South African rural crisis of the 1930s and 1940s. These migrants – often referred to as '*plaas-jappies*' or 'country bumpkins' – moved to Cape Town's traditional working class districts, where they encountered an old and established multicultural urban society.[23] As these districts changed – becoming poorer, increasingly coloured, and more conflict-ridden – gang cultures developed. Ironically, the first gangs emerged as a vigilante response to rising crime levels, as an attempt to control the menace of the '*skollie*', or thug.[24] Economic need and increasing repression by the police, however, rapidly led to gang members developing more classic criminal entrepreneurial activities.[25] But from the 1960s onwards the apartheid regime began to forcibly remove people from the old working class neighbourhoods in the centre of Cape Town to council housing on the Cape Flats, some fifteen kilometres from the city centre. This caused significant disruptions to all local social activity, including that of the gangs, which were scattered across the vast expanse of the new townships, and it took a full decade for gangs to re-emerge as a significant Capetonian social feature, albeit now in a distinct Cape Flats version.[26]

Having lived through forced removals and being brought up on tales of injustices, these new gangs were particularly hostile towards dominant white society. Although the coloured townships can in general be said to have had a precarious and strained relationship with the struggle, and especially with African 'comrades' who often themselves did not trust coloured activists either, gangsters rapidly became involved in the struggle along very similar lines to gangs in Johannesburg. Indeed, many of the gangsters talked continuously of their activism against the whites and the Apartheid regime, often explicitly identifying themselves as having been part of a 'vanguard'. This zeal and antagonism towards the dominant white society was not confined to the struggle years, however. In 1999, one drug-dealing gangster called Mattie claimed: 'Actually this [the drug-dealing] is all because of the whites, *die vokkers*. We still fight them. We fight *die boere* [the police] and we only go steal in white areas. And you know, we really suffered. They beat us and put us in jail'.

Such a view of gangsterism was echoed more generally among the wider township population. When the largest drug dealer in Mattie's township, Kelly, was killed by unknown assassins in March 1998, the community was abuzz with stories of his bravery vis-à-vis the white police.[27] Furthermore, Kelly was explicitly portrayed as having tried to live up to the model of the 'social bandit'. He was rumoured to have donated money to old age homes, lent to the cash-strapped, and regularly disciplined those who transgressed the norms of acceptable behaviour in the township. Kelly was by no means the only gangster to engage in such forms of social solidarity; Daniel Reed has described how Cape Town township gangs were often founded with the explicit intention of defending their local communities.[28] Furthermore, in the post-apartheid era, there exists a widespread notion among African and coloured gang members that they must protect their territory, referred to as '*die agterbuurde*', or the back streets, in opposition to white society.[29] Indeed, there can often be an almost symbiotic relationship between gangs and the local community. In her study of gender in a coloured Cape Town township, Elaine Salo shows how young men in gangs formed a strategic alliance with women in the community.[30] The women, often the mothers of the young men, would exonerate their gang-related practices in return for their respect for the women and defence of territory. An important element allowing for the legitimisation of such alliances was the past association of gang violence with the struggle.

But nowhere within the Cape Flats world of gangsters are revolutionary associations more prominent than in prison. South African prisons are very violent and are dominated by organised gang structures, referred to as the number gangs – 26, 27 and 28.[31] Although these gangs originated in and around Cape Town, they are now national in scope. Despite the fact that coloureds only account for 9 per cent of the total South African population, these dominate both the prison and the gangs, partly because for almost a century they have been vastly over-represented in jail – relative to population size, in 1993 there were four times as many coloureds in jail as Africans – and they stay longer, often because they commit gang-related crimes in prison that lead to an extension of their imprisonment. The gangs relate quite clearly to notions of masculinity, insofar as to be a member of one of these gangs is to be an '*ndota*' ['man' in iziZulu]. Inmates become *ndotas* through an initiatory ritual process of stabbing a warder and subsequently submitting to the consequent violent punishment and solitary confinement. In the process the incumbent has to exhibit solidarity (he must do it for the advancement of the gang), stoicism (he must not show pain) and measured restraint (he must not mortally wound the warder). In this way, the prison gangs 'transform… the [institutional prison] violence from a tool of mortification into a form of nourishment' of masculine assertion.[32]

At the same time, however, such practices clearly also lend themselves to an understanding of gangs as being in a constant state of struggle against whites and dominant society, and fuel a narrative of antagonism and resistance to the state in which *ndotas* pay the highest price as a revolutionary vanguard. In contradiction to this narrative, however, stand gang-related practices both in prison and in the townships. While gangs, in and out of prison, represent themselves in a revolutionary manner, they are in fact arguably reproducing the very oppression, physical as well as discursive, against which they purport to act.

First of all, when we move from the level of narrative to practice, we realise that many of the elements of gang narratives break down: they do steal from their own; they maim and kill (sometimes incidentally) fellow township residents; they sell drugs and engage in numerous illicit economic activities that have toxic social consequences; and they fight each other, often with dramatic consequences for local communities. Gang members – and other youth as well – often engage in these practices for reasons of individual or group survival: there are few employment opportunities in the context of a wider South African economy that is characterised by highly segmented and constrained labour markets.

Secondly, while group membership may be seen as imperative for personal survival, as the police increasingly target young coloured men in arbitrary ways, the existence of gangs has facilitated – or necessitated, depending on one's point of view – a constant security presence of the state in the townships. To this extent, while the gangs claim to protect their local communities, their presence and practices are what allows for further oppression. Gang membership has also become the reason for the continued stereotyping of the coloured townships on the Cape Flats.

Finally, gangs as social structures are also inherently conservative. Rather than challenging the over-arching (capitalist and racial) structures of prison and society, they reproduce the system, which does allow for their continued existence and (male) dominance. Both township and prison have been turned into domains that are run by *ndotas* and where, as the saying goes in Cape Town, 'the rest are made women out of'. To paraphrase Philippe Bourgois, the gangs reproduce patriarchy on the streets.[33] If this is revolution, then the gangs themselves appear to be its sole beneficiaries.

GANGS AS WAR MACHINES

Although gang members in Nicaragua and South Africa often explicitly seek to justify their social practices by associating them discursively with revolution, such invocations in many ways constitute little more than attempts to mitigate the stigma of barbarism that is so often levelled at gangs and their violence. While gangs often do draw some level of support from the local neighbourhood communities within which they emerge (not least as sons, neighbours or friends), arguably all this does is 'blur' violent gang practices. In the final analysis, gangs in both Managua and Cape Town are really not fighting 'for' anything but themselves. Although they can plausibly be said to be fighting 'against' wider structural circumstances of economic exclusion and racism, most of the time the behaviour patterns of gang members are clearly motivated principally by their own interests rather than the active promotion of any form of collective good. To this extent, their association with revolution must be seen principally as part of a sub-cultural repertoire – which also includes particular narratives and practices of gang warfare, initiations, and bodily performances[34] – that allows gangs to articulate themselves as concrete institutional forms within particular historical contexts of economic and political hardship and flux.

For this reason, we suggest that gangs are better conceived through the notion of the 'war machine' rather than as vanguard revolutionary violence or modern-day forms of barbarism. Deleuze and Guattari elaborate this notion to discuss social phenomena that direct their actions against domination, but without necessarily having well-defined battle lines or standard forms of confrontation.[35] A 'war machine' does not display political consciousness; it is not directed towards establishing an alternative form of authority; it simply destabilises (in the words of Deleuze and Guattari, it 'deterritorialises') authority. Such a characterisation of the 'war machine' is in many ways reminiscent of Walter Benjamin's famous 'destructive character', who is 'always blithely at work', just 'clearing away' and 'reduc[ing] to rubble'. This is particularly apt in relation to gangs considering that Benjamin contended that 'the destructive character is young and cheerful'.[36] Yet viewing gangs as 'war machines' does potentially open up somewhat more 'utopian' associations than the impoverished options of Benjamin's 'destructive character'. The 'war machine', as Malene Busk has pointed out, 'inhabits territory as pure deterritorialization', and in doing so constitutes itself in fundamental contradiction to the realm of what Deleuze and Guattari call 'the majority', that is to say dominant society.[37] A 'war machine' is thus a 'minority' that is differentiated from 'the majority' not in terms of its size, but in relation to the fact that it occupies space in a radically different manner. A 'majority' sediments a particular type of order, entrenches itself and occupies space in a universalising way, while a minority is a 'line of flight', unstable, ambiguous, and 'ever-moving'.[38]

This is a vision that arguably resonates rather well with the ambiguities of gangs as we have described them in Managua and Cape Town. Their violence is not directed against authority in any proactive sense of promising a (revolutionary) alternative, but nevertheless engages with authority, imposing often ephemeral and highly contradictory but fundamentally different forms of order to those projected by dominant society. As such, gangs could arguably be seen as providing glimpses of the fact that alternatives to the present are possible: they are constituted as 'a point that would stand outside the temporality of the dominant order' in a contemporary epoch that seems otherwise barren of plausible emancipatory revolutionary projects.[39]

At the same time, however, as Deleuze and Guattari themselves are at great pains to point out, 'the majority' and 'the minority' should not be seen as distinct domains, as they are inseparable partners. The value of the concept of the 'war machine' is that it allows us to transcend easy and ultimately unproductive binary notions of 'power' and 'resistance', 'oppressor' and 'oppressed', or 'moral society' versus 'barbarians', and focuses instead on the systemic articulations between different poles in society. The need for such a nuanced view is particularly clear when considering the way that gangs are increasingly policed around the world. Since the 1980s, states have arguably been waging something of a global 'war on crime', which has fundamentally shaped gangs and their actions worldwide. Originating in the US, but rapidly spreading to Europe and the global South, including in particular Central America and South Africa, this 'war' has notably involved the proliferation of new forms of policing, including in particular the seemingly contradictory approaches of 'community policing' and 'zero tolerance',[40] which in actual fact can be seen as very similar forms of authority,[41] insofar as elements of both approaches are drawn from – or resemble – counter-insurgency strategies.[42]

Although it might initially seem strange to compare extremely violent counter-insurgency practices with contemporary law-enforcement efforts against crime, the grammar of the two is remarkably similar. Community policing as well as counter-insurgency operations are often described as 'psycho-politico-security projects' (to use the military lingo) that combine both development and security elements.[43] Specific areas – 'gang-affected areas', for example – are to be 'pacified', through a combination of partnerships, development initiatives and 'targeted' security interventions. Similarly, both counter-insurgency and 'zero tolerance' policing operate on the basis that authorities must strike hard against the first signs of 'social decay'.[44] Finally, both strategies are based on a binary opposition between 'law abiding citizens' and 'criminals', and impose a stark either/or logic that allows for little of the ambiguity that is the hallmark of gangs – and indeed life more generally – in both Cape Town's townships and Managua's slums. In Central America, for example, the 'Mano Dura' – 'hard hand' – anti-gang strategy was introduced in 2003, allowing for the arrest of individuals from the age of 12 onwards, simply for having tattoos or dressing in particular ways;[45] while in South Africa, multiple legal reforms and social development initiatives have systematically sought to categorise and identify 'deserving' and 'undeserving' populations, in order to attend to their 'needs' differently, so to speak.[46]

The deployment of such counter-insurgency strategies logically suggests the existence of insurgents, and begs the question of whether revolutionary potential is not being attributed to gangs. By fostering the production of predictable, visible frontlines and enemies, dominant society could be said to be extending an imagined subversive agency to gangs, which might perhaps be able to inspire revolution, very much along the lines that Fanon described in *The Wretched of the Earth*. Certainly, this is an idea that can be said to be implicit in James Holston's recent analysis of the violent *Primeiro Comando da Capital* (PCC) gang in São Paulo, Brazil, as a form of 'insurgent citizenship'.[47] Highlighting the paradoxical fact that the PCC formulates its demands on the Brazilian state on the basis of invocations of human rights and the rule of law, in a context where both of these are lacking, he contends that this makes these demands into an almost revolutionary statement. At the same time, he concludes that such a form of 'insurgent citizenship' ultimately delegitimises the already fragile Brazilian democracy, without offering much that is positive in its place.

Deleuze and Guattari, however, warn us against associating either the 'minority' or the 'majority' with good or evil.[48] This suggests that what is really at stake with 'war machines' such as the PCC or the gangs of Managua and Cape Town is less the actual meanings of their behaviours and practices, and more the potential that their existence represents. In this respect, though, the articulation of gangs and policing practices resembles what Foucault discerned regarding the social production of 'delinquency' – a means of stifling youthful forms of resistance to oppression and injustice by constructing these as a concern of court rooms and prisons rather than of the streets.[49] In other words, even if gangs can be seen as potentially offering a glimpse of the possibility of emancipatory social change, the tragic truth is that in the final analysis their existence in fact actively suppresses the perception of such potential transformation, suggesting that the chance for utopia has come and gone in Nicaragua and South Africa – for now.

NOTES

1 USAID, *Central America and Mexico Gangs Assessment*, Washington: United States Agency for International Development, 2006.

2 Max G. Manwaring, *Street Gangs: The New Urban Insurgency*, Carlisle: Strategic Studies Institute, US Army War College, 2005; S. Boraz and T. Bruneau, 'Are the *Maras* Overwhelming Governments in Central America?', *Military Review*, November-December, 2006, pp. 36-40.

3 Teresa P.R. Caldeira, *City of Walls: Crime, Segregation, and Citizenship in São Paulo*, Berkeley: University of California Press, 2000.

4 Stanley Cohen, *Folk Devils and Moral Panics: The Creation of the Mods and the Rockers*, Oxford: Basil Blackwell, 1972; Sebastian Huhn, Anika Oettler and Peter Peetz, 'Exploding Crime? Topic Management in Central American Newspapers', GIGA Working Paper No. 33, German Institute of Global and Area Studies, Hamburg, 2006.

5 Mauricio Rubio, *De la Pandilla a la Mara: Pobreza, Educación, Mujeres y Violencia Juvenil*, Bogotá: Universidad Externado de Colombia, 2007.

6 Hans Magnus Enzensberger, *Civil Wars: From L.A. to Bosnia*, New York: The New Press, 1994.

7 Frantz Fanon, *The Wretched of the Earth*, London: Penguin, 1990 [1961], pp. 54.

8 Barry Krisberg, *The Gang and the Community*, San Francisco: R&E Research Associates, 1975; John Hagedorn, *People and Folks: Gangs, Crime and the Underclass in a Rustbelt City*, Chicago: Lakeview Press, 1988; Sanyika Shakur, *Monster*, New York: Penguin Books, 1993.

9 Gerald D. Suttles, *The Social Order of the Slum: Ethnicity and Territory in the Inner City*, Chicago: University of Chicago Press, 1968.

10 Gilles Deleuze and Felix Guattari, *A Thousand Plateaus: Capitalism and Schizophrenia*, London: Continuum, 1988, pp. 351-423.

11 Demobilised *Contra* youth were also involved, albeit to a much lesser extent, and were generally concentrated in a few specific neighbourhoods of the country's cities.

12 Hannah Arendt, *On Violence,* New York: Harcourt Brace, 1969, p. 5. For further details, see Dennis Rodgers, 'Living in the Shadow of Death: Gangs, Violence, and Social Order in Urban Nicaragua, 1996-2002', *Journal of Latin American Studies*, 38(2), 2006, pp. 267-92; Dennis Rodgers, 'When Vigilantes Turn Bad: Gangs, Violence, and

Social Change in Urban Nicaragua', in David Pratten and Atreyee Sen, eds., *Global Vigilantes*, London: Hurst, 2007.

13 Ernest (Che) Guevara, *Venceremos: The Speeches and Writings of Che Guevara*, Edited by John Gerassi, New York: Simon and Schuster, 1969, p. 398. This analogy is all the more relevant considering the associations between *Sandinismo* and the 'Cult of Che' (see Roger Lancaster, *Thanks to God and the Revolution: Popular Religion and Class Consciousness in the New Nicaragua*, New York: Columbia University Press, 1988, pp. 132 and 185).

14 Not all Managua gang members were pro-*Sandinista*. The increased political polarisation that followed the 1990 elections led to a spatial re-organisation of the city's population. New neighbourhoods emerged and coalesced, some pro-*Sandinista* and others pro-*Contra*. The post-electoral return of refugees also greatly contributed to the formation of the latter; the gang members in *barrio* Enrique Bermúdez (named after the commander of the *Contra* Northern Military Front during the war in the 1980s) were in no way sympathetic to *Sandinismo*, for example. Instead, this particular gang's solidarity was grounded in identification with the historical experiences of the *barrio* Enrique Bermúdez population's opposition to the *Sandinista* regime, just as gang members in Julio's gang were discursively pro-*Sandinista* as a result of their neighbourhood's local historical association with *Sandinismo*.

15 See Dennis Rodgers, 'Managua', in Kees Koonings and Dirk Kruijt, eds., *Fractured Cities: Social Exclusion, Urban Violence and Contested Spaces in Latin America*, London: Zed, 2007 for details.

16 Dennis Rodgers, 'A Symptom called Managua', *New Left Review*, 49, 2008, pp. 103-20.

17 'African' was one of four racial categories employed by the Apartheid regime to divide the heterogeneous South African population. Each of these categories – white, Indian, African or coloured – gave access to different resources and privileges. They continue to be used today in post-Apartheid South Africa, both pro-actively and pejoratively. For further details, see William Beinart, *Twentieth Century South Africa*, Oxford: Oxford University Press, 2001; Steffen Jensen, *Gangs, Politics and Dignity in Cape Town*, London: James Currey, Johannesburg: Wits University Press, and Chicago: University of Chicago Press, 2008; Alistair Sparks, *The Mind of South Africa: The Story of the Rise and Fall of Apartheid*, London: Heineman, 1990.

18 For elaboration, see Dunbar Moodie, *Going for Gold: Men, Mines and Migration*, Berkeley: University of California Press, 1995; Clive Glaser,

Bo-Tsotsi: The Youth Gangs of Soweto, 1935-1976, Cape Town: David Philips, 2000; Gary Kynoch, *We Are Fighting the World: A History of the Marashea Gangs in South Africa, 1947-1999*, Athens: Ohio University Press, 2005; and Monique Marks, *Young Warriors: Youth Politics, Identity and Violence in South Africa*, Johannesburg: Witwatersrand University Press, 2001.

19 See Frederick Thrasher, *The Gang: A Study of 1,313 Gangs in Chicago*, Chicago: University of Chicago Press, 1927 for the classic study.

20 Aletta Norval, *Deconstructing Apartheid Discourse*, London: Verso, 1996.

21 Glaser, *Bo-Tsotsi*; Belinda Bozzoli, *Theatres of Struggle and the End of Apartheid*, Johannesburg: Wits University Press, 2004.

22 Eric Hobsbawm, *Primitive Rebels: Studies in Archaic Forms of Social Movement in the 19th and 20th Centuries*, London: W.W. Norton and Co., 1965.

23 John Western, *Outcast Cape Town*, Berkeley: University of California Press, 1996.

24 See Jensen, *Gangs, Politics and Dignity*; Elaine Salo, 'Respectable Mothers, Tough Men and Good Daughters: Producing Persons in Manenberg Township, South Africa', unpublished PhD dissertation, Department of Social Anthropology, Emory University, Atlanta, USA, 2004.

25 Don Pinnock, *The Brotherhoods: Street Gangs and State Control in Cape Town*, Cape Town: David Philips, 1984, pp. 23-30.

26 Jensen, *Gangs, Politics and Dignity*.

27 Steffen Jensen, 'Of Street Gangsters and Drug Dealers: Power, Mobility and Violence on the Cape Flats', *Focaal*, 36, 2000, pp. 105-16.

28 Daniel Reed, *Beloved Country: South Africa's Silent Wars*, Oxford: BBC, 1994.

29 Steffen Jensen, 'Capetonian Back Streets: Territorializing Young Men', *Ethnography*, 7(3), 2006, pp. 275-302.

30 Salo, 'Respectable Mothers'.

31 These have something of a mythical origin, with the standard narrative being that they were founded at the beginning of the 20th century when a man-turned-prophet, Po, recruited two men, Nongoloza and Kilikijan to revolt against colonial and capitalist exploitation. These two men became the forefathers of the 27 and the 28, while the 26 gang emerged inside prison as a compromise between the two older gangs. Jonny Steinberg, *Nongoloza's Children: Western Cape Prison Gangs during and after Apartheid*, Johannesburg: Centre for the Study of Violence and Reconciliation, 2004.

32 Ibid., p. 25.

33 Philippe Bourgois, *In Search of Respect: Selling Crack in El Barrio*, Cambridge: Cambridge University Press, 1996.

34 For elaboration, see Dennis Rodgers, 'Joining the Gang and Becoming a *Broder*: The Violence of Ethnography in Contemporary Nicaragua', *Bulletin of Latin American Research*, 27(4), 2007, pp. 444-61; Jensen, 'Capetonian Back Streets'.

35 Deleuze and Guattari, *A Thousand Plateaus*, pp. 351-423.

36 Walter Benjamin, 'The Destructive Character', in W. Benjamin, *Reflections: Essays, Aphorisms, Autobiographical Writings*, Edited by P. Demetz, New York: Schocken Books, 1986, pp. 301-3.

37 Malene Busk, 'Mikro-politik – Politisk Filosofi hos Gilles Deleuze', in Carsten Bagge-Lautsen and Anders Berg Sørensen, eds., *Den ene, den anden, den tredje: Politisk identitet, andethed og fællesskab I moderne fransk tænkning*, Copenhagen: Forlaget Politisk Revy, 1999, p. 146.

38 Deleuze and Guattari, *A Thousand Plateaus*, pp. 351-61.

39 Alain Badiou, 'The Communist Hypothesis', *New Left Review*, 49, 2008, p. 37.

40 See Loïc Wacquant, 'The "Scholarly Myths" of the New Law and Order Doxa', *Socialist Register 2006*, pp. 93-115, and his earlier 'How Penal Common Sense Comes to Europeans: Notes on the Transatlantic Diffusion of the Neoliberal "Doxa"', *European Societies* 1(3). 1999, pp. 319-52.

41 Many researchers have highlighted how community policing is not very different from 'zero tolerance' strategies. For example, based on an analysis of community policing in the UK, the US and South Africa, Bill Dixon entitles an article 'Zero Tolerance: The Hard Edge of Community Policing', *African Security Review*, 12(3), 2000, pp. 73-78.

42 Lars Buur, Steffen Jensen and Finn Stepputat, eds., *The Security-Development Nexus: Manifestations of securitization and Sovereignty in South Africa*, Uppsala: Nordic Africa Institute Press, 2007, pp. 29-32.

43 John McCuen, *The Art of Counter-Revolutionary War: The Strategy of Counter-Insurgency*, New York: Stackpole Books, 1966.

44 Such action is often referred to as being 'preventive' rather than 'reactive' (see William Bratton, 'Zero Tolerance', in Norman Dennis, ed., *Zero Tolerance: Policing a Free Society*, London: The IEA Health and Welfare Unit, 1998).

45 See Dennis Rodgers, 'Slum Wars of the 21st Century: Gangs, "*Mano Dura*", and the New Geography of Conflict in Central America', *Development and Change*, forthcoming.

46 Steffen Jensen, 'The South African Transition: From Development to Security?', *Development and Change,* 36(3), 2005, pp. 551-70; Jensen, *Gangs, Politics and Dignity*.

47 James Holston, *Insurgent Citizenship: Disjunctions of Democracy and Modernity in Brazil*, Princeton: Princeton University Press, 2007.

48 Deleuze and Guattari, *A Thousand Plateaus*, p. 227.

49 Michel Foucault, *Discipline and Punish: The Birth of the Prison*, Translated by Alan Sheridan, London: Penguin, 1977.

EMANCIPATION AND THE LEFT: THE ISSUE OF VIOLENCE

MICHAEL BRIE

In the past six years more children have died globally as a result of starvation and preventable diseases than humans perished in the six years of the Second World War. Every three seconds a human life that just began ceases to exist in a cruel way. At the same time in these same three seconds $120,000 are being spent on military armaments world wide. There exists a fundamental contradiction between the alleged constraints of globalisation and human rights.

In the face of such outrageous injustice, an imperial war in the name of a 'war on terror', and the simultaneous expansion of the surveillance state, and confronted with the self-enrichment of the mega-rich and the increasing impoverishment of broad segments of society, resistance becomes a necessity. Brecht's words are up-to-date: 'That you have to resist/ If you don't want to perish/ That you will surely understand'.

And yet, what do we make of peaceful demonstrations if they do not manage to block the US military machine and its allies? What is the purpose of non-violent blockades if they cannot enforce an ecological sea-change? Why speak and criticise if we find that our arguments turn out to be toothless? Are non-violent actions really more than narcissistic surrogate undertakings without any consequences for the First Class passengers on the *Titanic*?

It is twenty years since the Soviet system collapsed. The remaining powers of the West have declared themselves victorious, in order to simply continue what they had been doing all along, and even making it worse. This includes the arms race, as much as the destruction of the ecological foundations of human life, the exploitation of nature and human beings at one and the same time. If we want to avoid despair in face of the contradiction between the necessary and the real, we will have to turn radical and fight for fundamental change. But what route can lead us out of lethargy?

In the aftermath of the Chernobyl catastrophe of 1986, one of the sharpest independent German thinkers of the 20th century, Günther Anders, called for the adoption of counter-violence. In the interest of 'future world peace and the continued existence of the human species', he argued, it was necessary 'to consider the transition from protest to self-defence and from self-defence to a counter-attack'. He concluded: 'In short, as it was in Hitler's wars but also in Kennedy's and Johnson's Vietnam War, we have to consider as enemies, and treat accordingly, those who compel us to do that which in principle is taboo for us, namely to kill'. Insofar as counter-violence aimed at a violence-free future, it was legitimate. 'Anyone who has been a contemporary of Verdun and Auschwitz and Hiroshima, of Algeria and Vietnam and, and, and... cannot and must not become or be or remain an advocate of non-violent action at all costs... to act in self-defence against threats of violence and especially acts of violence is not only legitimate but, in fact, also a duty… Those who are preparing the annihilation of millions of people of today or tomorrow… or who at least risk doing so, must vanish, must be stopped'.[1] This diagnosis of our times has not changed much. In face of the already-existing global catastrophe, what could be more legitimate than counter-violence? Is violence not the only force which really has any meaning? And even if one dismisses all that, is it not necessary to show critical solidarity with those who make a decision in favour of violence?

Anyone who is convinced that capitalism must not be the last word of history is obliged to search for alternatives. And anyone who claims that the emergency is so big that we must not continue on the path we are currently on is compelled to point to a way out of the crisis. So the question has to be posed again with complete clarity: is violence in the last instance not the only radical means to bring about radical change? In the history of the left, has the renunciation of violence not also entailed in practice a renunciation of the goal of changing society fundamentally? All larger and smaller reforms, all 'improvements' here and there, the small or half-baked compromises – have they been anything more than an excuse, because one could not or did not want to resort to violence?[2]

WHAT IS VIOLENCE?

But what actually is violence? Is it not everywhere, and hence also nowhere? Is not every pore of human social life characterised by it? Do we not find violence lurking behind every labour contract? In what follows the concept of violence will have the very narrow sense of the 'deliberate physical harm to humans by humans'.[3] A deed becomes violent whenever the person who commits it consciously strives to hurt another person, whenever it deliberately threatens their bodily or mental integrity, whenever it purposefully causes another person's (deadly) fear. However useful a much larger concept of violence may be in other contexts, there appears to be a need for a concept that captures this concrete form of human behaviour towards other people, i.e. a behaviour that consciously seeks to physically or mentally destroy another person. Violence consciously or purposefully breaks into the inner existential shelter of another person, i.e. in that room in which there is no other hiding-place, a room from which there is no escape – the body of a human being.

What is so frightening, whenever there is debate about violence exercised in the name of a 'good cause', is the lack of empathy felt towards the person against whom the violence is directed. Violence is turned into a mere technique, a message, a symbol, a means of political action that does not differ from any other, that is more or less useful in a given situation. Violence may indeed be all that. As opposed to every other form of human interaction, however, violence is by its own nature *speechless*. Whatever purpose it may be serving, regardless of the message it is supposed to 'convey', in the first instance violence makes the person whom it hits 'silent and hushed in horror'[4] – like an uncontrollable scream. And precisely because violence is silent, speaking about it is so important.

The concept of violence adopted here, then, is clearly distinct from the concept of structural violence as it has been introduced to the debate by Johan Galtung: 'We must speak of violence whenever humans are influenced in such a way that their actual somatic and mental self-realization is smaller than their potential self-realization' – be it through a diminished life expectancy, illiteracy, lies and indoctrination, etc. He writes: 'Here no one makes an appearance who could immediately harm another person. Violence is built into the system and expresses itself through unequal power relations'.[5] It is my contention that such a definition does not even broach the issue of the consequences of rule itself, and the inequality of the distribution of life chances connected to it. Such rule does exert violence, as defined in this essay, as a means; however, it cannot be reduced to it. Another line needs to be drawn vis-à-vis the concepts of symbolic or cultural violence which represent, propagate or legitimise rule.[6]

Furthermore, violence understood as it is here has also to be distinguished from wilful damage to property, civil disobedience, sit-down demonstrations and blockades, etc. Violence is action that seeks to degrade subjects to mere things and uses this as a means to exert power, whereas damage to property and other forms of non-violent resistance and civil disobedience leave the political opponent physically unharmed. What they do is to factually or symbolically limit his power (the power to move, etc.). For the ruling class, violence is always the *ultima ratio,* i.e. whenever its own means of power fail. Violence is its final and decisive 'word'. In the concentration and annihilation camps of the German fascists, rule and the system of absolute violence merged into one.[7]

This violence of rulers must, certainly, be distinguished from counter-violence, i.e. the resort to violence by those who defend themselves against oppression, exploitation and annihilation. It is the violence of the rebellious, the political resistance that resorts to violence. Its aim is the negation of rule. It is used in order to defend oneself. And if it is used to achieve power it may be used to consolidate a new order of rule.

THE RIGHT TO RESIST

When I use the term 'resistance' it implies all forms of direct action that transcend the exercise of one's own democratic rights in conformity with the law (for example, legal demonstrations, meetings, appeals).[8] Resistance is always also a violation of existing laws and hence illegal. The existing state of legality is consciously surpassed. The person who decides in favour of resistance is consciously breaking the law and has to reckon with legal prosecution. However, what are the other consequences?

It was Immanuel Kant who developed the principle of the categorical primacy of a state of legality under public laws vis-à-vis any perceivable violation of this state of legality. The evils resulting from resistance would loom so large that even the worst state of legality was more desirable, since otherwise civil war would threaten. However, is this understanding still applicable today? May we really expect citizens to leave to the Supreme Court the question of whether laws or government action harm the dignity of humans, and to hope that free political speech and elections will really put an end to any state of existential emergency? Must every violation of the state of legality really lead to a war of all against all, to civil war?

It was by a democratically elected government that the Federal Republic of Germany was led to a war of aggression against Yugoslavia, and this war, which violated existing international law, was assented to by the Supreme Court as well as the President. The constitutional forms (including a constitutional appeal) were not sufficient to prevent Germany's participation in this war. As a justification, the German government pointed to a humanitarian emergency in Kosovo (an imminent genocide). However, inasmuch as a war of aggression is necessarily connected to the killing of a large number of people (according to different sources, between five and ten thousand people died as a consequence of the NATO attacks), even for the opponents of the war a crisis of conscience arose, namely to be co-responsible as German citizens for the murder of other people.

The construction and maintenance of nuclear power plants has also continuously raised similar questions: in face of the long-term consequences for future generations, and the potential threats they present (accidents, the consequences of terrorist attacks, etc.), is legality really reconcilable with the protection of the indefeasible dignity and physical integrity of human beings? To take two other examples, policies which in the eyes of many are not sufficiently effective to prevent global warming, and which therefore accept the deaths of large numbers of people; or a global economic order that partially contributes to the fact that states are incapable of providing their populations with basic rights to education and health services; both raise questions in relation to which the right to resist might be justified. It is also being discussed in terms of the introduction of genetically engineered plants, and in relation to abortion *versus* the protection of human embryos.

What happens if a minority – even if it is a small one – comes to the conclusion that the dignity of humanity is being harmed, that human rights are being systematically violated? Is one then justified in asking them to subject themselves permanently to the processes provided for in the constitution, to restrict themselves to mere speech, rushing from one meeting to the next, while being unable to see a way of averting the emergency that they perceive? How are they supposed to behave when they have become convinced that there is no chance of reaching a solution in due time through constitutional procedures, when they believe that the lobby interests which are opposing the free process of democratic opinion formation are so strong as to render clarification, truth and enlightenment impossible?

In short, under the conditions of a democratic state functioning on the premises of the rule of law, within what limits do citizens actually have a right to do more than they are allowed by the constitution and the criminal code? In what situations may citizens even feel it to be a duty to proclaim an extralegal state of emergency? Under what conditions do they have the right to turn against decisions made by the state?

Let us consider the possibility, for example, that within the next few years Germany were to experience a nuclear catastrophe comparable to the one in Chernobyl – be it only as a consequence of terrorist attacks. How would the state's refusal to shut down all the nuclear power plants affect the constitutionally-guaranteed 'dignity of the human being'? Would we not have to accuse everyone who did not resist of failure? A democratic constitution cannot lay down the forms that resistance might take, since there always remains the question of whether they are going to prove sufficient to deal with the emergency. It is therefore impossible for the democratic order to free itself from the impulse of rebellion. *In the innermost core of democracy there always beats a revolutionary heart which places the ideals of human rights above the constitutional order.*[9]

Moreover Article 1 of the United Nations' 'Universal Declaration of Human Rights' of December 10, 1948, states that all human beings are born 'free and equal in terms of dignity and rights', and in the preamble there is a further formulation – something unique in international law – which is a positive individual right to resistance against 'tyranny and oppression'.[10] But when and how can these rights be defended? Since the democratic left is bound to defend the legitimacy of its resistance to the constitution's legal institutions on the basis of the same constitution, it is confronted with the question of what kinds of resistance are compatible with the goal defending the dignity of Man and defending human rights. It is necessary to determine the legitimate means of such resistance.

Resistance which goes beyond mere words and which breaks applicable law (otherwise it would not be resistance) conjures up the danger of civil war. Blocking the access route to the G8 Summit in Heiligendamm was, of course, against the law. To attack members of the police force is not part of the right to demonstrate. The attempt to prevent the transport of nuclear waste by sit-down demonstrations and blockades is not legal. The same applies to the destruction of genetically engineered seeds. Their *legitimacy*, however, cannot simply be challenged by declaring them to be illegal. But where is the limit?

Political action that is ready to commit illegal acts in the name of the dignity of Man and human rights is inevitably deeply contradictory. On the one hand it is proclaiming an extralegal emergency and hence an open conflict with the state. On the other hand such political action does this by invoking precisely this state's constitutional order and fundamental rights. This implies that those who are claiming the right to resist for themselves are taking back from the parliament their sovereignty vis-à-vis the state. A left minority is effectively arguing – simply by making the transition to resistance – that for their own actions they are claiming a legitimacy transcending that of the democratic state. As Malcolm X proclaimed in 1963: 'We are declaring our right on this earth... to be a human being, to be respected as one and to own the rights of human beings in this society, on this planet, on this day. This we are going to enforce by all means necessary...'.[11] But this risks putting ourselves on the verge of a transition from the legal order to civil war. What *means*, however, are necessary for the legitimate end, and what means destroy it? Under which conditions is violence a legitimate and expedient means of the struggle for liberation? When does resistance have to remain non-violent in order to be justified and appropriate?

VIOLENCE IS A CRIME

The question of the *expediency* of violence is not at all identical with the question of its *legitimacy*. This becomes apparent when the question is raised whether torture is legitimate if, by its application, other human beings can be saved; or whether shooting down a passenger airplane which is aimed at a stadium full of people is legitimate. There exist many good arguments for the expediency of such judgments. However, are there also arguments that justify them? To distinguish between the expediency and the legitimacy of the means may appear to be hairsplitting. And yet for those who become victims of political violence it remains a question of life and death.

It was Walter Benjamin who pointed towards a difference which is crucial for this debate. According to Benjamin, one should inquire into not only the goals but also the means. And this one should do 'without regard for the ends purpose they serve'. He argued that it was necessary to develop 'mutually independent criteria both of just ends and of justified means'. Benjamin rejected the view that violence is 'a raw material, the use of which is in no way problematical, unless force is misused for unjust ends'. Independently of the ends pursued, 'the question would remain open whether violence, as a principle, could be a moral means even to just ends'.[12]

Walter Benjamin posed this question of the ethics of violence immediately after the First World War which had driven Europe, the self-proclaimed 'Treasure of Civilisation', into the horror in which 10 million people died and 20 million were wounded. Similarly, other thinkers of the modern age such as Thomas Hobbes, John Locke, Hugo Grotius, Samuel von Pufendorf, Christian Wolff, Charles de Montesquieu and Immanuel Kant developed their positions based on the experience of the religious and civil wars of the 16th and 17th centuries. What they had in mind was to stop the killing and to enforce ideally non-violent judicial forms of interaction both within and between states. The goal was to put a leash on violence.

For some, violence is a means among many, more or less reasonable, more or less useful, more or less appropriate in a concrete case. For others, the application of violence in political struggles is literally breaking a taboo. Something indefeasible is touched upon: the right of the other to physical integrity, and internal and external peace. Something becomes endorsed, tolerated or even promoted that as a matter of principle cannot be permitted. For whoever thinks that it is 'appropriate' to violently threaten other human beings claims to be the master of other people's lives and deaths. It is precisely this claim which marks the all-important difference from the point of view of the person affected by violence. Once it has taken the shape of violence, for those who become its victims, political communication transforms itself into injury, mutilation, the crippling of their bodies, or into murder.

Moreover, violent political *resistance* goes beyond the threat to the individual as well. Because it is political, it relates to the whole. Every politically motivated attack on individual representatives of the state attacks the legal order as such, disturbs the legal peace *in toto*, declares a citizens' war against the order of the state. Regardless of how limited its focus may be, every violent political action is characterised by this horizon. What it symbolises is civil war. It does not merely threaten individuals, it threatens everyone.

The survival of *homo sapiens* has always depended on the limited usage of his capacity to murder. And yet, who is going to stop him? The 'nature' of Man, his historical heritage as a species, does not get in the way of it. His emotional inhibitions did not suffice to stop him from the copious murder of small children. 'Reason' does not take effect without the reasonable who, in the war of all against all, are murdered first. Humankind has been compelled to construct barriers against killing time and time again. The weapons that Man has now developed allow him to kill his fellow human beings with unprecedented ease and 'efficiency'. At the same time, the command or lack of command of these increasingly effective weapons splits the human race like no other biological species on this earth. And no other species is capable of annihilating itself. The cycle of violence always generates new counter-violence and an ever more unhampered readiness to make use of it, too. The ongoing maximisation of the power of annihilation, and the inequality in respect of who commands this power, makes it more necessary than ever to construct barriers against the implementation of our potential for violence.

Human civilisation can now only survive if a minimum criterion of ethical behaviour is established and respected. Kant's categorical imperative raises the protection of human life above all other goals. The maintenance of the community of humans through the protection of the right to life of every human being is given a higher importance than any perceivable other end. To threaten or annihilate one human being means to threaten humankind itself – as an ethical entirety and, if the murder is not stopped, as a race.

In his novel *The Brothers Karamazov*, Dostoyevsky took the question of the ethical legitimation of violence to its limits: in order to save the happiness of humankind in its entirety, in order to save it, would it be justified to kill 'only' a single child? Sacrificing an individual as a means to the salvation of all! But – solely a means! The former US Secretary of State Madeline

Albright thought in completely other dimensions when in 1996 she was asked by CBS whether the interests of the USA were worth the death of 500,000 Iraqi children and replied that it was a difficult choice, but 'it was worth the price'.

During the twentieth century, acting on the responsibility of states, at least 160 million defenceless people were murdered – 4,650 people on average on every day of the 36,500 days of the century – three civilian deaths in every one of the more than 50 million minutes of the century. In the preceding 25 centuries there were a total of 130 million people who became victims of such murders.[13] Never before had the lives of human beings been abused so instrumentally as they were during the 20th century. The ever-greater ends appeared to be justifying ever more arbitrary means. And some states which had emerged from socialist and communist revolutions contributed immensely to this balance sheet of violence.

Yet as opposed to all preceding eras, modernity has 'defined itself as an anti-violence project and turned the rational order and the pacification of social internal space into the all-dominant topic'.[14] Violence was meant to serve the protection of the individual and an order of peace, internally as well as externally. At the same time this entailed 'forcing the world to be different from what it was'.[15] The opposition between the pretension of pacification and the will to change (resulting from it) has to be mediated in an emancipative way or else it will lead to barbarism.

Theodor Adorno formulated the demand that 'Auschwitz [must] never happen again'.[16] The left today has to add that the Gulag, the murders of the Chinese cultural revolution, the Killing Fields of the Khmer Rouge, must never recur. To defy barbarism within the field of politics means overcoming a way of thinking and acting from mere expediency, of 'instrumental' reason. The person who conceives of the means of political action merely through the perspective of their expediency 'relates to them as does the dictator to humans. He knows them inasmuch as he is able to manipulate them… as a substrate of rule'.[17]

The rejection of violence in political struggles should not be played down as a merely instrumental argument. What is at stake is nothing less than the defence of the political-ethical protective barrier which has to be constructed over and over again in order for Auschwitz never to happen again. The existential horror of the application of politically motivated violence must never be explained away by considerations of expedience, because it is the most important emotional barrier against backslides into barbarism. After Stalin and Mao, after Pol Pot, the notion shared by parts of the left that radicalness is identical with the violent nature of the means is no longer innocently naïve. The radical aim 'to overthrow *all those conditions* in which man is an abased, enslaved, abandoned, contemptible being' must never be confused with extremism of the means.

THE EXPEDIENCE OF COUNTER-VIOLENCE

But is it really possible to do without violence completely? Is this not – in the best case – self-deluding, and a legitimation for not doing anything that would do justice to the pretence of real change? Is not *any* rebellion better than mere acceptance of the status quo, or – worse still – an agreeable accommodation with it? ('In the time of betrayal/ The scenery is beautiful', wrote the poet Heiner Müller in 1958.)

If we accept that violence against human beings is *in itself* illegitimate and criminal, under what conditions is it not barbarism when is used for 'transparent, humane ends'?[18] Are there not situations in which political violence can make sense, while at the same time not negating the end – a more humane society, free from violence? Are there not conditions in which it may it be politically necessary to make the transition to violence against other human beings? Why should the global struggle against hunger not be pursued through the means of violence; why should the struggle for minimum wages or for more democracy or against the use of nuclear energy not be pursued by means of violence? Why should not soldiers of the US Army, stopping in Germany on their way to Iraq, become targets for political murder – not to mention George W. Bush, who is undoubtedly responsible for war crimes?

If one really does take the position seriously, that violence by humans against humans is always a crime, and if one does follow the position taken here, namely that one may only resort to such violence in a situation of utmost emergency, then there exists only one situation in which it does not completely contradict humane ends: *the situation of a lack of alternatives*. There exists only one humane grounds for the exercise of physical force against other humans for political ends, i.e. if one has no other means at one's own disposal. And yet, what does this mean?

Only when the state denies the access to the most elementary conditions of survival, when the state's monopoly of force has dissolved, when we are dealing with a totalitarian regime or a dictatorship, may violence become an acceptable political means of resistance inside the state. For example, violence may be understood as action resulting from an immediate emergency if human beings who are threatened with death by starvation take by force grain silos guarded by the police or the army. The dissolution of the state's monopoly of force through the acquiescence or even promotion of death squads may lead to a situation where the protection of one's own life and the life of others cannot be guaranteed without armed force. Totalitarian regimes are those which oppress any expression of free speech and the opportunity for free association and organisation for the purpose of collective will formation. Dictatorships are characterised by the fact that the rulers cannot be replaced through free elections with a universal franchise. In all of these cases, in the absence of alternatives, violence may contribute to the immediate creation of the conditions of survival or the safeguarding of the most elementary conditions of a politics free from violence.

If one does follow this argument, then political violence by non-state actors is justifiable in terms of relating to humane ends when, and *only* when, it aims *directly* at making itself superfluous. This political violence has two legitimate goals: first, to end the killing of human beings; and/or, second, to create the elementary conditions of democracy. It is either about physical survival or about the creation of the conditions of being able to peacefully sort out political conflicts. The moment in which violence is executed for ends going beyond these two goals – for example, deterrence or 'educational' purposes' – it ceases to support legitimate ends and sets its own ends of oppression, exploitation and annihilation.

COUNTER-VIOLENCE UNDER LIBERAL DEMOCRACY

Why do so many who speak out in favour of violence, or act towards it in critical solidarity, speak so half-heartedly about it? Why is it played down, and its consequences linguistically belittled? Why do we not find proud avowals of it? The reason is simple: if political resistance resorts to the means of violence, the step towards symbolic civil war has been taken. Stones and molotov cocktails, sticks and clubs are the weapons of the weak in this war. They imagine weapons and declare war without really engaging in it. Until now it restricted to some individual combats, it is still subjected to certain rules of the game, there are rarely fatalities. As yet, while it is not open war, its shadow is hurrying on ahead. The smoke of burning police cars, or the sight of citizens and policemen beating each other, appear to the public as an impending war directed against society as a whole.

The arguments continuously brought forward on behalf of violence under the conditions of political democracy are fourfold. First, reference is made to the toppling of Salvador Allende in Chile in 1973. On this view, as soon as democratic elections lead to real changes being made to power and property relations – i.e. in situations in which elections really have any meaning – their results will be destroyed by military force. But why does this not lead to the conclusion that the control of the existing military force needs to be improved? Why should the erection of a leftist dictatorship be a better solution than the protection of democracy against right-wing putschists? And if, in order to protect democracy, a democratically-elected government declares a state of emergency, and hence is compelled to abrogate, for a certain period of time, basic rights, this must not lead to a continued suspension of democracy and the obstruction of the free formation of public opinion and plural elections. Let us hear Rosa Luxemburg again, who criticised the establishment of the Bolshevist dictatorship in the following words: 'Without universal elections, an unlimited freedom of the press and of assembly, and free contest of ideas, the life in every public institution dies down, turns into a pseudo-life in which the bureaucracy remains the only active element… a dictatorship indeed, but not the dictatorship of the proletariat but rather the dictatorship of a handful of politicians'.[19]

The resistance to Communist rule in the state socialist countries shows that even under the conditions of a dictatorship, democracy and non-violence may in the end prove to be more successful than any violent action. For decades, at least after 1968, the often very small, very weak, always persecuted opposition managed to generate a culture of conflict resolution that was far superior to that of the state. Even mass movements were disciplined – to the point where the marshals of opposition marches, with their wristbands that proclaimed 'non-violence', became the most important precondition for averting bloodshed. The state powers, which had always invoked the will of the people and humanist goals, were morally disarmed, and the servants of the Communist state were able to decide in favour of non-violence. Due to the longstanding interplay between non-violent opposition and the Communists who saw their power as a means to advance to a more humane society, it was possible for the 'velvet revolution', the 'peaceful turn' to occur, once even in the eyes of its supporters state socialism no longer embodied a superior perspective.

The second objection to the position of non-violence under the conditions of a secure political democracy is the thesis that only violence is capable of arousing 'the masses' and intimidating 'the rulers'. Historical facts suggest exactly the opposite: political violence evokes civil war. It threatens everyone and everybody. In the best case an alliance between the citizens and the ruling elites emerges that aims at collectively fending off the slide into the barbarism of dehumanised violence. And in the shadow of such an alliance the rulers are able simultaneously to try to roll back democratic citizens' rights and expand the realm of unchecked surveillance and the exercise of force. The rulers are encouraged to secure their rule by also using repression, and the ruled start to believe that being so ruled is the precondition of national peace.

The third argument of those advocating violent political resistance assumes that it is the representatives of the state, or the people protected by it, who are the obstacle to the goal pursued. They would have to be threatened or got rid of (how and where to?) in order for the goal to be realised. If, however, basic political rights are secured and free elections are conducted regularly, who is then forcefully standing in the way of changing the economic, social and political order? A successful assassination of Hitler would undoubtedly have been expedient, given that the entire state power within national socialism was comprised in the 'Führer'. His earlier death would have saved millions of human beings' lives. Under the conditions of free elections, however, and guaranteed fundamental rights, political rulers are elected by the citizens and can also be removed by them. Given that this path is open, no violent path can be shown to be rational for the purpose of humanity. Violent attacks on policemen and policewomen (with the exception of a situation of endangered life) are even less sustainable. Pointing to obstacles hampering the way of a sea-change in politics does not justify violence.

The true 'obstacles' to a change towards a more just, more ecological, more democratic and more peaceful society are those who tolerate unjust, un-ecological and un-peaceful conditions – the majority of all the citizens. If the majority within a given society does not change, then there is no real solidaristic emancipation but only the more or less frequent exchange of the top personnel. If this is the case, what leftist would demand the annihilation of the majority of the population as a condition of a new politics? On the contrary, the preconditions of a solidaristic and collective self-transformation of the majority have to be created. This, however, can only occur through non-violent means.

A fourth objection to non-violence is that representative democracy in most states is confronted by a global dictatorship of large corporations and financial institutions. The political representatives of states can be voted out, but the managers of the multinational firms and hedge funds are accountable only to the owners of capital. This is, without a doubt, one of the biggest challenges to solidaristic emancipation. Political democracy necessitates social democracy. However, the latter cannot last permanently without economic democracy. The task is not to wage a 'war' against corporate bosses, but rather to democratise economic power and economic sectors and financial institutions which are not under democratic control.[20]

On the Western left there are, as yet, hardly any open advocates of violence. However, there exists a false and blind tolerance, a false laisser-faire which considers throwing a stone or a molotov cocktail into the side of a police car a legitimate form of protest and a path to emancipation, and seeks to build alliances with others who take this course. Reaction, resistance, counter-force *can* be the onset of liberation. As expressions of protest against rule they contain the dignity of rebellion. Even the crudest revolt is at least *revolt*; blind anger goes beyond mere endurance and toleration. However, as a mere reflex of oppression, exploitation or exclusion, counter-force is initially no more than the other side of rule. To this extent, it is not different, it is only against. Often it, imitates in the rawest form the means of domination, and sometimes even make these more brutal. It can also be aimed at scapegoats, and can become self-destructive. The step towards emancipation does not begin with resistance itself but only then when rebellion turns solidaristic.

RESISTANCE UNDER NEOLIBERALISM

Everything that has been said so far has been aimed at showing why under liberal democracy violence is neither a legitimate nor an expedient means of action. This, however, does not explain why in the name of 'another world', a more humane, more democratic, more peaceful world some people do resort to violence. There exist many arguments for it and one very understandable reason – their deeply felt powerlessness: 'Use of force is… also failure of power'.[21] Counter-violence is (also) the desperate hope of gaining power.

There are many causes of this despair amongst leftists, as well as a view of the world which is itself one-dimensional: not only did the dictatorial path taken by Bolshevism and the Soviet Union fail, but so did the reform strategy of left social democracy – judged by its goal of overcoming a world dominated by capital. In the eyes of many leftists, the participation of leftists in governments does not appear to be achieving anything beyond a more benign administration of the status quo. Often too the claim is heard that it is precisely these participations in governments which have paved the way for another wave of commodification. Never before in the history of the world have so many free elections taken place, yet at the same time a sober realisation is spreading how little this has meant for social and ecological progress. Even wars of aggression have been legitimated in the name of democratisation.

In the centres of capitalism Fordism dissolved the resilient milieus of the proletarians and created what seemed to Marcuse to be a 'one dimensional society' based on technological-administrative domination and its sublimation in the consumerist desires of the dominated. They became accomplices of their own subjugation, negating the possibility of new forms of existence. Now, in the name of freedom, neoliberal capitalism seems to be replacing this one-dimensional technological-administered world with a one-dimensional marketised world. The external command of the factory and the large organisation is replaced by the internal guidance of market-conforming behaviour where failure in the markets becomes individualised, and punished by exclusion. The neoliberal constellation of rule differs from rule in earlier periods in history. Even wars are supposed to lead to free elections and guaranteed basic political rights for the defeated. In the capitalist centres this appears particularly valid. Much more intensely than ever before the ruled appear to be integrated as *independent subjects* into the structures of rule. The global war against terror, to make use of this formula, conducted without front lines, without hinterlands, without central commands and without prisoners, is the military reflection of the global competition of 'network enterprises' on the markets.[22]

Such a view of the world generates despair: how can there be resistance to such domination if it has been internalised by the dominated in such a way that it has turned into a part of them? What sense does it make to de-elect the rulers, if those rulers are interchangeable? Why make a revolution if competition between economic regions captures the new state powers as well? But this view of the world as a one-dimensional closed system is a construct, which generates hopelessness. There are alternatives. Actually existing societies have very different countenances.[23] Even neoliberal capitalism is characterised by the conflicting tendencies of the logic of capital and the logic of the social.[24] The Empire is coming up against forces of an alternative order. The marketisation of society generates new potentials of individual desire, agency, self-determination and solidarity. The new subjectivity within neoliberalism can also be transformed into an independent emancipation movement. It is a chance, nothing more, but also nothing less. People who invoke democracy and simultaneously undermine it will suddenly find themselves in a position of needing to justify themselves vis-à-vis new democratic movements. The person who proclaims freedom as the highest aim is not going to be able to avoid debating the necessary preconditions of freedom. The person who makes self-determination into the highest value will have to confront the question on what conditions this self-determination ultimately depends. The person who promotes globalisation and equal market rights for all is no longer going to be able to avoid the problem of a just global order.

From the moment when rule no longer manifests itself primarily through the foreclosure of the self-determination of individuals and social groups, but attempts to channel it instead, from the moment when rule tries to conceal its violent nature in order to remain rule, spaces of liberation can be created. This is because we are not dealing with a totalitarian-fascist opponent. The historical model of the labour movement, along with the majority of movements against colonialism and racism, have been characterised by the idea of countering the power of the rulers with a mirror-image of counter-power, but with new and different goals. At least as a historical step towards a social transition this appeared to be inevitable. The forces opposing capitalism, imperialism, colonialism and militarism imagined themselves as armies with generals, officers and soldiers, bound together by an ideology of irreconcilability with the enemy.

It is true for all forms of rule that they prove to be very stable as long as they are capable of creating a culture 'in which the dominated permanently have to struggle against the dominators within the limits that the latter have set up for them'.[25] To destabilise the rule of neoliberalism, new routes to solidaristic emancipation must be found. If rule is achieved through the subjectivity of the ruled, through the expansion of the forms of their self-determination and democratic participation, through conditioning, and by punishing refusal with exclusion, the struggle for a solidaristic emancipation can and must change. If rule relies not primarily on the state but rather on the 'inherent necessities' of unleashed markets, which are also enforced by state action, then the struggle over the state and within the state is not going to suffice. More than ever before is there a need for emancipatory-solidaristic *subjects* as both the condition for, and the consequences of, liberating struggles.

Currently, the emancipatory left is pursuing three strategies in order to overcome neoliberal capitalism and the violence emanating from it. These are the strategy of the rejection of wars, socially reactionary reforms and the new authoritarianism; the strategy of the development of autonomous spaces for the development of alternatives; and the strategy of comprehensive social transformation. These all begin, however, with the strategy of the simple 'no'. The worldwide demonstrations against the war on Iraq in February 2003 and the mobilisation in Germany against the Hartz IV labour market reforms did not stop these things, but they showed that the peoples of the world, citizens, are challenging the arrogance of the elites and their claims to rulership. The non-violent blockade of the land routes to the venue of the G8 summit in Heiligendamm was another case in point. The goal, to actually and effectively block the G8 summit and disconnect it from its infrastructure, was achieved.[26] At the same time, the security interests of the state were taken seriously. The fence which sealed off the centre of the convention was not supposed to be stormed. However, through civil disobedience it could be shown that the G8 summit was an illegitimate claim to power.

This strategy of the left, to confront neoliberalism with a life-affirming solidaristic 'no', to challenge every new war, every new counter-reform, every rolling-back of democracy and citizens' rights, does not only need demonstrations, rallies, voting for this party and support of these organisations which are resisting neoliberalism. When the entire economic, social and political order's obligation to the 'dignity' claims of the constitution appears to become lost, more is needed.[27]

Non-violent resistance is anything but passive. It is an active 'third way' between conflict avoidance and the violent playing-out of a conflict.[28] Among other things, the boycott of commodities and infrastructure, social boycotts, refusal to pay taxes, refusal to cooperate, rejection of distinctions and awards, civil disobedience, workplace and sympathy strikes and occupations as well as political strikes all belong to the category of non-violent resistance. Such resistance calls for the highest personal ethics, and for the extraordinary courage it takes to expose oneself to someone else's violence while at the same time refusing to answer it with violence.

Civil disobedience has a double function: on the one hand it is directed at the 'population', the large majority of citizens, and it points to the fact that a constitutional emergency has come into being, a situation in which power may no longer legitimately rest with representative institutions. Acts of civil resistance are a 'form of political appeal'.[29] At the same time, such acts of resistance are supposed to increase the 'costs' of state action in enforcing the specific interests of the state.

In his empirical study of the extra-parliamentary protests of the 1970s and the 1980s, Thomas Balistier concludes that protest which makes the transition to destruction can also lead to violence: 'Its actors have dismissed the strategy of non-violent protest; they organise and practise open militancy, whose goal contains the qualitatively different dimension of the threat of damage. Destruction and attempted destruction is a product of, and produces temporary or permanent, communicationlessness… As a rule, these concrete behaviour patterns actually… neither advance the social movements nor the resolution of the conflict. On the contrary, they lead into a dead-end street at whose end we can find the paramilitarian victory of the state powers and quite often also the collapse of the protest itself'.[30] To cross the line between the destruction of things and violence against persons does not take much, even if for the new social movements of recent decades – unlike the Red

Army Fraction and the Movement 2nd June of the 1970s – injuring or killing human beings never became a direct goal.

When this line is crossed, the means vitiate the end. Instead of dynamising the contradiction between the claims of the constitution and reality, what becomes actualised is the contradiction between internal peace and civil war. Under the conditions of a democratic state based on the rule of law, the use of violence is not only illegitimate but in the highest degree inexpedient. Citizens are immunised to the concerns of the protest; its actors are delegitimised and become isolated as 'anarchists' and 'terrorists'. Pressure is not increased on political power to change gear, but rather on civil society to refrain from any form of protest, let alone resistance, in order to avoid slipping into civil war.

Moreover, the 'no' to violence is necessary so that barbarism is never again perpetrated in the name of socialism. The barbarism of unhampered capitalism must be stopped and foreclosed so that the necessary spaces for emancipation can really emerge. Sober impatience and engaged patience are called for. Chances have to be seized so that the despairing do not pick up stones and the rebellious do not become discouraged.

Finally, rolling back violence in social and interpersonal relations is also very closely linked to any strategy for a peaceful revolution transcending capitalism. It is only going to be successful if we succeed in 'making life more interesting, making individuals less powerless and creating a society in which more opportunities exist to practise love and integrity, a society which functions in the name of life'.[31]

NOTES

1 Günther Anders, *Gewalt – ja oder nein. Eine notwendige Diskussion*, Edited by Manfred Bissinger, München: Knaur, 1987, pp. 103-4, 144-5.

2 In the course of its history the left has discussed this issue over and over again. Thomas Müntzer's despairing call to the members of his revolutionary league of 1525 to join the Peasant Uprising is still echoing in our ears: 'On with it, on with it as long the fire's burning hot. Do not let your sword turn cold, do not slow down. Weld swiftly on Nimrod's anvils, throw their tower to the ground'. Thomas Müntzer, 'An die Allstedter. Manifest an die Mansfeldischen Berggesellen', in S. Streller, ed., *Hutten, Müntzer, Luther,* Volume One, Berlin: Aufbau Verlag, 1970, p. 264. From his prison cell Louis Blanqui wrote: 'Weapons and organization – those are the decisive means of progress, the sole serious means to end misery. He who has iron, also has bread. One surrenders

to the bayonets, unarmed lots are swept away like husk. France, peppered with armed workers – that marks the advent of socialism. In the face of the armed proletariat anything is going to vanish: obstacles, contumacies, impossibilities. But for those proletarians who are passing their time with ridiculous street promenades, freedom trees and euphonic advocate's phrases, for them there is holy water to start with, then insults and finally canister shots and always misery. Let the people choose'. Louis Blanqui, 'Warnung an das Volk', in J. Höppner and W. Seidel-Höppner, eds., *Von Babeuf bis Blanqui. Französischer Sozialismus und Kommunismus vor Marx*, Volume 2, Leipzig: Verlag Philipp Reclam, 1975, p. 525.

3 Gertrud Nummer-Winkler, 'Überlegungen zum Gewaltbegriff', in W. Heitmeyer and H.-G. Soeffner, eds., *Gewalt, Entwicklungen, Strukturen, Analyseprobleme*, Frankfurt am Main: Suhrkamp, 2004, p. 28. I would add 'and psychological' – M.B. At the least, ever since the publication of the instructions for 'contactless torture' (long term sleep-deprivation for prisoners in Stalin's caves of torture, the confrontation of bound prisoners with cold and heat in Guantanamo belong to this category as well), we also have to include these 'indirect forms' of the deliberate destruction of human beings. In what follows, violence is understood in the sense of the Latin term *violentia* and is sharply distinguished from the exercise of power (*potentia*) or rule (*potestas*).

4 Kurt Röttgers, 'Spuren der Macht und das Ereignis der Gewalt', in K. Platt, ed., *Reden von Gewalt*, München: Wilhelm Fink, 2002, p. 80.

5 Johan Galtung, *Strukturelle Gewalt. Beiträge zur Friedens – und Konfliktforschung*, Reinbek : Rowohlt Verlag, 1975, pp. 9, 12.

6 On the concepts of symbolic and cultural violence compare: Dieter Kinkelbur, 'Sozialformen der Gewalt', in W. Kempf, ed., *Konflikt und Gewalt. Ursachen – Entwicklungstendenzen – Perspektiven. Schriftenreihe des Österreichischen Studienzentrums für Frieden und Konfliktlösung*, Volume 5, Münster: Agenda Verlag, 2000, p. 26f.

7 A 'dense description' of this absolute violence is provided by Wolfgang Sofsky, *Die Ordnung des Terrors: Das Konzentrationslager*, Frankfurt am Main: Fischer, 2004.

8 Compare on the debate about the definition of forms of action: Thomas Balistier, *Straßenprotest. Formen oppositioneller Politik in der Bundesrepublik Deutschland zwischen 1979 und 1989*, Münster: Westfälisches Dampfboot, 1996, p. 24ff. Direct actions are, first and foremost, 'refusals, impediments, squattings and destructions' (p. 129).

9 See Klaus Peters, *Widerstandsrecht und humanitäre Intervention*, Köln: Heymanns, 2005, p. 194.

10 On the genesis of this right see: Bodo Missling, *Widerstand und Menschenrechte. Das völkerrechtlich begründete Individualwiderstandsrecht gegen Menschenrechtsverletzungen*, Tübingen: Helga Köhler, 1999, p. 106ff.

11 Quoted from: http://de.wikipedia.org/wiki/Malcolm_X.

12 Walter Benjamin, 'Critique of Violence', in Benjamin, *Reflections*, New York: Harcourt Brace Jovanovich, 1978, pp. 277-8.

13 Rudolph J. Rummel, *Statistics of Democide. Genocide and Mass Murder since 1900*, London: Münster, 1998.

14 Sebastian Scheerer, 'Verstehen und Erklären von Gewalt – ein Versprechen der Moderne', in G. Albrecht, O. Backes and W. Kühnel, eds., *Gewaltkriminalität zwischen Mythos und Realität*, Frankfurt am Main: Suhrkamp, 2001, p. 148.

15 Zygmunt Baumann, 'Gewalt – modern und postmodern', in M. Miller and H.-G. Soeffner, eds., *Modernität und Barbarei. Soziologische Zeitdiagnose am Ende de 20. Jahrhunderts*, Frankfurt am Main: Suhrkamp 1996, p. 36.

16 Theodor W. Adorno, 'Erziehung nach Auschwitz', in Adorno, *Erziehung zur Mündigkeit. Vorträge und Gespräche mit Hellmut Becker 1959-1969*, Edited by Gerd Kadelbach, Frankfurt am Main: Suhrkamp, 1970, p. 92, available at: http://schule.judentum.de/nationalsozialismus/adorno.htm.

17 Max Horkheimer and Theodor Adorno, *Dialektik der Aufklärung*, Frankfurt am Main: Fischer Wissenschaft, 1988, p. 15.

18 Adorno, 'Erziehung nach Auschwitz', p. 131.

19 Rosa Luxemburg, 'Zur russischen Revolution', in Luxemburg, *Gesammelte Werke*, Volume 4, Berlin: Dietz, 1974, p. 362.

20 See Alex Demirovi , *Demokratie in der Wirtschaft. Positionen – Probleme – Perspektiven*, Münster: Westfälisches Dampfboot, 2007; Heinz J. Bontrup et al., *Wirtschaftsdemokratie. Alternative zum Shareholder-Kapitalismus*, Hamburg: VSA, 2006.

21 Kurt Röttgers, 'Im Angesicht von Gewalt', in U. Erzgräber and A. Hirsch, eds., *Sprache und Gewalt*, Berlin: Berliner Wissenschafts-Verlag, 2001, p. 55.

22 Compare the contributions by Christina Kaindl, Morus Markard, Lutz Brangsch, Katrin Reimer, Alex Demirovic, Volker Caysa, Werner Ruf, Erhard Crome and Rainer Rilling in Michael Brie, ed., *Schöne neue Demokratie – Elemente totaler Herrschaft*, Berlin: Karl Dietz, 2007.

23 Cornelia Heintze, 'Wohlfahrtsstaat als Standortvorteil. Deutschlands Reformirrweg im Lichte des skandinavischen Erfolgsmodells', Rosa-Luxemburg-Stiftung Sachsen, 2005.

24 Dieter Klein and Michael Brie, 'Elementare Fragen neu bedenken. Kapitalismus, Sozialismus, Eigentum und Wege der Veränderung', *Standpunkte der RLS*, 2, 2007.

25 Ashis Nandy, *Der Intimfeind. Verlust und Wiederaneignung der Persönlichkeit im Kolonialismus*, Translated by Lou Marin, Nettersheim: Graswurzelrevolution, 2008, p. 79.

26 Quoted in Komitee für Grundrechte und Demokratie, *Gewaltbereite Politik und der G8-Gipfel*, Köln: Komitee für Grundrechte und Demokratie, 2007, p. 73.

27 For a Christian perspective see Dagmar Neuhäuser, 'Aufgewacht "aus dem Schlaf der Sicherheit". Bewegte Christen solidarisieren sich – das Beispiel der G8-Proteste 2007', in J. Dellheim, S. Teune and A. Trunschke, eds., *Ziehen wir an einem Strang? Gewerkschaften, soziale Bewegungen, Nichtregierungsorganisationen, Parteien*, Schkeuditz: Schkeuditzer Buchverlag, 2007, p. 40ff.

28 Barbara Müller and Christine Schweitzer, 'Gewaltfreiheit als Dritter Weg zwischen Konfliktvermeidung und gewaltsamer Konfliktaustragung', in Kempf, ed., *Konflikt und Gewalt*, p. 82-111.

29 John Rawls, *Eine Theorie der Gerechtigkeit,* Frankfurt am Main: Suhrkamp, 1979, p. 404.

30 Balistier, *Straßenprotest*, p. 107f.

31 Erich Fromm, 'Violence and Its Alternatives: An Interview with Frederick W. Roevekamp', 1968, available from http://www.erich-fromm.de.

THE DEFENCE OF HUMANITY REQUIRES THE RADICALISATION OF POPULAR STRUGGLES

SAMIR AMIN

Compared with preceding political systems, capitalism has historically fulfilled certain progressive functions: it has freed the individual from many constraints imposed by earlier systems, it has developed productive forces on an unprecedented scale, it has fused multiple communities into the nations that we know, it has laid the foundations of modern democracy. Yet all these achievements have been marked and limited by capitalism's class nature: the 'free' individual is in fact nothing more than 'a well-off male bourgeois', while the persisting patriarchate has kept most of the female half of humanity in subordinate positions. In the opulent centres of the system, capitalism has no longer much to offer beyond a consumerism that is alienating and destructive and of the relationships of human fraternity, blocking the genuine emancipation of women, and the liberating dimension of the practice of democracy. It must be made clear that its 'advantages' are also distributed in an increasingly unequal manner under the dictatorship of plutocracies, supported by their monopoly over the media, reducing democracy to practices devoid of meaning and scope, and thereby destroying its legitimacy. The forceful opening of new fields for the expansion of the dominance of the established plutocracies – the privatisation of public services (education, health) and the infrastructures which provide for basic needs (water, electricity, housing, transports) always end in the exacerbation of inequalities and the destruction of the fundamental social rights of the popular classes. The short-term rationality of calculating the return on equity is an invitation to an explosion of criminal or potentially criminal developments (especially through biogenetics).

Modern imperialism has nothing to offer to the large majorities of peoples in Asia, Africa and Latin America (75 per cent of the population of the planet); there, the continuation of its development, beneficial as it may be to a privileged few, requires the massive impoverishment of the others (in particular the peasants who make up close to half of humanity). The rights of nations have been reserved for those belonging to the dominant centres, while those of the dominated and colonised peripheries have been systematically denied. As the successes of its global expansion have increased, the limitations of capitalism have grown steadily, today reaching tragic dimensions. The continuation of the domination of capital over the totality of these peripheries, the peoples of which are as a result in constant revolt (revolt is not revolution but creates conditions for it) requires the militarisation of globalisation. This rules out any genuine democratisation or social progress for those peoples.

At the global level accumulation, driven by the exclusive logic of profit, means: the depletion of non-renewable resources (oil in particular), the irreversible destruction of biodiversity and the accelerated destruction of the natural bases of the reproduction of all life on the planet. This destruction also results in increasingly unequal access to the short term 'benefits' which global capitalism provides. When President George Bush I declared that 'the American way of life is not negotiable', he was effectively ruling out any general 'catching up' for most of the world, since this could only mean that the imperialist nations (first the United States, but behind them the Europeans and the Japanese who had already caught up) would continue to insist on priority of access to the resources of the whole planet. Contemporary globalised capitalism no longer offers an adequate framework for the pursuit of human emancipation. Capitalism is not only a system based on the exploitation of workers; it has become the enemy of all of humanity. As such, it must be considered as an 'obsolete' system – one may even say 'senile', despite the apparent successes of its ongoing expansion. The defence of humanity requires that we change to fundamental principles other than those which govern the globalised capitalist/imperialist accumulation and reproduction.

THE NECESSARY RADICALISATION OF POPULAR STRUGGLES

The aggressions of globalised oligopolistic capital under the control of financial plutocracies clash with the growing resistances of the peoples of the entire planet, with reactions which make counterattacks a real possibility. So far, however, the resistances and the ripostes have been crumbling away. In the opulent countries of central capitalism these resistances are still largely concerned with defending past gains that are being daily whittled away by neo-liberal policies. In some peripheral societies reactions crystallise around backward-looking culturalist projects, which, by definition, are incapable of meeting the challenges of the twenty-first century. Most of the movements currently in conflict with the power of the plutocracies do not question the fundamental principles of capitalism, even though they are the cause of the social tragedies of which their popular audiences are victims. These movements grapple with the consequences of the system, without concerning themselves sufficiently with the mechanisms which have initiated them. That is the reason why the struggles have not yet succeeded in shifting the balance of power in favour of the popular classes, even if they may have won some significant victories here and there. The radicalisation of struggles – which I take to mean their becoming aware of the obsolete character of capitalism – governs their capacity to produce positive alternatives. It is necessary and possible.

Despite the extreme variety of the objective conditions of the insertion of the working classes and their nations into the contemporary capitalist/ imperialist system, all the peoples of the world aspire to social progress, to a genuine democratisation, and to peace. To be radical today is not to separate but to bring together the different dimensions of the challenge:

i. Democratisation of the management of all aspects of political, economic, social, family, business, school, neighbourhood and national life, must be associated with social progress for all, starting with the most destitute. Genuine democratisation is inseparable from social progress. The defence of human rights, the right to work, 'equal opportunity' for men and women everywhere, however legitimate these rights may be (and they are), is not enough; more must be achieved by involving people in a global project initiating a transition towards socialism. Diversity in vision, though respectable not only for what it is but also because it is enriching, must not be an insurmountable obstacle to the construction of the unity of the working classes and the internationalism of peoples.

ii. The independence and sovereignty of states, nations and peoples must be respected and a polycentric international system must be built on this basis. Unfortunately, many militants of the movements in struggle, notably in the opulent countries of the imperialist centre, reject the idea of the defence of nations, hastily putting this in the same category as aggressive chauvinism. Yet defending the rights of nations is a condition for reducing significantly the conflicts of interest resulting from inequality in capitalist development, for substituting for brutal power struggles an obligation to negotiate, and for eliminating the unending war of the North against the South which characterises our epoch. This means the construction of 'united fronts' – the renewal of the united fronts of the Non-Aligned and the Tricontinental movements in particular – around common objectives. It also means replacing the existing institutions serving globalised financial capital – the WTO, the IMF, the World Bank, NATO, the European Union, and other regional projects such as the proposed Free Trade Agreement of the Americas, or the free trade arrangements between the European Union and the countries of Africa, the Caribbean and the Pacific – by other institutions of global management. Some steps have been taken in this direction, especially in Latin America with the ALBA project, and, for what it is worth, Mercosur; and in Asia with the Shanghai group. But we are still far from having managed to put the existing institutions to flight, even if they have already lost their legitimacy in the eyes of the peoples.

Radicalisation, understood in the terms I have outlined, is synonymous with the politicisation of struggles and the affirmation of the socialist alternative. By politicisation is meant the awareness that there is no social movement which can claim an 'a-political' character, even if the disgust with politics as we know it may seem a legitimate response to the cynical means by which the established political forces, including the existing centre-left political parties, seek to sustain themselves.

FACING IMPERIALIST AGGRESSION: THE CASE FOR ARMED RESISTANCE

For the moment, radicalisation requires that priority be given to defeating the project of military control of the planet, at the service of plutocratic globalisation. The current period is one of renewed imperialist deployment, associating the partners of the above-mentioned triad. This association, which makes me describe imperialism as being henceforth 'collective' (as opposed to the imperialisms of the past, continuously involved in mutual conflict) means the unconditional alignment of the subordinate partners to the US. Europeans, without calling into question the leadership of Washington, may wish for a greater participation in the formulation of a common strategy and for sharing the benefits to be derived from it less unequally. In any case, this imperialist deployment constitutes a new 'hundred years' war' of the North against the South, which is a continuation of the unending aggression being carried out since 1492.

The way globalised plutocracies view the world is represented by the insipid term of 'globalisation', as if the latter could not assume a form other than that which it does at the present. Actually, the violence of the contradictions which oppose the interests of the peoples and nations of the peripheries to those of the dominant sections of globalised capital has become so acute that the globalisation in question has had to be militarised, guaranteed by the military control of the planet proclaimed by Washington. The deployment of over 600 US military bases distributed over the whole planet is intended to establish the domination of Washington over the whole world, including its subordinate associates in the triad, compelled – for lack of comparable military and political means – to align themselves with the unilateral hegemony of the United States.

The United States and their associates have developed a new military doctrine, aimed at giving them an 'absolute superiority' over all their adversaries – the peoples and the nations of the South. No doubt this superiority is nothing new. Produced by the unequal character inherent to the development of capitalism, it has enabled the North since 1492 to assert itself against the South, at the price of long wars of colonial conquest. This absolute superiority was called into question for some time by Soviet military power, as well as by the military and political self-assertion of the countries of liberated Asia (China, Vietnam) and a few others (e.g. Cuba). The new political conjuncture and the imbalances which characterise it has led the dominant classes of collective imperialism to imagine a new model of 'war' which would no longer require the occupation of land and the difficulties and risks involved in it. In the new model 'war' is reduced to massive aerial bombardment (to which victims cannot give a similar response), and to the destruction of the infrastructures and the victims' means of survival. This form of 'war' does not even exclude the possibility of resorting to nuclear weapons – 'if necessary' according to G.W. Bush. The aim of this form of war is quite simply to terrorize entire populations, or even, in case of resistance (described as 'suicidal' by the new military experts of the Pentagon) to eradicate them (genocide). The United States is a terrorist state, a rogue state 'par excellence'. Speeches on international law, humanitarian law, and democracy have no meaning whatsoever in face of these realities. The new war technology seemed to its inventors to present a second advantage: a 'zero dead war' (for the aggressors, naturally). This 'requirement' reflected a marked development in the societies of the North, in which the butcheries of earlier times were no longer acceptable. The doctrine of 'zero dead' would be capable, according to its originators, of making people accept the genocide of others. That may unfortunately be the case with respect to the people of the United States, at this juncture. Regarding the peoples of Europe, the authorities have so far opted for silence.

The peoples of the South can meet the challenge only through preparation – including military preparation – that is adequate to the confrontation. 'Disarm, we are going to attack you' proclaim the media in the service of imperialism. To this invitation, the strangeness of which is only matched by its ignoble character, the peoples and the states of the South have only one answer: to develop their military capabilities to the required level and forms adequate to deter the enemy. The twentieth century witnessed the deployment of the national liberation movements of the peoples of the periphery. Many popular movements have been compelled to take up arms to respond to the violent interventions of imperialism. They have done so victoriously, and formulated an appropriate military theory and a strategy, models of which have been supplied by the Chinese people's army and by guerrillas in Vietnam, Algeria, Cuba and the Portuguese colonies. Their effectiveness rested on the double principle of a wide popular mobilisation (involving the politicisation of the armed forces and their participation in the progressive social transformations that were on the agenda), and on the acquisition of suitable combat equipment and techniques. The military writings of the Bolsheviks, Mao Zedong and Amilcar Cabral gave shape to the theory of the 'fish in water', made possible by the fact that the enemy was fighting on the terrain of peripheral societies in revolution.

In the capitalist Third World national liberation struggles have led to the construction of local bourgeois authorities of diverse natures, ranging from neo-colonial submission, to the radical bourgeois attempt to secure a 'new international economic order'. The military doctrine of most Third World states is a function of their political and social character, in other words of the illusions of the project of which their national bourgeoisies are the bearers. In this framework, armed forces have been conceived primarily as internal police forces. This being so, the radical ideologies derived from the national liberation movements initiated a process whereby this conception could be challenged: but they remained prisoners of the bourgeois character of the ruling class, which cannot tolerate the substitution of 'armed people' for the concept of a conventional army.

Moreover, the conception of the diplomatic game which was meant to support the nation in its conflict with imperialism rested on the Soviet alliance, which was expected to provide modern armaments and to keep alive the threat of a more sustained intervention if the need arose. At the same time, however, these regimes never conceived of a conflict with imperialism other than a temporary one. This is why, in the Arab world, they thought they could drive a wedge between their direct enemy (Israel) and its American and European allies: they kept their two options open on the diplomatic front, the Soviet alliance being capable of being modulated (or even abandoned) should the West take serious steps towards the recognition of their rights. We know how radical regimes have fallen in this trap and, even before the disappearance of the Soviet Union, have themselves initiated a rapprochement with the United States and Europe, without receiving anything in return. On the contrary, the enemy took advantage of the opportunity to overthrow nationalist regimes and bring to an end any radical tendencies, and submit the countries in question to compradorisation.

Today, within the framework of the United States' project and collective imperialism, rapid deployment forces have been put in place to avoid the aggressor being bogged down in endless wars. Their logic is that of pre-emptive war, embarked upon 'before it is too late', that is before popular national political and social forces manage to seize power. The goals of rapid deployment are to overthrow any government deemed incapable of blocking the emergence of a radical popular movement, or any government forced, through weakness or demagogy, to call into question the imperialist status quo. This strategy means that the takeover must be perfectly controlled; in other words that a new government can be put in place during the operation. Military means must be capable of hitting hard in a short time to destroy the ability to organise resistance. But it must also be at little human cost to the aggressors – i.e., there must be an insignificant number of their corpses lying on the ground.

As a counterpoint, the creation of a deterrent force in the service of the people of the Third World is not a question of pure military technique and armament, but primarily a political question. Hence the creation of this force must necessarily be based on two pillars: a popular army (the ideal of the 'armed people'), and effective military means. The political objective of the rapid deployment force being to overthrow a regime, it is essential to make this objective impossible (or at least extremely difficult). A dictatorial government, accepted out of passivity, will always remain vulnerable, even if, in spite of its undemocratic character, for one reason or another it is targeted by the West. A real popular national government, supported by a popular army in its image, reduces considerably the vulnerability inherent in the status of 'underdeveloped' country. Rapid intervention then becomes ineffective in the sense that the imperialist order can only be restored by the military occupation of the country, compelling the adversary to fight on the terrain of the attacked. In that situation imperialism then has no other option, other than that of committing a genocide by massive bombardment (even nuclear), which would require a real 'fascisation' of Western societies.

The recent developments in the Middle East, following invasions by the armies of the United States and its faithful allies (Israel, in particular, and some European countries) are a good illustration of the points made here: the 'easy' initial victory in the invasion of Iraq, the political failure of Washington's project and the rise of resistance (in spite of the inadequacies which characterise it), and the failure of the Israeli army in face of the popular resistance in south Lebanon. While the United States' project, backed by their subordinate European and Israeli allies, aims to establish military control over the whole planet, the Middle East has been chosen, in line with this perspective, as a 'first strike' region.

This is for four reasons: (i) it has the most abundant oil resources of the planet, and their direct control by the United States would give Washington a privileged position, placing its allies – Europe and Japan – and their potential rivals (China) in an uncomfortable position of dependence with respect to energy supplies; (ii) it is located at the heart of the ancient world and makes it easier to maintain a permanent military threat against China, India and Russia; (iii) the region is currently going through a process of weakening and confusion which enables the aggressor to secure an easy victory, at least in the initial stage; (iv) the United States has a staunch ally in the region, Israel, which has nuclear weapons, and has long harboured the goal of splitting up the region into micro-states along ethnic or religious lines.

The implementation of the project is advanced: Palestine, Iraq, and Afghanistan are occupied and destroyed, Syria and Iran are openly threatened. But the bankruptcy of the project is no less visible; people's resistance does not weaken, as was particularly seen in Lebanon where an effective armed resistance showed why it is necessary, today more than ever, to defend the people's inalienable right to armed resistance. However one cannot be satisfied with armed popular resistance as the only possible response to aggression. It is necessary to supplement its potential dissuasive power with effective, modern 'anti-rapid deployment forces' equipment. Dissuasion requires that a Third World country have, in spite of the massive destruction which it undergoes following a first strike, a significant response capacity, inflicting thereby heavy losses on the rapid deployment forces or on targets located in the enemy camp. In this situation, rapid intervention becomes an uncertain adventure. Mobile missiles provide one answer to the issue of the required means of dissuasion, since the probability is high that they will escape destruction by a first strike. The question of the 'proliferation of nuclear weapons', and more particularly the threat under which imperialists keep Iran accused of developing a 'dangerous' nuclear capacity, is also relevant here.

It is not our intention to develop here the analyses called for by the 'Islamic revolution'. From the point of view of what interests us here I will make only two observations. The first is that the regime of political Islam in Iran is not by nature incompatible with the integration of the country into the globalised capitalist system. The second is that the Iranian nation as such is a 'strong nation' whose major components – both working classes and ruling classes – do not accept the integration of their country into the globalised system in a weak position. There is of course a contradiction between these two dimensions of Iranian reality, and the second accounts for the orientations of Teheran's foreign policy which show a will to resist foreign diktats. The fact remains that it is Iranian nationalism – powerful and, in my opinion, historically quite positive – which explains the success of the 'modernisation' of the scientific, industrial, technological and military capacities undertaken by the successive regimes of the Shah and Khomeinism. Iran is one of the rare states of the South (with China, India, Korea, Brazil and perhaps some others, but not many!) to have a 'national middle-class' project. Whether the realisation of this project is or is not in the long run possible (and I believe it is not) is not the object of our discussion here. Today this project exists, it is definitely there.

It is precisely because Iran is in this position that towards the end of the Bush II administration the United States threatened the country with a new 'preventive' war. Yet the claim that this was just about the nuclear capacities that Iran is developing is dubious. Why shouldn't this country – like all others – have a right to it, up to and including becoming a nuclear military power? By what right can the imperialist powers award themselves, and certain regional allies, a monopoly of weapons of mass destruction? Can one lend credence to the imperial discourse according to which 'democratic' nations will never make use of them, as 'rogue states' would? The 'non-proliferation' treaty in itself never went far enough, even if – under pressure – many states of the South subscribed to it, while the nuclear powers of the North failed to implement their part in it. Denuclearisation must apply to all, starting with the over-equipped countries, the United States first, and it must also apply to its allies who are not signatories to the treaty. Failing that, proliferation, far from increasing risks, could contribute to their reduction, as some French military experts have openly argued.

The states and the peoples of the three continents are confronted with the same challenge that imperialist capitalism always represented for them. But the economic situation which characterises our period is unfavourable to the fast development of their capacity to respond to aggression, the comprador bourgeoisies being by and large those who monopolise power there. Under these conditions, priority must be given to the organisation of armed popular defence, whose effectiveness has been shown in southern Lebanon. Defending the absolute right of popular organisations under these conditions becomes a major responsibility for all (and this is why the very idea of 'disarming Hezbollah' must be treated as unacceptable). At the same time, the development of popular struggles must have the objective of removing from power the local comprador classes or, at least, forcing them to cohabit with the organisations of popular forces. Indeed, the conditions are ripe for a new liberation wave.

The Bolivarian revolution in progress in Chavez's Venezuela constitutes perhaps a possible road to radicalisation. With the victories gained by other peoples in Latin America, it is no longer Cuba which is isolated on the continent; it is Washington that faces the prospect of isolation. One also observes promising signs of the rebuilding of a front of the South in the debates at the United Nations and the WTO, aided by the strength of anti-imperialist opinion on Asia and Africa. Conditions are evolving that will, among other things, make possible the necessary development of the military capacities of dissuasion. Of course even the more anti-imperialist governments will advance projects of a strictly 'national' nature rather than give priority to advancing the interests of the working classes. Here also a radicalisation of the struggles is the only means of increasing the chances of moving towards the formation of popular and democratic political broad alliances with adequate power to move towards fundamental changes in each respective nation state.

The importance that I have given to the military dimension of the challenge is essential. This is because the area of the 'Greater Middle East' is today central to the conflict which opposes the imperialist leader to the peoples of the whole world. Derailing the project of the establishment in Washington is the condition for giving progressive forces in any area of the world the opportunity to assert themselves. Failing that, all these advances will remain extremely vulnerable. That does not mean that the importance of struggles led in other areas of the world – in Europe, in Latin America, and elsewhere – can be underestimated. It only means that they must fit into a global perspective which requires defeating Washington in the area that it chose for its first criminal strike at the beginning of the 21st century.

THE MODERATE OPTIONS: ARGUMENTS AND LIMITS

The radicalisation of struggle is not an option chosen by many social movements today. The arguments put forward to justify the adoption of moderate positions are numerous. In general what is invoked is the realism necessary to avoid becoming isolated in a far left ghetto. This is all the more so insofar as small radical minorities are indeed likely to be strongly tempted, once more, to proclaim themselves 'avant-gardes', to refuse systematically the criticism of others, and to turn a blind eye to the rapid transformations which affect contemporary societies. These arguments are serious. Yet beyond the important questions they raise – to which it is necessary to provide answers – they also often mask dubious analyses of the situation, reflecting political and ideological stances and related strategic options which must equally be subjected to criticism.

The page of the first historical wave of experiments carried out in the name of socialism having been turned, capitalism appears to many as the last frontier of our time ('the end of history'). Its description at the outset of this essay as senile, against all the indications of its successes, which are constantly in the news, could even make one smile. Under these conditions, popular movements feel compelled to adhere to capitalist logic, to give their struggles only modest objectives – above all pushing back 'neoliberalism' of course – but only with a view to promoting the alternative of a 'capitalism with a human face'. The analysis which I have proposed prohibits such conclusions. This is because the redoubled violence in the relations of domination of capital which characterises our time is not the product of the extravagances of extreme neoliberalism, but a requirement of the reproduction of capital under contemporary conditions. This is what makes capitalism an obsolete system, although certainly not in the sense that it is going to disappear on its own, dying peacefully of 'natural' causes, but rather in the sense that its reproduction will require from now on the exercise of increasing violence. We have thus reached the stage when people must get rid of it, threatened as they are, otherwise, with the prospect of seeing humanity condemned to barbarity.

This analysis does not rule out the possibility that popular classes propose immediate objectives for their struggles, undoubtedly modest, but necessary to regain confidence in their power. But in my opinion it should be stressed that these possible victories will remain vulnerable and fragile as long as they are not part of a movement which, while gradually gaining power, assigns to itself the goal of leaving capitalism behind. Many militants of our time – especially in the centres of the world imperialist system – no longer believe that the struggles can fit into a system of independent nations which, according to them, have lost their relevance because of deepening globalisation. And because the relationship between nation and state cannot be dissolved, they develop strategies which deliberately ignore the question of the power of the state and substitute for struggles against the state, struggles in 'civil society'. And by the same token they challenge the relevance of 'party politics', since the life of existing political parties is concerned with the combat for state power at the national level. The absolute priority often given by Europeans to the objective of 'saving Europe', as if the 'Europe' in question could be other than what it is – which is not likely in the foreseeable future – is also based on ignoring the obvious relevance of the diversity of national realities in Europe today. But the over-representation of the moderate currents within many social forums, which can be easily explained by the disparity of means (among other things, financial), also constitutes a serious threat to the future of popular struggles and is hampering their necessary radicalisation.

To me these 'moderate' arguments appear to be founded on hastily-conceived *a priori* reasoning. Globalisation is not a given 'objective' process which inevitably sweeps over everything. The globalisation that currently exists is really a strategy, promoted by the authorities of the dominant plutocracies. One cannot substitute for it 'another globalisation' without destroying this one first, and for that, it is necessary to restore the dignity of nations and the sovereignty of peoples and states. 'Civil society' or the 'multitude' today have not already become subjects of history (as Negri claims); they remain fully conditioned by social relations peculiar to capitalism. Political parties undertake their action – as a very general rule – within the framework of the reproduction of capitalism as if they were themselves convinced of its timelessness. Criticisms of parties are thus perfectly well-founded. But one will not reduce the scope of their discouraging practice by ignoring them, but by inventing new forms of political organisation of the working classes. Admittedly, within this framework parties are governed by the 'logic of organisation', while radicalisation calls for a 'logic of struggle' to prevail. But the logic of organisation dominates in the majority of 'civil society movements' today, as well as in the 'big parties'. The logic of struggle will assert itself – gradually – only when the struggles themselves are radicalised.

These moderate arguments and analyses have a pre-eminent place in the choice of actions to be carried out. They give an uncritical legitimacy to 'humanitarian' actions, often going as far as the proclamation of a 'right' – even duty – of 'interference', being unaware of the objectives of imperialism (the real existence of which they underestimate or fail to recognise), which loom large behind these interventions. Can one be unaware of the fact that it is in the name of this 'duty of interference' that NATO (i.e. the United

States and its subordinate allies) actively contributed to the destruction of Yugoslavia, and that efforts are being made to give legitimacy to the occupation of Afghanistan and Iraq? Anti-militarist discourse is undoubtedly a product of commendable intentions. But it becomes reactionary when in its name one denies people under threat the right to arm themselves to resist the actual aggressions of contemporary imperialism. Acts of a 'terrorist' nature exist, this is undeniable. But the confusion in this field must be rejected: 'terrorism' is not cause, it is consequence; it is a product of the inadequacies of the answers given to real challenges with which peoples are confronted. The 'counter-terrorism' discourse has been prepared for nearly thirty years by the think tanks which conceived it as a political weapon of US imperialism. It is now taken up again without reflection on its origins, or criticism of it, alas even by a significant part of the lefts in the rich countries. The term 'terrorism' – vague to perfection – is used to dispose of the debate on violence – among other things, the violence of military aggressions, of the destruction of cities and villages by unpunished massive bombardments, designed to terrorize (the term is perfectly appropriate) entire populations. The discussion that is necessary on the left should concern how to respond to this first terrorism, to identify effective political and military means and to distinguish them from those which are not so.

HUMAN SHIELD

JOHN BERGER

This 'letter to a political prisoner' from John Berger's forthcoming epistolary novel is written in the person of a woman whose man is in jail for life on political grounds, and tells the prisoner to whom it was sent about how the writer, along with many other women, surrounded a factory building where seven wanted men were hiding and which was going to be attacked. Loosely based on an episode in Palestine as well as earlier incidents of the same kind in other places, it is both an amalgam and an invention….

Mi Guapo,

Tonight you are listening in your cell to my words as I write. I'm sitting up in bed. The pad is on my knees.

If I close my eyes I see your ears, the left one sticking out more than the right. My elder sister used to claim that human ears are like dictionaries and that, if you know how, you can look up words in them. Limpid, for instance, Limpid.

My mobile rang and there was Yasmina's clipped voice – finches chirp quickly like this when their tree is at risk – telling me that an Apache had been circling above the old tobacco factory in the Abor district, where seven of ours were hiding, and that the neighbouring women – and other women too – were preparing to form a human shield around the factory and on its roof, to prevent them shelling it. I told her I would come.

I put down the telephone and stood still, yet it was as if I was running. Cool air was striking my forehead. Something of mine – but not my body, maybe my name A'ida – was running, swerving, soaring, plummeting and becoming impossible to sight or get aim on. Perhaps a released bird has this sensation. A kind of limpidity.

I'm not going to send you this letter, yet I want to tell what we did the other day. Perhaps you won't read it until we are both dead, no, the dead don't read. The dead are what remains from what has been written. Much of what is written is reduced to ashes. The dead are all there in the words that stay.

By the time I got there, twenty women, waving white headscarves, were installed on the flat roof. The factory has three floors – like your prison. At ground level, lines of women with their backs to the wall, surrounded the entire building. No tanks, jeeps or Humvees yet to be seen. So I walked from the road across the wasteland to join them. Some of the women I recognised, others I didn't. We touched and looked at one another silently, to confirm what we shared, what we had in common. Our one chance was to become a single body for as long as we stood there and refused to budge.

We heard the Apache returning. It was flying slowly and low to frighten and observe us, its four-bladed rotor blackmailing the air below to hold it up. We heard the familiar Apache growl, the growl of them deciding and us rushing for shelter to hide – but not today. We could see the two Hellfire missiles tucked under its armpits. We could see the pilot and his gunner. We could see the mini-guns pointing at us.

Before the ruined mountain, before the abandoned factory, which was used as a makeshift hospital during the dysentery epidemic four years ago, some of us were likely to die. Each of us, I think, was frightened but not for herself.

Other women were hurrying down the zigzag path from the heights of Mount Abor. Its very steep there – you remember? – and they couldn't see the helicopter. They were holding on to each other and giggling nervously. It was strange to hear their laughter and the growling drone of the Apache together. I looked along the line of my companions, particularly at their foreheads, and I was convinced that some of them had felt something like I had. Their foreheads were limpid. When the stragglers from Mount Abor reached us, they adjusted their clothes and we warmly and solemnly embraced them.

The more we are, the larger the target we make, and the larger the target, the stronger we are. A weird, limpid logic! Each of us was frightened but not for herself.

The Apache was hovering above the factory roof, three floors higher in the sky, stationary but never still. We held one another's' hands and from time to time repeated each other's names. I was holding the hands of Koto and Miriam. Koto was nineteen and had very white teeth. Miriam was a widow in her fifties whose husband had been killed twenty years ago. Although I'm not going to send you this letter I change their names.

At that moment we heard the tanks approaching down the street. Four of them. Koto was stroking my wrist with one of her fingers. We heard the *Tannoy* voice announcing a curfew and ordering everyone to disperse and get indoors. The street on the other side of the wasteland was crowded, and I spotted several cameramen there. A few *decigrams* in our favour.

The immense tanks were now coming fast towards us, turrets turning to select their exact target.

The fear provoked by sounds is the hardest to control. The clatter of their tracks grappling and flattening whatever they drove over, the roar of their engines twisted into their suction noise, and the loudspeaker ordering us to disperse – all three becoming louder and louder, until they stopped in a line facing us, twelve metres away, and the muzzles of their 105 mm. cannons even closer. We didn't huddle, we stood apart, only our hands touching. A commander emerging from the hatch of the first tank informed us, speaking our language badly, that we would now be forced to disperse.

Do you know how much an Apache costs? I asked Kato out of the corner of my mouth. She shook her head. Fifty million dollars, I said between my teeth. Miriam kissed my cheek. I was expecting the rear door of one of the tanks to be pushed up and the soldiers to emerge, land on their feet and run us down. It would have taken no more than a minute. And it didn't happen. Instead the tanks turned and, following each other with a distance of 20 metres between each, they began slowly to circle our circle.

I didn't think it then, mi Guapo, but now writing to you in the middle of the night, I think of Herodotus. Herodotus from Halicarnasse, who was the first to write down stories about tyrants being made deaf to every god by the din of their own machines.

We could never have resisted the soldiers, they would have carted us off. The tanks, as they circled us, deliberately drew nearer – they were tightening the noose slowly around us.

You know how a cat measures her jump, the distance of it, landing on her four feet close together, on the very spot she calculated? This is what each of us had to do, measuring, not the distance of a leap, but its opposite – the precise amount of willpower needed to take the terrifying decision to stay put, to do nothing, despite fear. Nothing. If you underestimated the willpower needed, you'd break line and run before you realised what you were doing. The fear was constant but it fluctuated. If you overestimated, you'd be exhausted and useless before the end and the others would have to prop you up. Our holding hands helped because the calculating energy passed from hand to hand.

When the tanks had circled the factory once, they were no more than an arms length away from us. Through the netted vents of their hulls, we could see helmets, eyes, gloved hands.

More terrifying than anything else was the armoured plating, seen so close up! When each tank passed, it was this surface, the most impermeable ever created by man, that we couldn't avoid seeing, even if we sang – and we had now started singing – with its rounded blind rivets, its texture of an animal-hide so it never shines, its granite hardness and its shit colouring, the colouring not of a mineral but of decay. It was against this surface that we were waiting to be crushed. And facing this surface we must decide, second by second, not to move, not to budge.

My brother, shouted Koto, my brother says any tank can be destroyed if you find the right place and the right moment!

How were we able – all three hundred of us – to hold out as we did? The caterpillar treads were now a few centimetres from our sandals. We didn't move. We went on holding hands and singing to each other in our old women's voices. For this is what had happened and this is why we could do what we did. We had not aged, we were simply old, a thousand years old.

A long burst from a machine gun in the street. Positioned as we were, we couldn't see properly what was happening, so we made signs to our old sisters on the roof who could see better than us. The Apache hung menacingly above them. They made signs back and we understood that a patrol had fired on some running figures. Soon we heard the wail of a siren.

The suction of the next tank hemming us in, ruffled and billowed our skirts. Do nothing. We didn't budge. We were terrified. And in our shrill grandmother's voices, we were singing – We're here to stay! Each of us armed with nothing except a derelict uterus.

That's how it was.

Then one tank – we didn't immediately believe our dim eyes – stopped circling and headed off across the wasteland, followed by the next and the next and the next. The old women on the roof cheered, and we, still holding hands but now silent, began to side-step towards the left so that slowly, very slowly as befitted our years, we were circling the factory.

About an hour later, the seven were ready to slip away. We, their grandmothers, dispersed, remembering what it had been like to be young and then becoming young. And within ten minutes I heard the street news, passed from mouth to mouth: Manda, the music teacher, had been shot dead in the street. She was trying to join us.

The lute is like no other instrument, she once said, as soon as you balance a lute on your lap, it becomes a man! Manda!

For so long as I am alive, I am yours, mi Guapo.

ALSO AVAILABLE FROM LEFTWORD

SOCIALIST REGISTER 2008

Global Flashpoints

Reactions to imperialism and neoliberalism

Editors: Leo Panitch, Colin Leys

978-81-87496-75-5, pp. xiv+362, paperback

New forces of resistance have emerged to both American imperialism and neoliberalism. But how far do these forces represent a progressive alternative? This volume surveys the key flashpoints of resistance today.

The main arena of resistance to imperialism is the Middle East. Six essays explore the ambivalent nature of Islamic anti-imperialism, and the West's crucial role in making it so significant, as well as the different forms it takes as a political creed; and they provide particular insight into the relationship between religion and politics today in Iraq, Palestine and Turkey.

Resistance to neoliberalism has been seen most clearly in the 'pink tide' in Latin America. Seven essays evaluate the potential – or lack of it – for a 21st century socialism across the region, and especially in Venezuela, Bolivia, Mexico, and Argentina; while an interview with João-Pedro Stédile, leader of Brazil's Landless People's Movement, provides a unique perspective on class struggles in that country.

Three further essays look at recent reactions to neoliberalism and imperialism elsewhere – in Eastern Europe, in France, and in the heart of empire, the United States itself. The volume concludes with a symposium: three leading left economists analyse neoliberalism as a global regime of social and political control, and critically examine the left's response to it.

CONTRIBUTORS: Bashir Abu-Manneh, Gilbert Achcar, Aijaz Ahmad, Gregory Albo, Sabah Alnasseri, Elmar Altvater, Edur Velasco Arregui, Yildiz Atasoy, Asef Bayat, Emilia Castorina, Ana Esther Ceceña, Wes Enzinna, Marta Harnecker, Raghu Krishnan, Margarita López Maya, Kim Moody, William Robinson, Richard Roman, Alfredo Saad-Filho, João Pedro Stédile, G.M. Tamás, Adrien Thomas

SOCIALIST REGISTER 2007

Coming to Terms with Nature

Editors: Leo Panitch and Colin Leys

978-81-87496-69-4, pp. xvi+363, paperback

This volume develops a better eco-socialist understanding of contemporary capitalism, and advances the kind of politics that could lead to an ecologically sustainable as well as a democratic socialism. Beginning with a leading filmmaker's vivid images of the crisis, seventeen essays address:

How capitalism is capable of finding new fields of accumulation in nature
The significance of capitalism's historic dependence on fossil fuels
Why renewable energy is neglected by 'New Labour' in Britain
Environmental effects of China's growth

Eco-Populism and environmental degradation in Africa
How globalized capitalist agriculture is destroying the ecosphere
The truth about the Kyoto Protocol
Water, power and money
How capitalism profits from waste
The contradictions of consumerism
The world-wide conflicts generated by the environmental crisis
The limits of 'eco-localism' and 'market ecology'
Party-building for eco-socialists: lessons from the German Greens
The eco-socialist case for democratic planning

CONTRIBUTORS: Greg Albo, Almar Altvater, Henry Bernstein, Achim Brunnengräber, Daniel Buck, Elinor Harriss, Barbara Harriss-White, Minqi Li, Brenda Longfellow, Michael Löwy, Joan Martinez-Alier, Philip McMichael, Costas Panayotakis, Jamie Peck, Heather Rogers, Neil Smith, Erik Swyngedouw, Dale Wen, Frieder Otto Wolf, Philip Woodhouse

SOCIALIST REGISTER 2006

Telling the Truth

Editors: Leo Panitch and Colin Leys

pp. 296, paperback

Fifteen leading writers explore the problem of truth and the lack of it in thirteen original essays on: the cynical state; 'capitalist democracy'; the 'business community'; 'welfare reform'; 'law and order'; the media and the Iraq war; global poverty statistics; development economics; the politics of theatre; academic postmodernism; socialists and the problem of class; the history of truth.

CONTRIBUTORS: Atillio A Boron, Terry Eagleton, Barbara Ehrenreich, Ben Fine, Doug Henwood, Michael Kustow, Colin Leys, Robert W McChesney, David Miller, Frances Fox Piven, Sanjay G Reddy, John Sanbonmatsu, G M Tamas, Elisa Van Waeyenberge, LoicWacquant

Talking About Trees

Science, Ecology and Agriculture in Cuba

Richard Levins

978-81-87496-63-2, pp. 169, hardcover

"Levins' writing is compelling, as always, and makes a valuable contribution to our thinking about a sustainable alternative to the rapacious globalization ravaging the planet today."

Vijay Prashad

Understanding dynamic complexity is the central scientific problem of our time. We need to look at science itself as an object of study, a historically developed way of producing knowledge that creates a rich mix of insights and confusions. Our approach needs to be partisan, rejecting the notion that feeling is the enemy of reason or that a commitment to human well-being is an enemy of objectivity.

Richard Levins, an ex-tropical farmer turned Harvard University ecologist, biomathematician and philosopher of science, gives us his first book since the hugely influential *The Dialectical Biologist*. He argues for a good, combative, perceptive scientific method that is more reflective of the complex, dynamic world in which we live and more supportive of precautionary decisions.

Talking About Trees ranges widely, from personal narratives to theoretical discussions on the need for the precautionary principle in science. Levins offers a strong critique of the industrial-commercial pathway to development; in its place he promotes an alternative development pathway that emphasizes economic viability with equity, ecological and social sustainability and empowerment of the dispossessed.

RICHARD LEVINS is John Rock Professor of Population Sciences, Harvard School of Public Health, Harvard University, Boston, MA. He is author, along with Richard Lewontin, of *The Dialectical Biologist*, Harvard University Press, 1985.

The Darker Nations

A Biography of the Short-lived Third World

Vijay Prashad

978-81-87496-66-3, pp. 384, hardcover

> "At a time when the politicians and ideologues of the Washington Consensus appeal to former colonies to free themselves from history, Vijay Prashad stubbornly carries on, recalling a past without which it is impossible to understand the present."
>
> Tariq Ali

"The Third World was not a place," argues Vijay Prashad. "It was a project." This book is a paradigm-shifting history of both a utopian concept and global movement—the idea of the Third World. *The Darker Nations* traces the intellectual origins and the political history of the attempt to knit together the world's impoverished countries in opposition to the United States and Soviet spheres of influence in the decades following World War II, as nation after nation across Asia, Africa and South America gained political independence from colonial rule.

Traversing continents, Vijay Prashad's fascinating narrative takes us from the birth of postcolonial nations after World War II to the downfall and corruption of nationalist regimes. A breakthrough book of cutting-edge scholarship, it includes vivid portraits of Third World giants like Jawaharlal Nehru, Egypt's Nasser, and Indonesia's Sukarno—as well as scores of extraordinary but now-forgotten intellectuals, artists, and freedom fighters. *The Darker Nations* restores to memory the vibrant though flawed idea of the Third World, whose demise, Prashad ultimately argues, has produced a much impoverished international political arena.

VIJAY PRASHAD is a prolific writer and the author of several books, including four for LeftWord Books. He teaches at Trinity College, Connecticut, USA.